the dreaming

Volume II

by

Queenie Chan

TOKYOPOP®

HAMBURG // LONDON // LOS ANGELES // TOKYO

The Dreaming Vol. 2
Written and Illustrated by Queenie Chan

Production Artists - Jihye "Sophia" Hong & Courtney Geter
Cover Design - Anne Marie Horne
Copy Editor - Stephanie Duchin

Editors - Carol Fox & Paul Morrissey
Digital Imaging Manager - Chris Buford
Pre-Production Supervisor - Erika Terriquez
Art Director - Anne Marie Horne
Production Manager - Elisabeth Brizzi
Managing Editor - Vy Nguyen
VP of Production - Ron Klamert
Editor-in-Chief - Rob Tokar
Publisher - Mike Kiley
President and C.O.O. - John Parker
C.E.O. and Chief Creative Officer - Stuart Levy

A  Manga

TOKYOPOP Inc.
5900 Wilshire Blvd. Suite 2000
Los Angeles, CA 90036

E-mail: info@TOKYOPOP.com
Come visit us online at www.TOKYOPOP.com

ISBN: 1-59816-383-3
First TOKYOPOP printing: November 2006
10 9 8 7 6 5 4 3
Printed in the USA

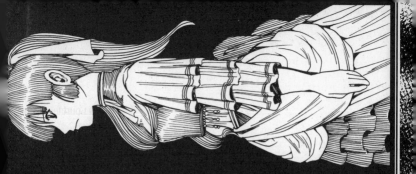

Table of Contents

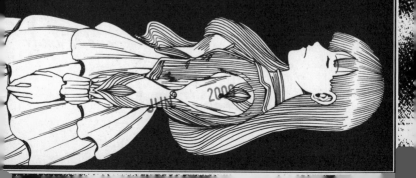

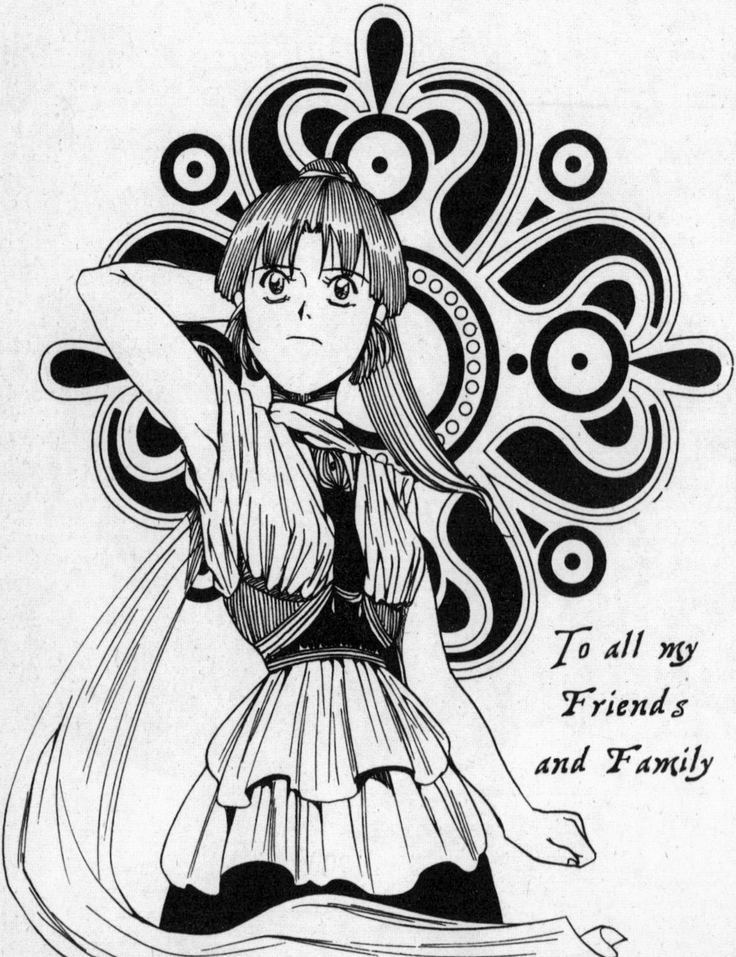

To all my
Friends
and Family

Chapter 8
Remembrance

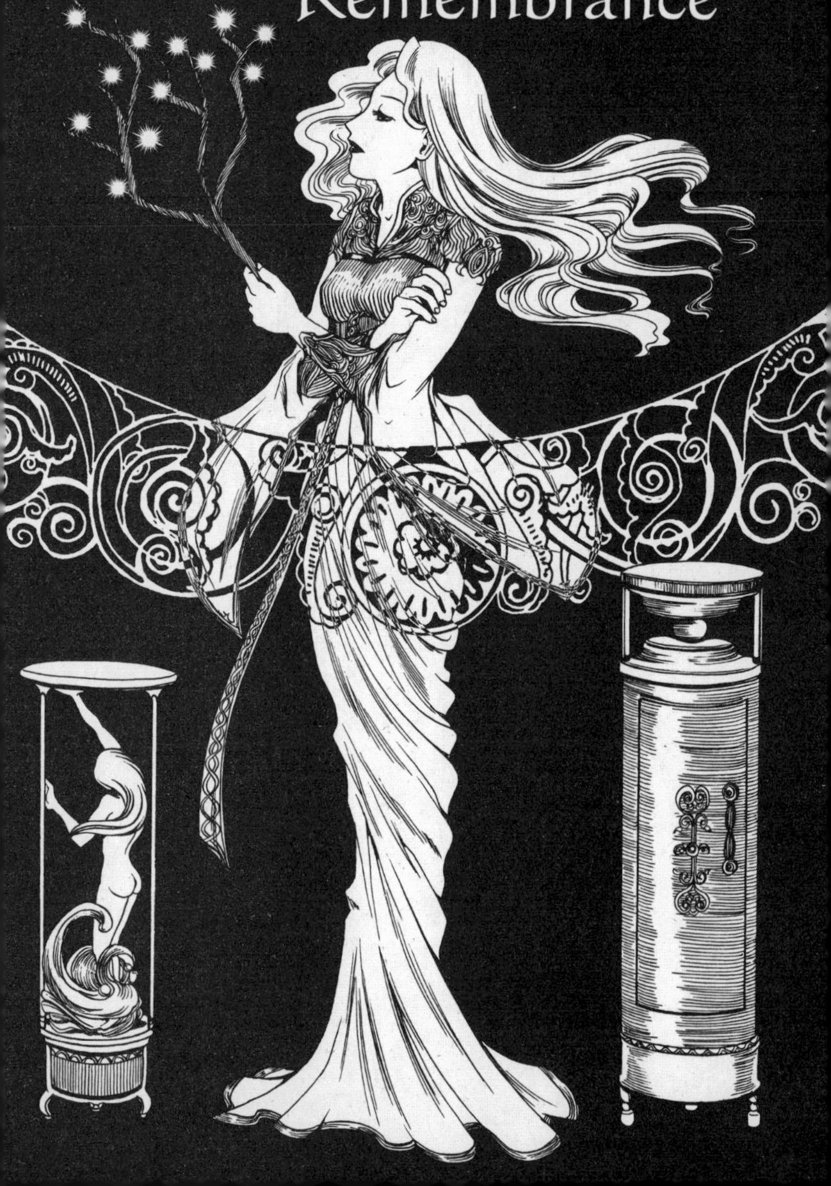

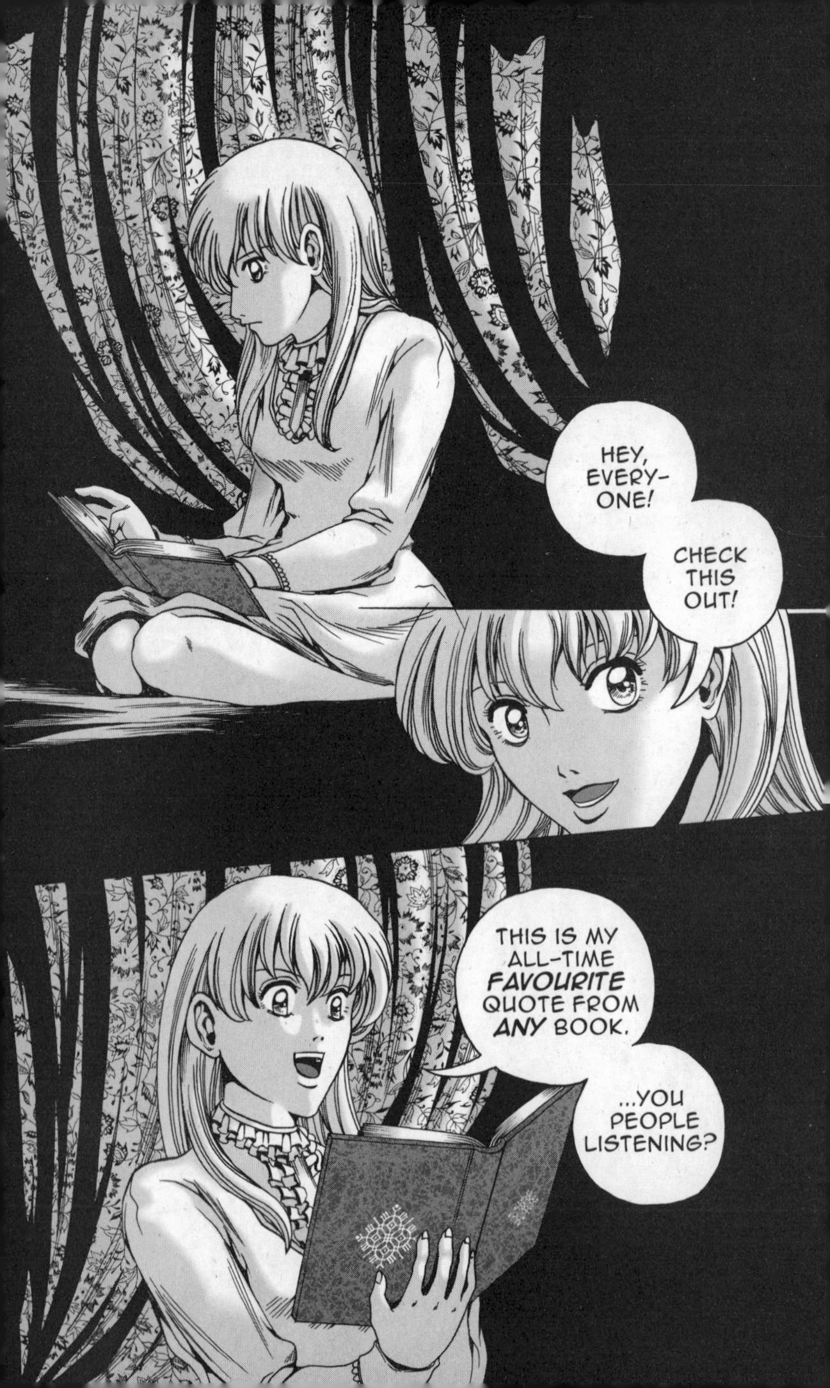
HEY, EVERY-ONE!
CHECK THIS OUT!
THIS IS MY ALL-TIME **FAVOURITE** QUOTE FROM **ANY** BOOK.
...YOU PEOPLE LISTENING?

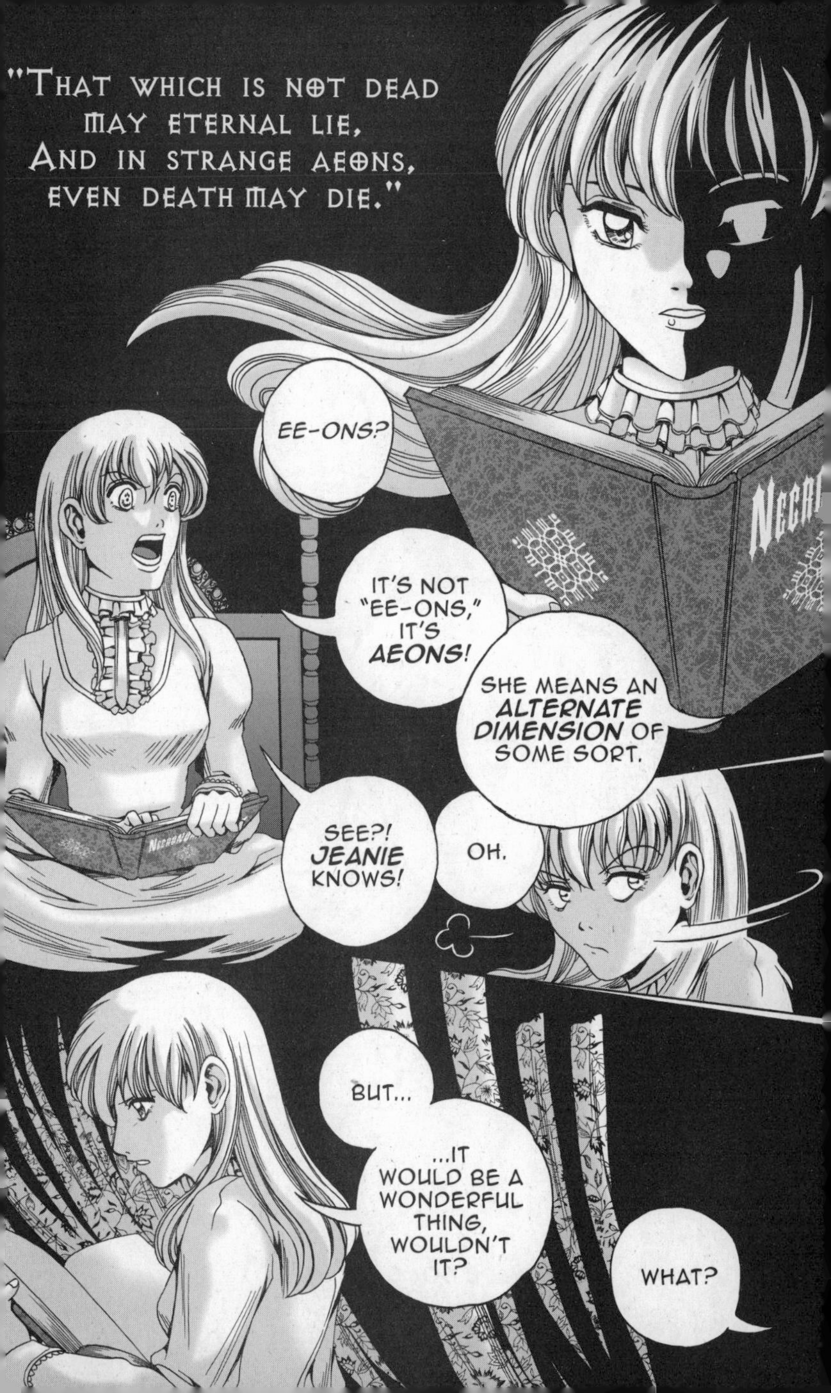
"That which is not dead may eternal lie, And in strange aeons, even death may die."
EE-ONS?
IT'S NOT "EE-ONS," IT'S AEONS!
SHE MEANS AN ALTERNATE DIMENSION OF SOME SORT.
SEE?! JEANIE KNOWS!
OH.
BUT...
...IT WOULD BE A WONDERFUL THING, WOULDN'T IT?
WHAT?

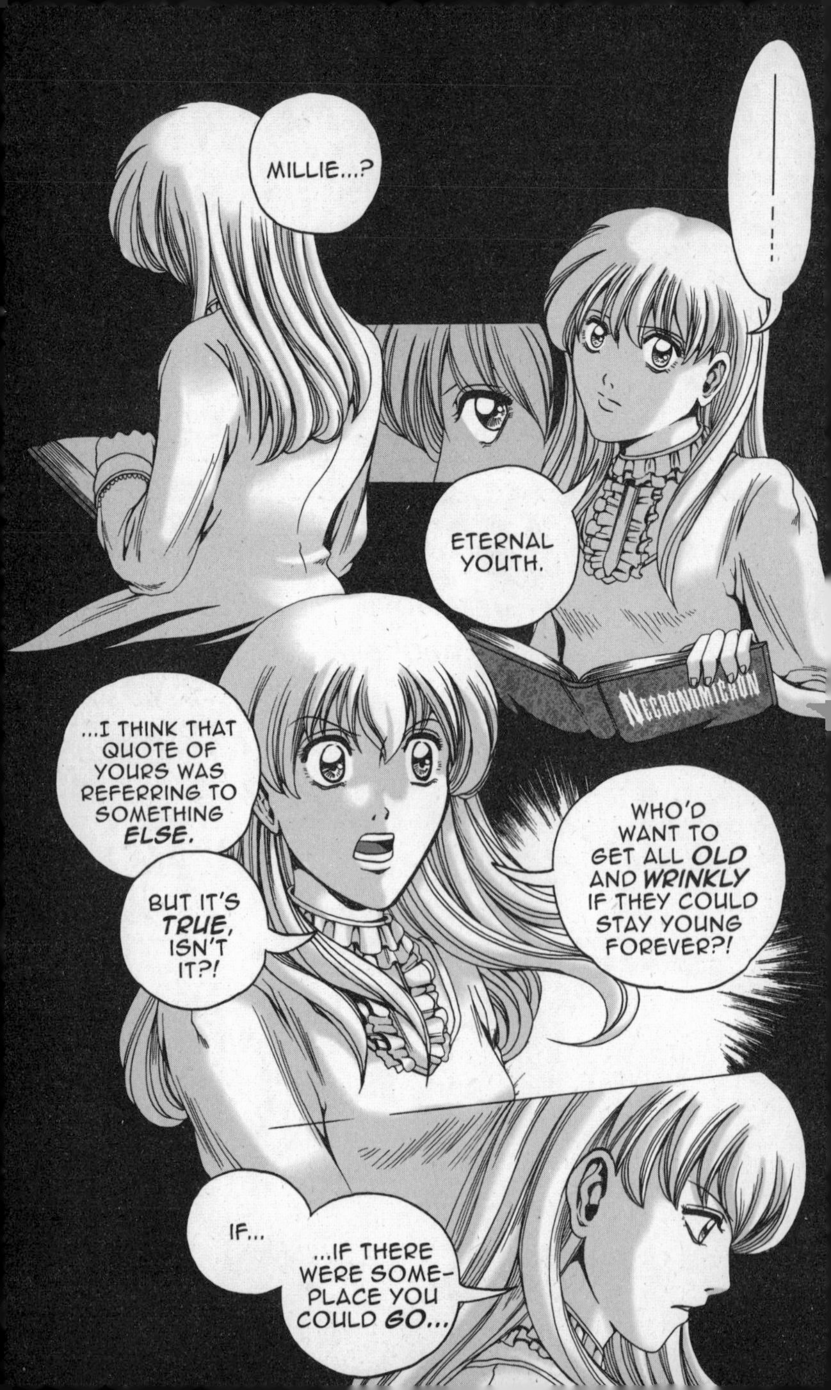
MILLIE...?
!
ETERNAL YOUTH.
NECRONOMICRON
...I THINK THAT QUOTE OF YOURS WAS REFERRING TO SOMETHING ELSE.
BUT IT'S TRUE, ISN'T IT?!
WHO'D WANT TO GET ALL OLD AND WRINKLY IF THEY COULD STAY YOUNG FOREVER?!
IF...
...IF THERE WERE SOME-PLACE YOU COULD GO...

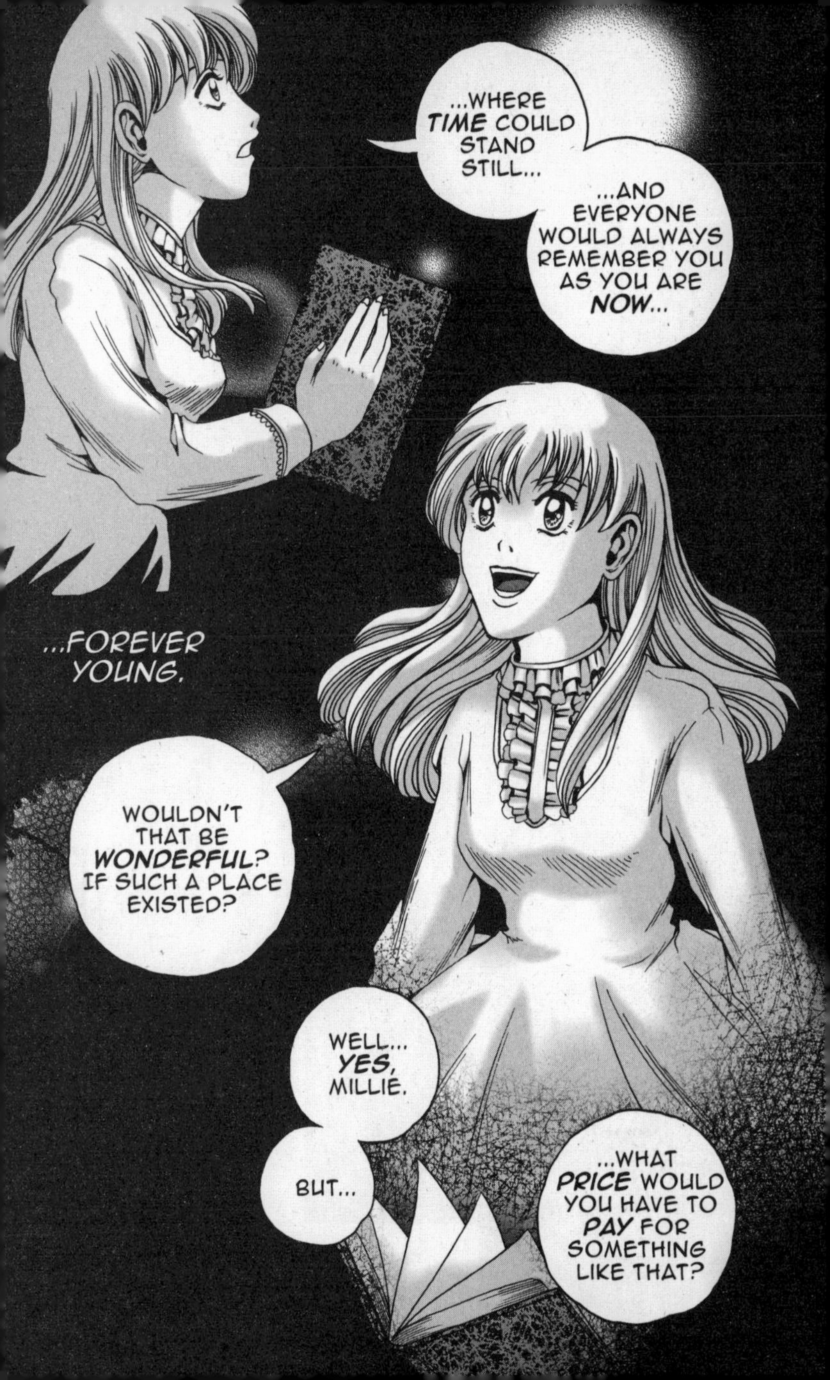
...WHERE TIME COULD STAND STILL...
...AND EVERYONE WOULD ALWAYS REMEMBER YOU AS YOU ARE NOW...
...FOREVER YOUNG.
WOULDN'T THAT BE WONDERFUL? IF SUCH A PLACE EXISTED?
WELL... YES, MILLIE.
BUT...
...WHAT PRICE WOULD YOU HAVE TO PAY FOR SOMETHING LIKE THAT?

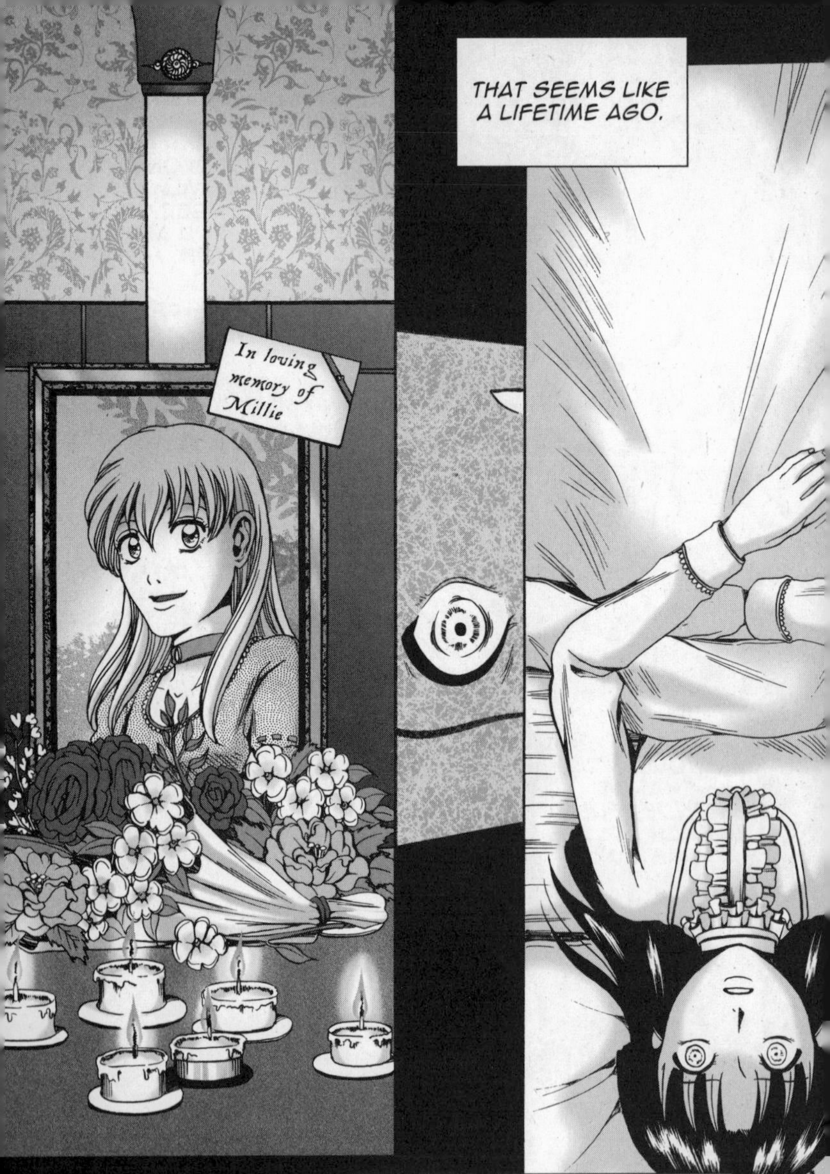
In loving memory of Millie
THAT SEEMS LIKE A LIFETIME AGO.

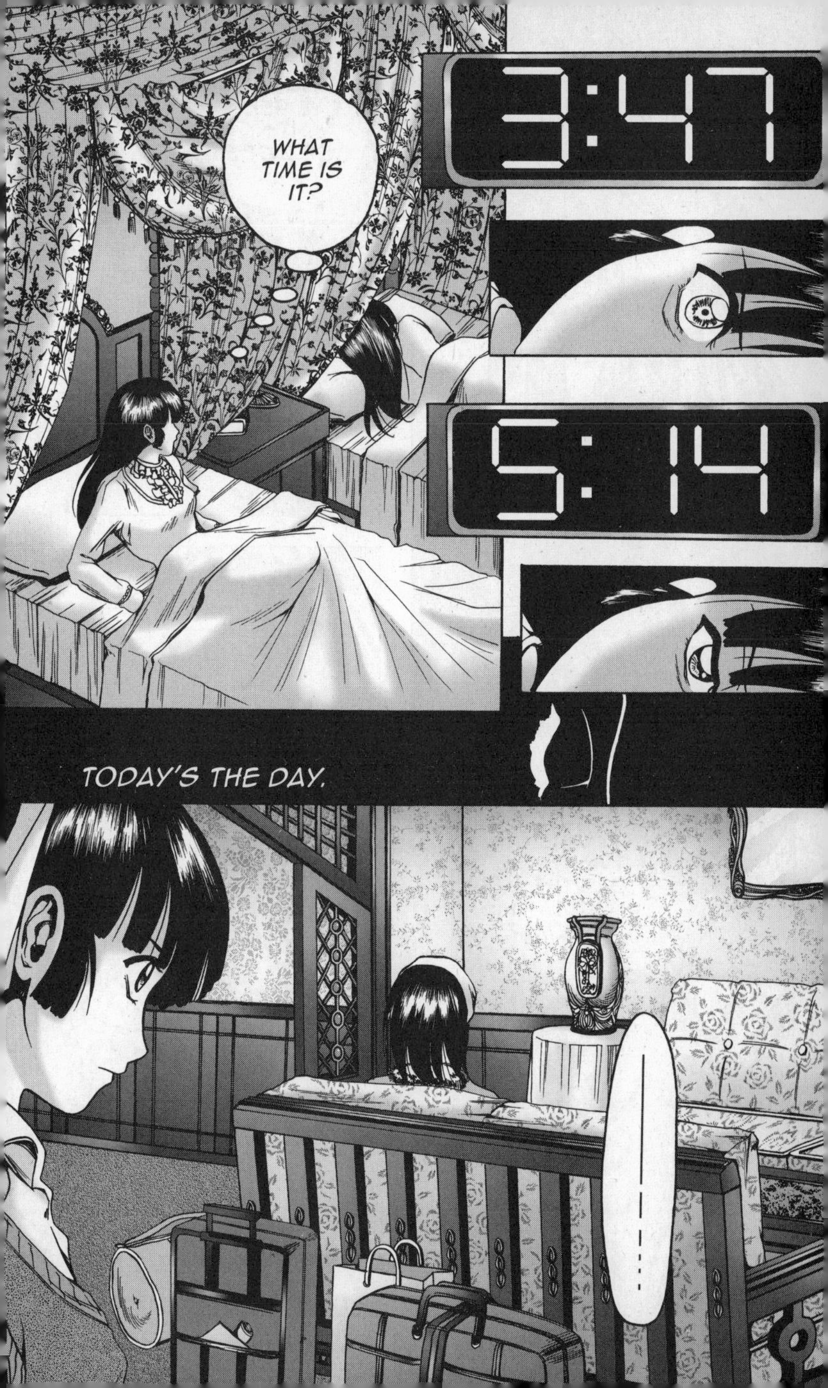
WHAT TIME IS IT?
3:47
5:14
TODAY'S THE DAY.
......

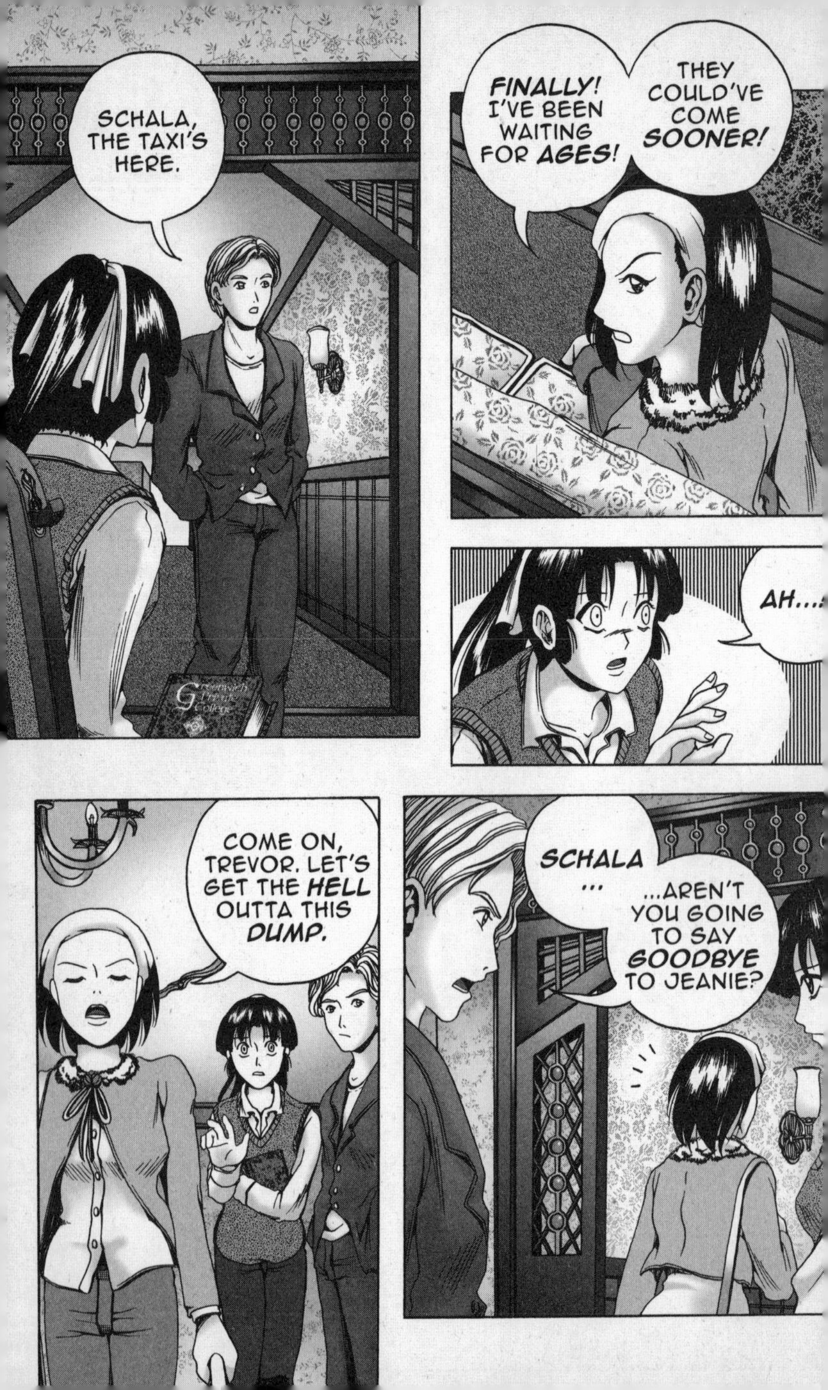
SCHALA, THE TAXI'S HERE.
FINALLY! I'VE BEEN WAITING FOR AGES!
THEY COULD'VE COME SOONER!
AH....
COME ON, TREVOR. LET'S GET THE HELL OUTTA THIS DUMP.
SCHALA ...
...AREN'T YOU GOING TO SAY GOODBYE TO JEANIE?

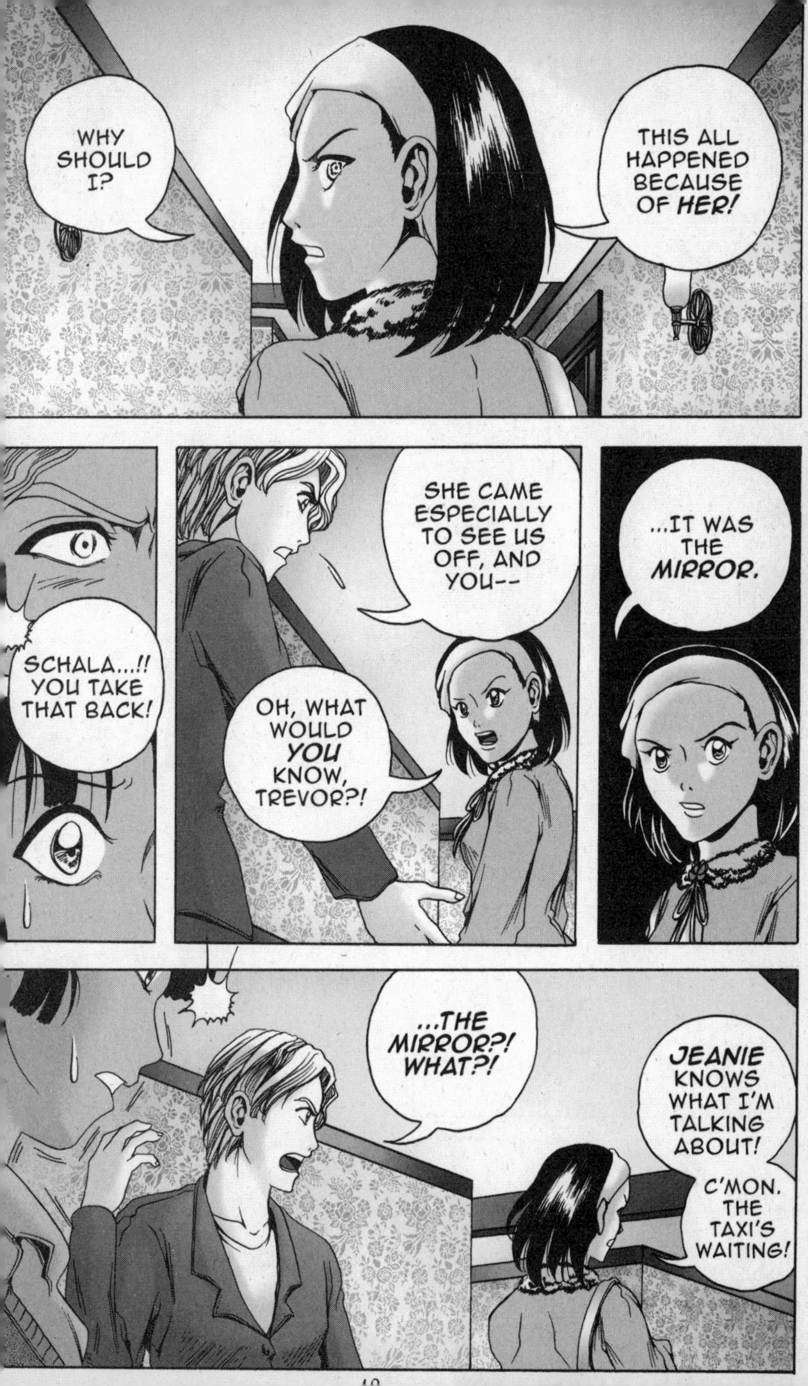
WHY SHOULD I?
THIS ALL HAPPENED BECAUSE OF HER!
SCHALA...!! YOU TAKE THAT BACK!
SHE CAME ESPECIALLY TO SEE US OFF, AND YOU--
OH, WHAT WOULD YOU KNOW, TREVOR?!
...IT WAS THE MIRROR.
...THE MIRROR?! WHAT?!
JEANIE KNOWS WHAT I'M TALKING ABOUT!
C'MON. THE TAXI'S WAITING!

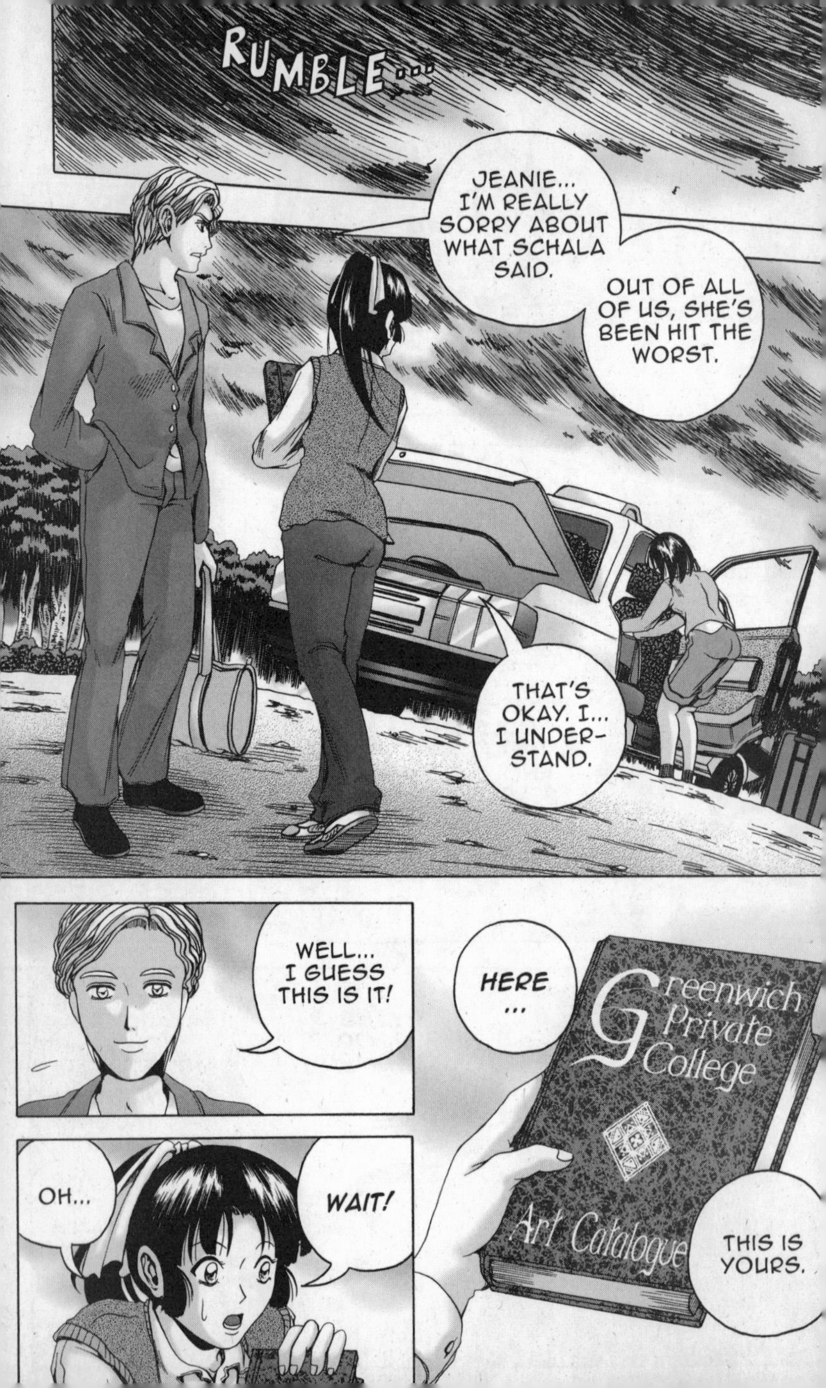
RUMBLE...
JEANIE... I'M REALLY SORRY ABOUT WHAT SCHALA SAID.
OUT OF ALL OF US, SHE'S BEEN HIT THE WORST.
THAT'S OKAY. I... I UNDERSTAND.
WELL... I GUESS THIS IS IT!
HERE ...
Greenwich Private College
Art Catalogue
OH...
WAIT!
THIS IS YOURS.

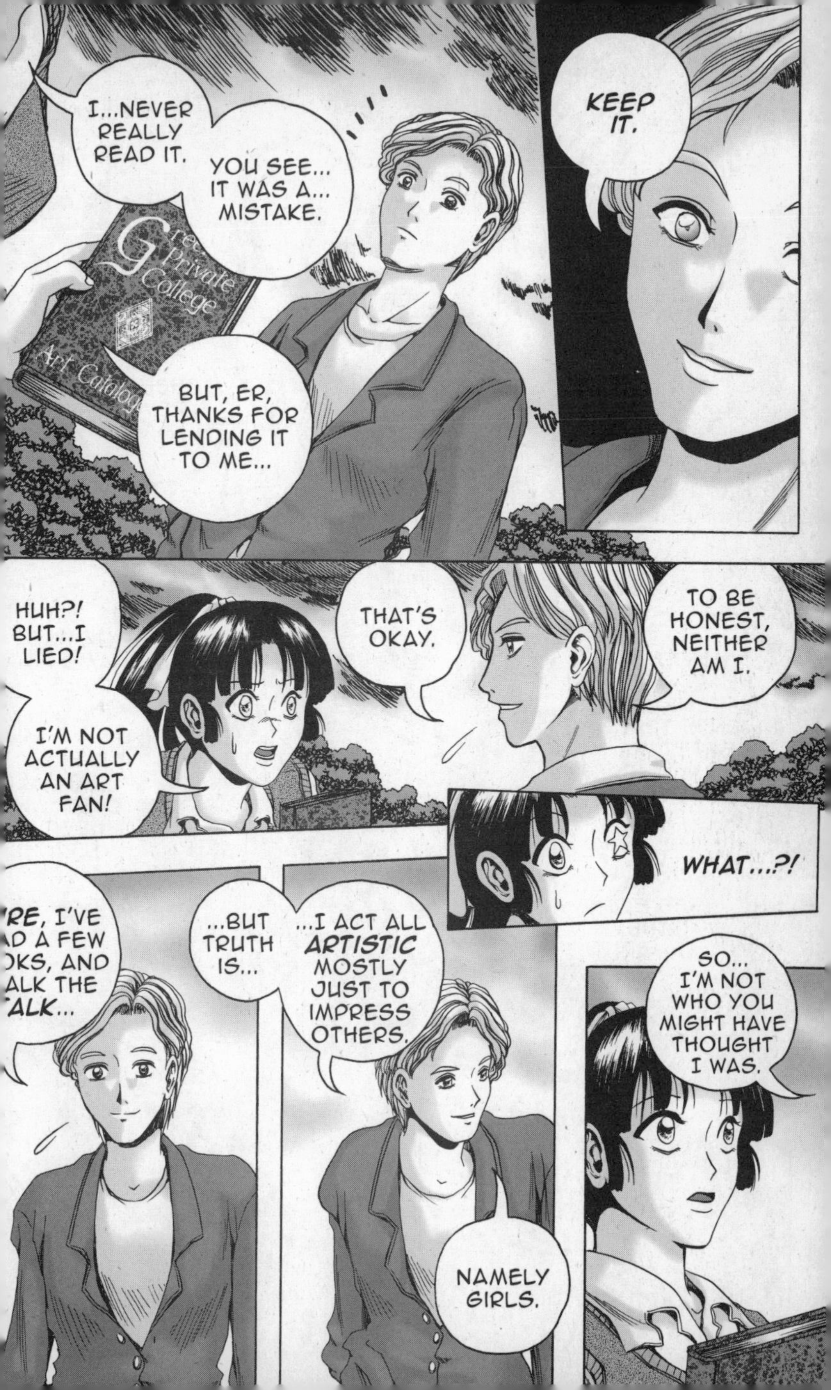
I...NEVER REALLY READ IT.
YOU SEE... IT WAS A... MISTAKE.
Great Private College Art Catalog
BUT, ER, THANKS FOR LENDING IT TO ME...
KEEP IT.
HUH?! BUT...I LIED!
I'M NOT ACTUALLY AN ART FAN!
THAT'S OKAY.
TO BE HONEST, NEITHER AM I.
WHAT...?!
RE, I'VE D A FEW OKS, AND ALK THE ALK...
...BUT TRUTH IS...
...I ACT ALL ARTISTIC MOSTLY JUST TO IMPRESS OTHERS.
NAMELY GIRLS.
SO... I'M NOT WHO YOU MIGHT HAVE THOUGHT I WAS.

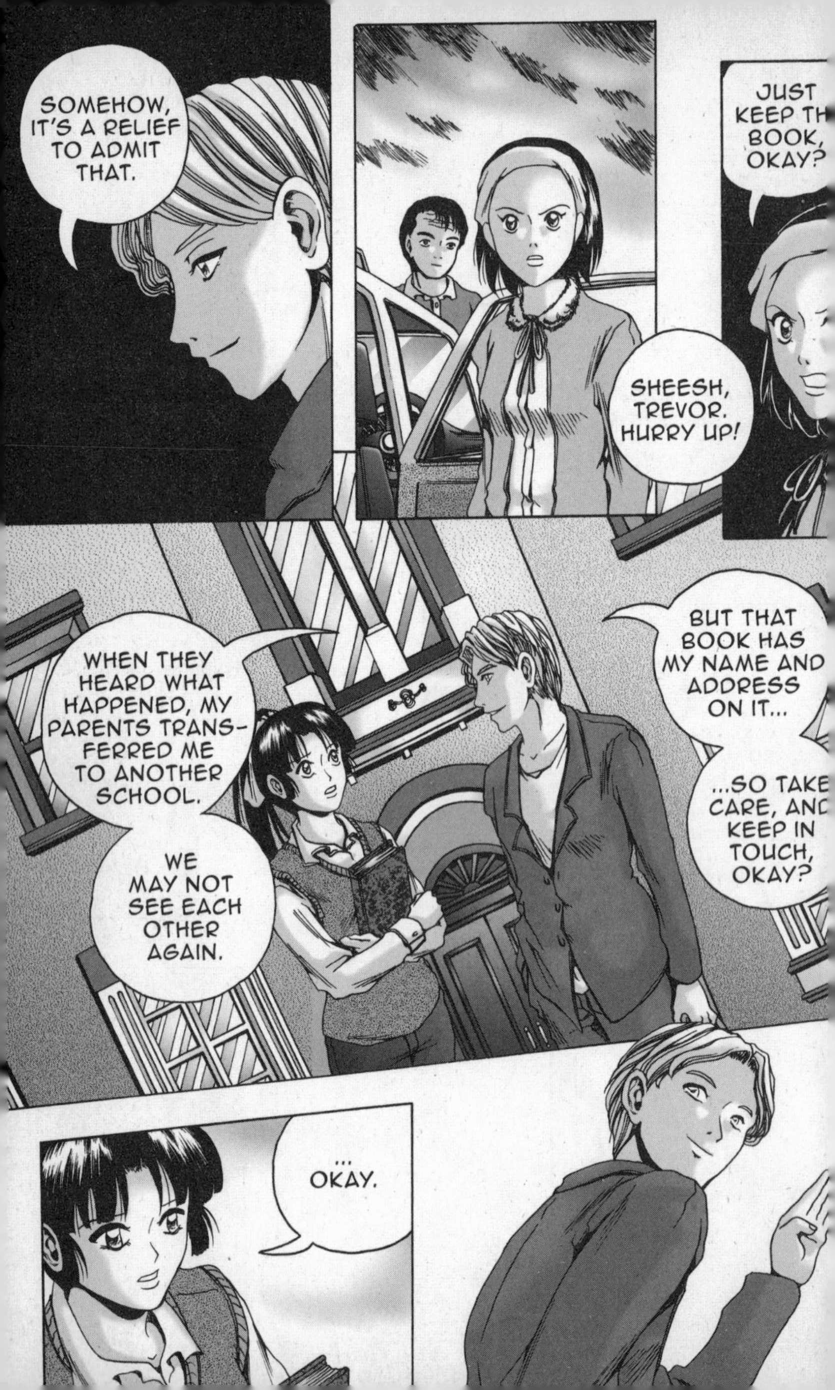
SOMEHOW, IT'S A RELIEF TO ADMIT THAT.
SHEESH, TREVOR. HURRY UP!
JUST KEEP TH BOOK, OKAY?
WHEN THEY HEARD WHAT HAPPENED, MY PARENTS TRANS-FERRED ME TO ANOTHER SCHOOL.
WE MAY NOT SEE EACH OTHER AGAIN.
BUT THAT BOOK HAS MY NAME AND ADDRESS ON IT...
...SO TAKE CARE, AND KEEP IN TOUCH, OKAY?
... OKAY.

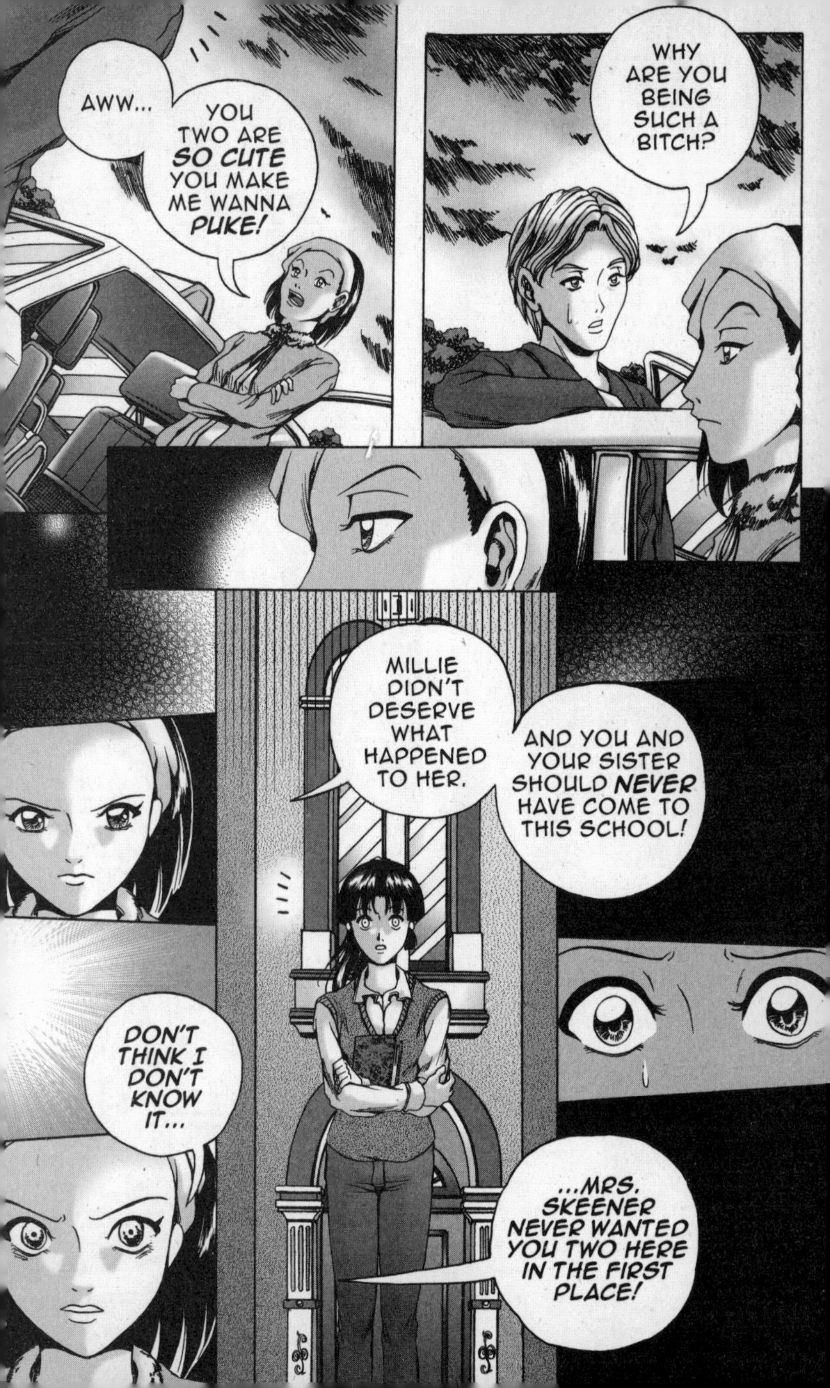
AWW...
YOU TWO ARE SO CUTE YOU MAKE ME WANNA PUKE!
WHY ARE YOU BEING SUCH A BITCH?
MILLIE DIDN'T DESERVE WHAT HAPPENED TO HER.
AND YOU AND YOUR SISTER SHOULD NEVER HAVE COME TO THIS SCHOOL!
DON'T THINK I DON'T KNOW IT...
...MRS. SKEENER NEVER WANTED YOU TWO HERE IN THE FIRST PLACE!

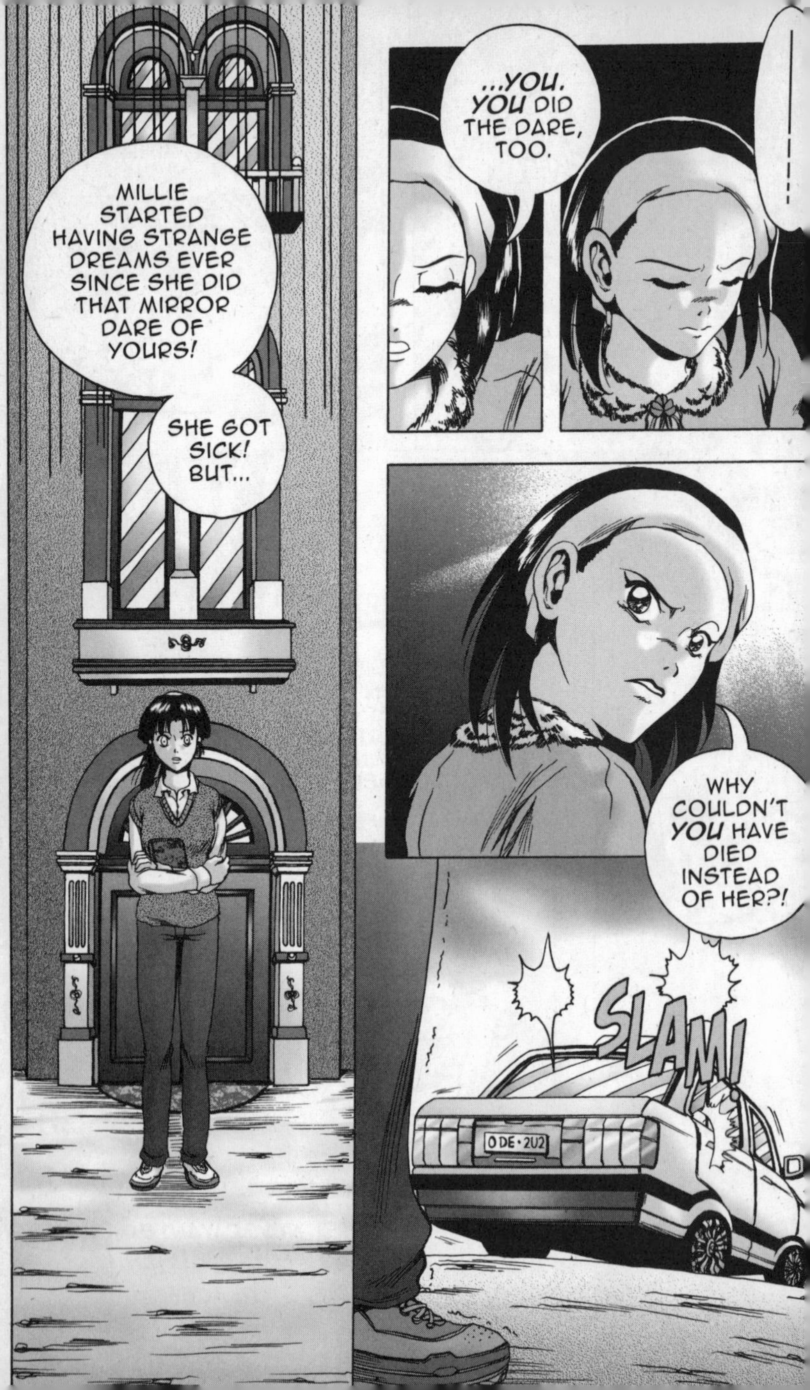
MILLIE STARTED HAVING STRANGE DREAMS EVER SINCE SHE DID THAT MIRROR DARE OF YOURS!
SHE GOT SICK! BUT...
...YOU. YOU DID THE DARE, TOO.
WHY COULDN'T YOU HAVE DIED INSTEAD OF HER?!
SLAM!
ODE·2U2

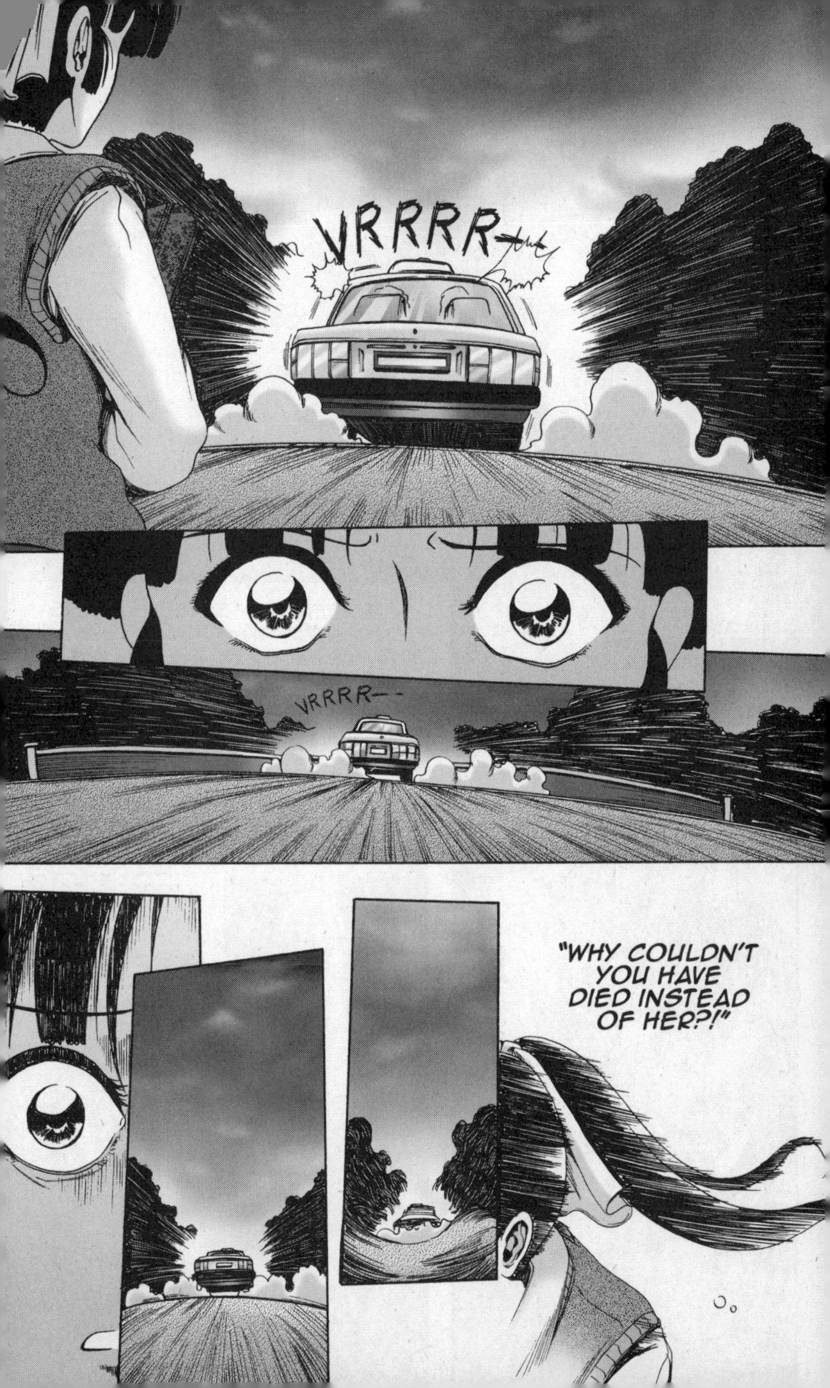
VRRRR
VRRRR
"WHY COULDN'T YOU HAVE DIED INSTEAD OF HER?!"

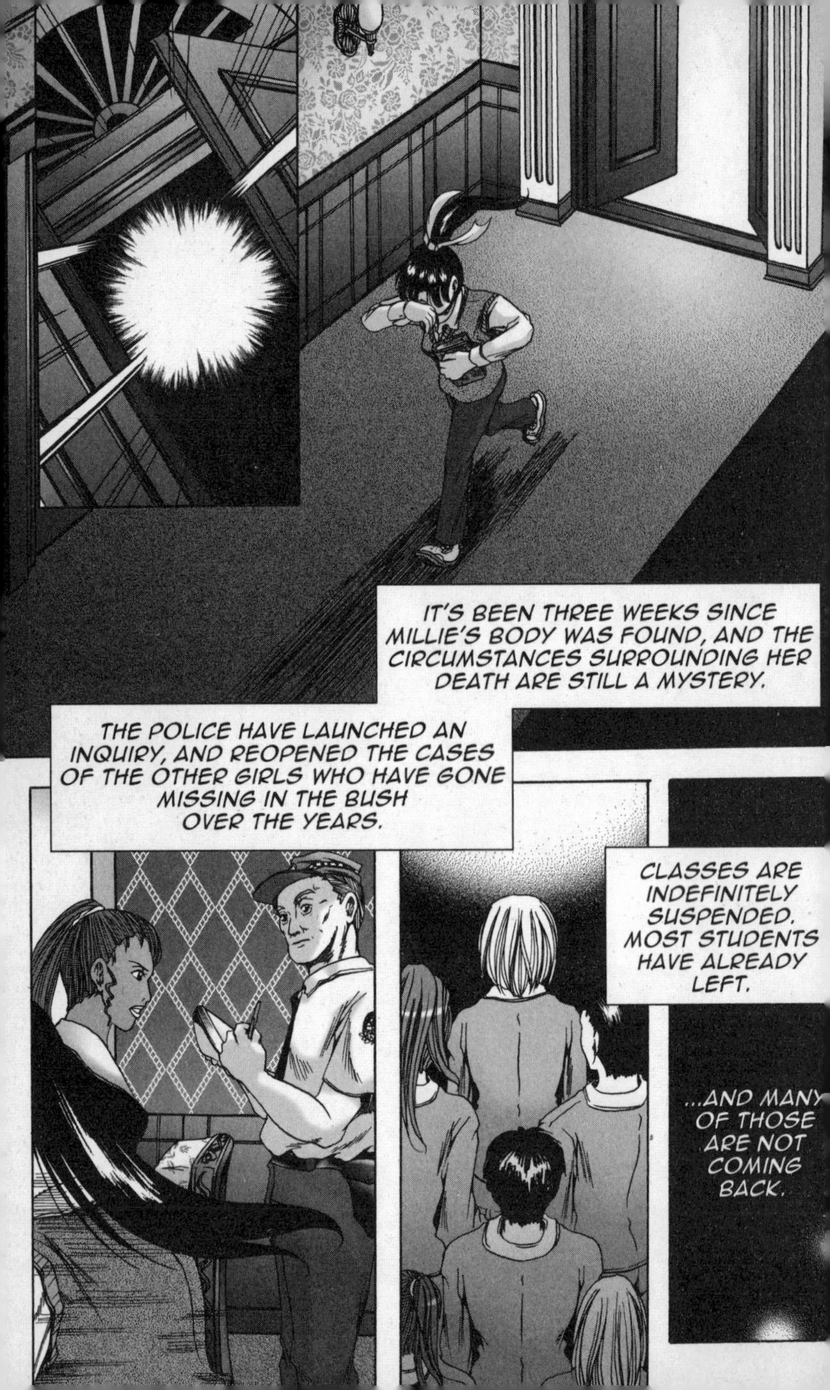
IT'S BEEN THREE WEEKS SINCE MILLIE'S BODY WAS FOUND, AND THE CIRCUMSTANCES SURROUNDING HER DEATH ARE STILL A MYSTERY.
THE POLICE HAVE LAUNCHED AN INQUIRY, AND REOPENED THE CASES OF THE OTHER GIRLS WHO HAVE GONE MISSING IN THE BUSH OVER THE YEARS.
CLASSES ARE INDEFINITELY SUSPENDED. MOST STUDENTS HAVE ALREADY LEFT.
...AND MANY OF THOSE ARE NOT COMING BACK.

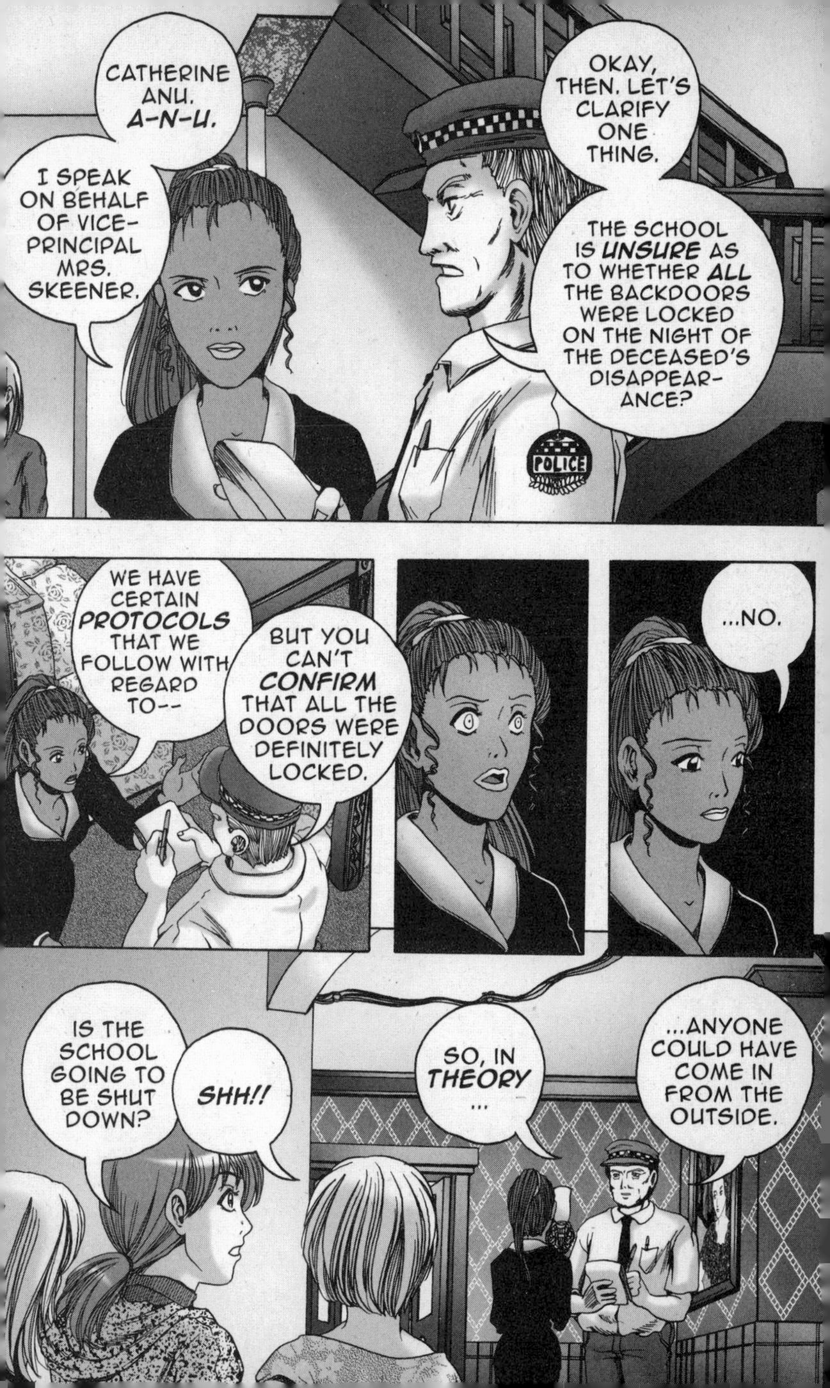
CATHERINE ANU. A-N-U.
I SPEAK ON BEHALF OF VICE-PRINCIPAL MRS. SKEENER.
OKAY, THEN. LET'S CLARIFY ONE THING.
THE SCHOOL IS UNSURE AS TO WHETHER ALL THE BACKDOORS WERE LOCKED ON THE NIGHT OF THE DECEASED'S DISAPPEAR-ANCE?
POLICE
WE HAVE CERTAIN PROTOCOLS THAT WE FOLLOW WITH REGARD TO--
BUT YOU CAN'T CONFIRM THAT ALL THE DOORS WERE DEFINITELY LOCKED.
...NO.
IS THE SCHOOL GOING TO BE SHUT DOWN?
SHH!!
SO, IN THEORY ...
...ANYONE COULD HAVE COME IN FROM THE OUTSIDE.

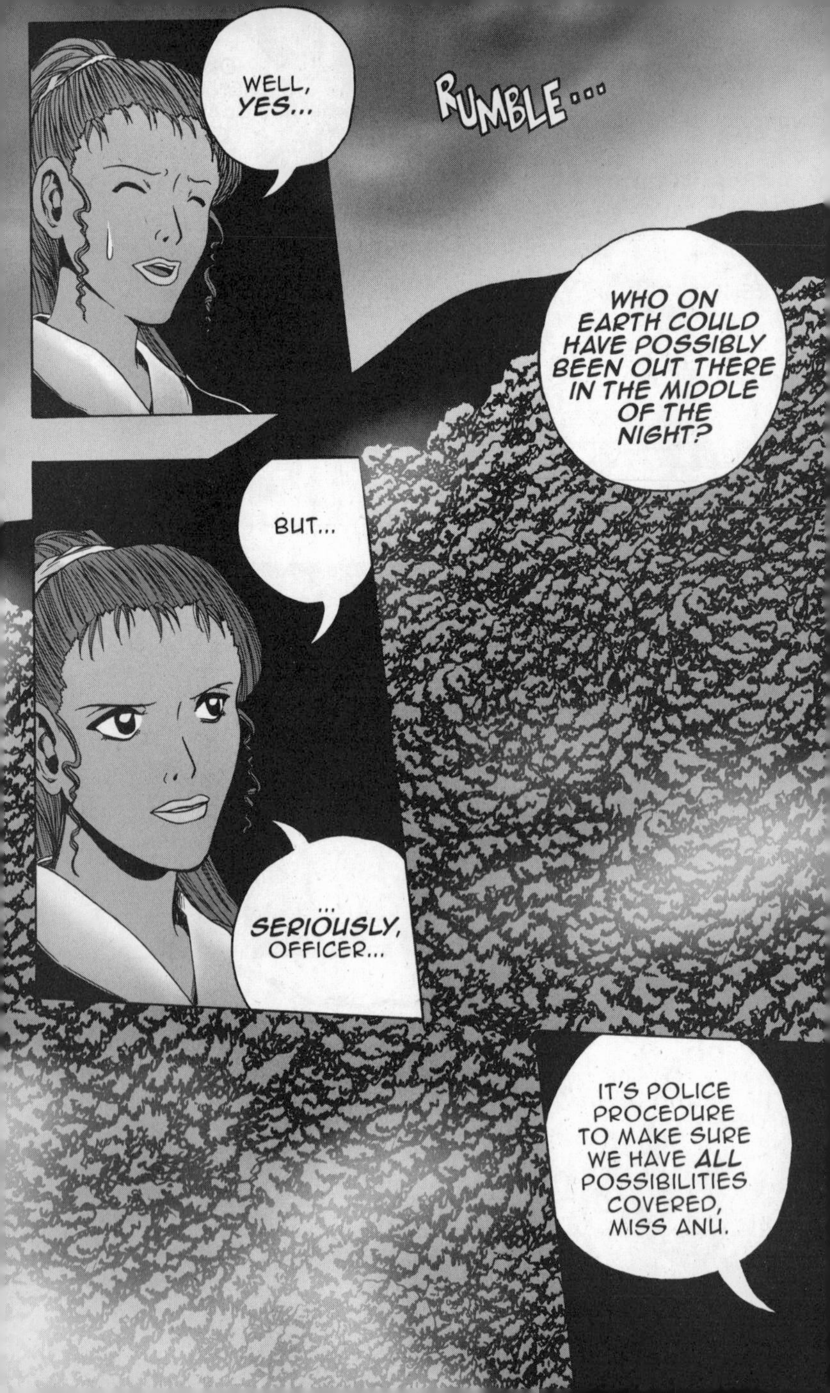
WELL, YES...
RUMBLE...
WHO ON EARTH COULD HAVE POSSIBLY BEEN OUT THERE IN THE MIDDLE OF THE NIGHT?
BUT...
... SERIOUSLY, OFFICER...
IT'S POLICE PROCEDURE TO MAKE SURE WE HAVE ALL POSSIBILITIES COVERED, MISS ANU.

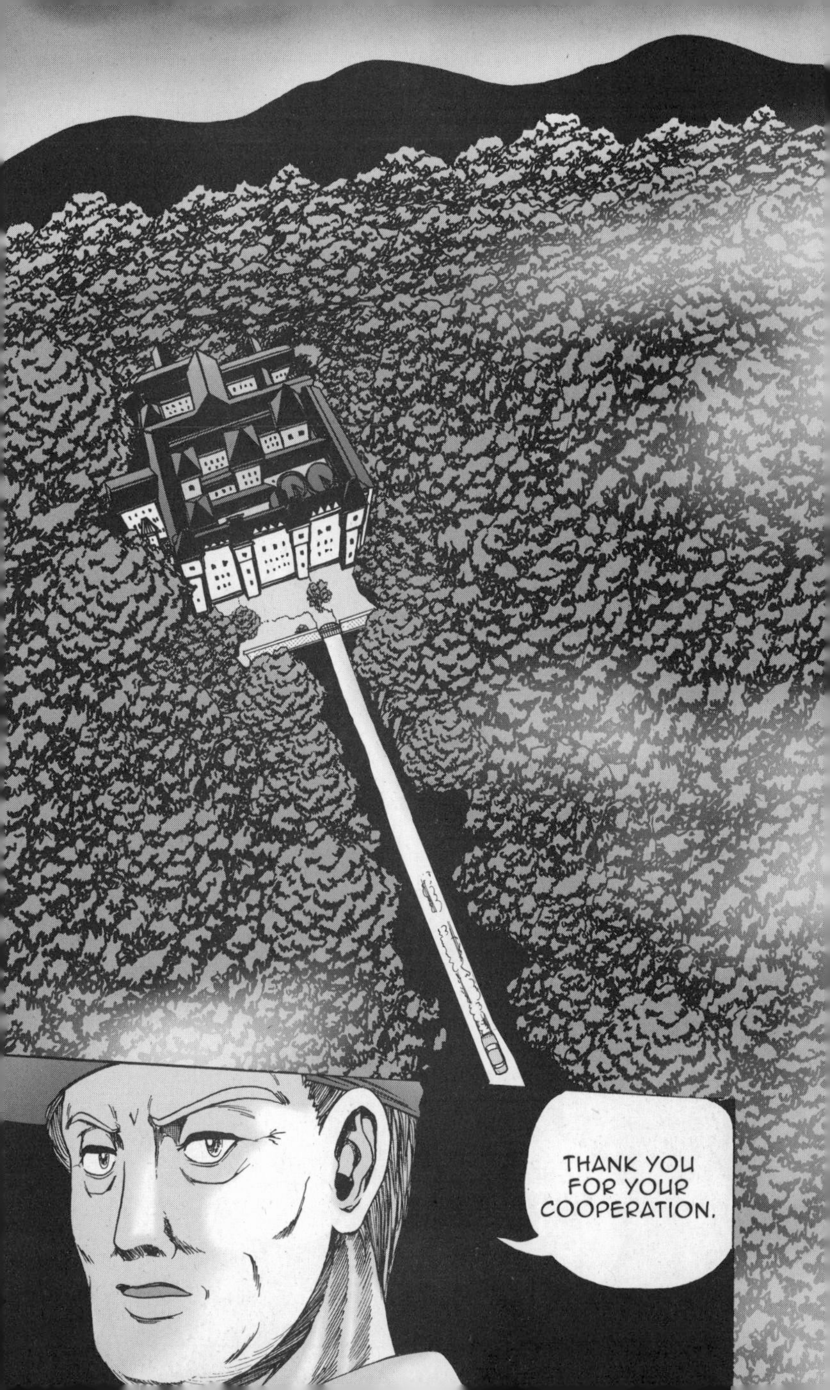
THANK YOU FOR YOUR COOPERATION.

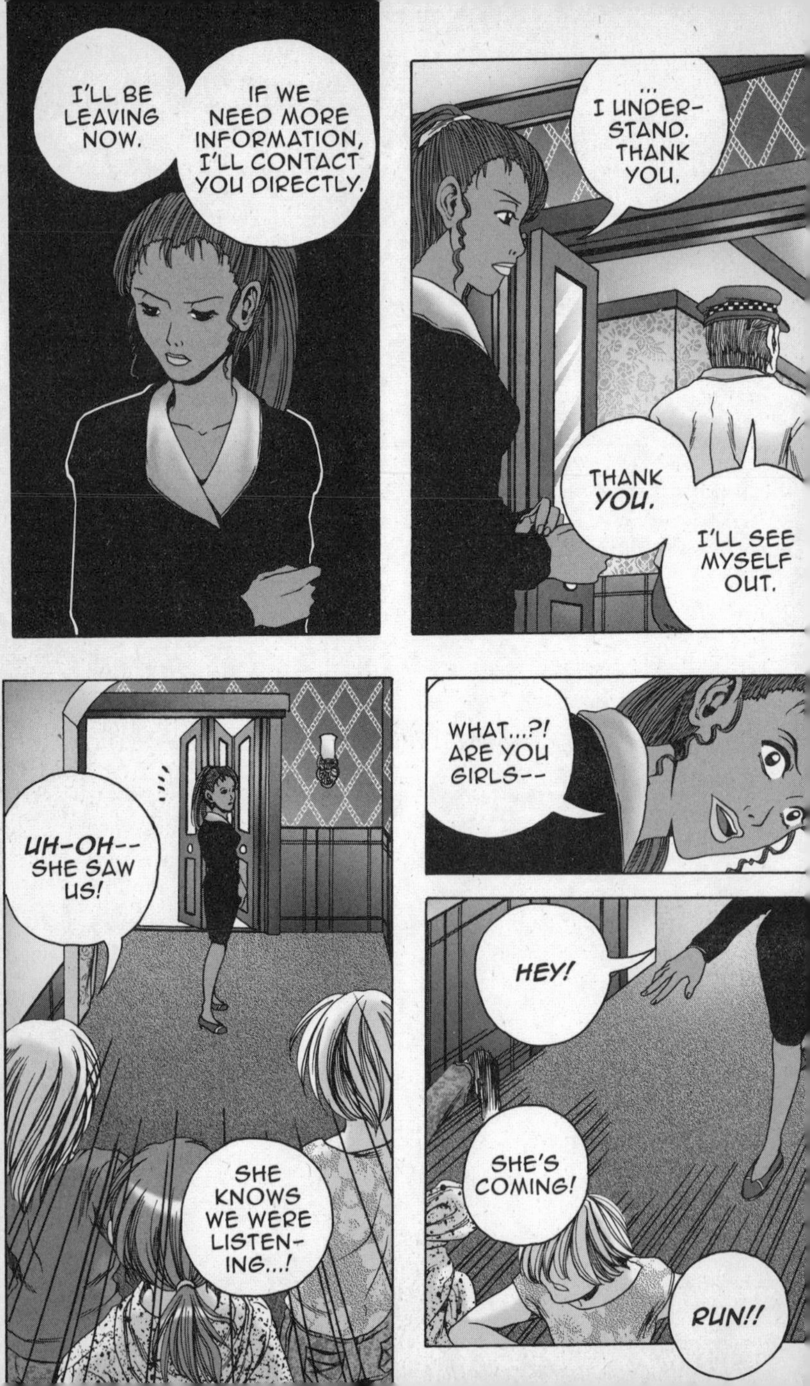
I'LL BE LEAVING NOW.
IF WE NEED MORE INFORMATION, I'LL CONTACT YOU DIRECTLY.
... I UNDER-STAND. THANK YOU.
THANK *YOU.*
I'LL SEE MYSELF OUT.
UH-OH-- SHE SAW US!
SHE KNOWS WE WERE LISTEN-ING...!
WHAT...?! ARE YOU GIRLS--
HEY!
SHE'S COMING!
RUN!!

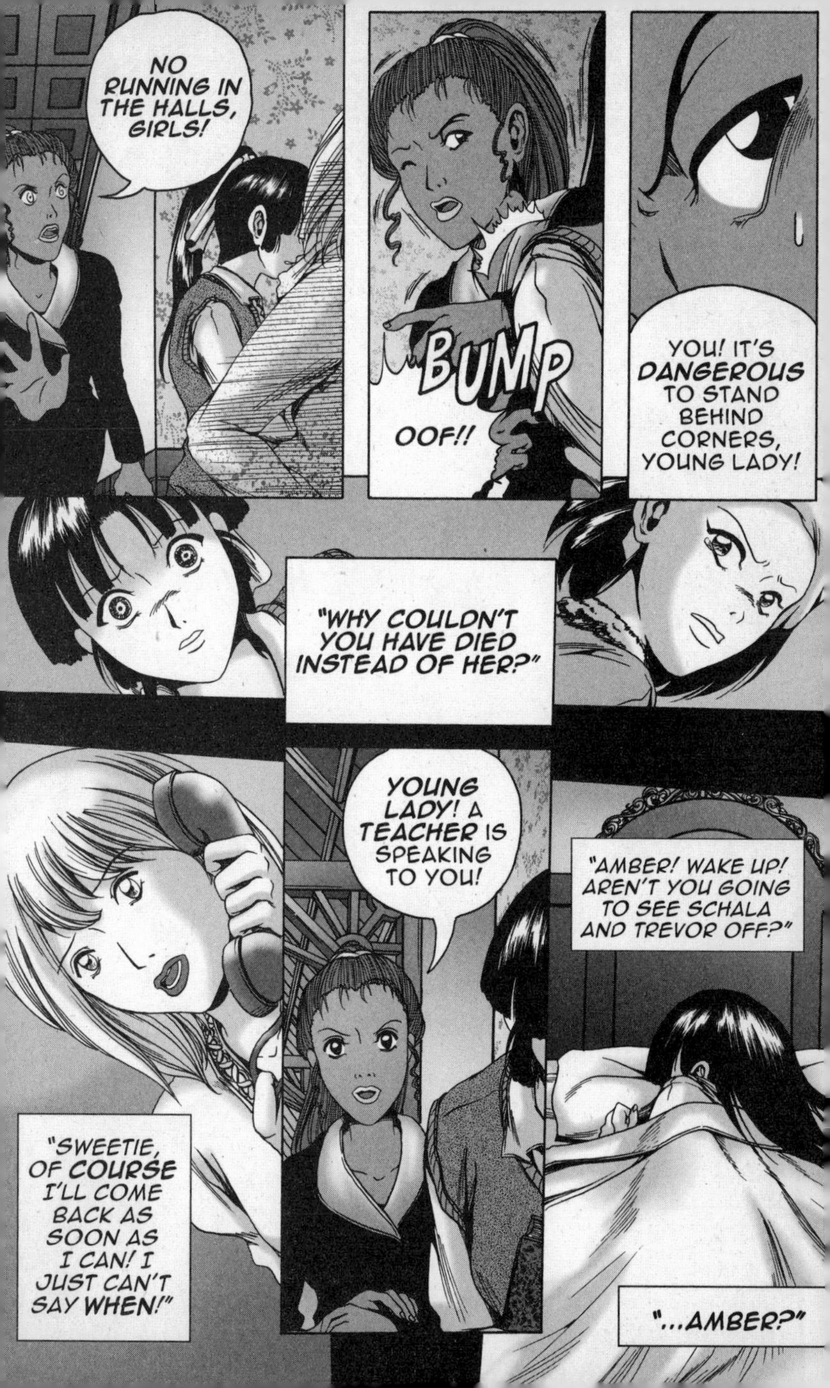
NO RUNNING IN THE HALLS, GIRLS!
BUMP
OOF!!
YOU! IT'S DANGEROUS TO STAND BEHIND CORNERS, YOUNG LADY!
"WHY COULDN'T YOU HAVE DIED INSTEAD OF HER?"
"SWEETIE, OF COURSE I'LL COME BACK AS SOON AS I CAN! I JUST CAN'T SAY WHEN!"
YOUNG LADY! A TEACHER IS SPEAKING TO YOU!
"AMBER! WAKE UP! AREN'T YOU GOING TO SEE SCHALA AND TREVOR OFF?"
"...AMBER?"

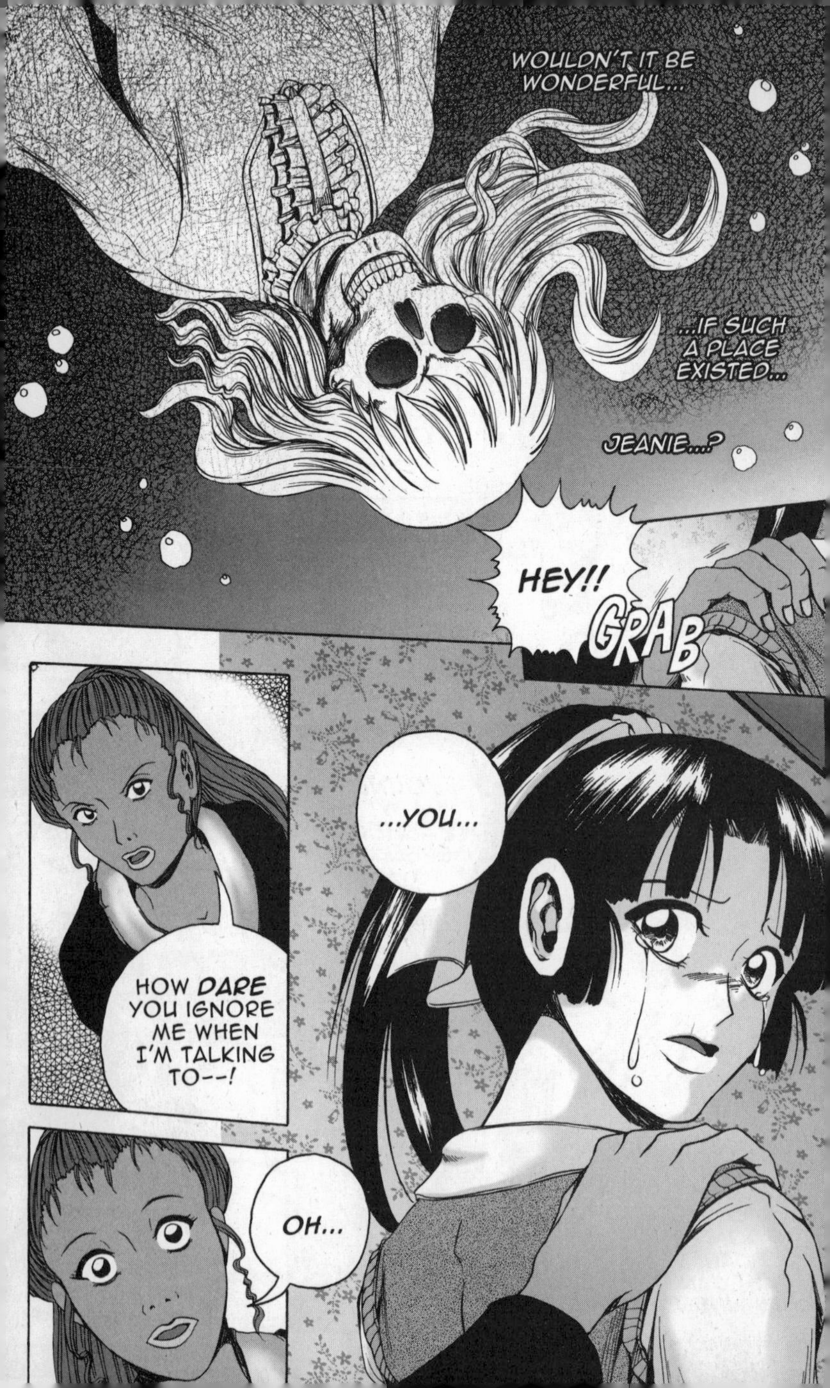
WOULDN'T IT BE WONDERFUL...
...IF SUCH A PLACE EXISTED...
JEANIE...?
HEY!!
GRAB
...YOU...
HOW DARE YOU IGNORE ME WHEN I'M TALKING TO--!
OH...

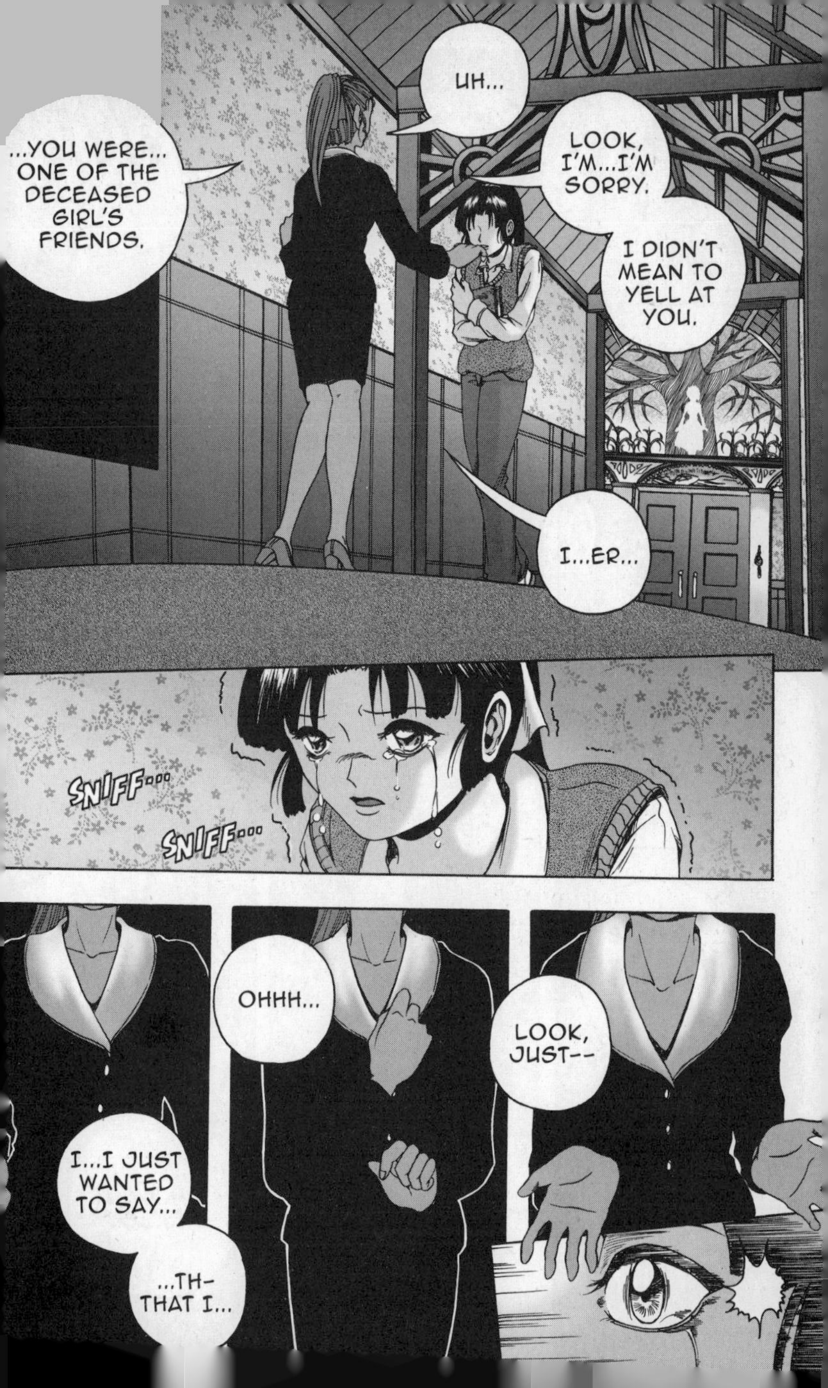
...YOU WERE... ONE OF THE DECEASED GIRL'S FRIENDS.
UH...
LOOK, I'M...I'M SORRY.
I DIDN'T MEAN TO YELL AT YOU.
I...ER...
SNIFF...
SNIFF...
I...I JUST WANTED TO SAY...
...TH-THAT I...
OHHH...
LOOK, JUST--

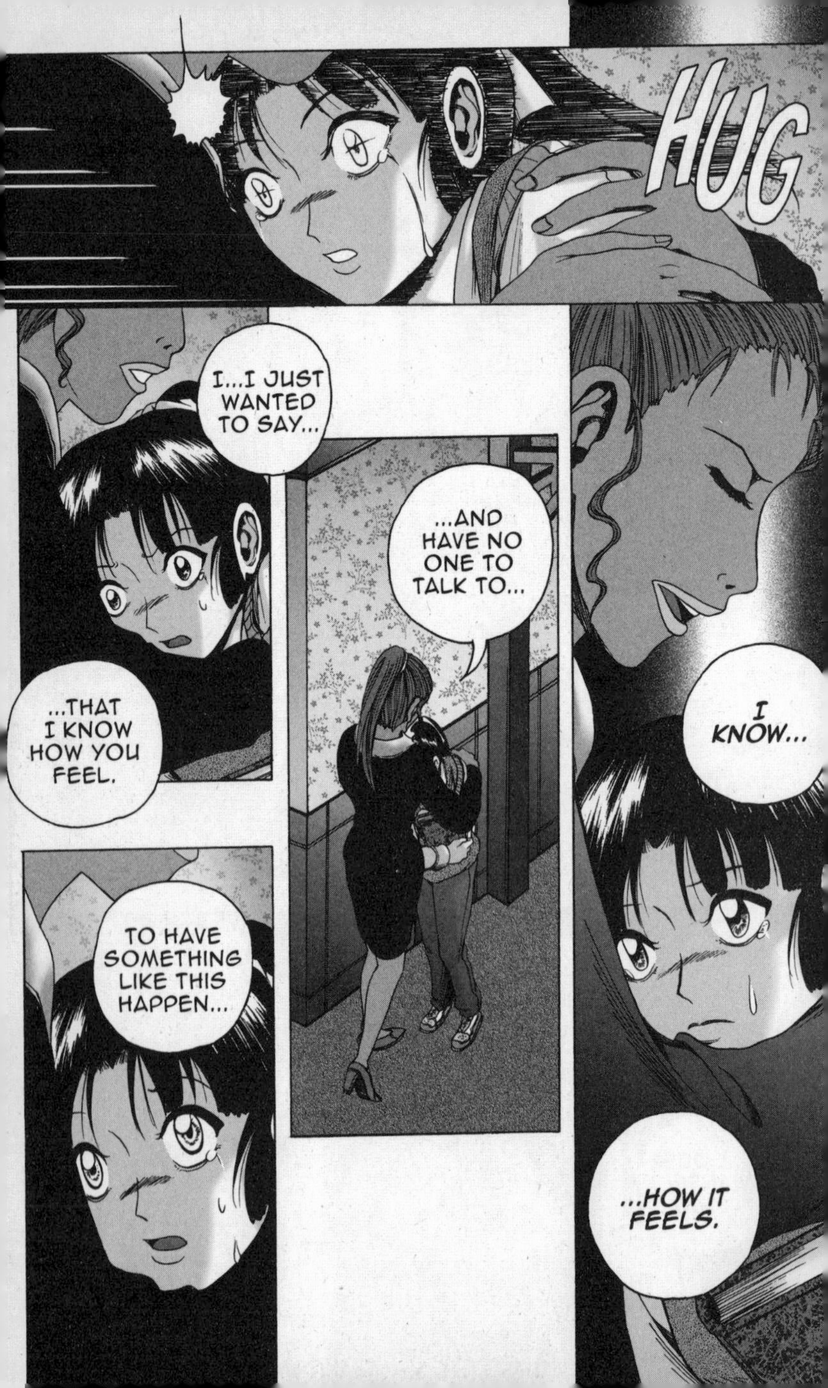
HUG
I...I JUST WANTED TO SAY...
...THAT I KNOW HOW YOU FEEL.
TO HAVE SOMETHING LIKE THIS HAPPEN...
...AND HAVE NO ONE TO TALK TO...
I KNOW...
...HOW IT FEELS.

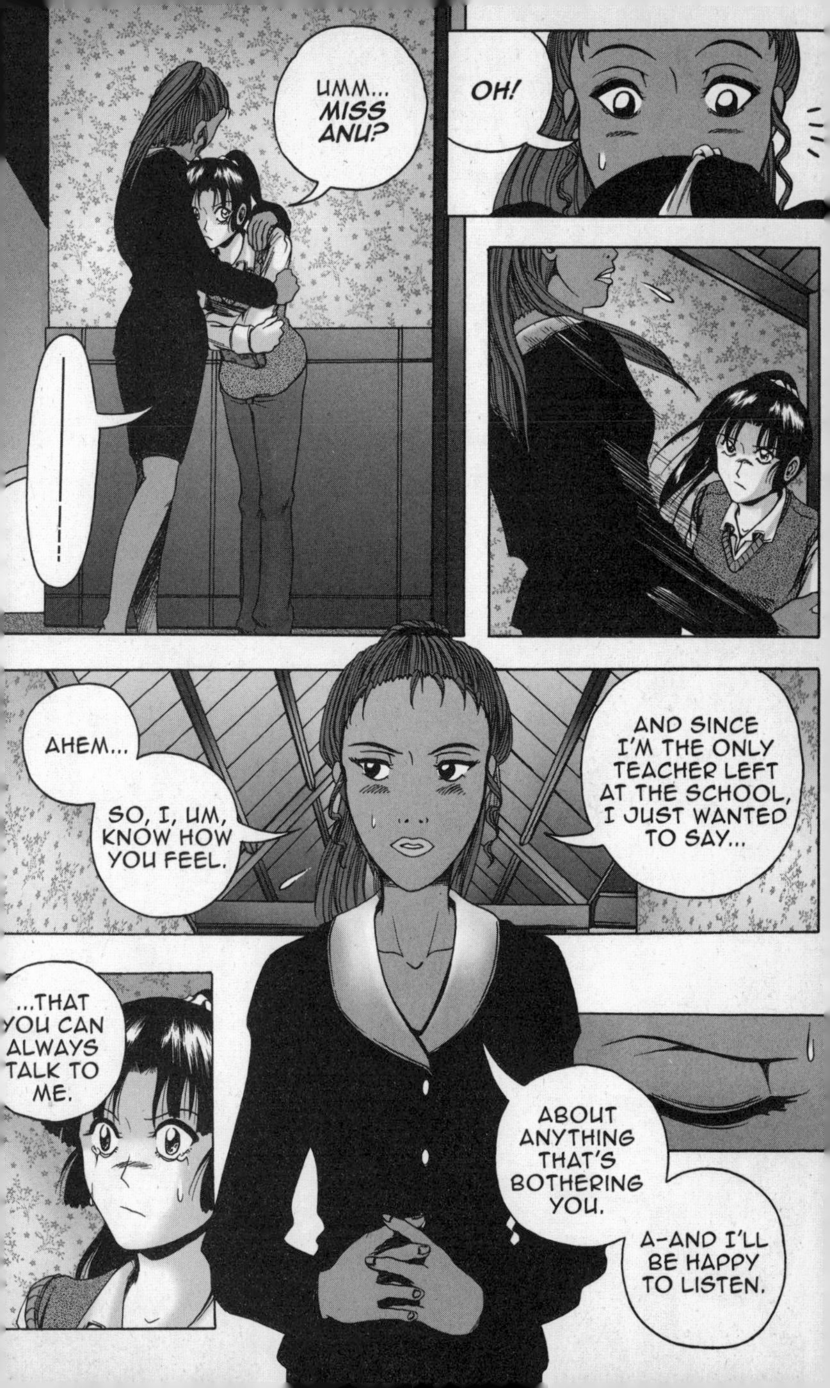
UMM... MISS ANU?
......
OH!
AHEM...
SO, I, UM, KNOW HOW YOU FEEL.
AND SINCE I'M THE ONLY TEACHER LEFT AT THE SCHOOL, I JUST WANTED TO SAY...
...THAT YOU CAN ALWAYS TALK TO ME.
ABOUT ANYTHING THAT'S BOTHERING YOU.
A-AND I'LL BE HAPPY TO LISTEN.

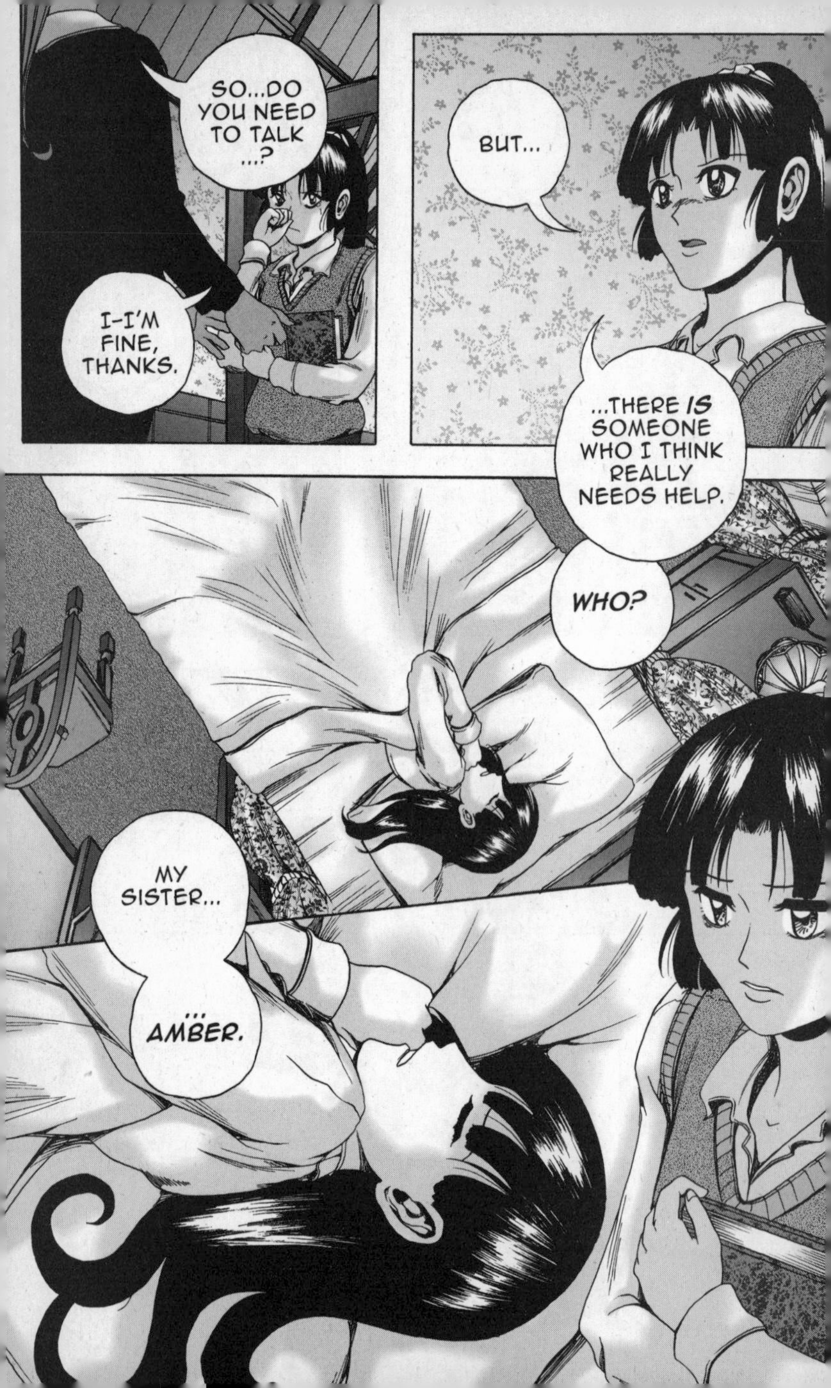
SO...DO YOU NEED TO TALK ...?
I-I'M FINE, THANKS.
BUT...
...THERE IS SOMEONE WHO I THINK REALLY NEEDS HELP.
WHO?
MY SISTER...
... AMBER.

Chapter 9
History of the School

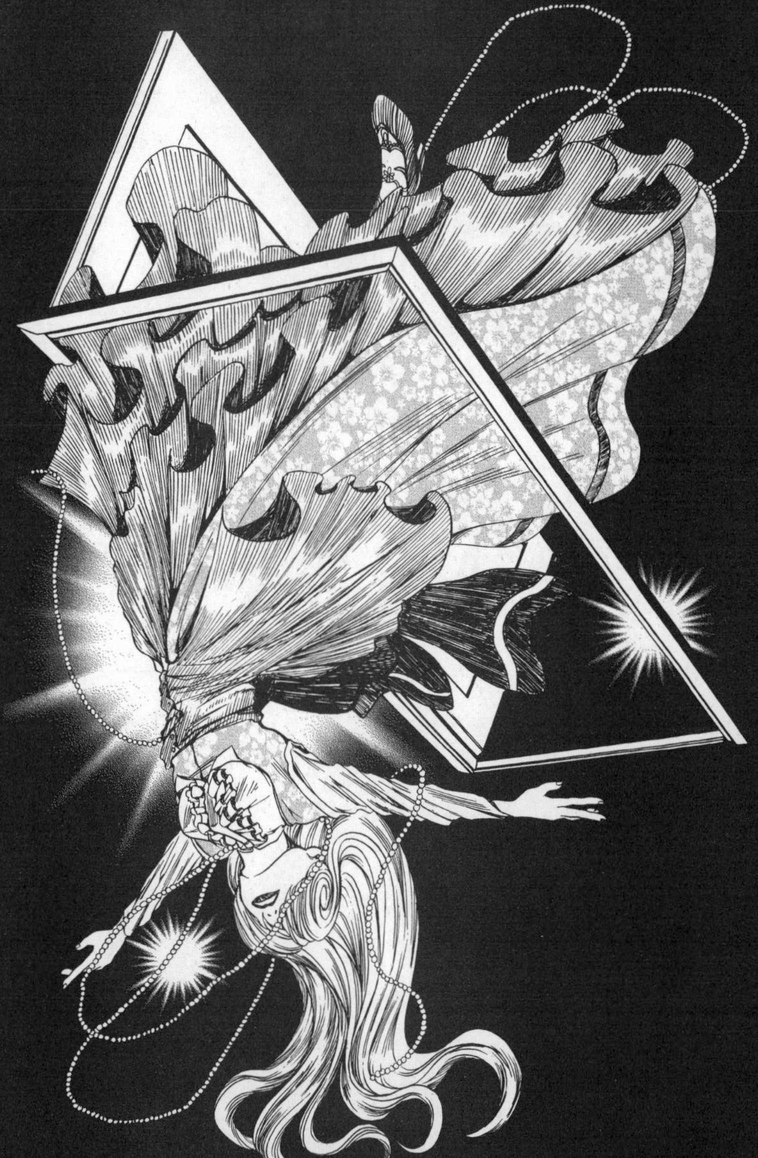

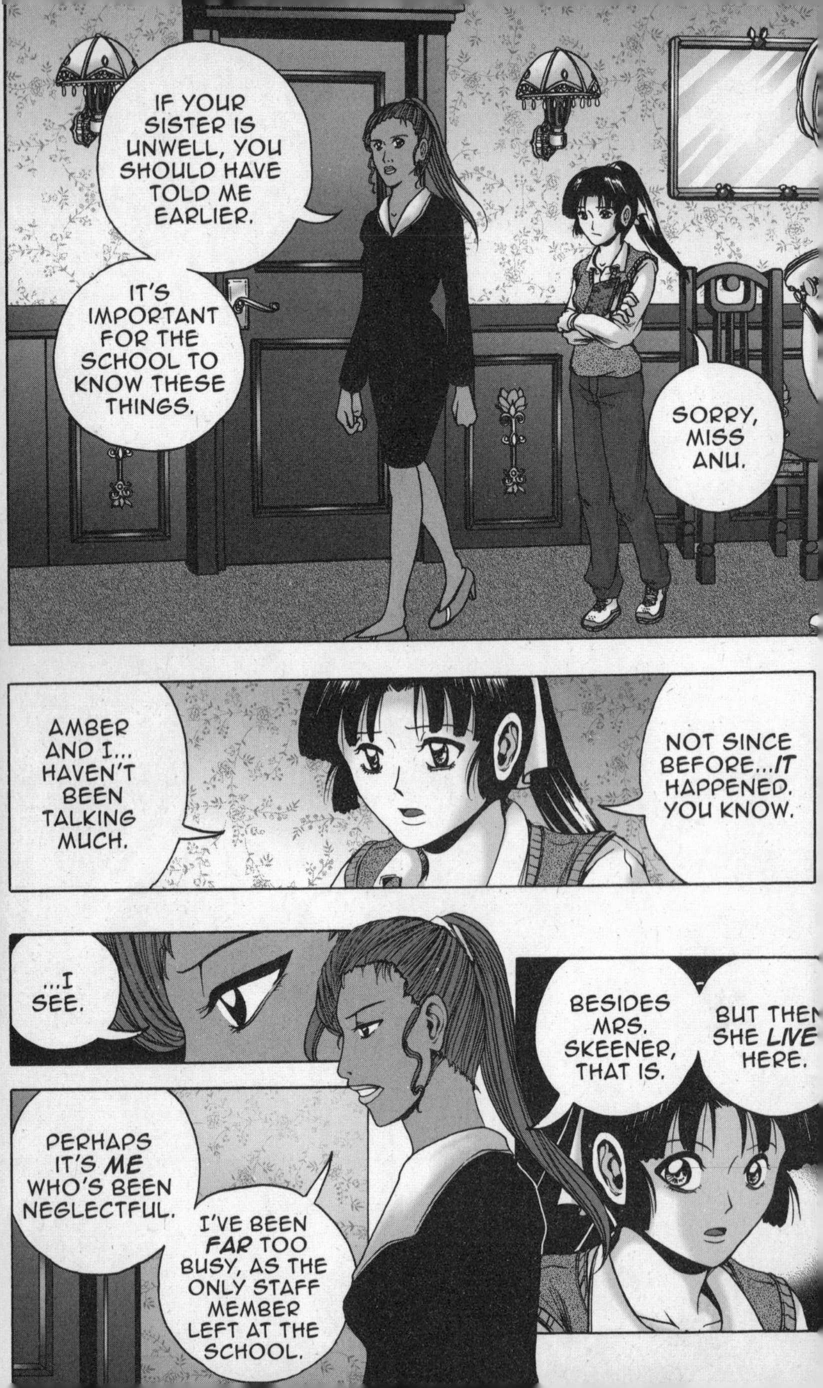
IF YOUR SISTER IS UNWELL, YOU SHOULD HAVE TOLD ME EARLIER.
IT'S IMPORTANT FOR THE SCHOOL TO KNOW THESE THINGS.
SORRY, MISS ANU.
AMBER AND I... HAVEN'T BEEN TALKING MUCH.
NOT SINCE BEFORE...*IT* HAPPENED. YOU KNOW.
...I SEE.
BESIDES MRS. SKEENER, THAT IS.
BUT THEN SHE *LIVE* HERE.
PERHAPS IT'S *ME* WHO'S BEEN NEGLECTFUL.
I'VE BEEN *FAR* TOO BUSY, AS THE ONLY STAFF MEMBER LEFT AT THE SCHOOL.

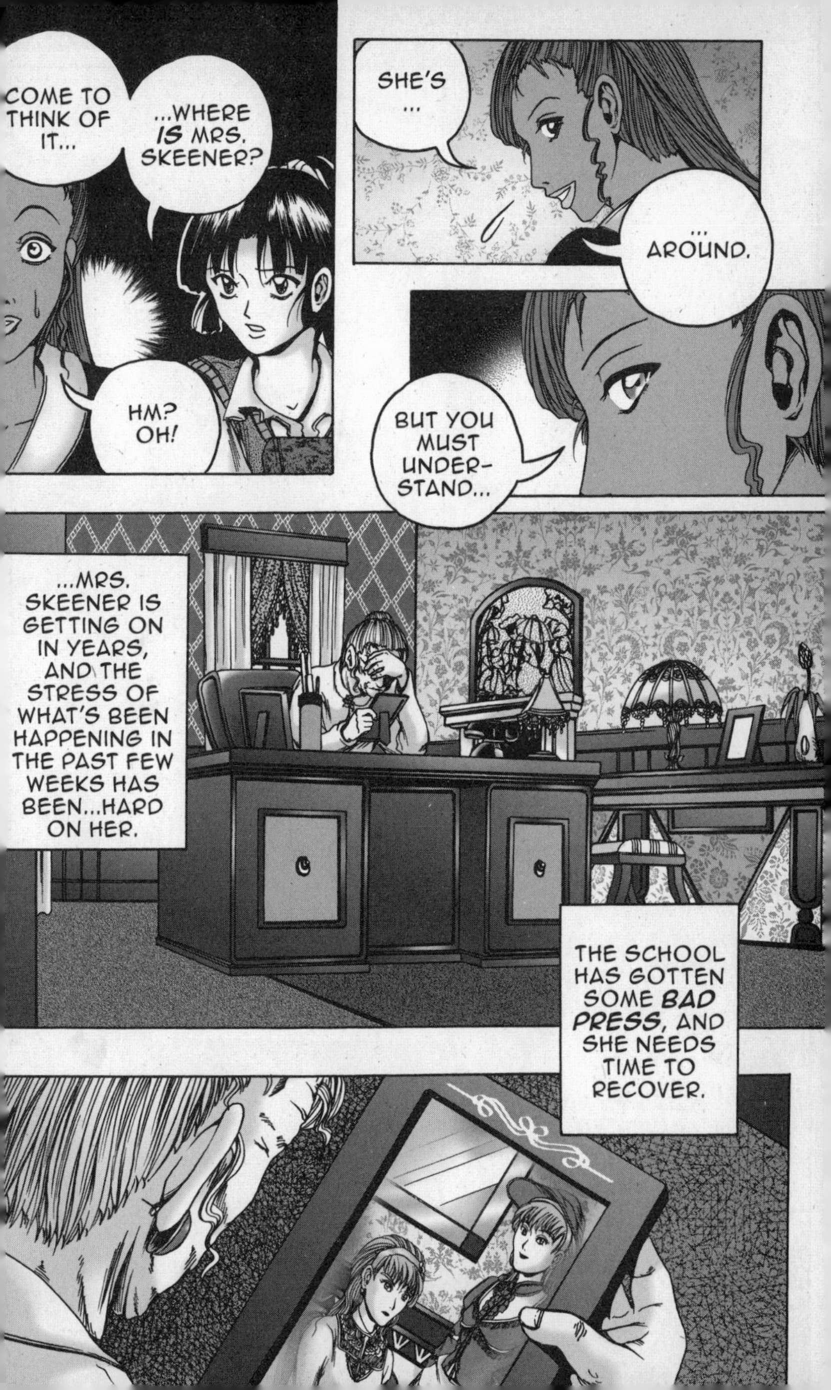
COME TO THINK OF IT...
...WHERE IS MRS. SKEENER?
HM? OH!
SHE'S ...
... AROUND.
BUT YOU MUST UNDER-STAND...
...MRS. SKEENER IS GETTING ON IN YEARS, AND THE STRESS OF WHAT'S BEEN HAPPENING IN THE PAST FEW WEEKS HAS BEEN...HARD ON HER.
THE SCHOOL HAS GOTTEN SOME BAD PRESS, AND SHE NEEDS TIME TO RECOVER.

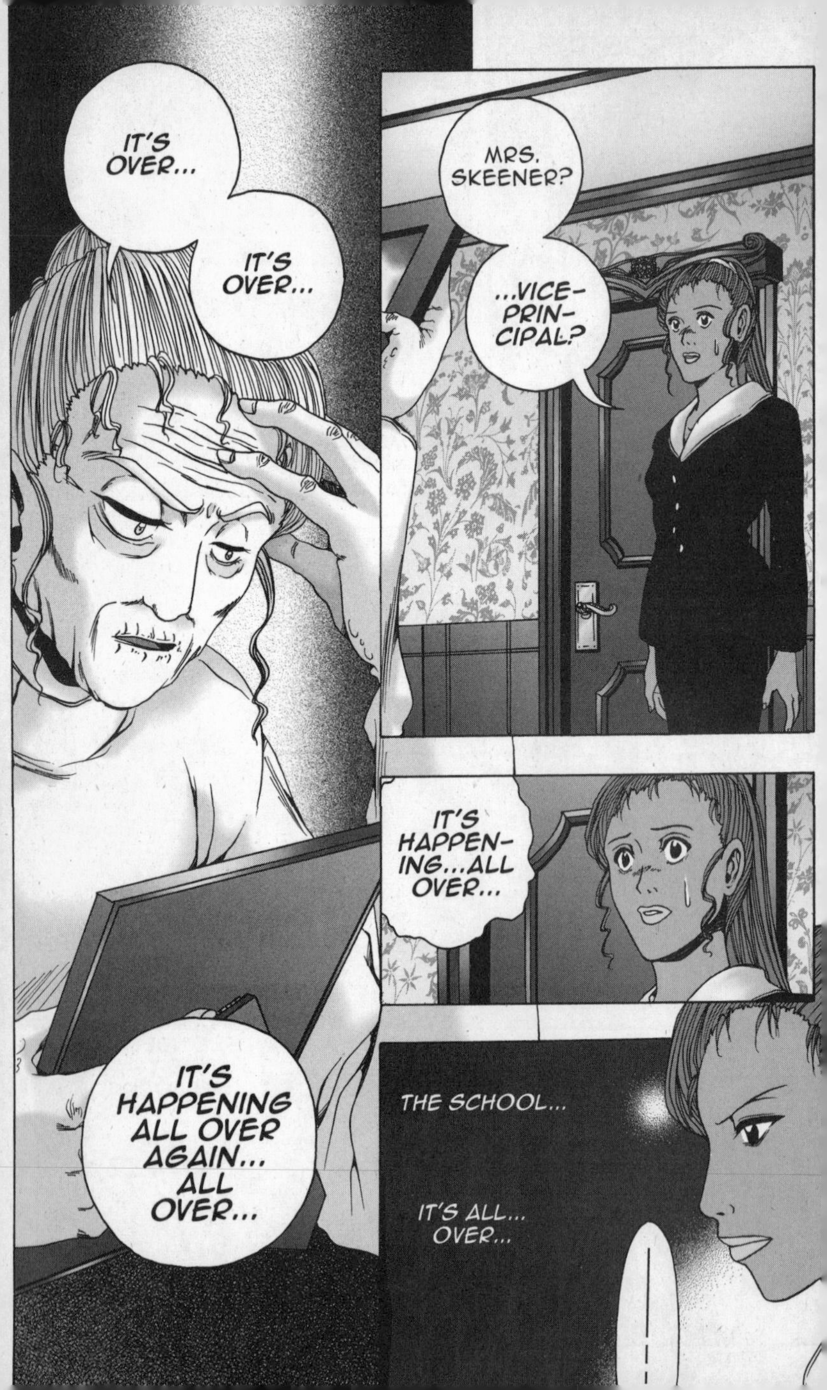
IT'S OVER...
IT'S OVER...
IT'S HAPPENING ALL OVER AGAIN... ALL OVER...
MRS. SKEENER?
...VICE-PRINCIPAL?
IT'S HAPPENING...ALL OVER...
THE SCHOOL...
IT'S ALL... OVER...

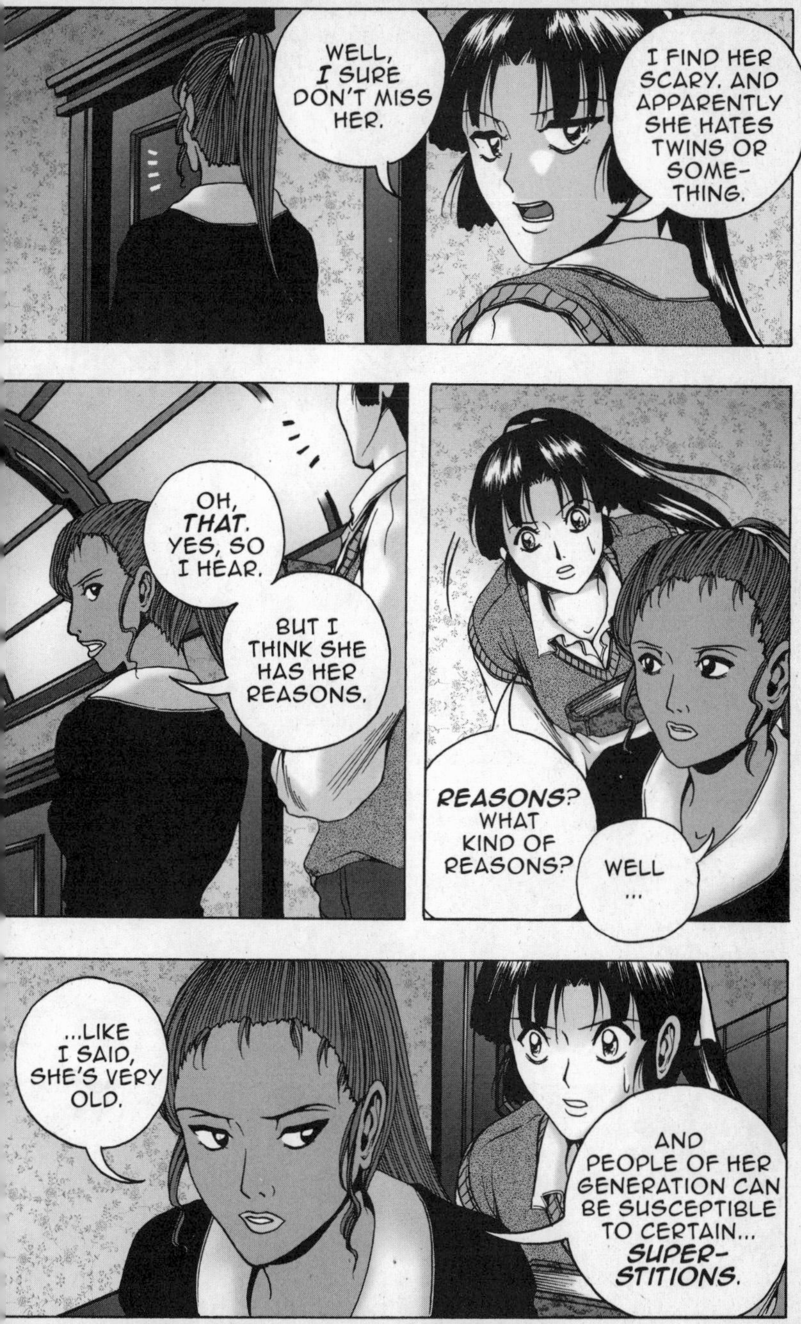
WELL, I SURE DON'T MISS HER.
I FIND HER SCARY. AND APPARENTLY SHE HATES TWINS OR SOME-THING.
OH, THAT. YES, SO I HEAR.
BUT I THINK SHE HAS HER REASONS.
REASONS? WHAT KIND OF REASONS?
WELL ...
...LIKE I SAID, SHE'S VERY OLD.
AND PEOPLE OF HER GENERATION CAN BE SUSCEPTIBLE TO CERTAIN... SUPER-STITIONS.

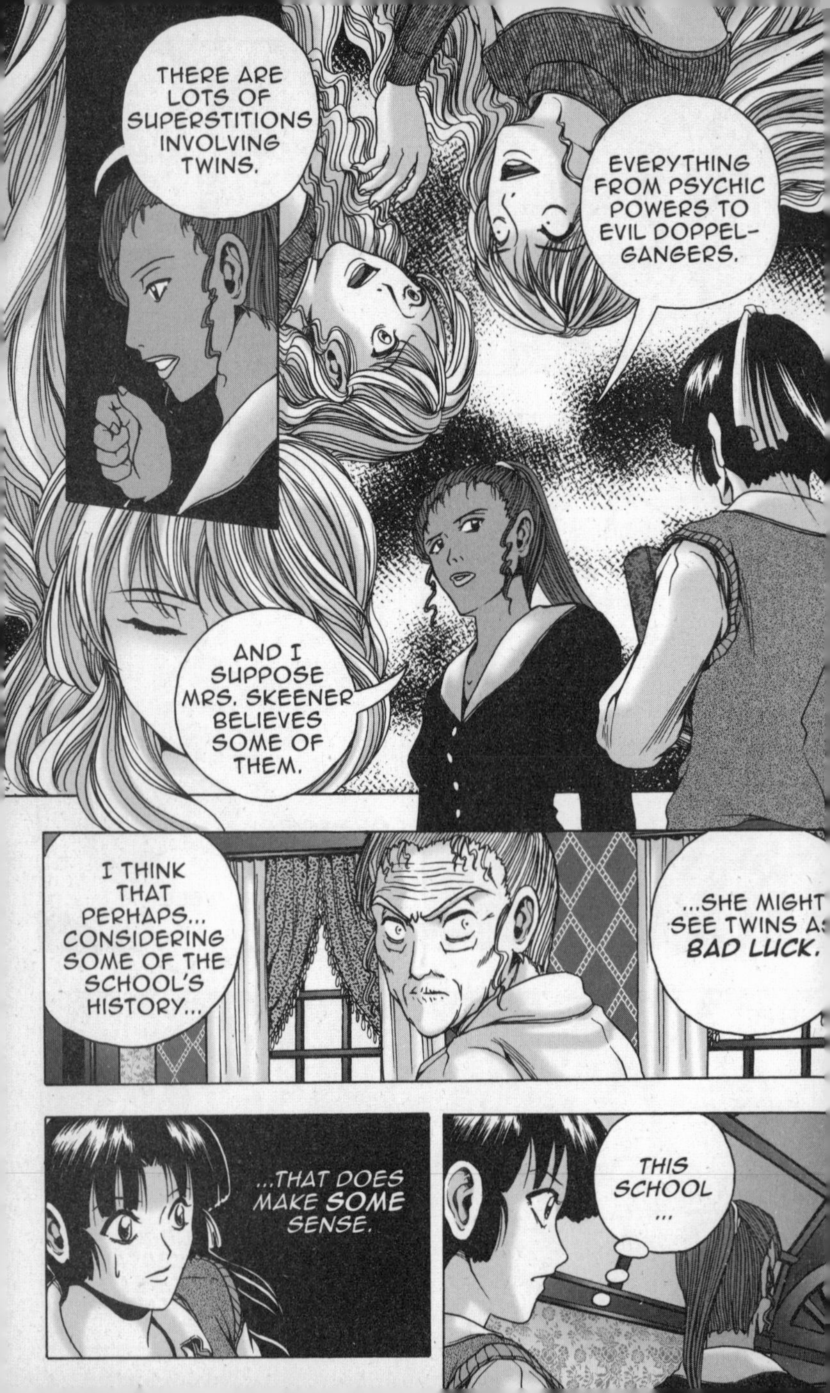
THERE ARE LOTS OF SUPERSTITIONS INVOLVING TWINS.
EVERYTHING FROM PSYCHIC POWERS TO EVIL DOPPEL-GANGERS.
AND I SUPPOSE MRS. SKEENER BELIEVES SOME OF THEM.
I THINK THAT PERHAPS... CONSIDERING SOME OF THE SCHOOL'S HISTORY...
...SHE MIGHT SEE TWINS AS BAD LUCK.
...THAT DOES MAKE SOME SENSE.
THIS SCHOOL ...

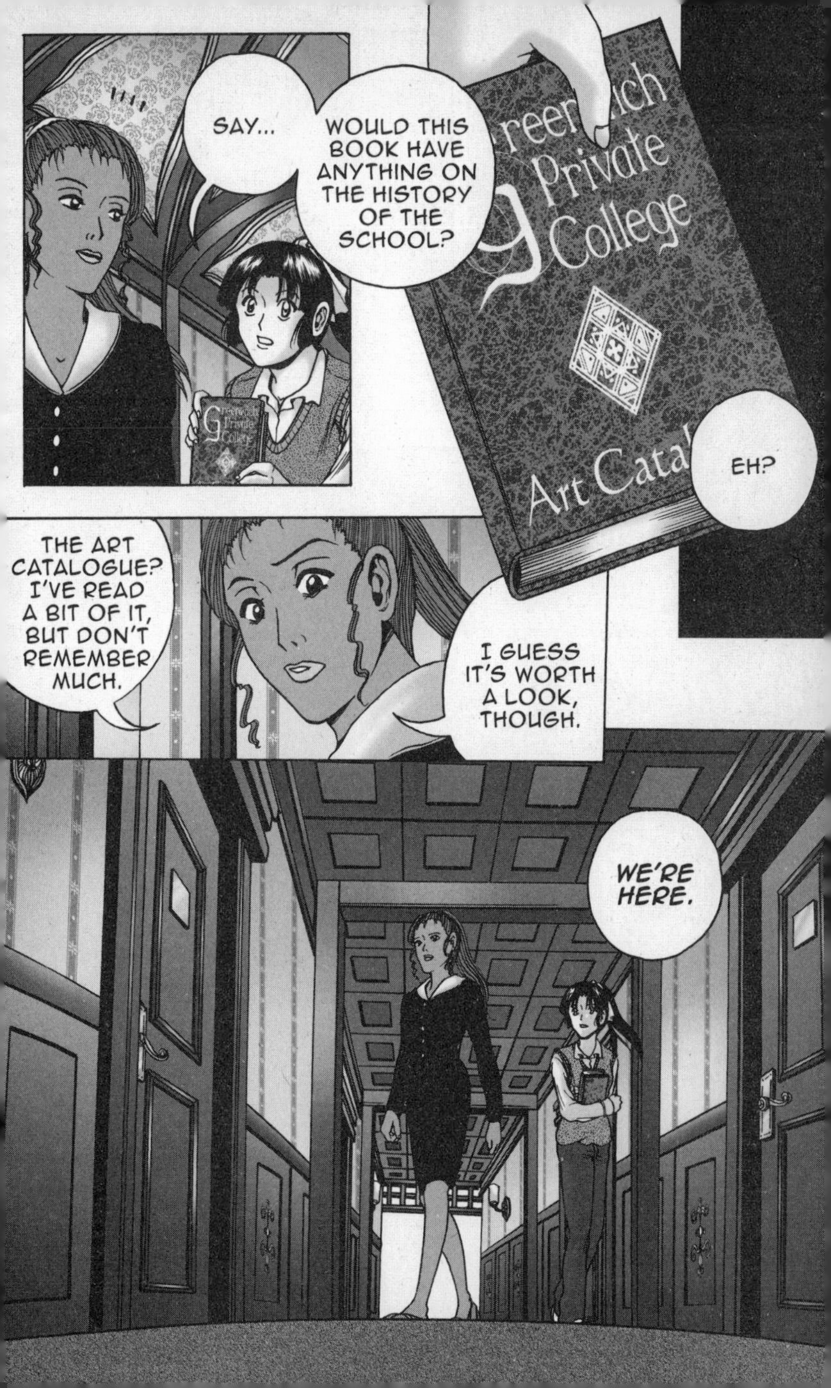
SAY...
WOULD THIS BOOK HAVE ANYTHING ON THE HISTORY OF THE SCHOOL?
EH?
THE ART CATALOGUE? I'VE READ A BIT OF IT, BUT DON'T REMEMBER MUCH.
I GUESS IT'S WORTH A LOOK, THOUGH.
WE'RE HERE.

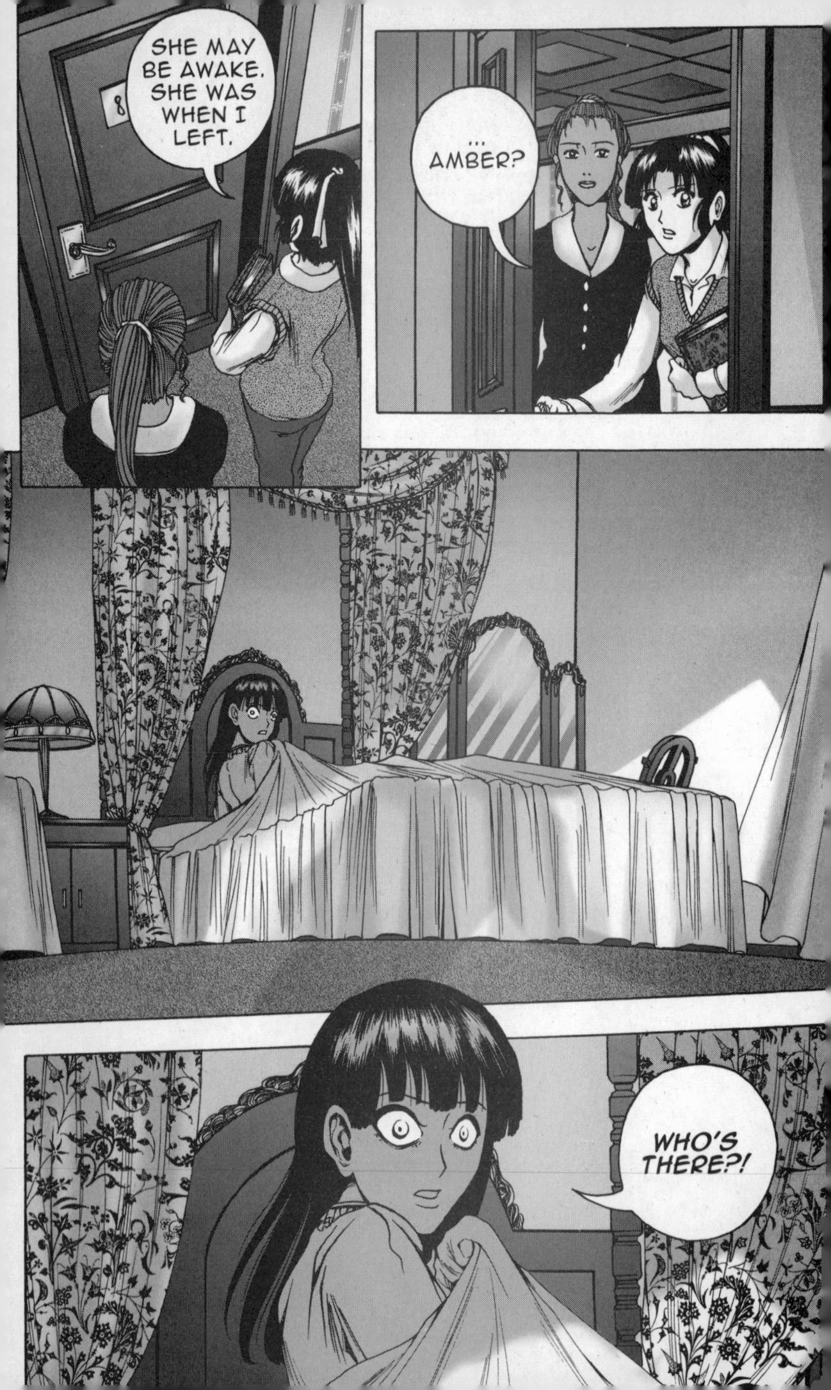
SHE MAY BE AWAKE. SHE WAS WHEN I LEFT.
... AMBER?
WHO'S THERE?!

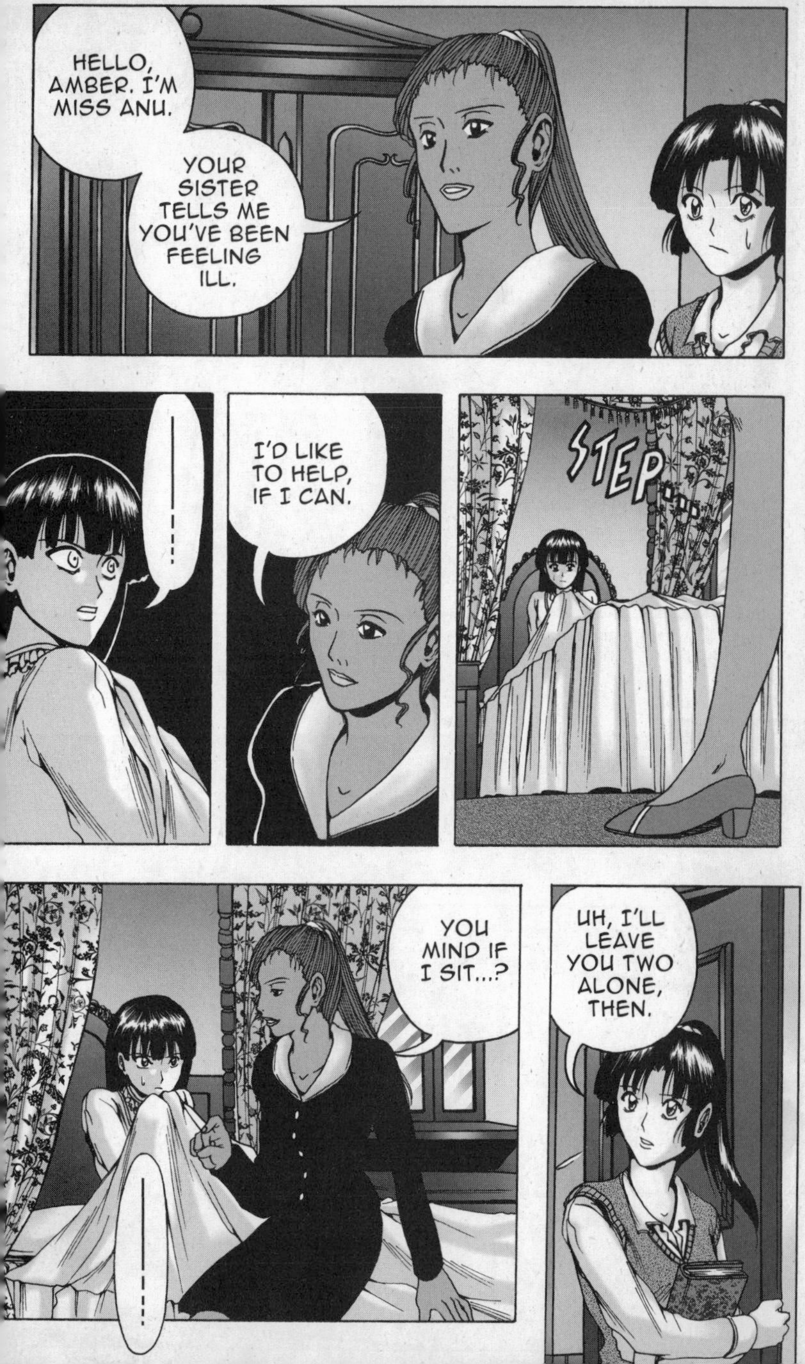
HELLO, AMBER. I'M MISS ANU.
YOUR SISTER TELLS ME YOU'VE BEEN FEELING ILL.
......
I'D LIKE TO HELP, IF I CAN.
STEP...
YOU MIND IF I SIT...?
......
UH, I'LL LEAVE YOU TWO ALONE, THEN.

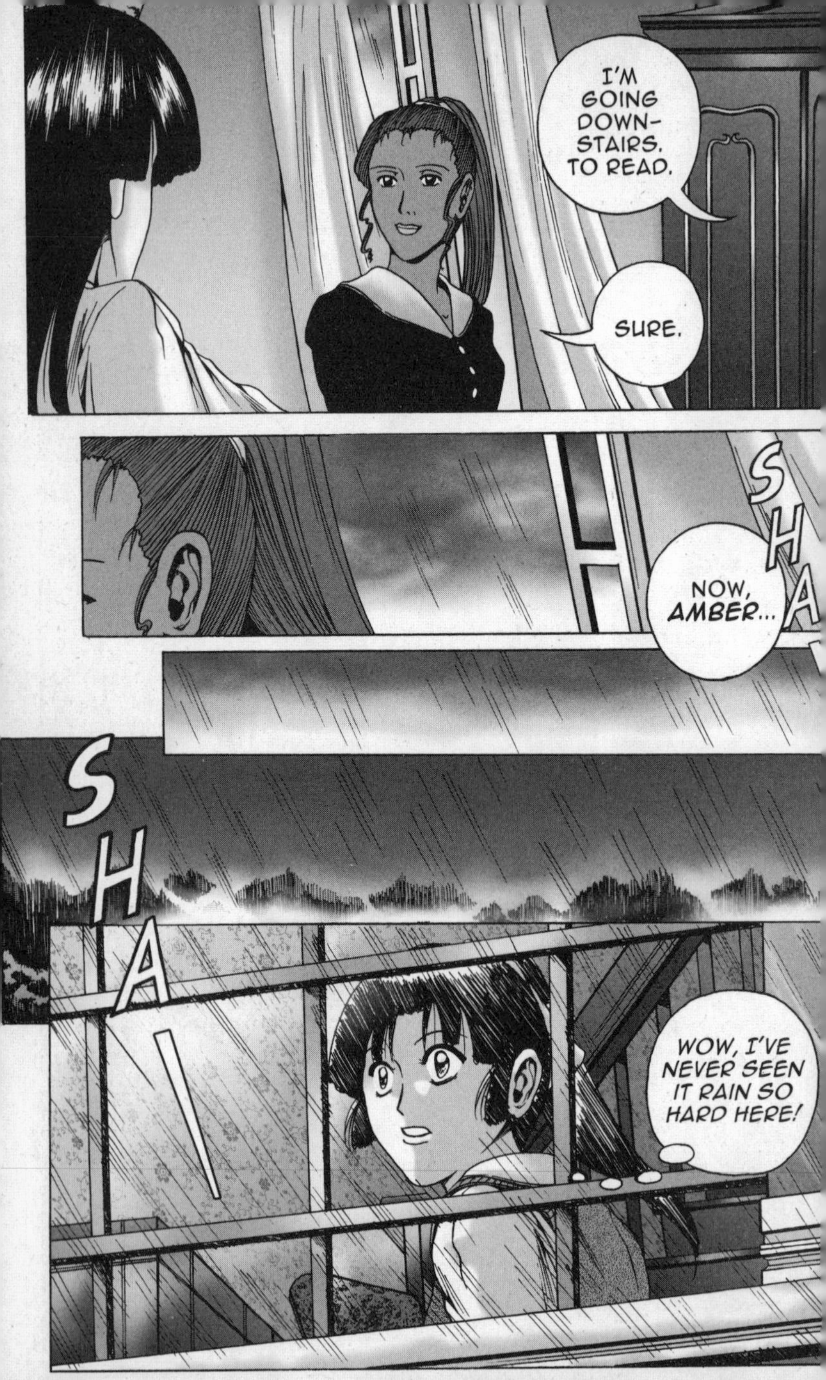
I'M GOING DOWN-STAIRS. TO READ.
SURE.
SHA
NOW, AMBER...
SHA!
WOW, I'VE NEVER SEEN IT RAIN SO HARD HERE!

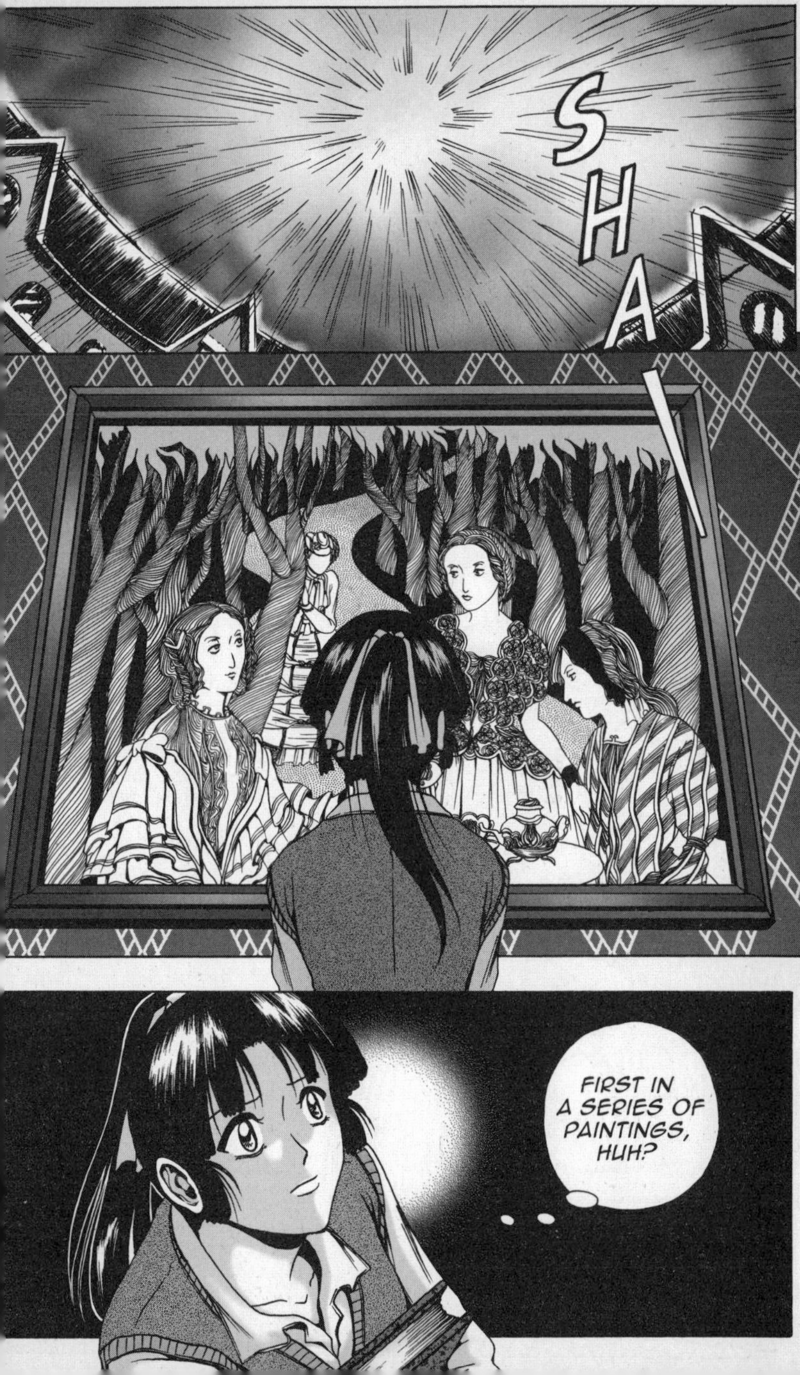
SHA
FIRST IN A SERIES OF PAINTINGS, HUH?

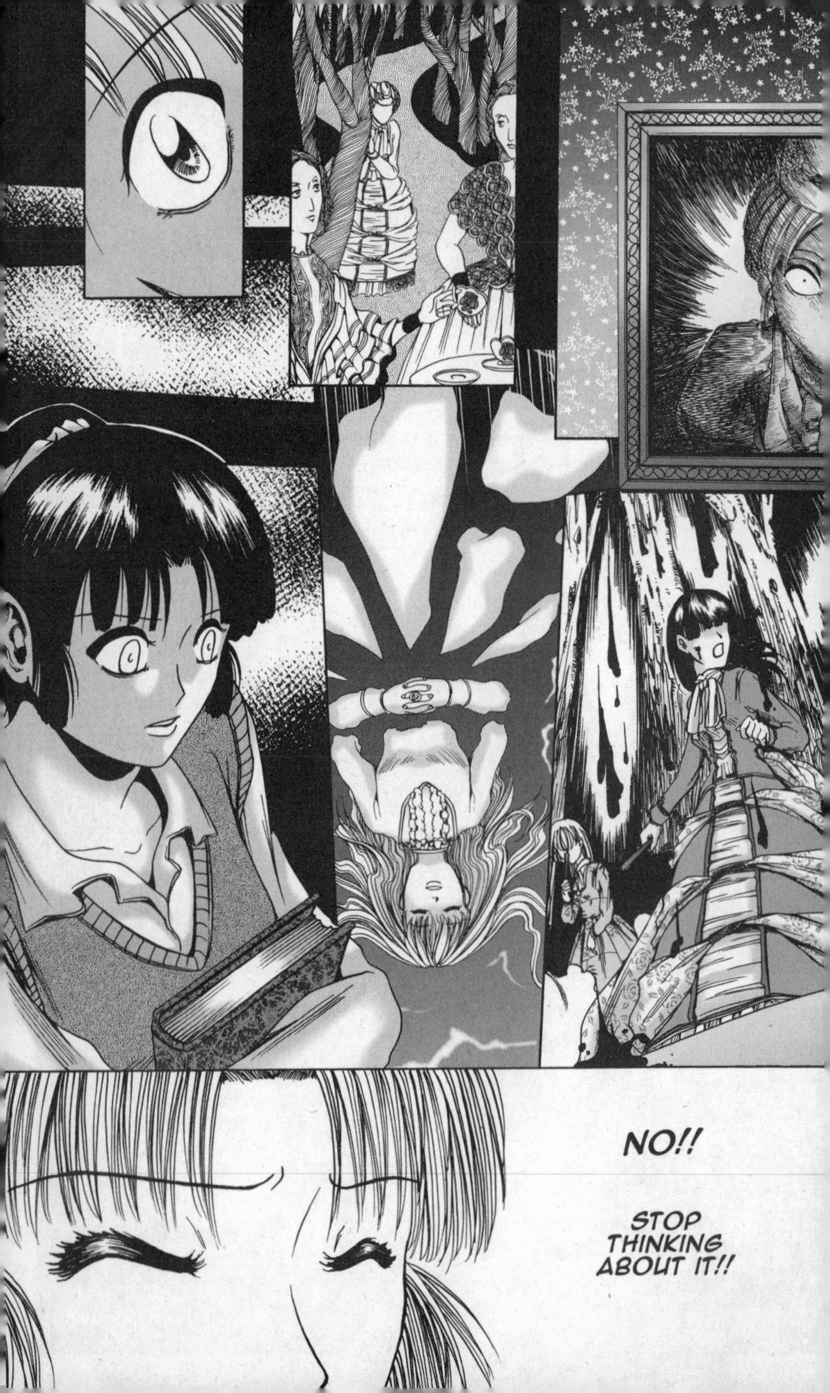
NO!!
STOP THINKING ABOUT IT!!

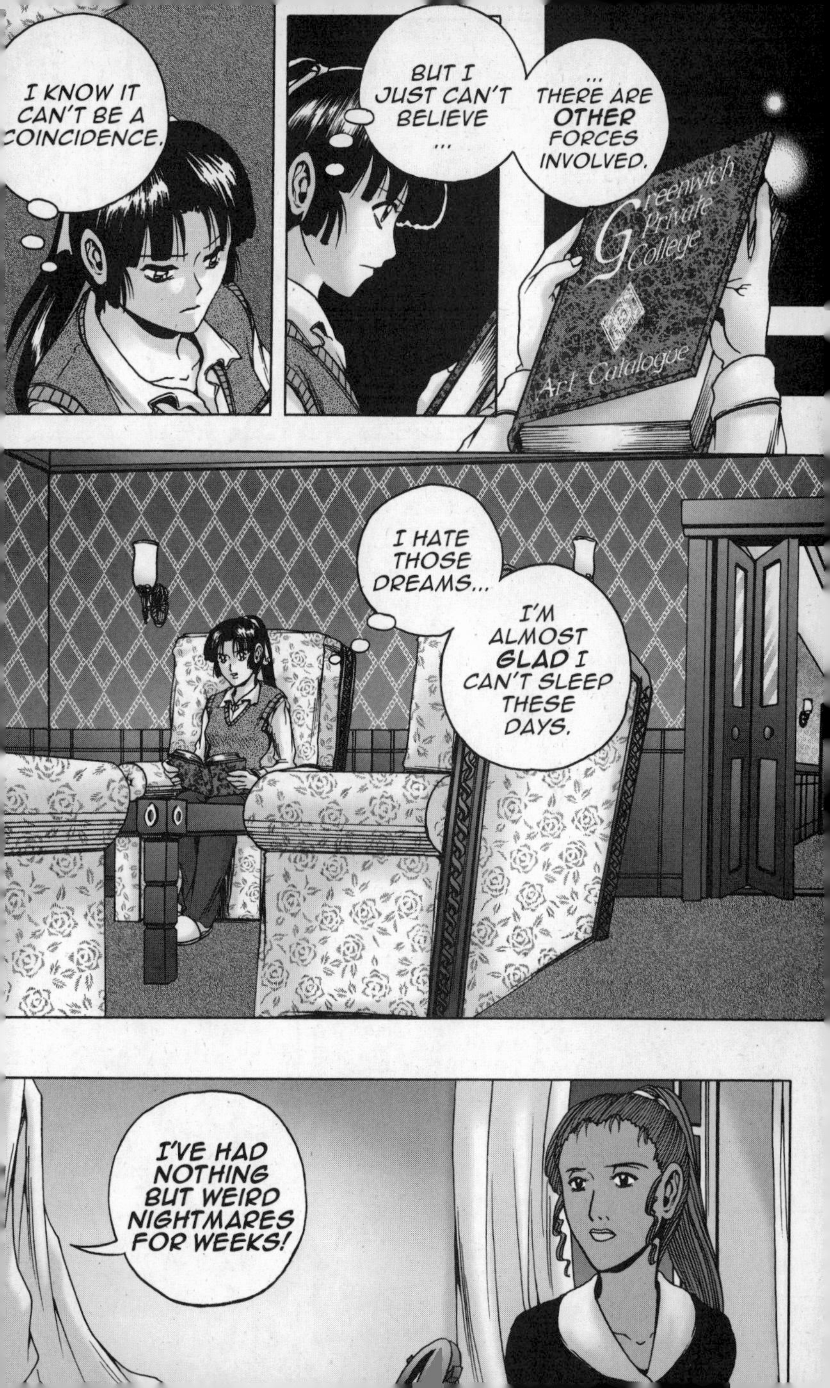
I KNOW IT CAN'T BE A COINCIDENCE.
BUT I JUST CAN'T BELIEVE ...
... THERE ARE OTHER FORCES INVOLVED.
Greenwich Private College Art Catalogue
I HATE THOSE DREAMS...
I'M ALMOST GLAD I CAN'T SLEEP THESE DAYS.
I'VE HAD NOTHING BUT WEIRD NIGHTMARES FOR WEEKS!

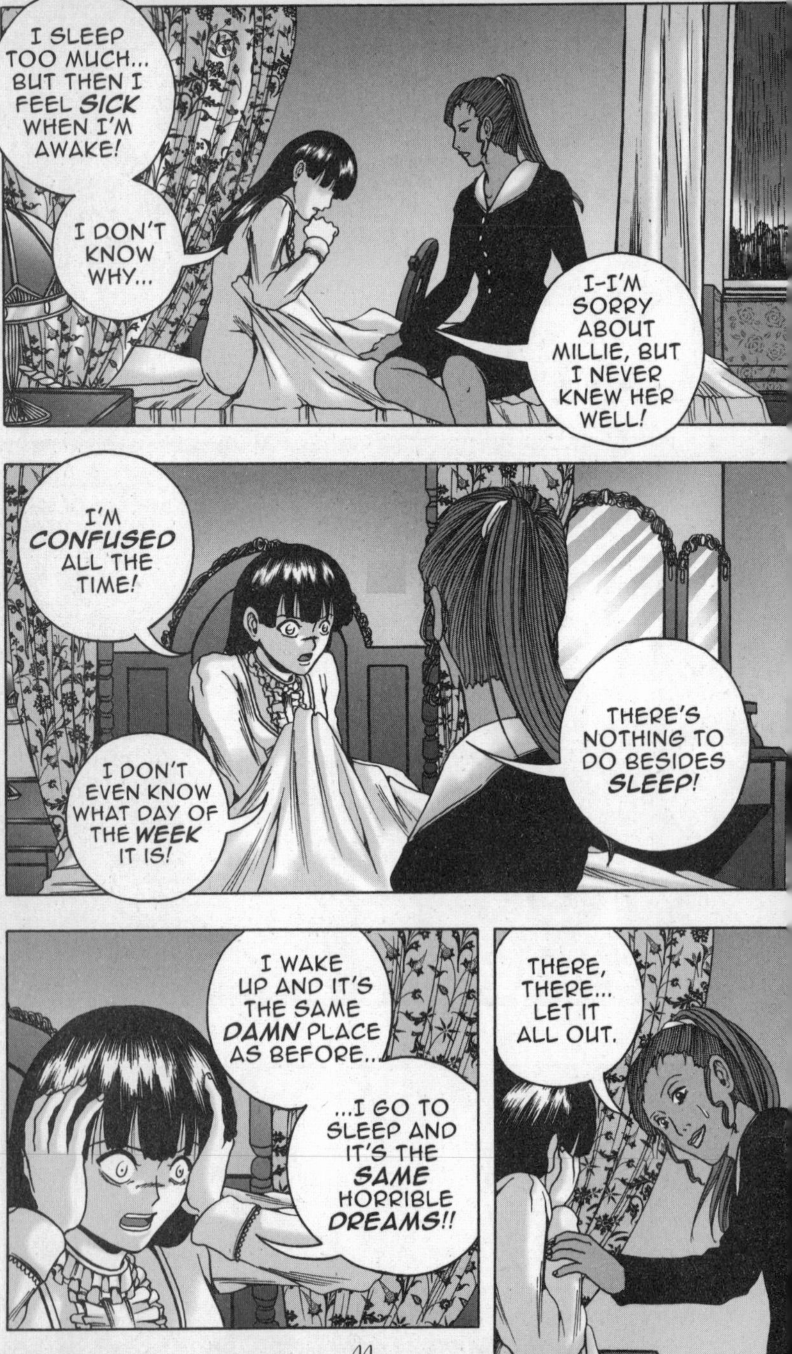
I SLEEP TOO MUCH... BUT THEN I FEEL SICK WHEN I'M AWAKE!
I DON'T KNOW WHY...
I-I'M SORRY ABOUT MILLIE, BUT I NEVER KNEW HER WELL!
I'M CONFUSED ALL THE TIME!
I DON'T EVEN KNOW WHAT DAY OF THE WEEK IT IS!
THERE'S NOTHING TO DO BESIDES SLEEP!
I WAKE UP AND IT'S THE SAME DAMN PLACE AS BEFORE...
...I GO TO SLEEP AND IT'S THE SAME HORRIBLE DREAMS!!
THERE, THERE... LET IT ALL OUT.

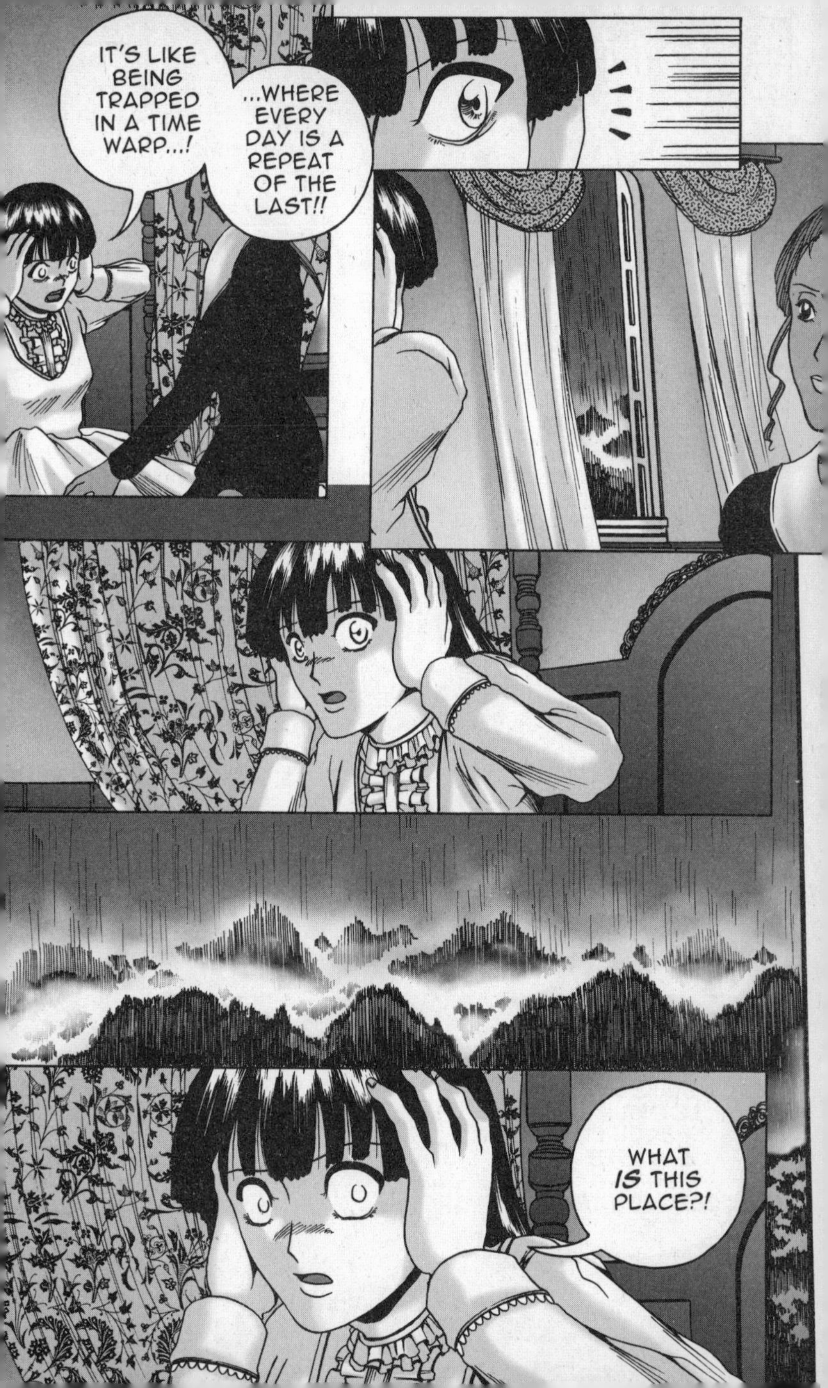
IT'S LIKE BEING TRAPPED IN A TIME WARP...!
...WHERE EVERY DAY IS A REPEAT OF THE LAST!!
WHAT *IS* THIS PLACE?!

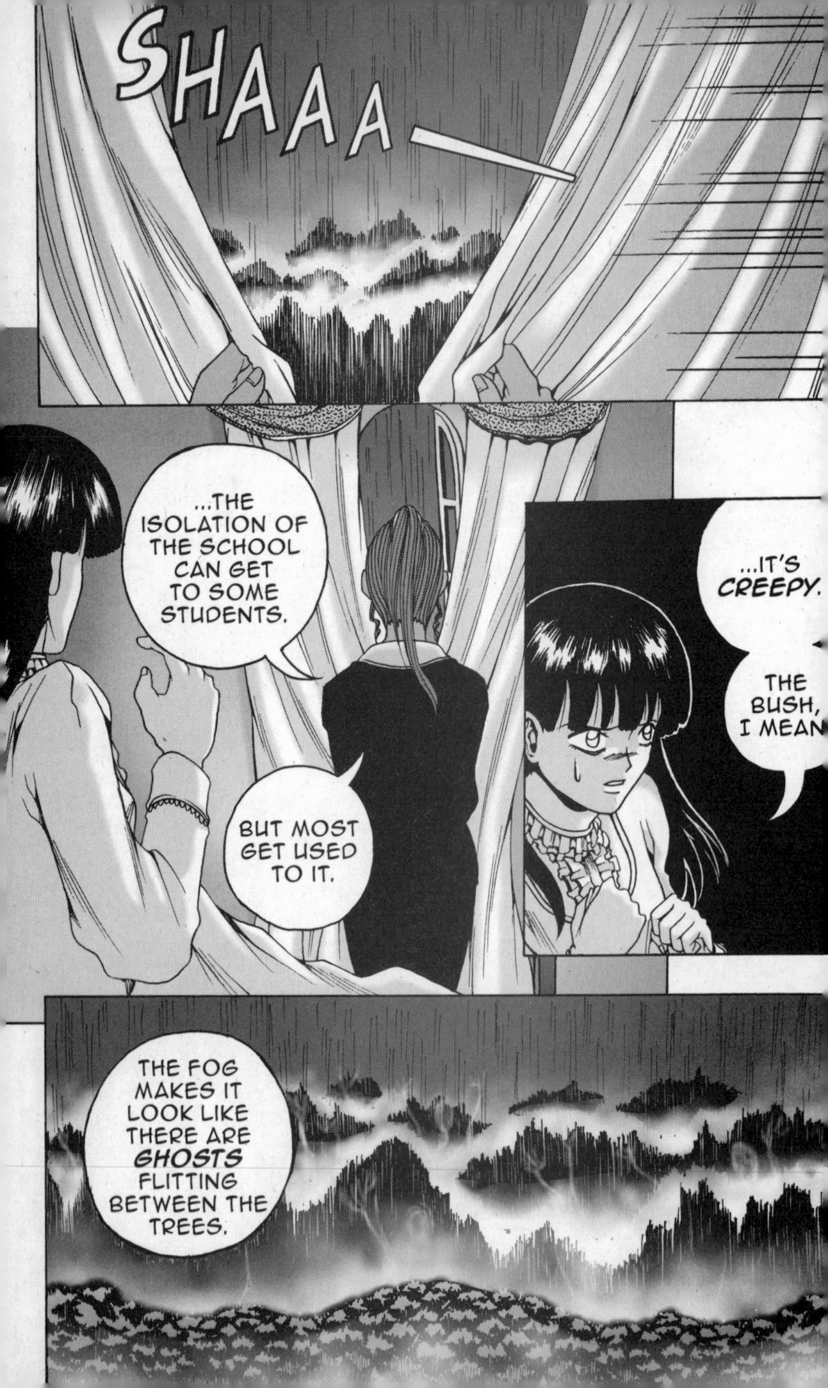
SHAAA
...THE ISOLATION OF THE SCHOOL CAN GET TO SOME STUDENTS.
BUT MOST GET USED TO IT.
...IT'S *CREEPY.*
THE BUSH, I MEAN
THE FOG MAKES IT LOOK LIKE THERE ARE *GHOSTS* FLITTING BETWEEN THE TREES.

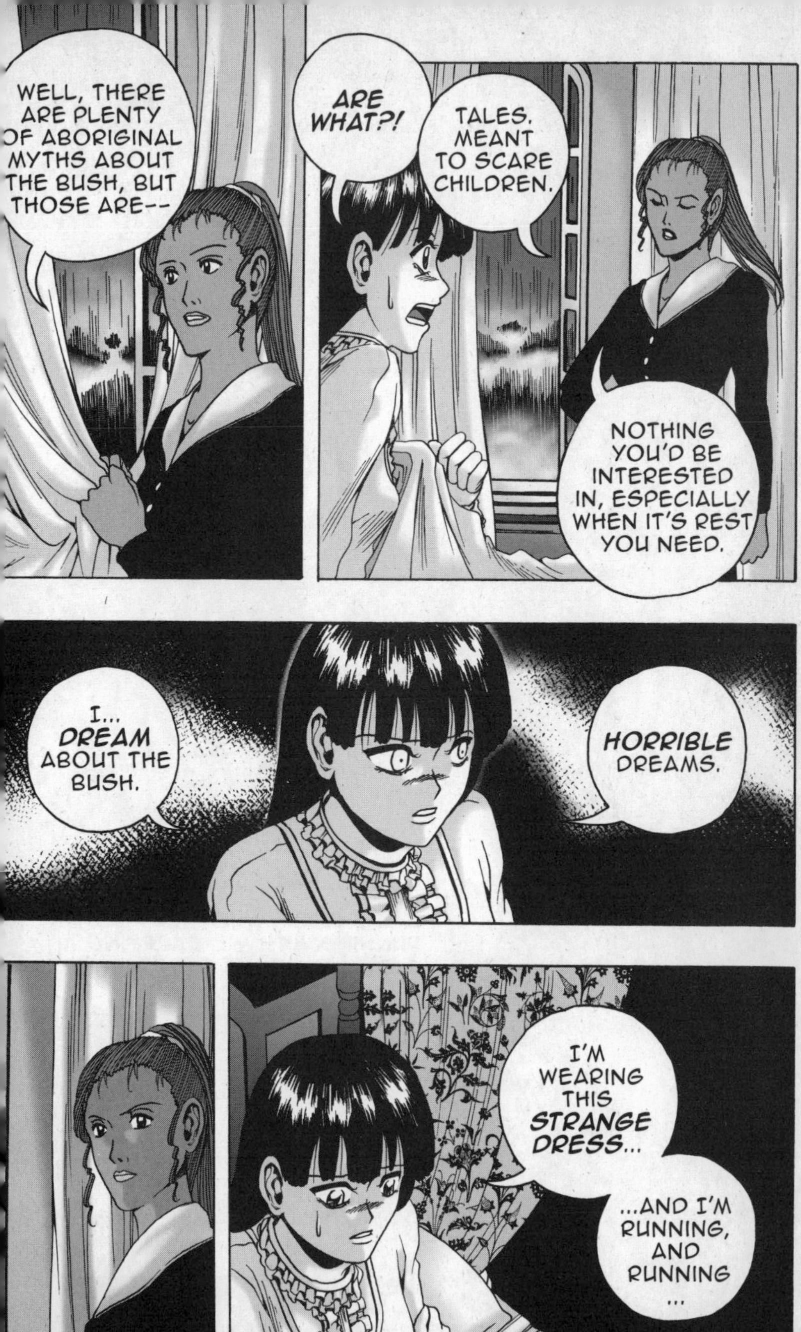

WELL, THERE ARE PLENTY OF ABORIGINAL MYTHS ABOUT THE BUSH, BUT THOSE ARE--
ARE WHAT?!
TALES. MEANT TO SCARE CHILDREN.
NOTHING YOU'D BE INTERESTED IN, ESPECIALLY WHEN IT'S REST YOU NEED.
I... DREAM ABOUT THE BUSH.
HORRIBLE DREAMS.
I'M WEARING THIS STRANGE DRESS...
...AND I'M RUNNING, AND RUNNING ...

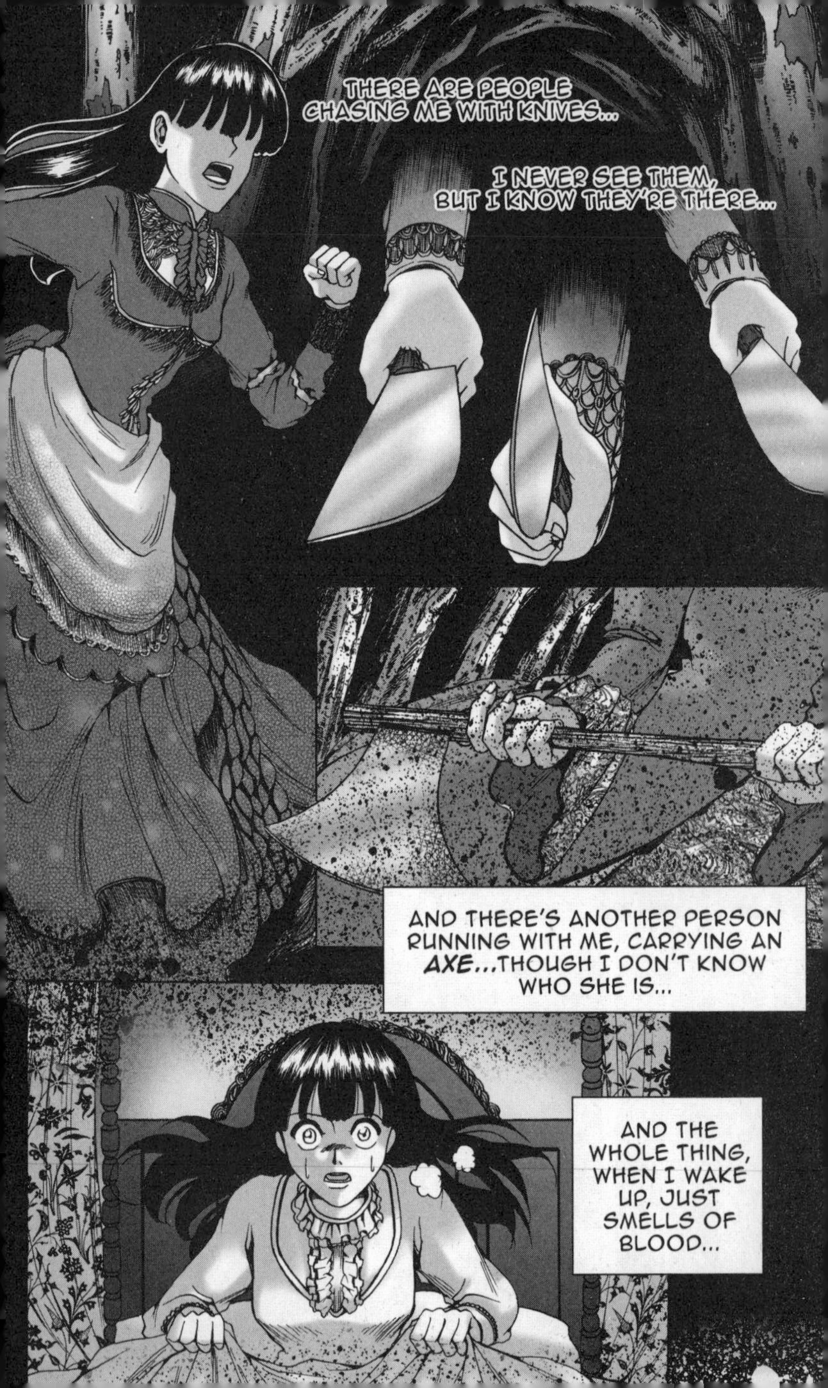
THERE ARE PEOPLE CHASING ME WITH KNIVES...
I NEVER SEE THEM, BUT I KNOW THEY'RE THERE...
AND THERE'S ANOTHER PERSON RUNNING WITH ME, CARRYING AN *AXE*...THOUGH I DON'T KNOW WHO SHE IS...
AND THE WHOLE THING, WHEN I WAKE UP, JUST SMELLS OF BLOOD...

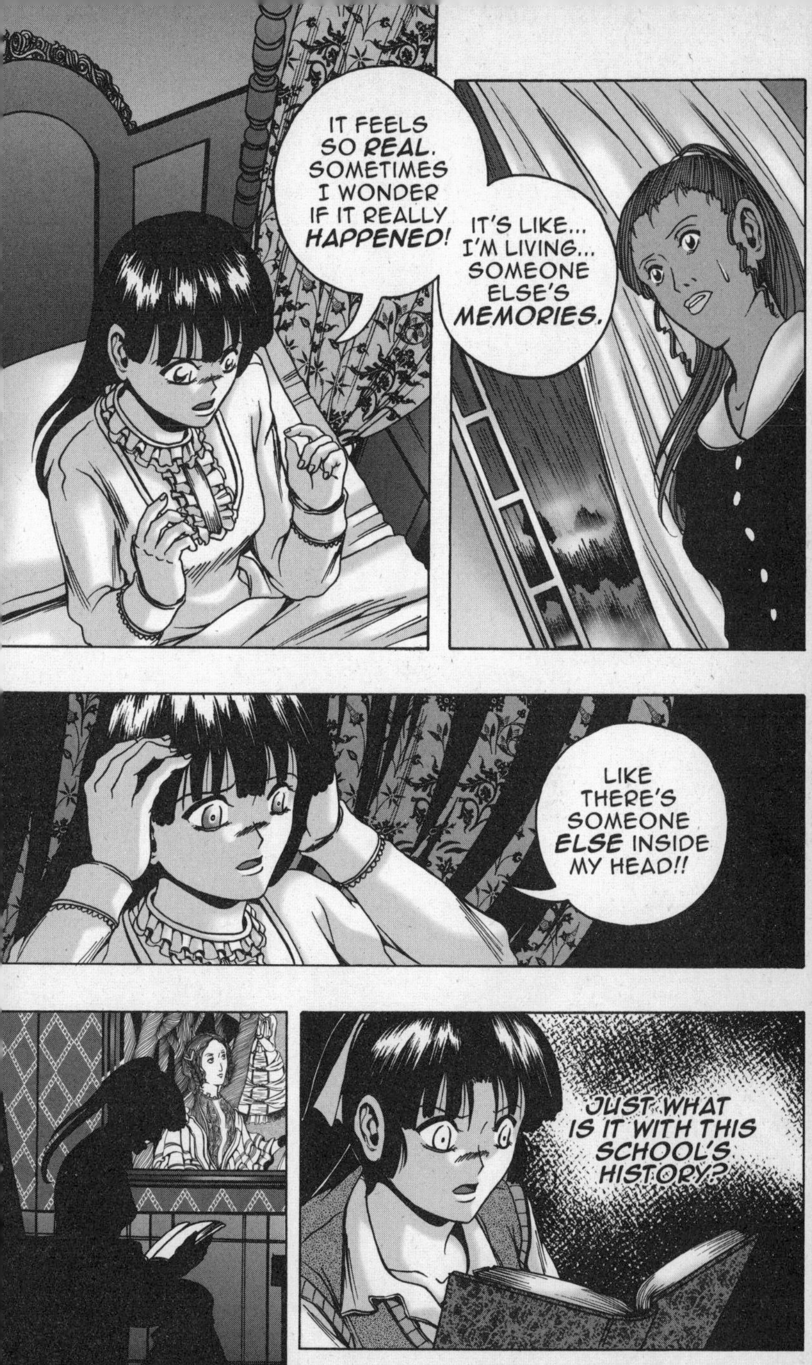
IT FEELS SO REAL. SOMETIMES I WONDER IF IT REALLY HAPPENED!
IT'S LIKE... I'M LIVING... SOMEONE ELSE'S MEMORIES.
LIKE THERE'S SOMEONE ELSE INSIDE MY HEAD!!
JUST WHAT IS IT WITH THIS SCHOOL'S HISTORY?

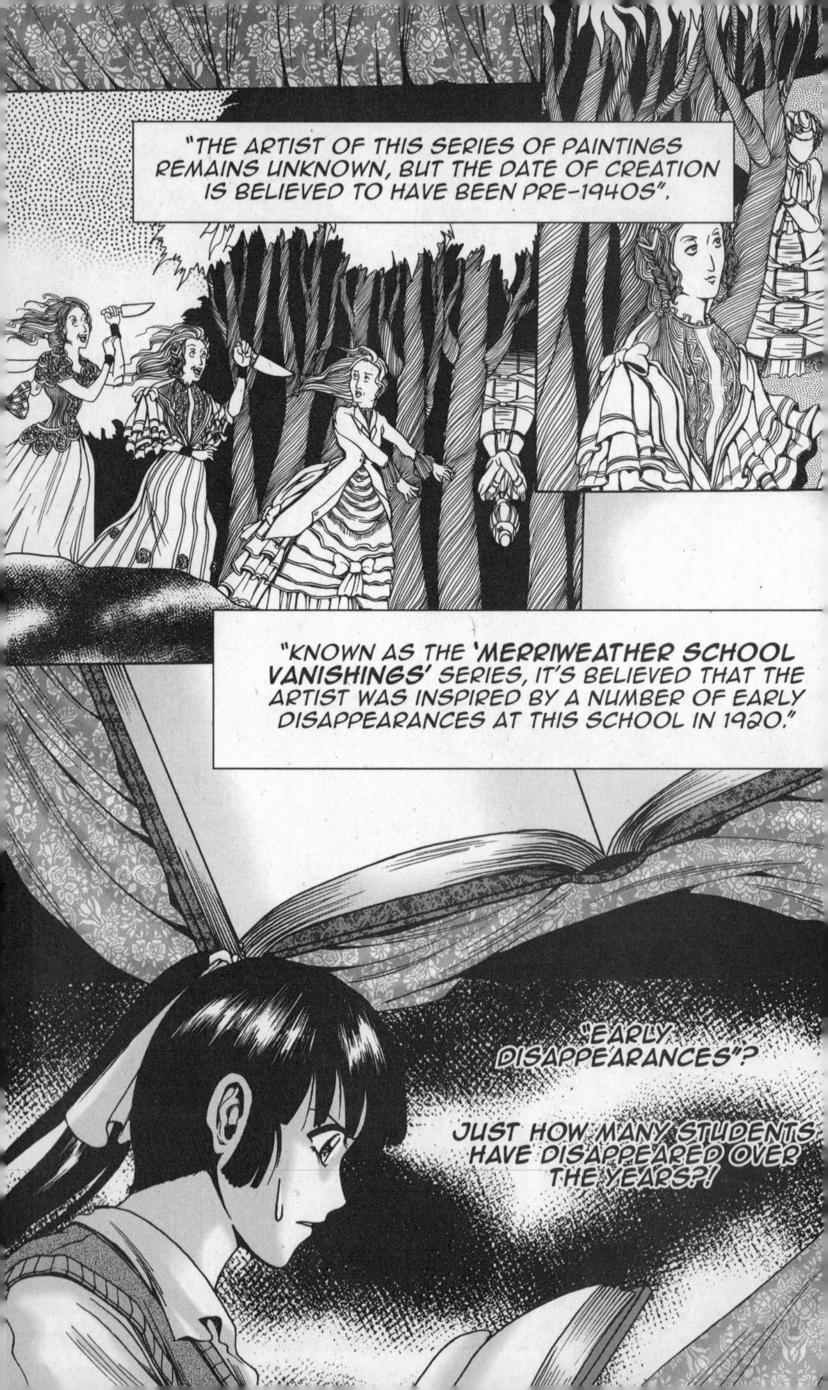
"THE ARTIST OF THIS SERIES OF PAINTINGS REMAINS UNKNOWN, BUT THE DATE OF CREATION IS BELIEVED TO HAVE BEEN PRE-1940S".
"KNOWN AS THE 'MERRIWEATHER SCHOOL VANISHINGS' SERIES, IT'S BELIEVED THAT THE ARTIST WAS INSPIRED BY A NUMBER OF EARLY DISAPPEARANCES AT THIS SCHOOL IN 1920."
"EARLY DISAPPEARANCES"?
JUST HOW MANY STUDENTS HAVE DISAPPEARED OVER THE YEARS?!

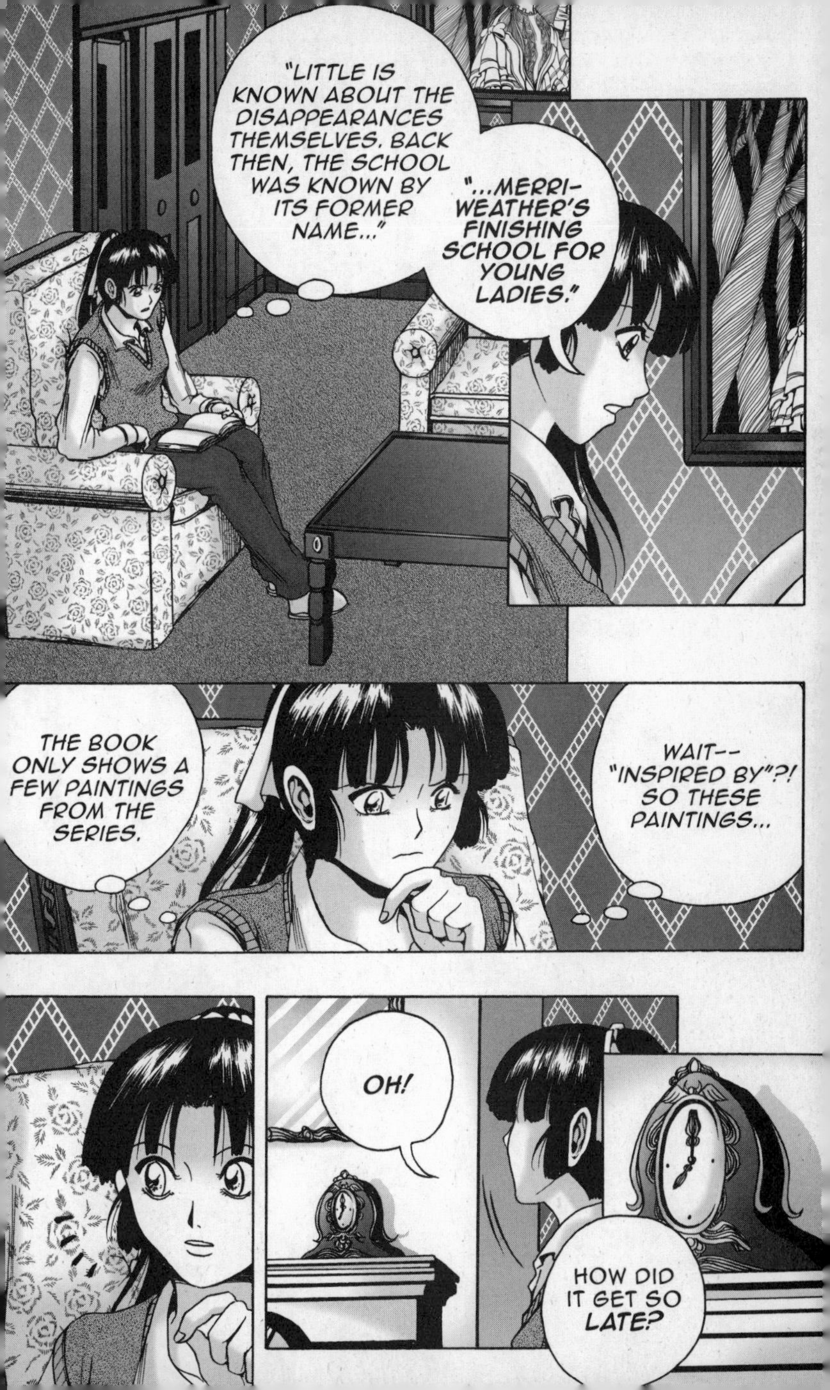
"LITTLE IS KNOWN ABOUT THE DISAPPEARANCES THEMSELVES. BACK THEN, THE SCHOOL WAS KNOWN BY ITS FORMER NAME..."
"...MERRI-WEATHER'S FINISHING SCHOOL FOR YOUNG LADIES."
THE BOOK ONLY SHOWS A FEW PAINTINGS FROM THE SERIES.
WAIT-- "INSPIRED BY"?! SO THESE PAINTINGS...
OH!
HOW DID IT GET SO LATE?

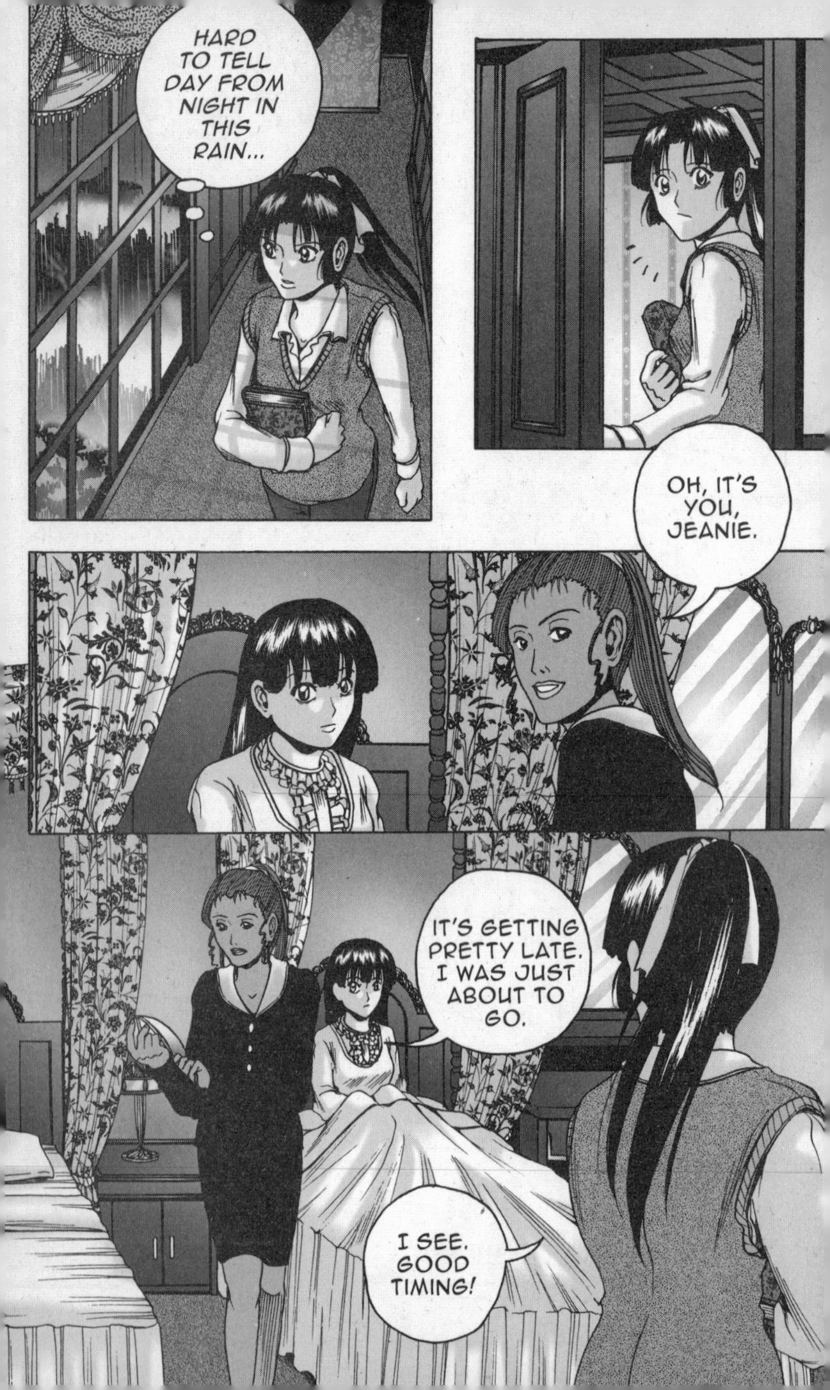
HARD TO TELL DAY FROM NIGHT IN THIS RAIN...
OH, IT'S YOU, JEANIE.
IT'S GETTING PRETTY LATE. I WAS JUST ABOUT TO GO.
I SEE. GOOD TIMING!

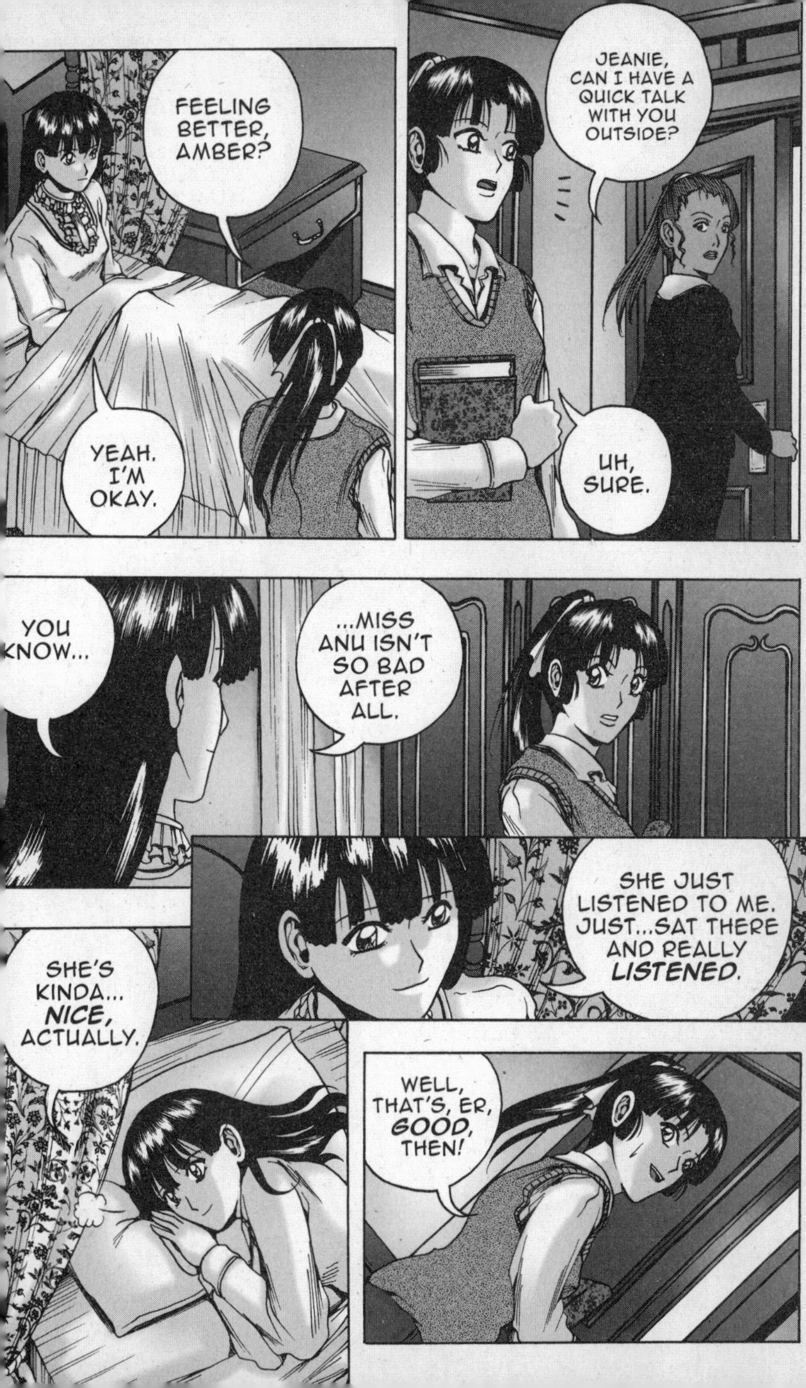
FEELING BETTER, AMBER?
YEAH. I'M OKAY.
JEANIE, CAN I HAVE A QUICK TALK WITH YOU OUTSIDE?
UH, SURE.
YOU KNOW...
...MISS ANU ISN'T SO BAD AFTER ALL.
SHE JUST LISTENED TO ME. JUST...SAT THERE AND REALLY **LISTENED**.
SHE'S KINDA... **NICE**, ACTUALLY.
WELL, THAT'S, ER, **GOOD**, THEN!

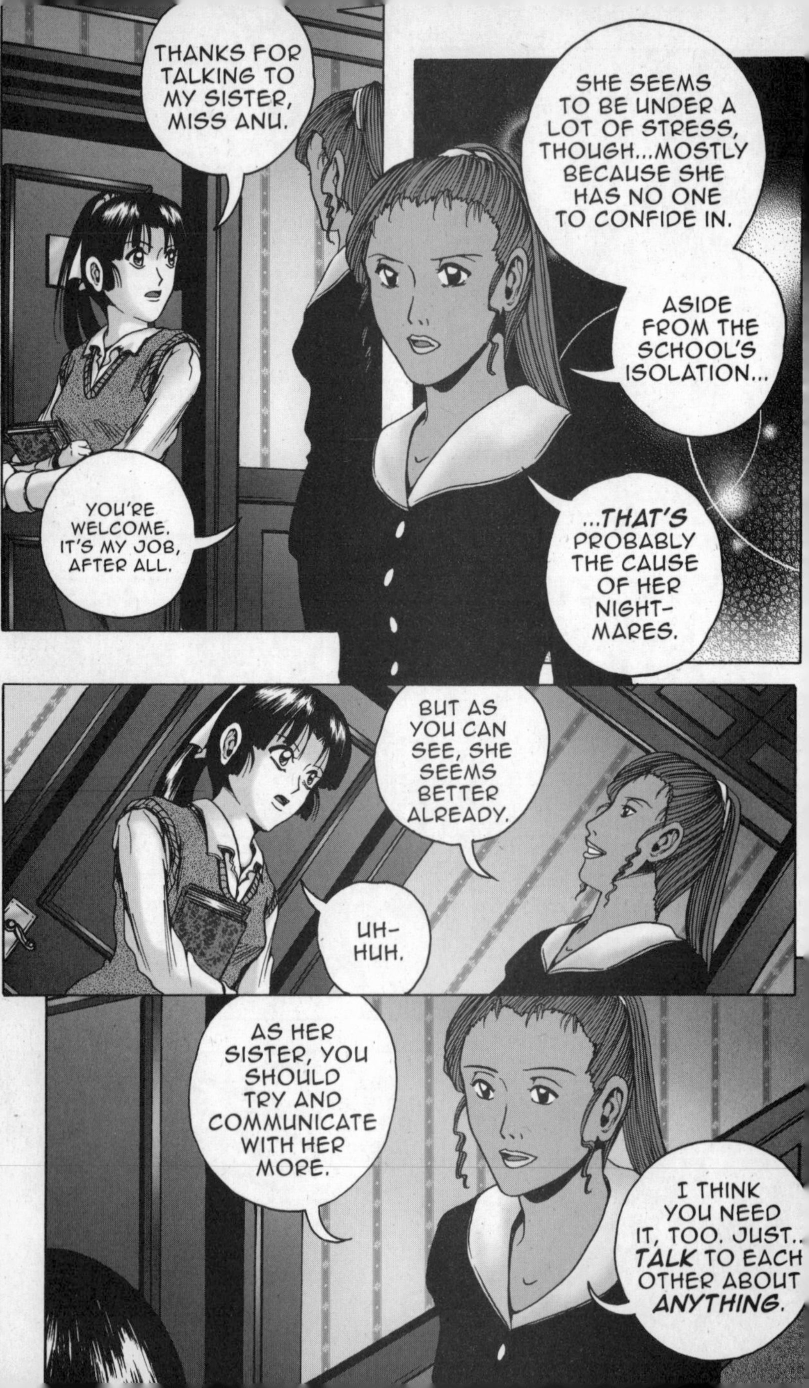
THANKS FOR TALKING TO MY SISTER, MISS ANU.
YOU'RE WELCOME. IT'S MY JOB, AFTER ALL.
SHE SEEMS TO BE UNDER A LOT OF STRESS, THOUGH...MOSTLY BECAUSE SHE HAS NO ONE TO CONFIDE IN.
ASIDE FROM THE SCHOOL'S ISOLATION...
...*THAT'S* PROBABLY THE CAUSE OF HER NIGHT-MARES.
BUT AS YOU CAN SEE, SHE SEEMS BETTER ALREADY.
UH-HUH.
AS HER SISTER, YOU SHOULD TRY AND COMMUNICATE WITH HER MORE.
I THINK YOU NEED IT, TOO. JUST.. *TALK* TO EACH OTHER ABOUT *ANYTHING*.

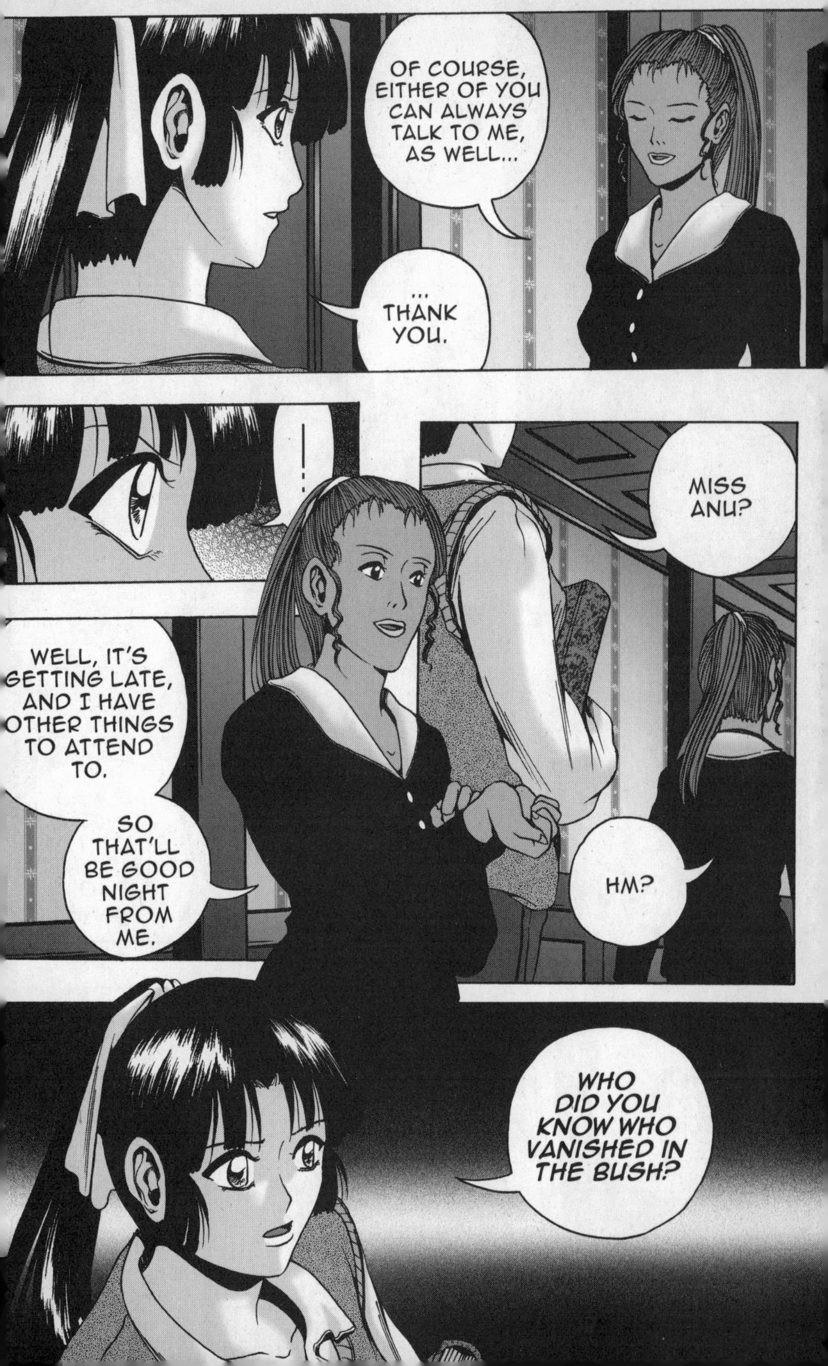
OF COURSE, EITHER OF YOU CAN ALWAYS TALK TO ME, AS WELL...
... THANK YOU.
!
MISS ANU?
WELL, IT'S GETTING LATE, AND I HAVE OTHER THINGS TO ATTEND TO.
SO THAT'LL BE GOOD NIGHT FROM ME.
HM?
WHO DID YOU KNOW WHO VANISHED IN THE BUSH?

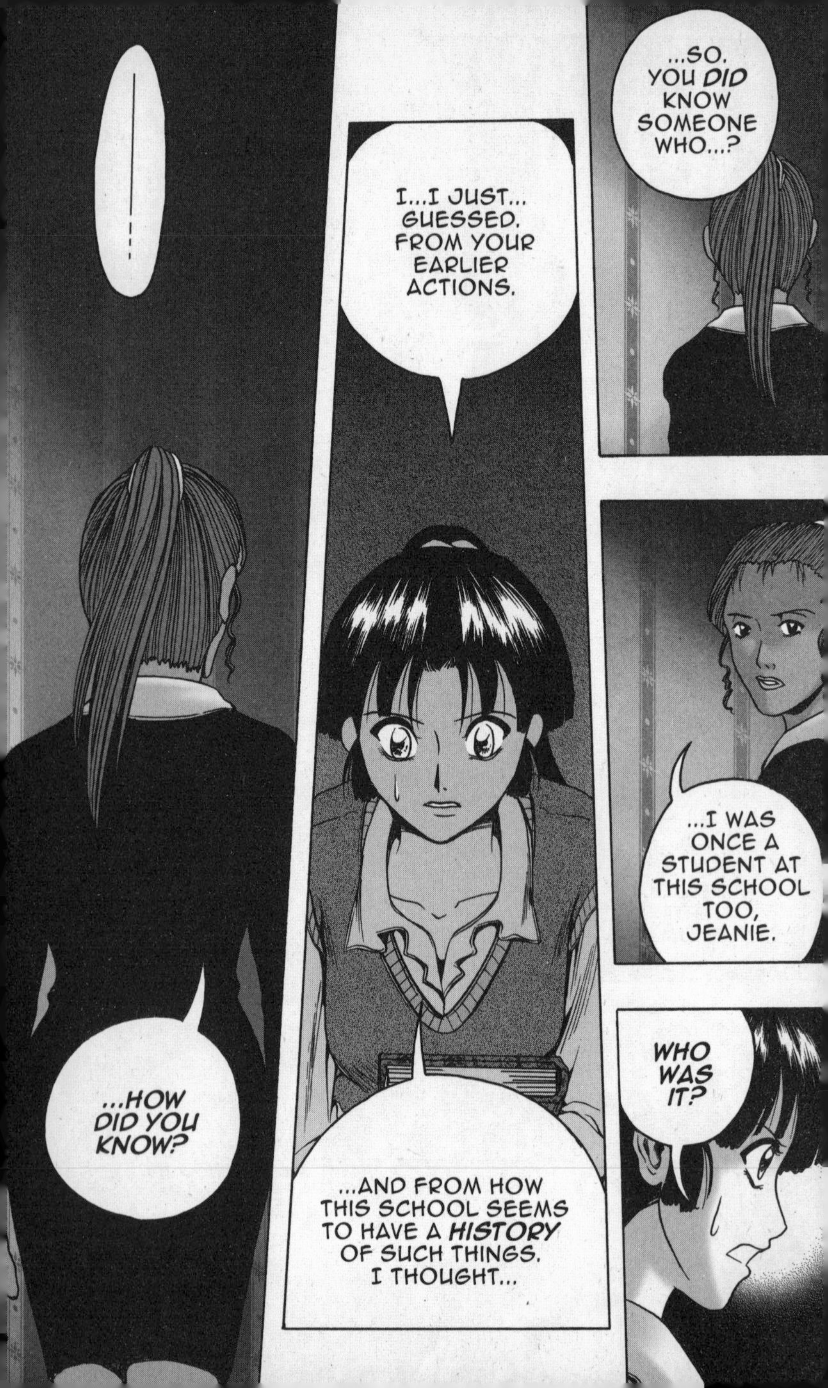
—!
...HOW DID YOU KNOW?
I...I JUST... GUESSED. FROM YOUR EARLIER ACTIONS.
...AND FROM HOW THIS SCHOOL SEEMS TO HAVE A *HISTORY* OF SUCH THINGS. I THOUGHT...
...SO. YOU *DID* KNOW SOMEONE WHO...?
...I WAS ONCE A STUDENT AT THIS SCHOOL TOO, JEANIE.
WHO WAS IT?

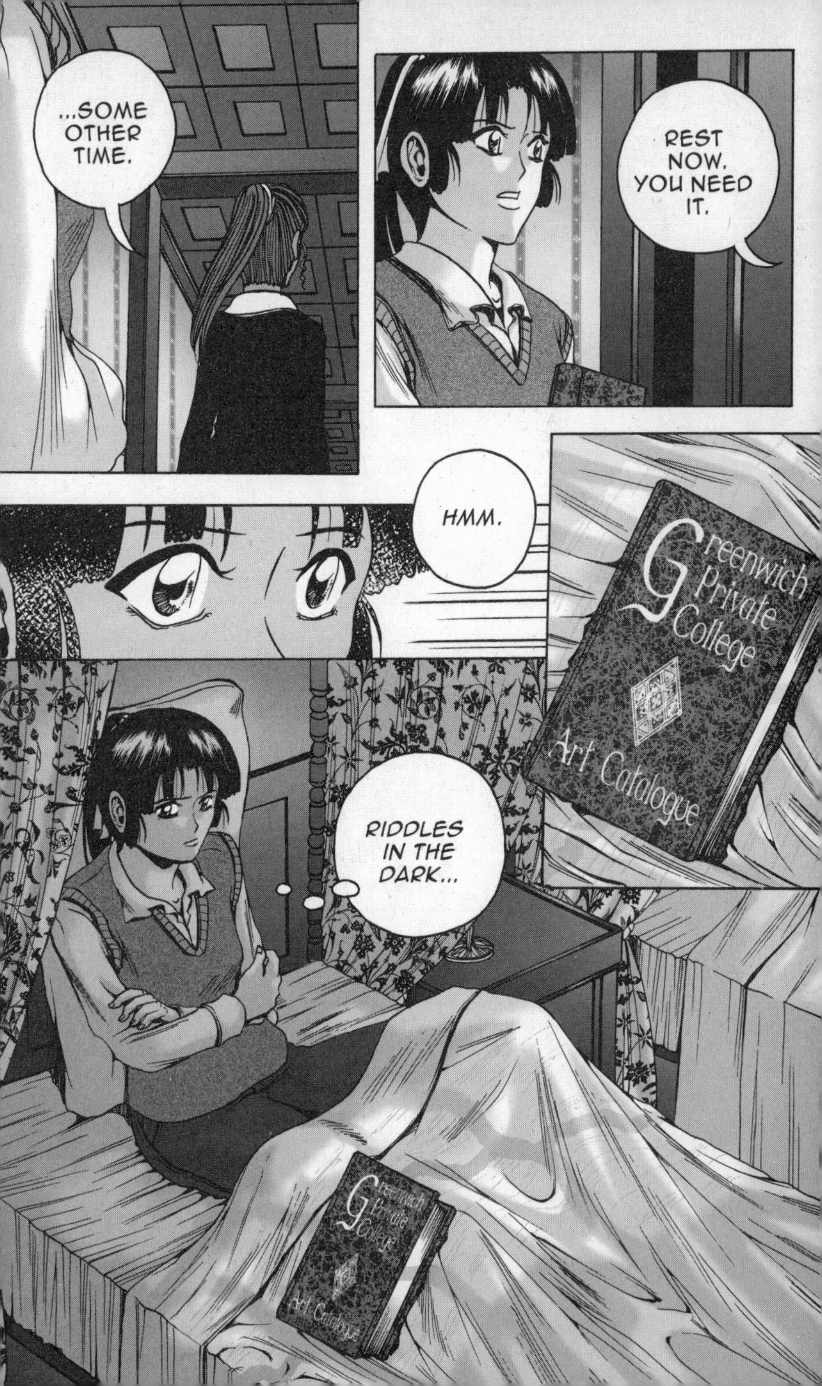
...SOME OTHER TIME.
REST NOW. YOU NEED IT.
HMM.
Greenwich Private College
Art Catalogue
RIDDLES IN THE DARK...

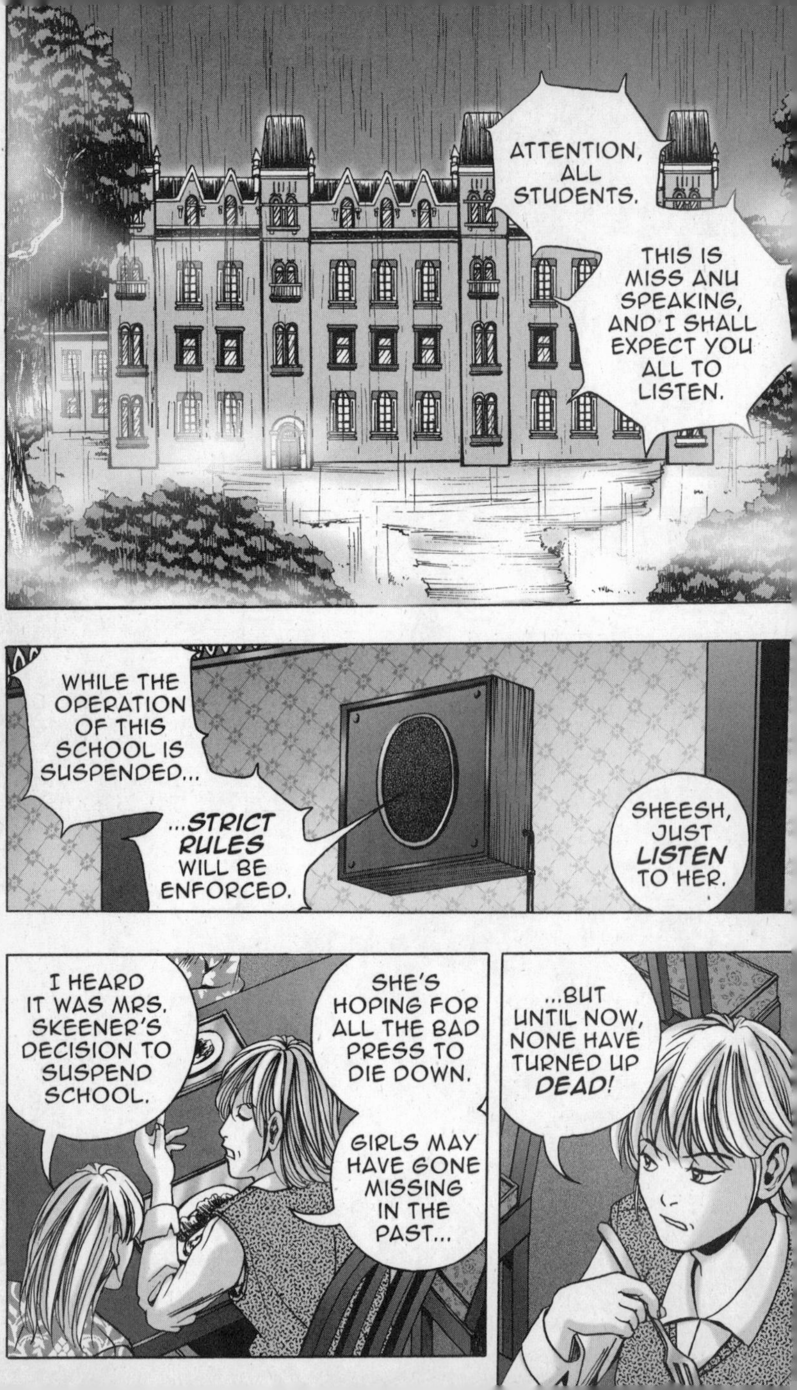
ATTENTION, ALL STUDENTS.
THIS IS MISS ANU SPEAKING, AND I SHALL EXPECT YOU ALL TO LISTEN.
WHILE THE OPERATION OF THIS SCHOOL IS SUSPENDED...
...STRICT RULES WILL BE ENFORCED.
SHEESH, JUST LISTEN TO HER.
I HEARD IT WAS MRS. SKEENER'S DECISION TO SUSPEND SCHOOL.
SHE'S HOPING FOR ALL THE BAD PRESS TO DIE DOWN.
GIRLS MAY HAVE GONE MISSING IN THE PAST...
...BUT UNTIL NOW, NONE HAVE TURNED UP DEAD!

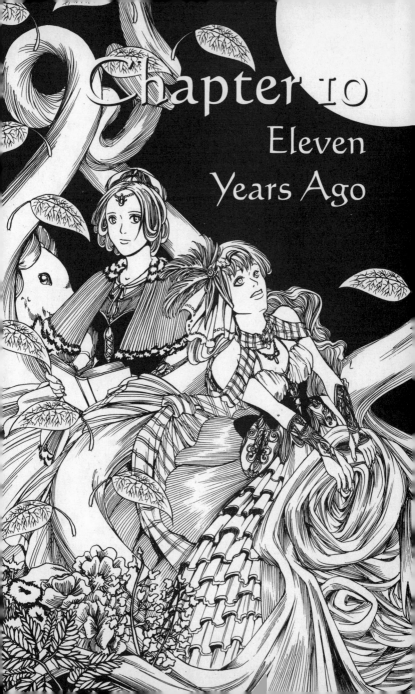

Chapter 10

Eleven Years Ago

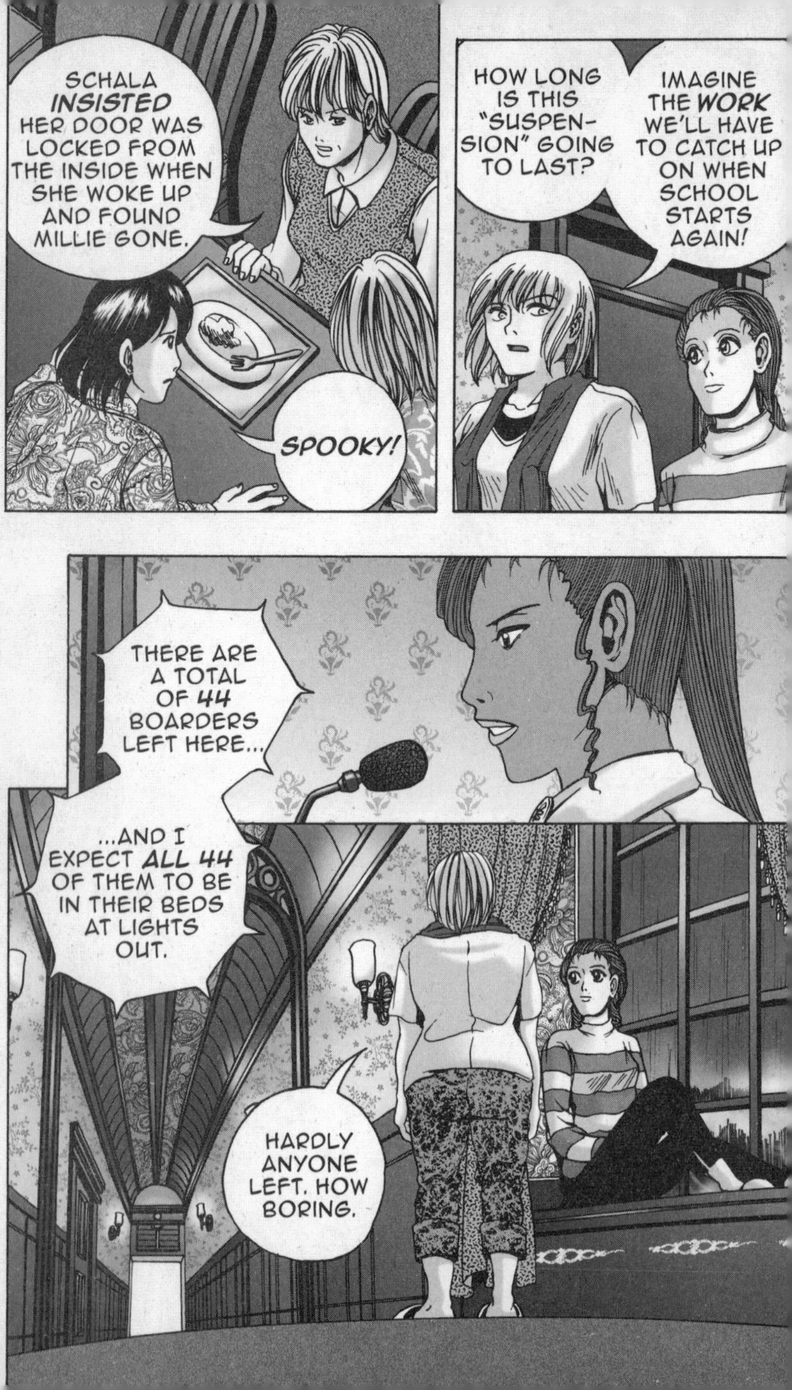
SCHALA INSISTED HER DOOR WAS LOCKED FROM THE INSIDE WHEN SHE WOKE UP AND FOUND MILLIE GONE.
SPOOKY!
HOW LONG IS THIS "SUSPENSION" GOING TO LAST?
IMAGINE THE WORK WE'LL HAVE TO CATCH UP ON WHEN SCHOOL STARTS AGAIN!
THERE ARE A TOTAL OF 44 BOARDERS LEFT HERE...
...AND I EXPECT ALL 44 OF THEM TO BE IN THEIR BEDS AT LIGHTS OUT.
HARDLY ANYONE LEFT. HOW BORING.

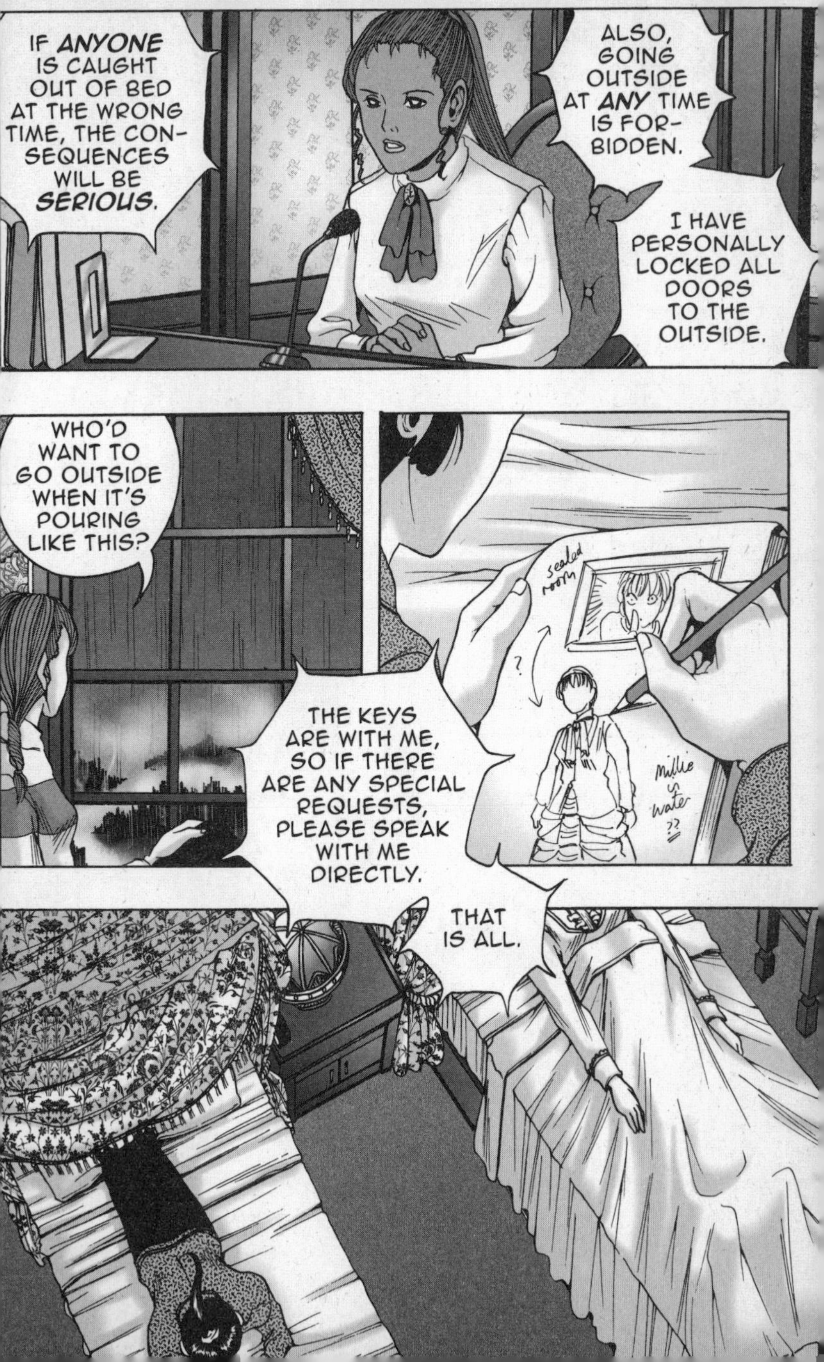
IF ANYONE IS CAUGHT OUT OF BED AT THE WRONG TIME, THE CONSEQUENCES WILL BE SERIOUS.
ALSO, GOING OUTSIDE AT ANY TIME IS FORBIDDEN.
I HAVE PERSONALLY LOCKED ALL DOORS TO THE OUTSIDE.
WHO'D WANT TO GO OUTSIDE WHEN IT'S POURING LIKE THIS?
sealed room
?
Millie is water ??
THE KEYS ARE WITH ME, SO IF THERE ARE ANY SPECIAL REQUESTS, PLEASE SPEAK WITH ME DIRECTLY.
THAT IS ALL.

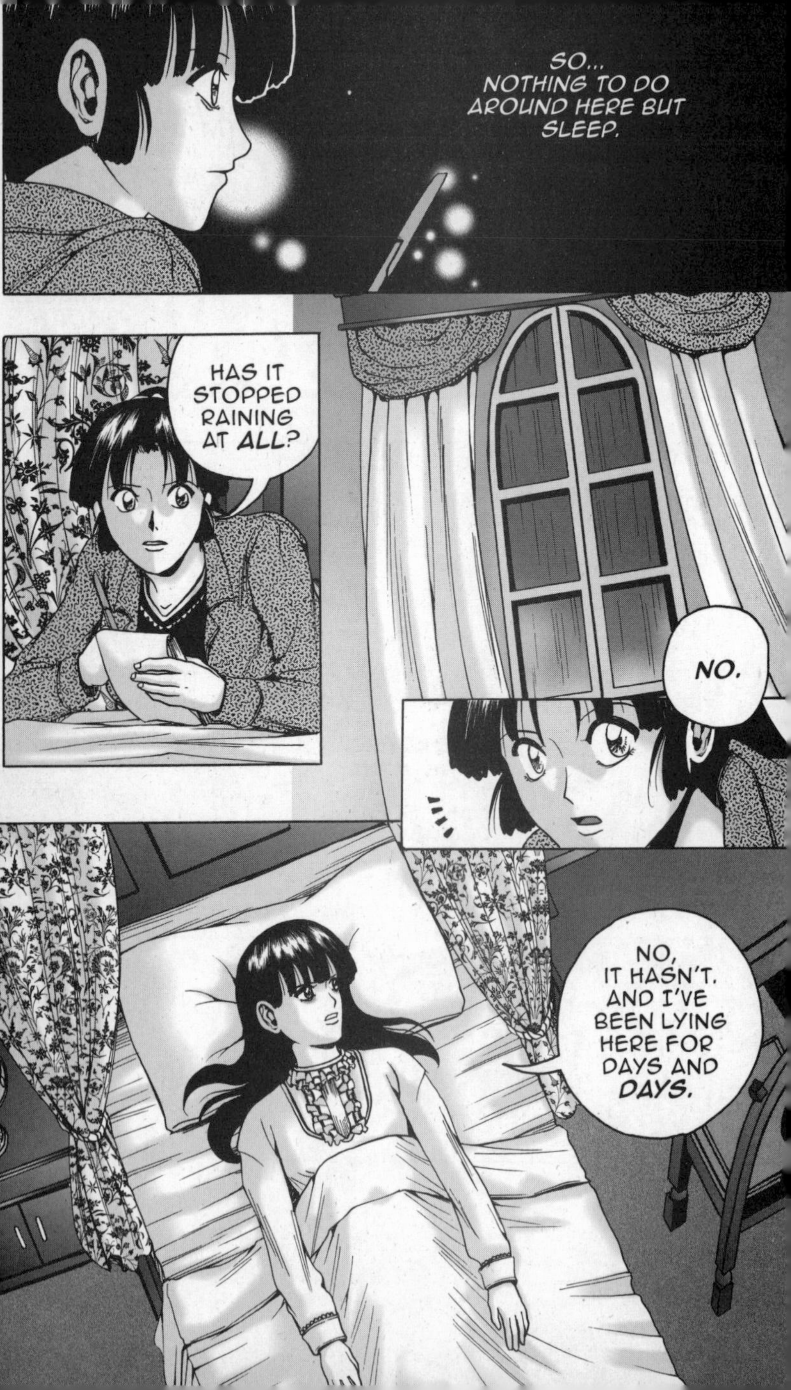
SO...
NOTHING TO DO
AROUND HERE BUT
SLEEP.
HAS IT
STOPPED
RAINING
AT ALL?
NO.
NO,
IT HASN'T.
AND I'VE
BEEN LYING
HERE FOR
DAYS AND
DAYS.

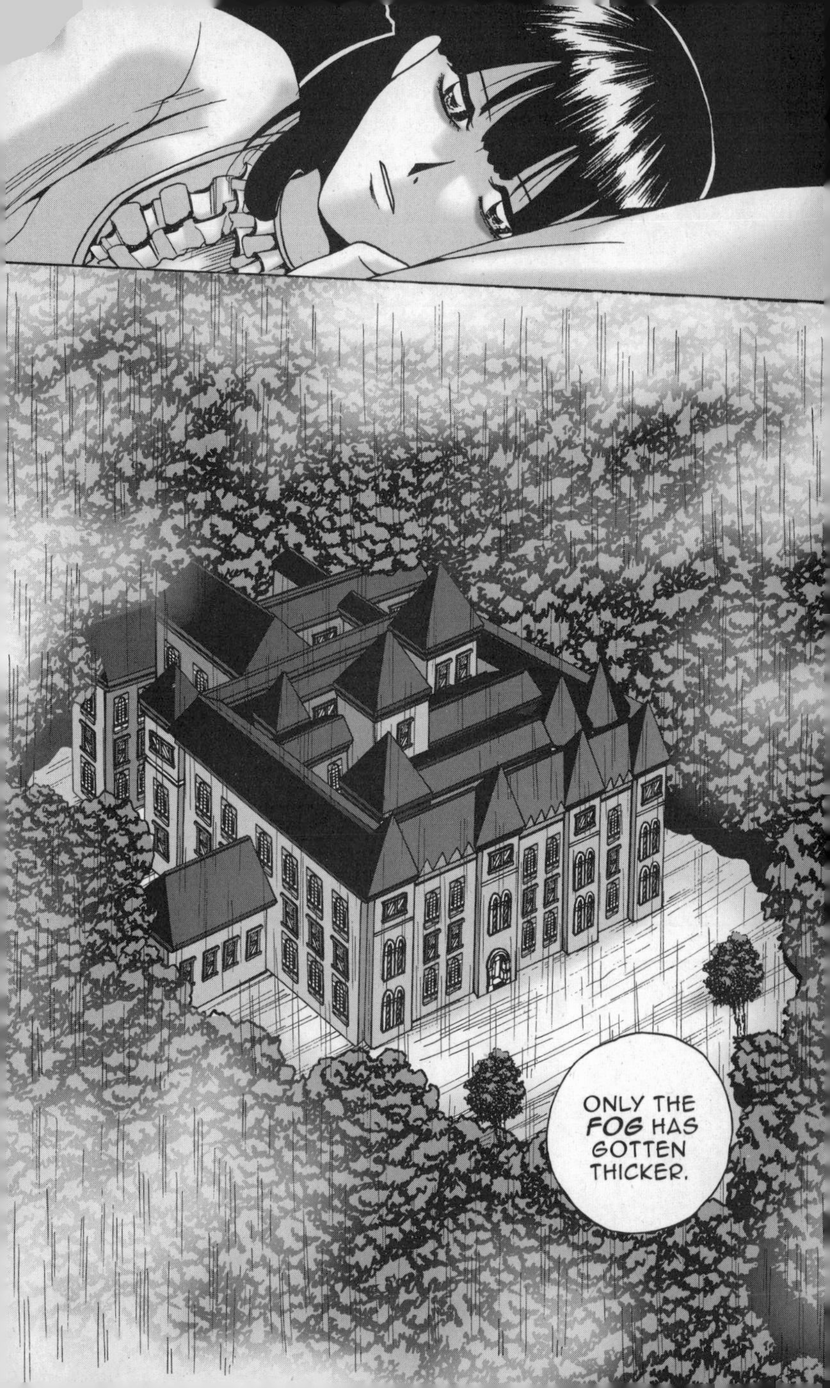
ONLY THE FOG HAS GOTTEN THICKER.

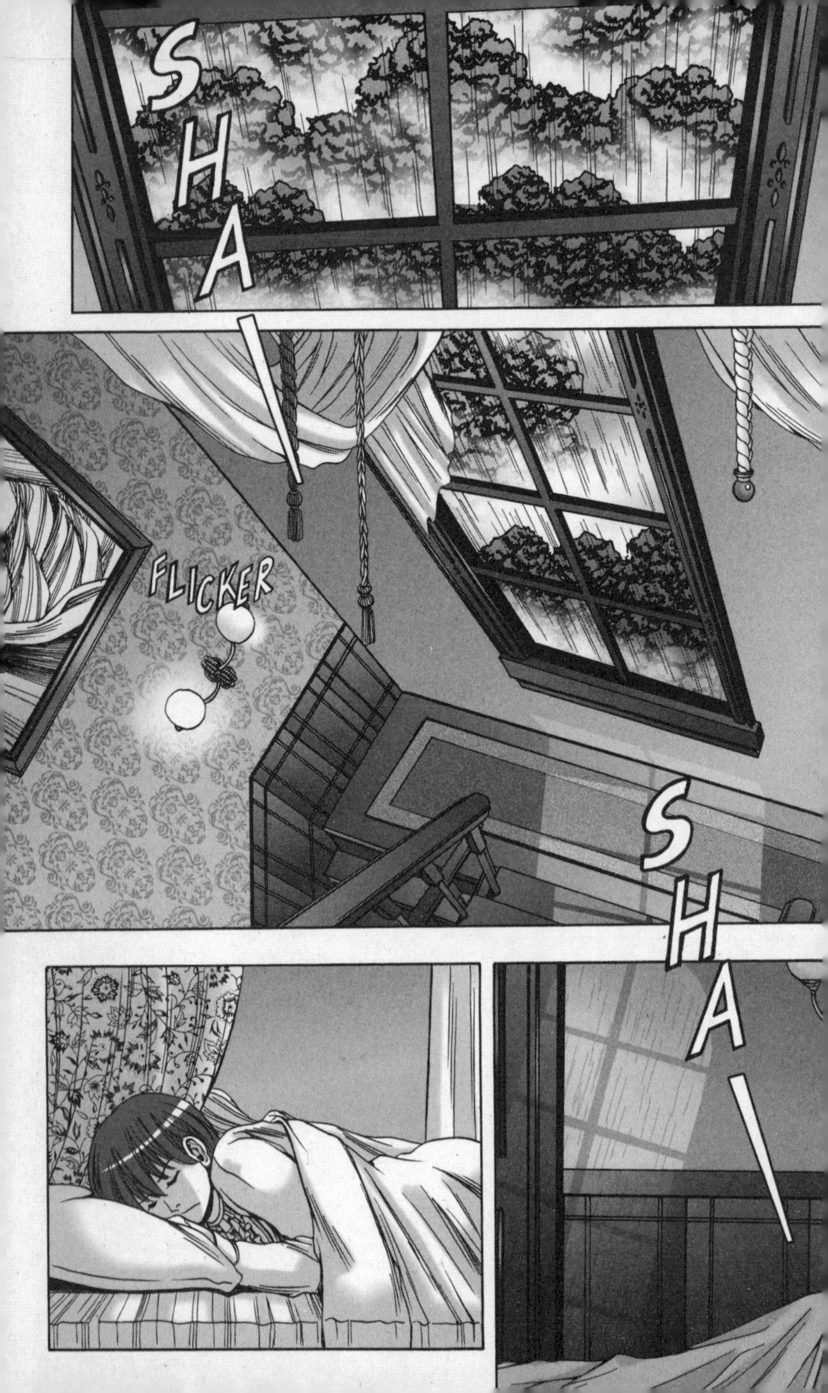
SHA!
FLICKER
SHA!

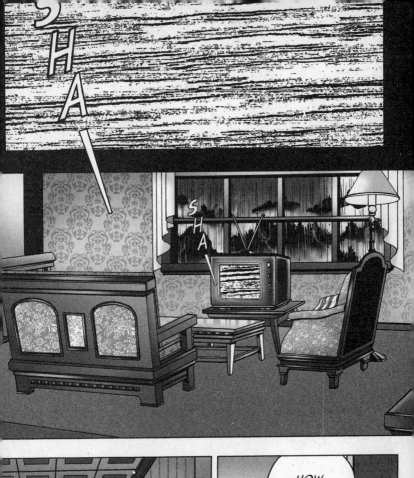

SHA

SHA

DRIP

HOW LONG HAS IT BEEN?

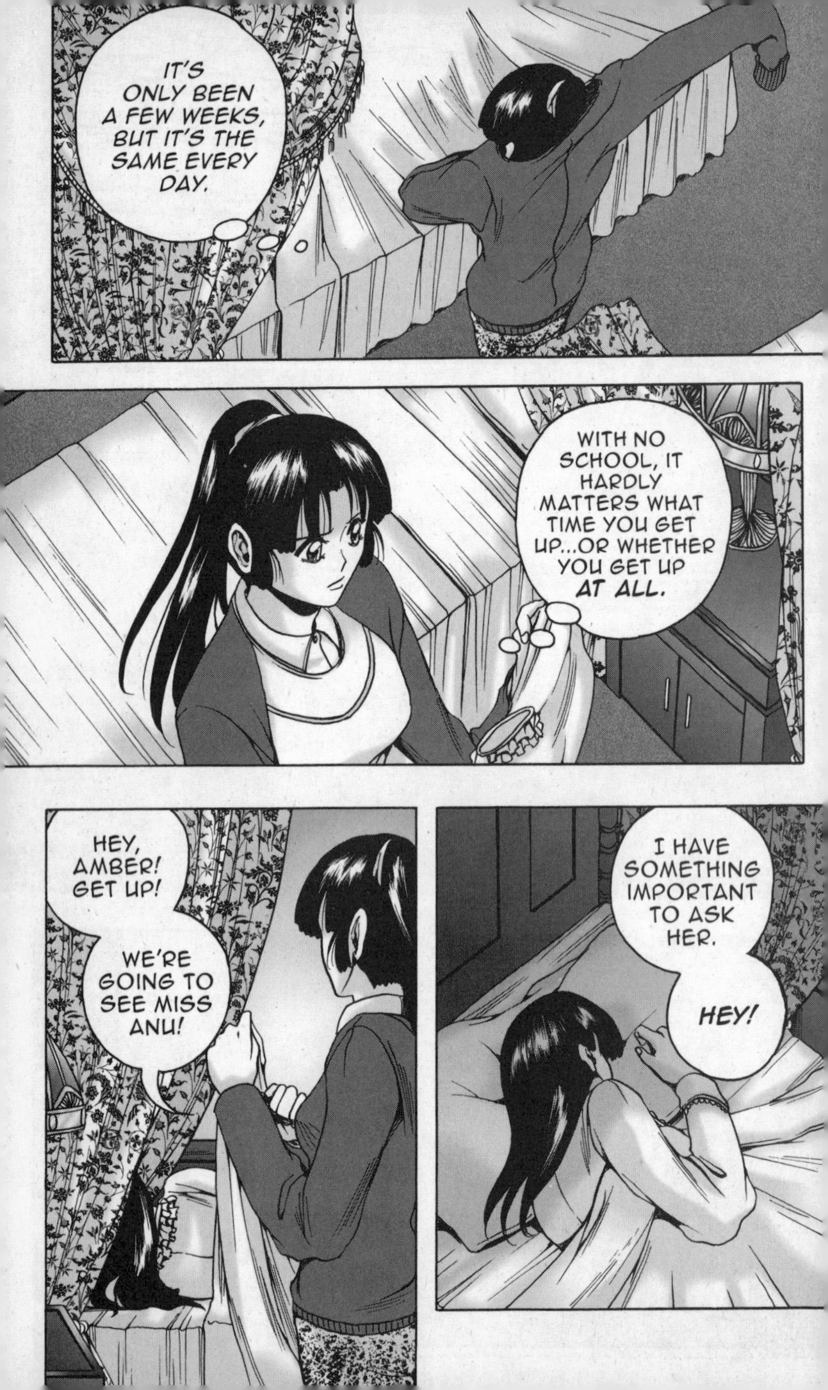
IT'S ONLY BEEN A FEW WEEKS, BUT IT'S THE SAME EVERY DAY.
WITH NO SCHOOL, IT HARDLY MATTERS WHAT TIME YOU GET UP...OR WHETHER YOU GET UP *AT ALL.*
HEY, AMBER! GET UP!
WE'RE GOING TO SEE MISS ANU!
I HAVE SOMETHING IMPORTANT TO ASK HER.
HEY!

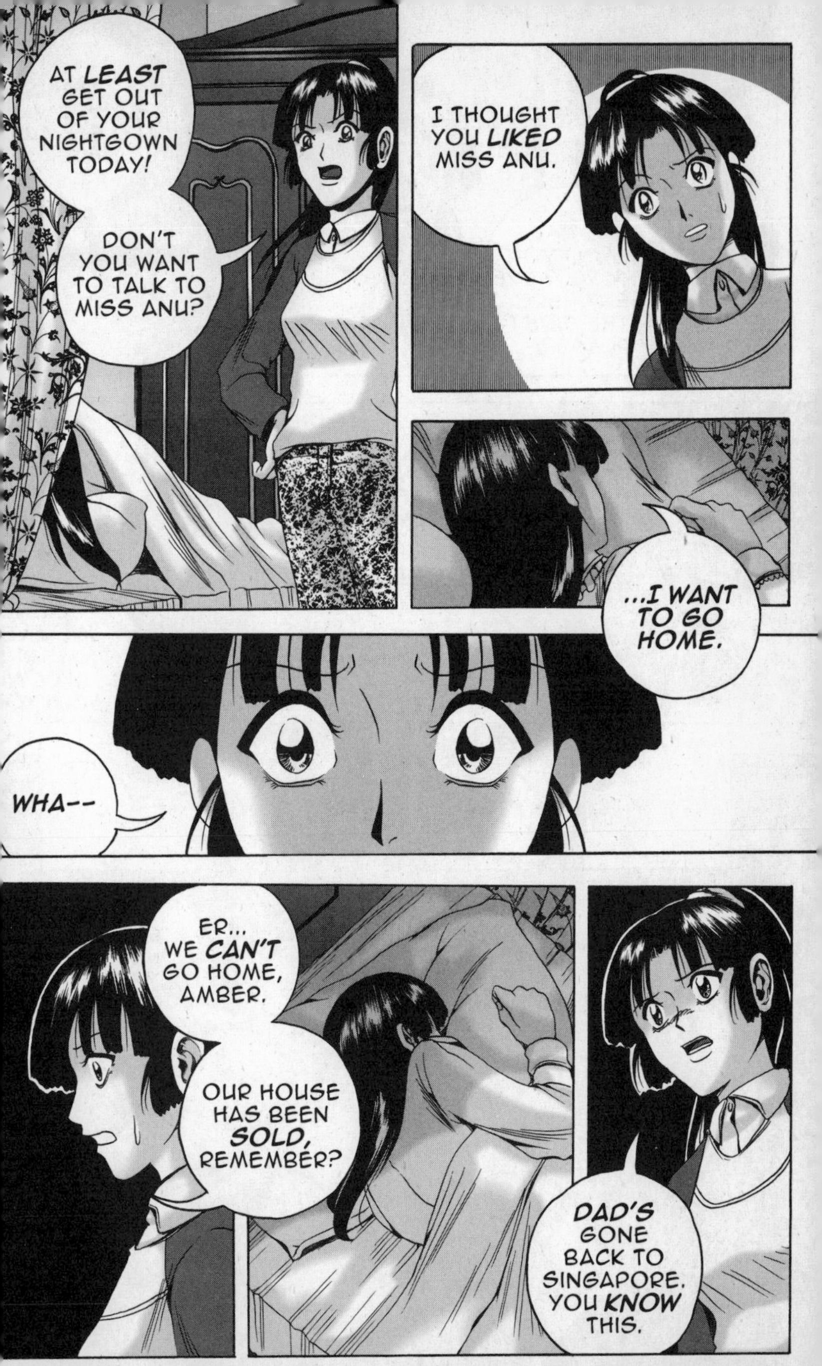
AT LEAST GET OUT OF YOUR NIGHTGOWN TODAY!
DON'T YOU WANT TO TALK TO MISS ANU?
I THOUGHT YOU LIKED MISS ANU.
...I WANT TO GO HOME.
WHA--
ER... WE CAN'T GO HOME, AMBER.
OUR HOUSE HAS BEEN SOLD, REMEMBER?
DAD'S GONE BACK TO SINGAPORE. YOU KNOW THIS.

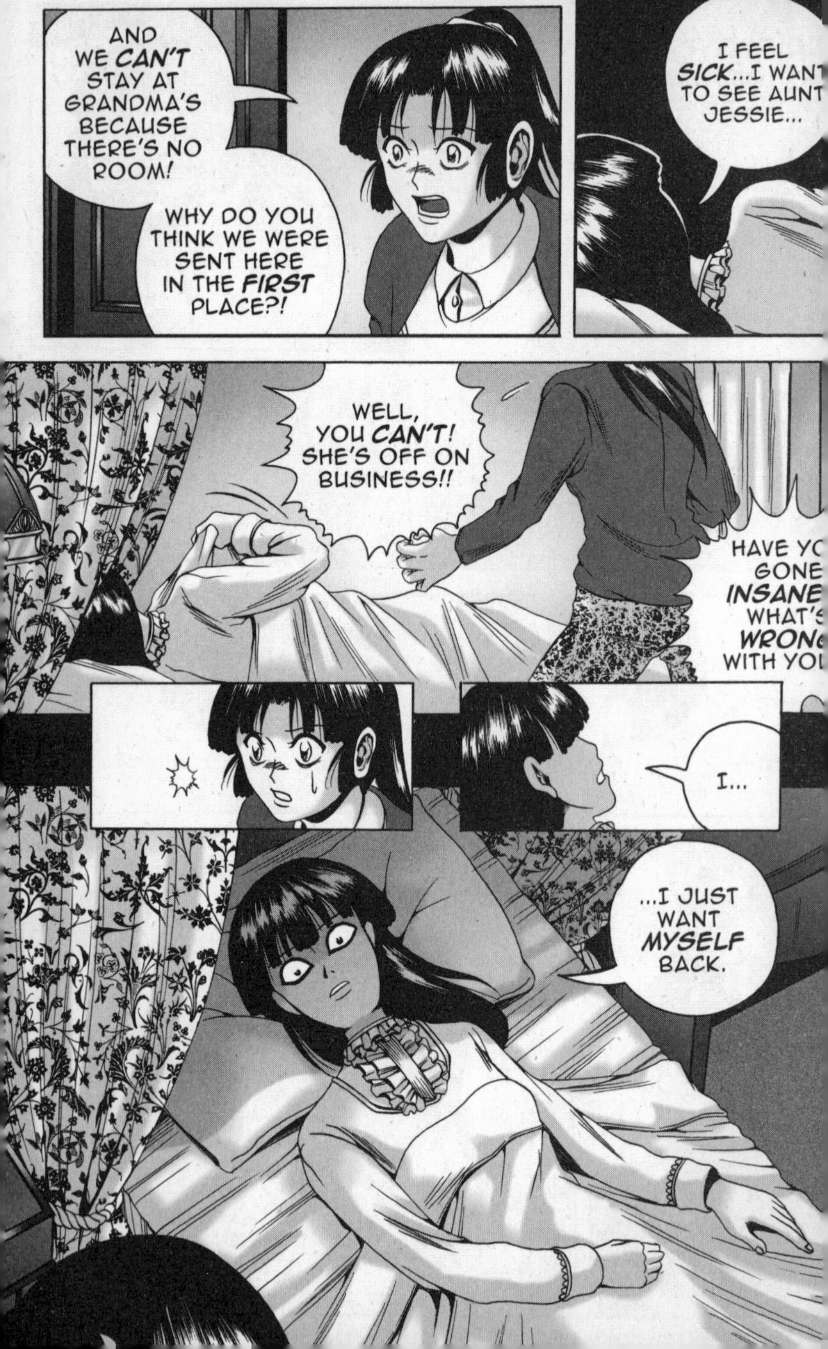
AND WE CAN'T STAY AT GRANDMA'S BECAUSE THERE'S NO ROOM!
WHY DO YOU THINK WE WERE SENT HERE IN THE FIRST PLACE?!
I FEEL SICK...I WANT TO SEE AUNT JESSIE...
WELL, YOU CAN'T! SHE'S OFF ON BUSINESS!!
HAVE YO GONE INSANE WHAT'S WRONG WITH YO
I...
...I JUST WANT MYSELF BACK.

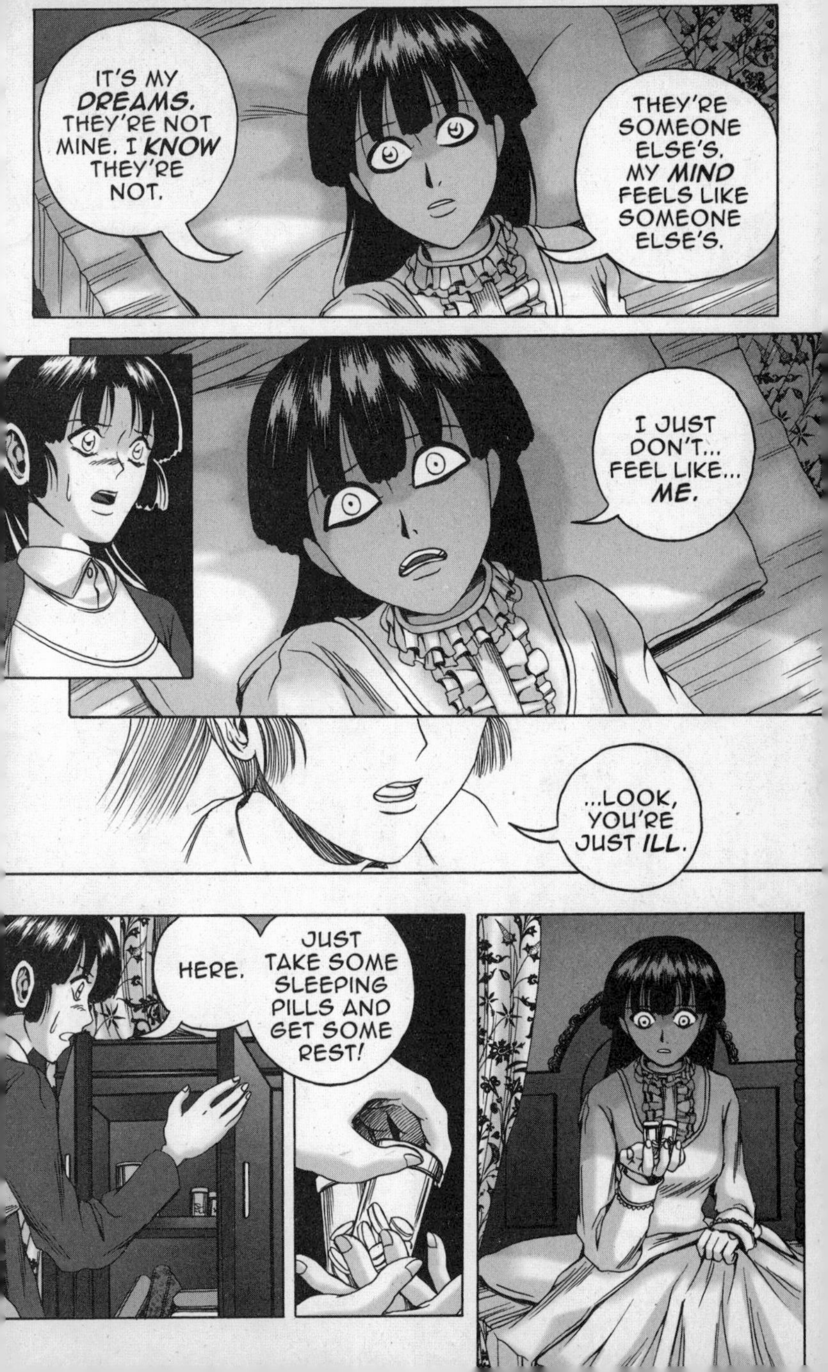
IT'S MY DREAMS. THEY'RE NOT MINE. I KNOW THEY'RE NOT.
THEY'RE SOMEONE ELSE'S. MY MIND FEELS LIKE SOMEONE ELSE'S.
I JUST DON'T... FEEL LIKE... ME.
...LOOK, YOU'RE JUST ILL.
HERE.
JUST TAKE SOME SLEEPING PILLS AND GET SOME REST!

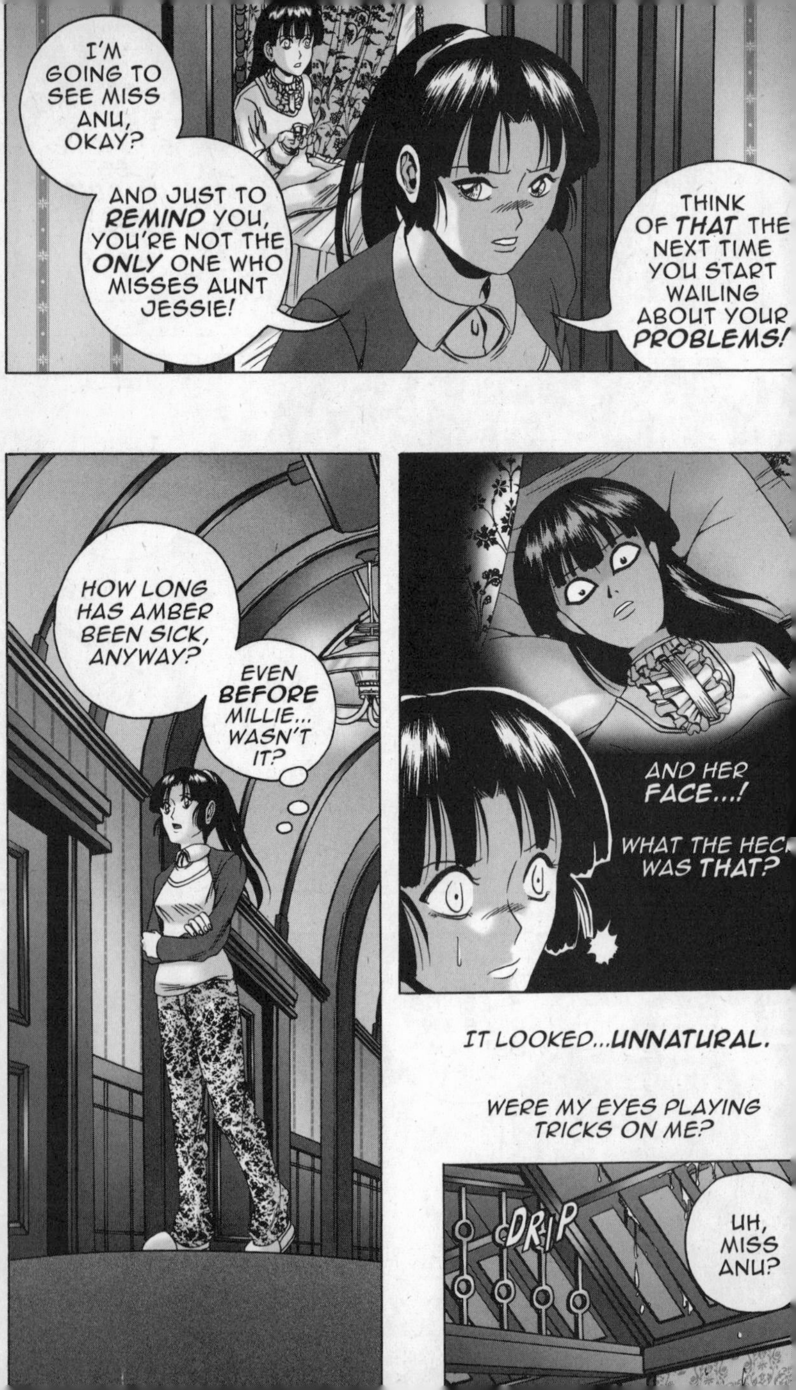
I'M GOING TO SEE MISS ANU, OKAY?
AND JUST TO REMIND YOU, YOU'RE NOT THE ONLY ONE WHO MISSES AUNT JESSIE!
THINK OF THAT THE NEXT TIME YOU START WAILING ABOUT YOUR PROBLEMS!
HOW LONG HAS AMBER BEEN SICK, ANYWAY?
EVEN BEFORE MILLIE... WASN'T IT?
AND HER FACE...!
WHAT THE HEC
WAS THAT?
IT LOOKED...UNNATURAL.
WERE MY EYES PLAYING TRICKS ON ME?
DRIP
UH, MISS ANU?

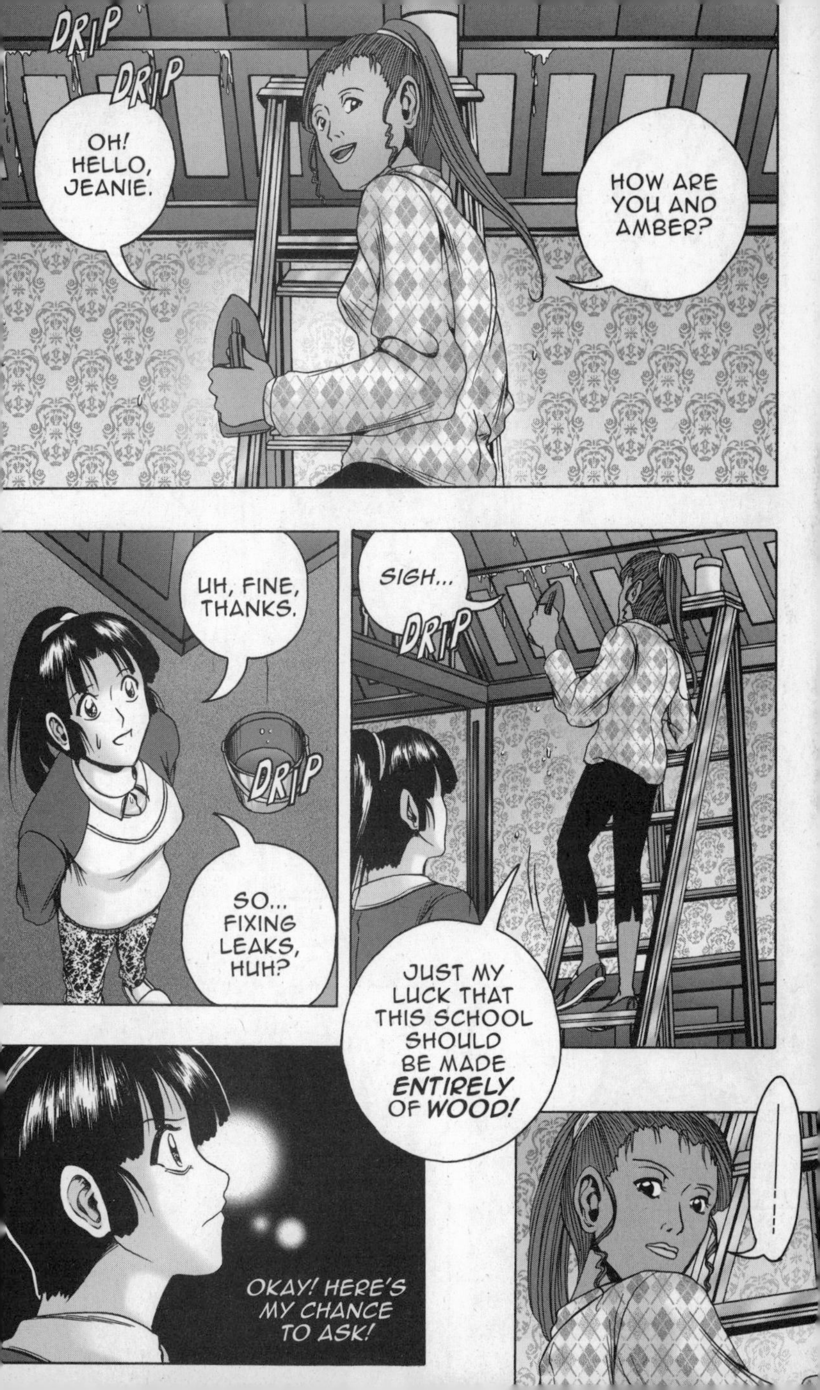
DRIP
DRIP
OH! HELLO, JEANIE.
HOW ARE YOU AND AMBER?
UH, FINE, THANKS.
DRIP
SO... FIXING LEAKS, HUH?
SIGH...
DRIP
JUST MY LUCK THAT THIS SCHOOL SHOULD BE MADE ENTIRELY OF WOOD!
OKAY! HERE'S MY CHANCE TO ASK!
...!

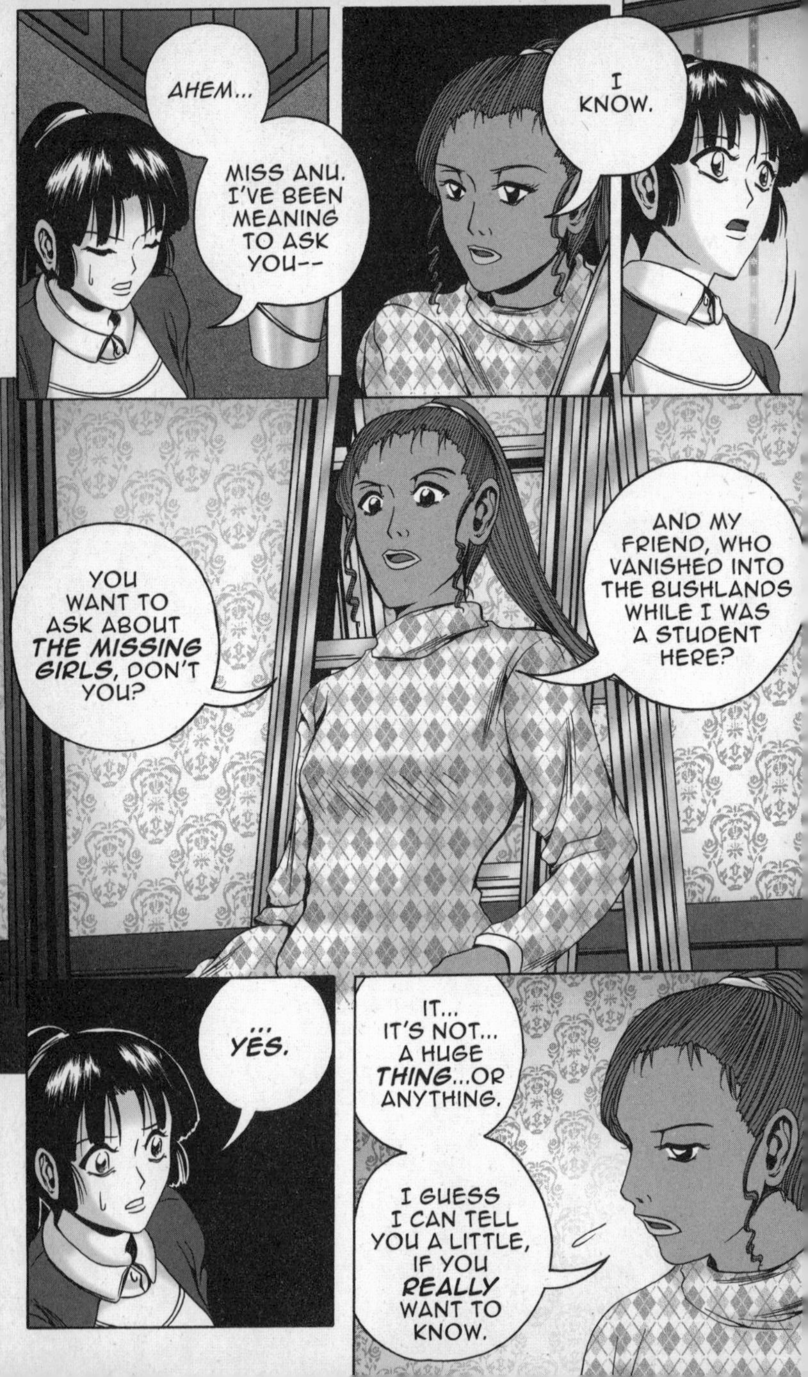
AHEM...
MISS ANU. I'VE BEEN MEANING TO ASK YOU--
I KNOW.
YOU WANT TO ASK ABOUT *THE MISSING GIRLS*, DON'T YOU?
AND MY FRIEND, WHO VANISHED INTO THE BUSHLANDS WHILE I WAS A STUDENT HERE?
... *YES.*
IT... IT'S NOT... A HUGE *THING*...OR ANYTHING.
I GUESS I CAN TELL YOU A LITTLE, IF YOU *REALLY* WANT TO KNOW.

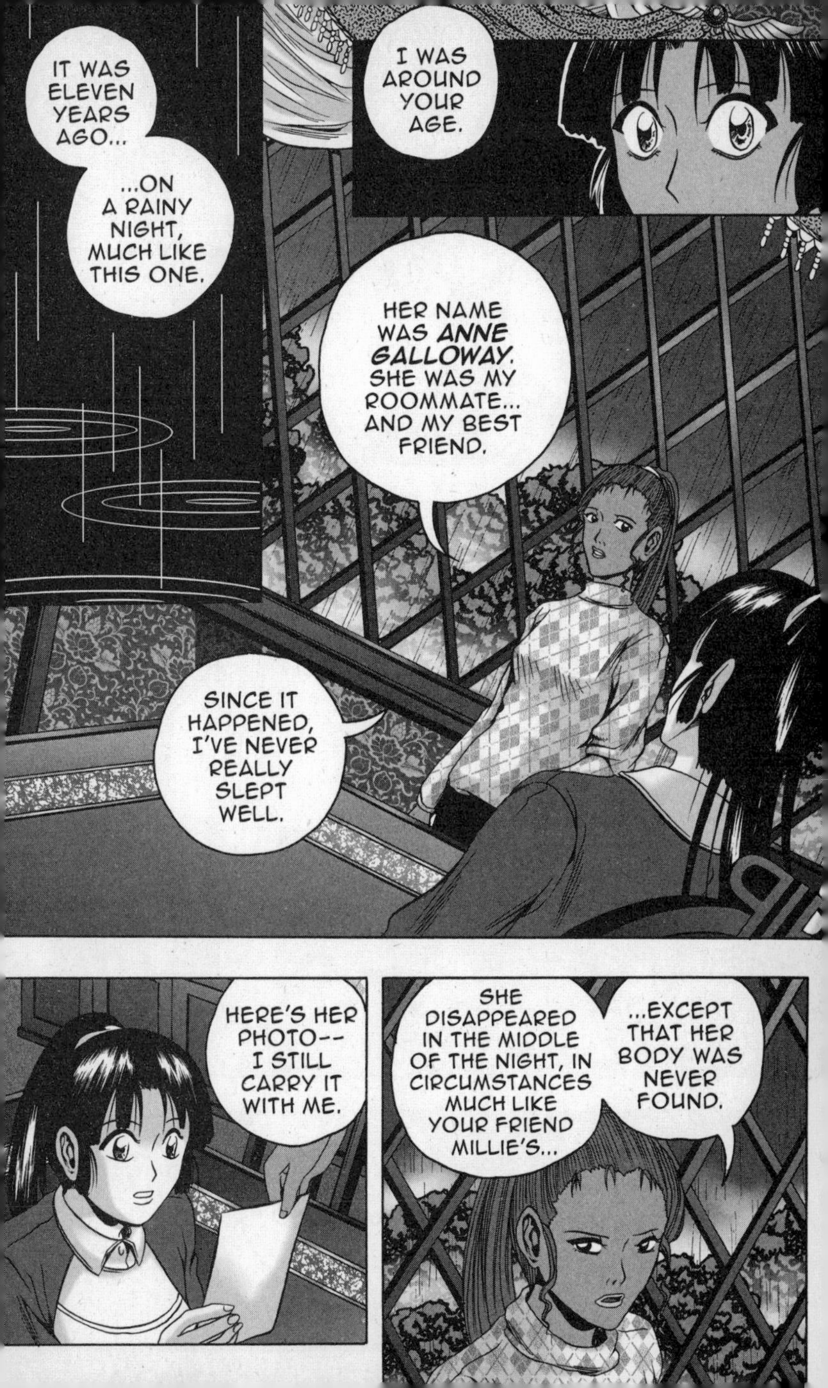
IT WAS ELEVEN YEARS AGO...
...ON A RAINY NIGHT, MUCH LIKE THIS ONE.
I WAS AROUND YOUR AGE.
HER NAME WAS ***ANNE GALLOWAY***. SHE WAS MY ROOMMATE... AND MY BEST FRIEND.
SINCE IT HAPPENED, I'VE NEVER REALLY SLEPT WELL.
HERE'S HER PHOTO-- I STILL CARRY IT WITH ME.
SHE DISAPPEARED IN THE MIDDLE OF THE NIGHT, IN CIRCUMSTANCES MUCH LIKE YOUR FRIEND MILLIE'S...
...EXCEPT THAT HER BODY WAS NEVER FOUND.

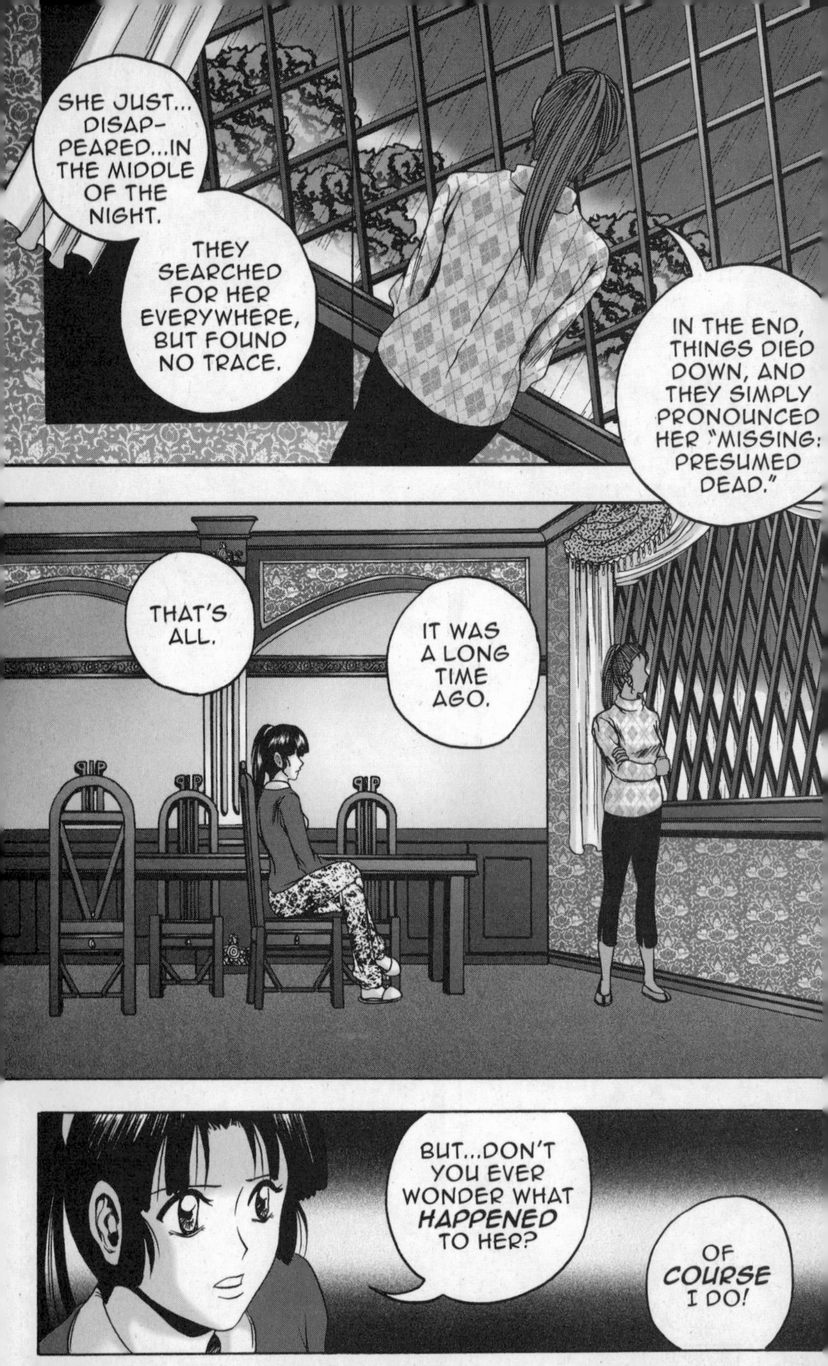
SHE JUST... DISAP-PEARED...IN THE MIDDLE OF THE NIGHT.
THEY SEARCHED FOR HER EVERYWHERE, BUT FOUND NO TRACE.
IN THE END, THINGS DIED DOWN, AND THEY SIMPLY PRONOUNCED HER "MISSING: PRESUMED DEAD."
THAT'S ALL.
IT WAS A LONG TIME AGO.
BUT...DON'T YOU EVER WONDER WHAT *HAPPENED* TO HER?
OF *COURSE* I DO!

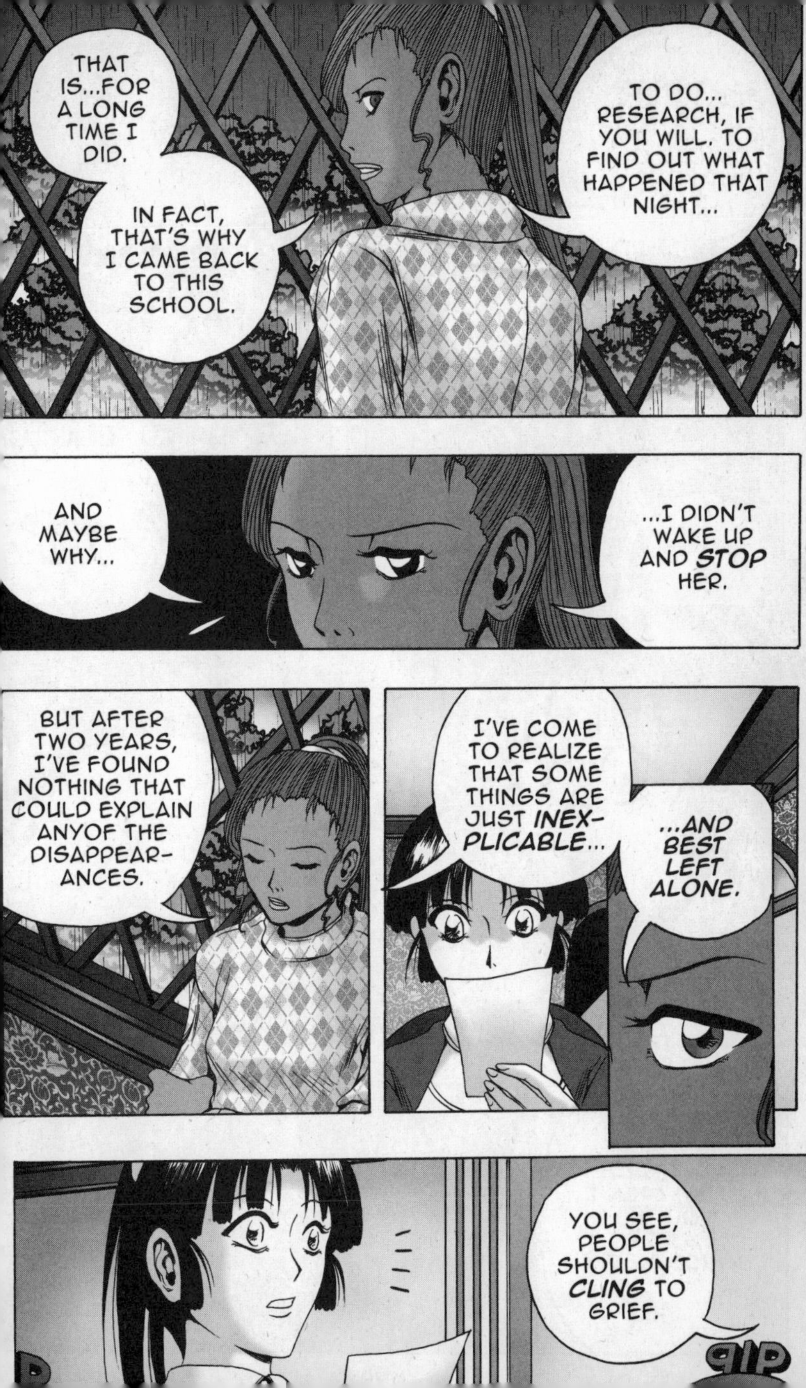
THAT IS...FOR A LONG TIME I DID.
IN FACT, THAT'S WHY I CAME BACK TO THIS SCHOOL.
TO DO... RESEARCH, IF YOU WILL. TO FIND OUT WHAT HAPPENED THAT NIGHT...
AND MAYBE WHY...
...I DIDN'T WAKE UP AND STOP HER.
BUT AFTER TWO YEARS, I'VE FOUND NOTHING THAT COULD EXPLAIN ANYOF THE DISAPPEAR-ANCES.
I'VE COME TO REALIZE THAT SOME THINGS ARE JUST INEX-PLICABLE...
...AND BEST LEFT ALONE.
YOU SEE, PEOPLE SHOULDN'T CLING TO GRIEF.

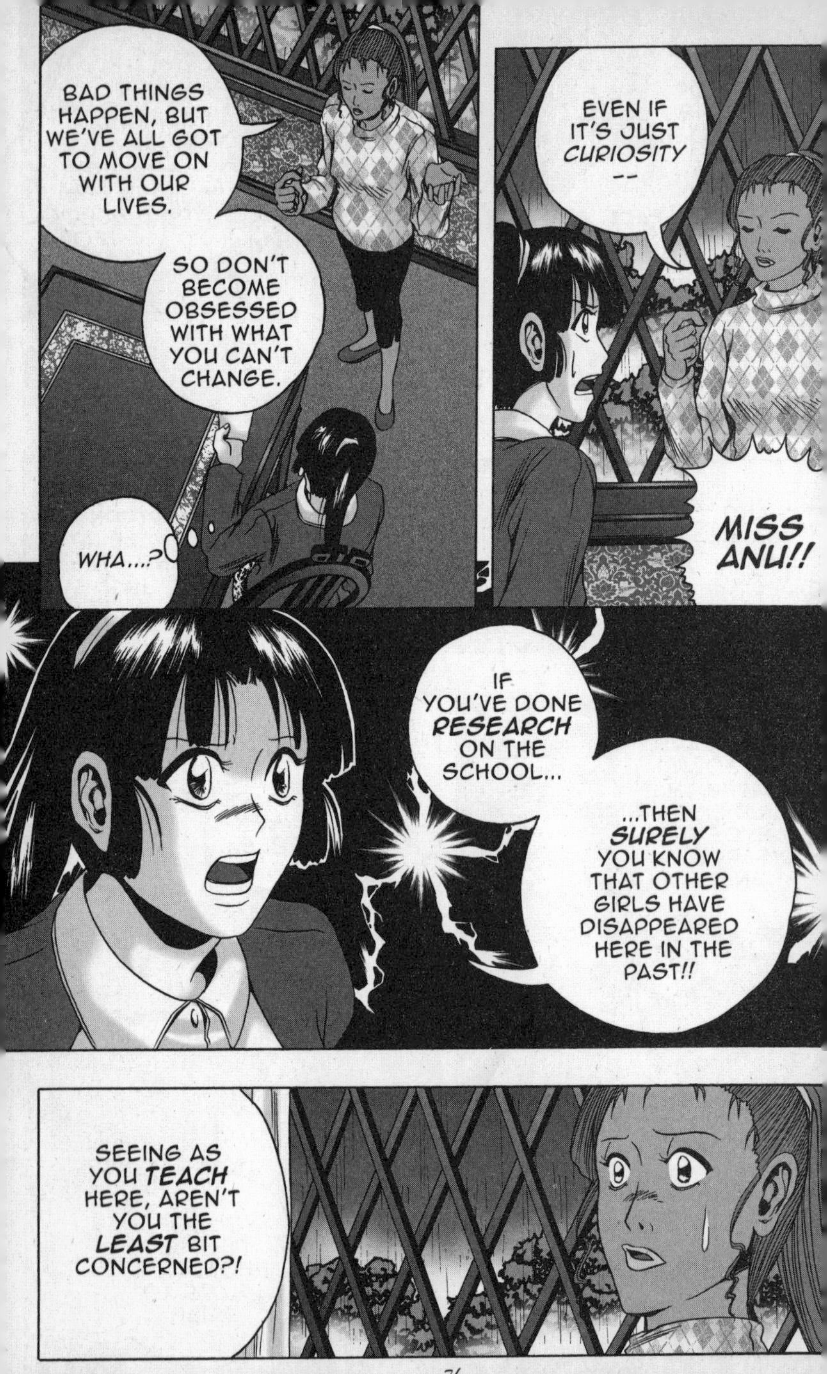
BAD THINGS HAPPEN, BUT WE'VE ALL GOT TO MOVE ON WITH OUR LIVES.
SO DON'T BECOME OBSESSED WITH WHAT YOU CAN'T CHANGE.
WHA...?
EVEN IF IT'S JUST *CURIOSITY* --
MISS ANU!!
IF YOU'VE DONE ***RESEARCH*** ON THE SCHOOL...
...THEN ***SURELY*** YOU KNOW THAT OTHER GIRLS HAVE DISAPPEARED HERE IN THE PAST!!
SEEING AS YOU ***TEACH*** HERE, AREN'T YOU THE ***LEAST*** BIT CONCERNED?!

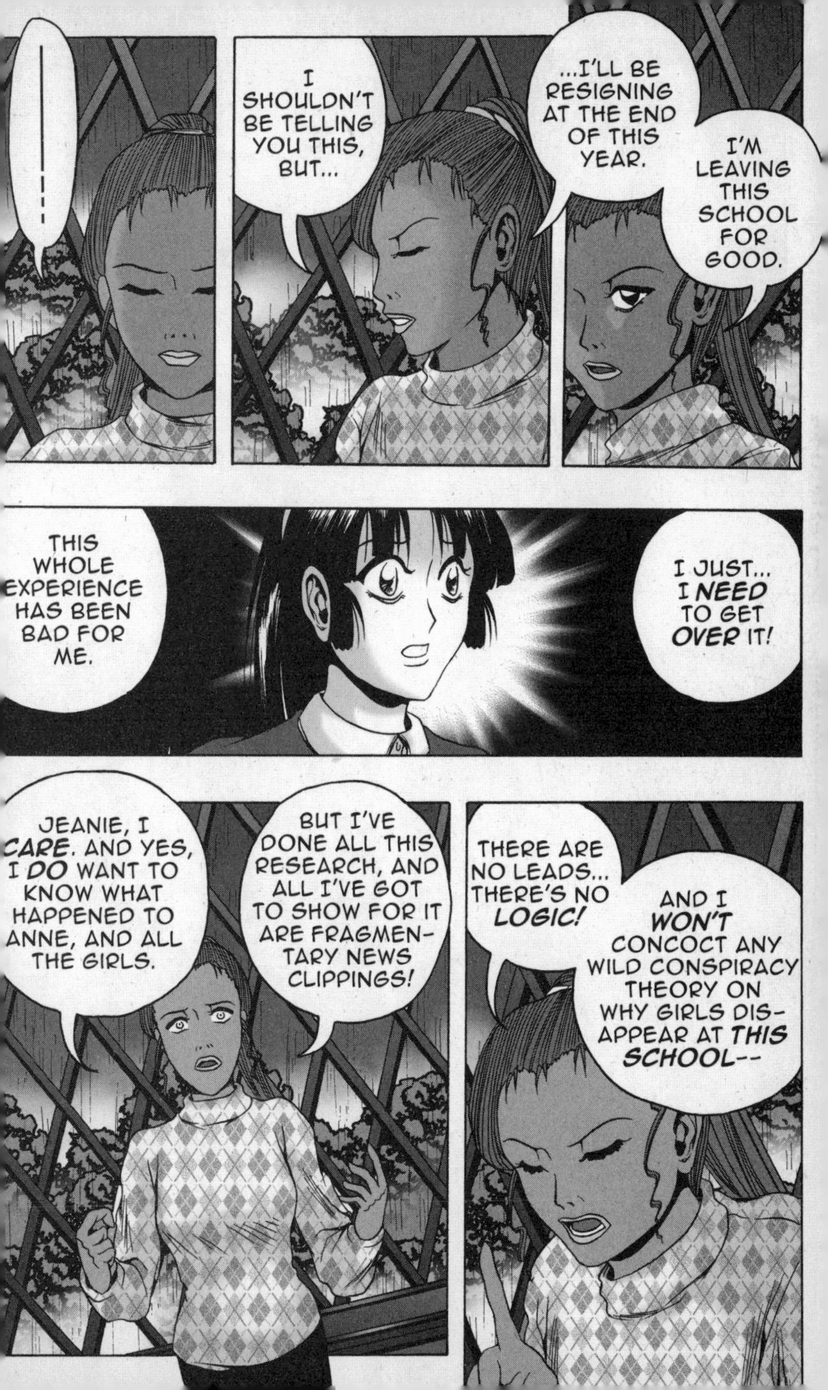

I SHOULDN'T BE TELLING YOU THIS, BUT...
...I'LL BE RESIGNING AT THE END OF THIS YEAR.
I'M LEAVING THIS SCHOOL FOR GOOD.
THIS WHOLE EXPERIENCE HAS BEEN BAD FOR ME.
I JUST... I *NEED* TO GET *OVER* IT!
JEANIE, I *CARE*. AND YES, I *DO* WANT TO KNOW WHAT HAPPENED TO ANNE, AND ALL THE GIRLS.
BUT I'VE DONE ALL THIS RESEARCH, AND ALL I'VE GOT TO SHOW FOR IT ARE FRAGMENTARY NEWS CLIPPINGS!
THERE ARE NO LEADS... THERE'S NO *LOGIC!*
AND I *WON'T* CONCOCT ANY WILD CONSPIRACY THEORY ON WHY GIRLS DISAPPEAR AT *THIS SCHOOL*--

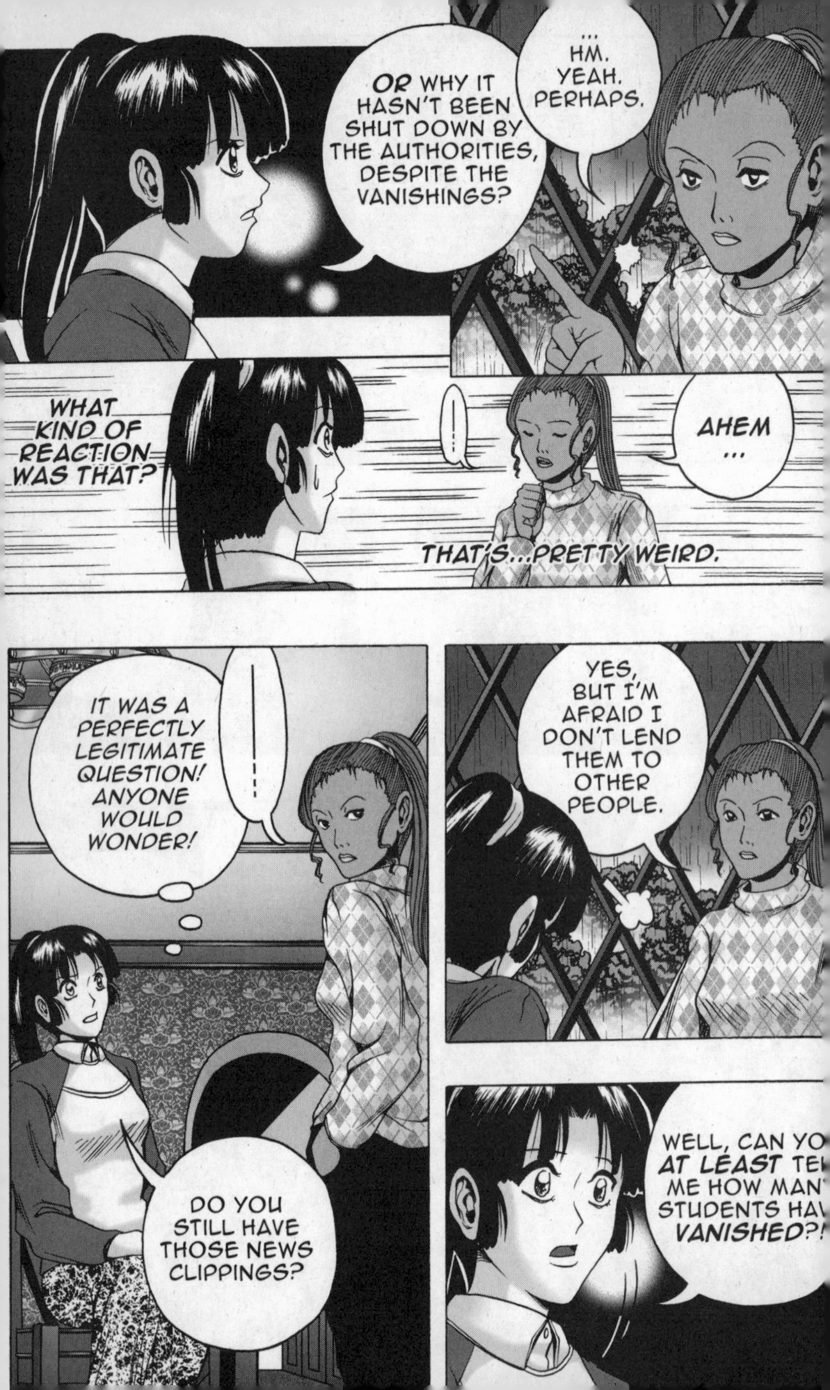
OR WHY IT HASN'T BEEN SHUT DOWN BY THE AUTHORITIES, DESPITE THE VANISHINGS?
... HM. YEAH. PERHAPS.
WHAT KIND OF REACTION WAS THAT?
!
AHEM ...
THAT'S...PRETTY WEIRD.
IT WAS A PERFECTLY LEGITIMATE QUESTION! ANYONE WOULD WONDER!
!
DO YOU STILL HAVE THOSE NEWS CLIPPINGS?
YES, BUT I'M AFRAID I DON'T LEND THEM TO OTHER PEOPLE.
WELL, CAN YO AT LEAST TE ME HOW MAN STUDENTS HA VANISHED?!

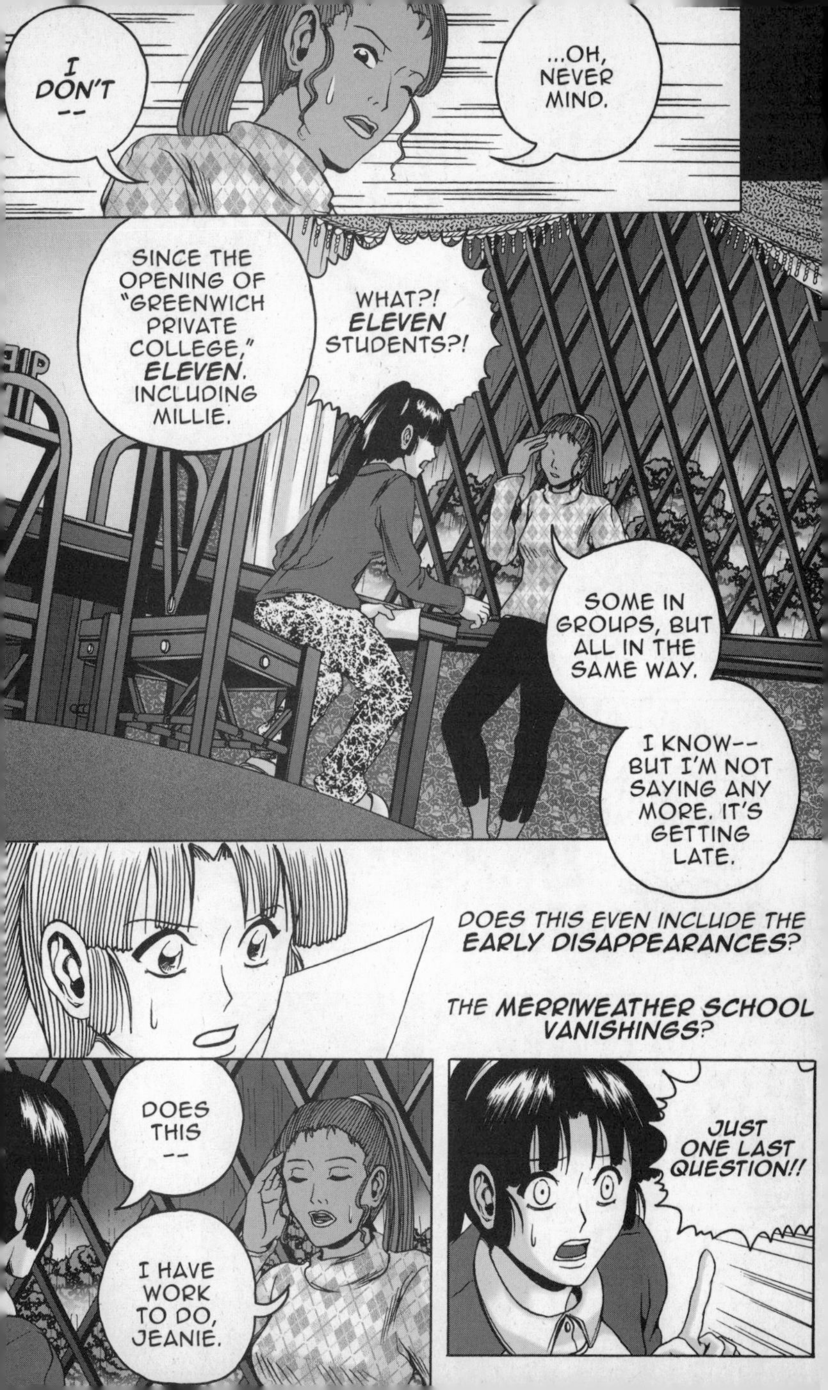
I DON'T --
...OH, NEVER MIND.
SINCE THE OPENING OF "GREENWICH PRIVATE COLLEGE," ELEVEN. INCLUDING MILLIE.
WHAT?! ELEVEN STUDENTS?!
SOME IN GROUPS, BUT ALL IN THE SAME WAY.
I KNOW-- BUT I'M NOT SAYING ANY MORE. IT'S GETTING LATE.
DOES THIS EVEN INCLUDE THE EARLY DISAPPEARANCES?
THE MERRIWEATHER SCHOOL VANISHINGS?
DOES THIS --
I HAVE WORK TO DO, JEANIE.
JUST ONE LAST QUESTION!!

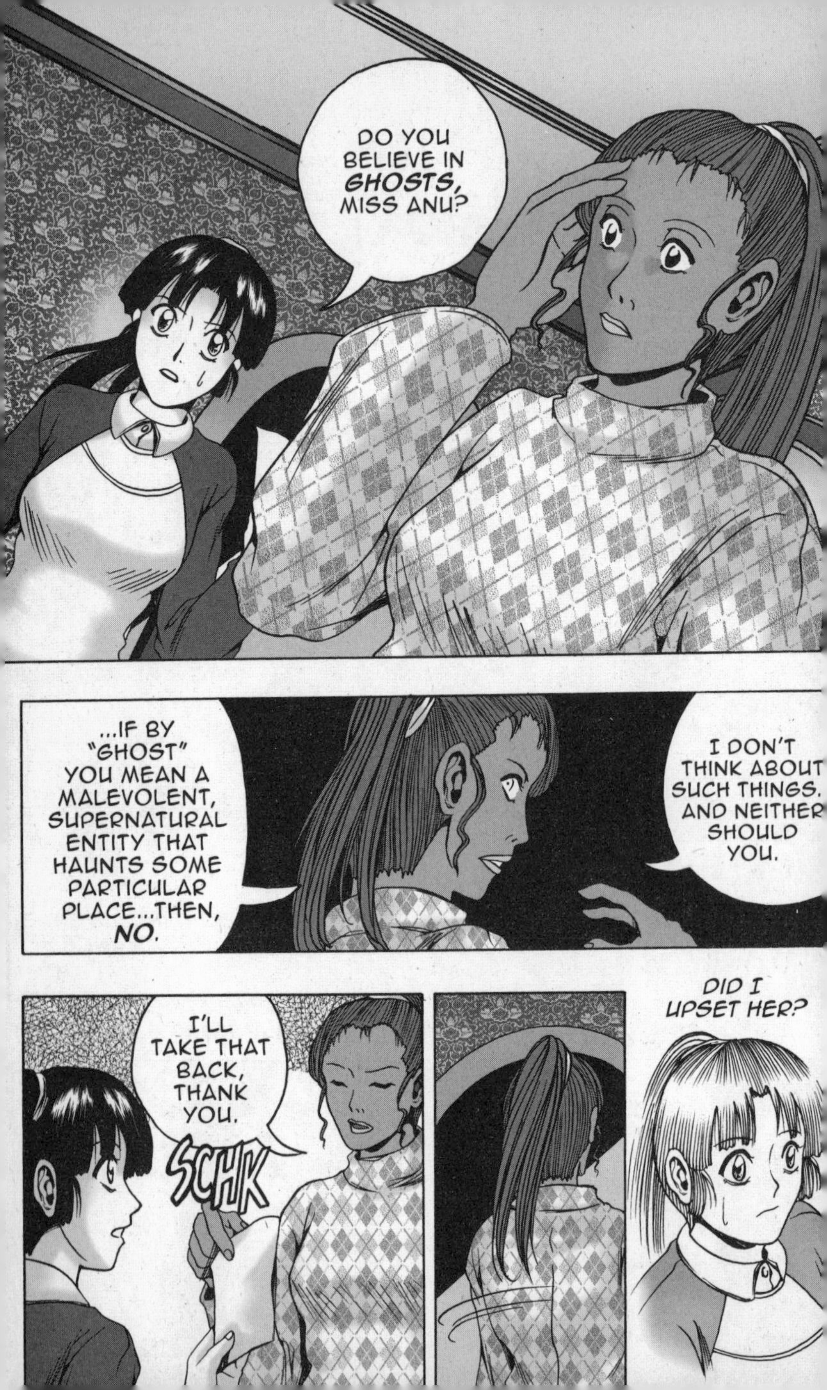
DO YOU BELIEVE IN GHOSTS, MISS ANU?
...IF BY "GHOST" YOU MEAN A MALEVOLENT, SUPERNATURAL ENTITY THAT HAUNTS SOME PARTICULAR PLACE...THEN, NO.
I DON'T THINK ABOUT SUCH THINGS. AND NEITHER SHOULD YOU.
I'LL TAKE THAT BACK, THANK YOU.
SCHK
DID I UPSET HER?

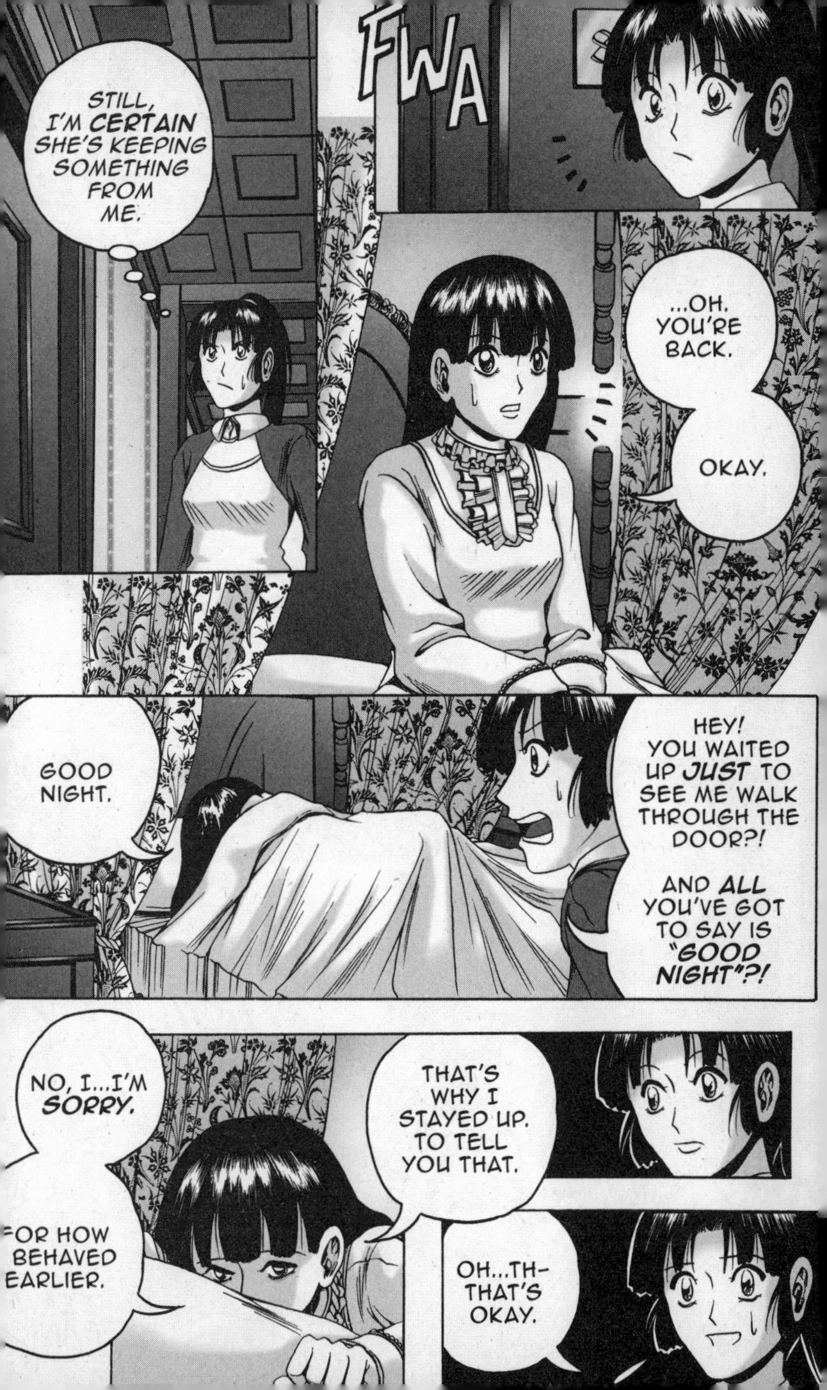
STILL, I'M CERTAIN SHE'S KEEPING SOMETHING FROM ME.
FWA
...OH. YOU'RE BACK.
OKAY.
GOOD NIGHT.
HEY! YOU WAITED UP JUST TO SEE ME WALK THROUGH THE DOOR?!
AND ALL YOU'VE GOT TO SAY IS "GOOD NIGHT"?!
NO, I...I'M SORRY.
FOR HOW BEHAVED EARLIER.
THAT'S WHY I STAYED UP. TO TELL YOU THAT.
OH...TH-THAT'S OKAY.

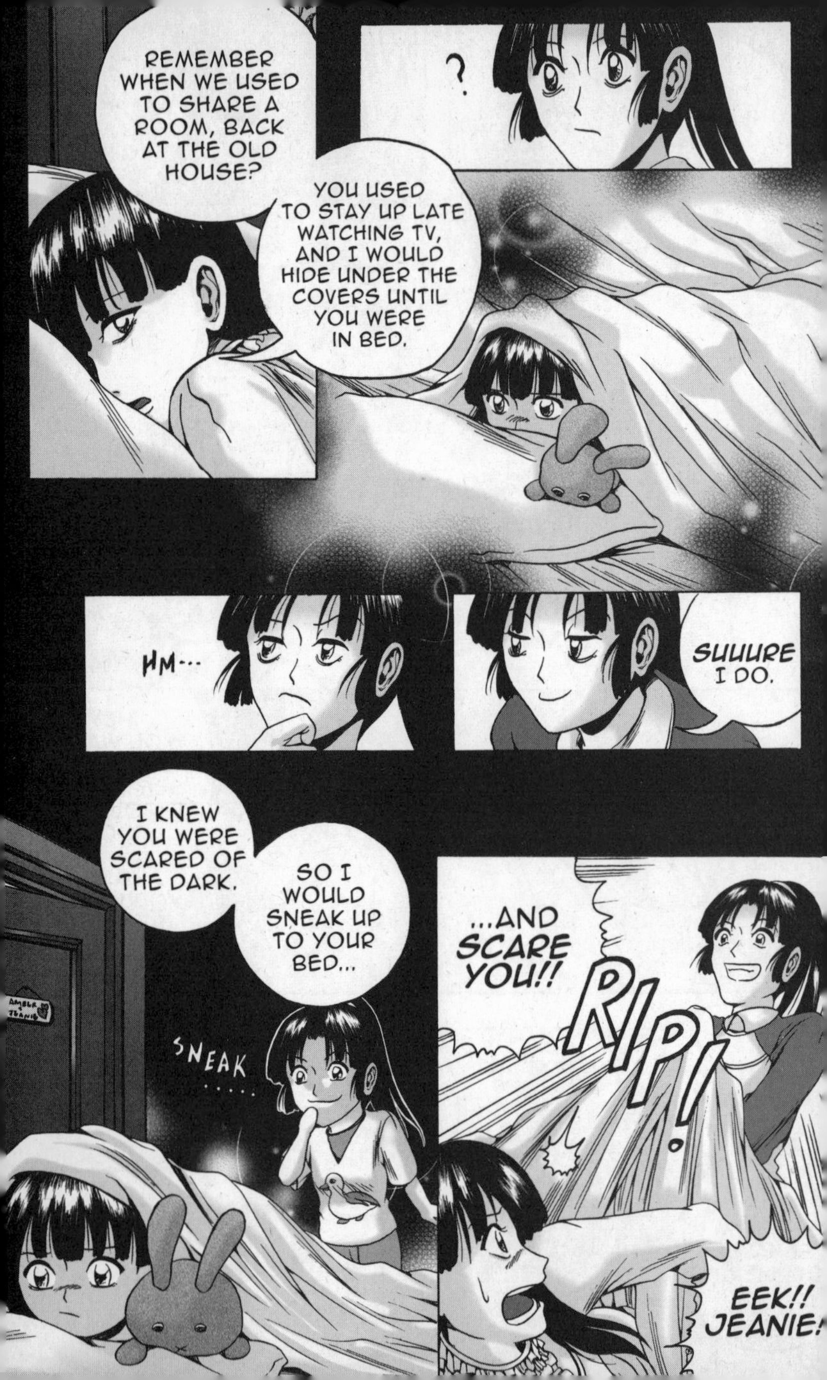
REMEMBER WHEN WE USED TO SHARE A ROOM, BACK AT THE OLD HOUSE?
?
YOU USED TO STAY UP LATE WATCHING TV, AND I WOULD HIDE UNDER THE COVERS UNTIL YOU WERE IN BED.
HM...
SUUURE I DO.
I KNEW YOU WERE SCARED OF THE DARK.
SO I WOULD SNEAK UP TO YOUR BED...
SNEAK .....
...AND SCARE YOU!!
RIP!
EEK!! JEANIE!

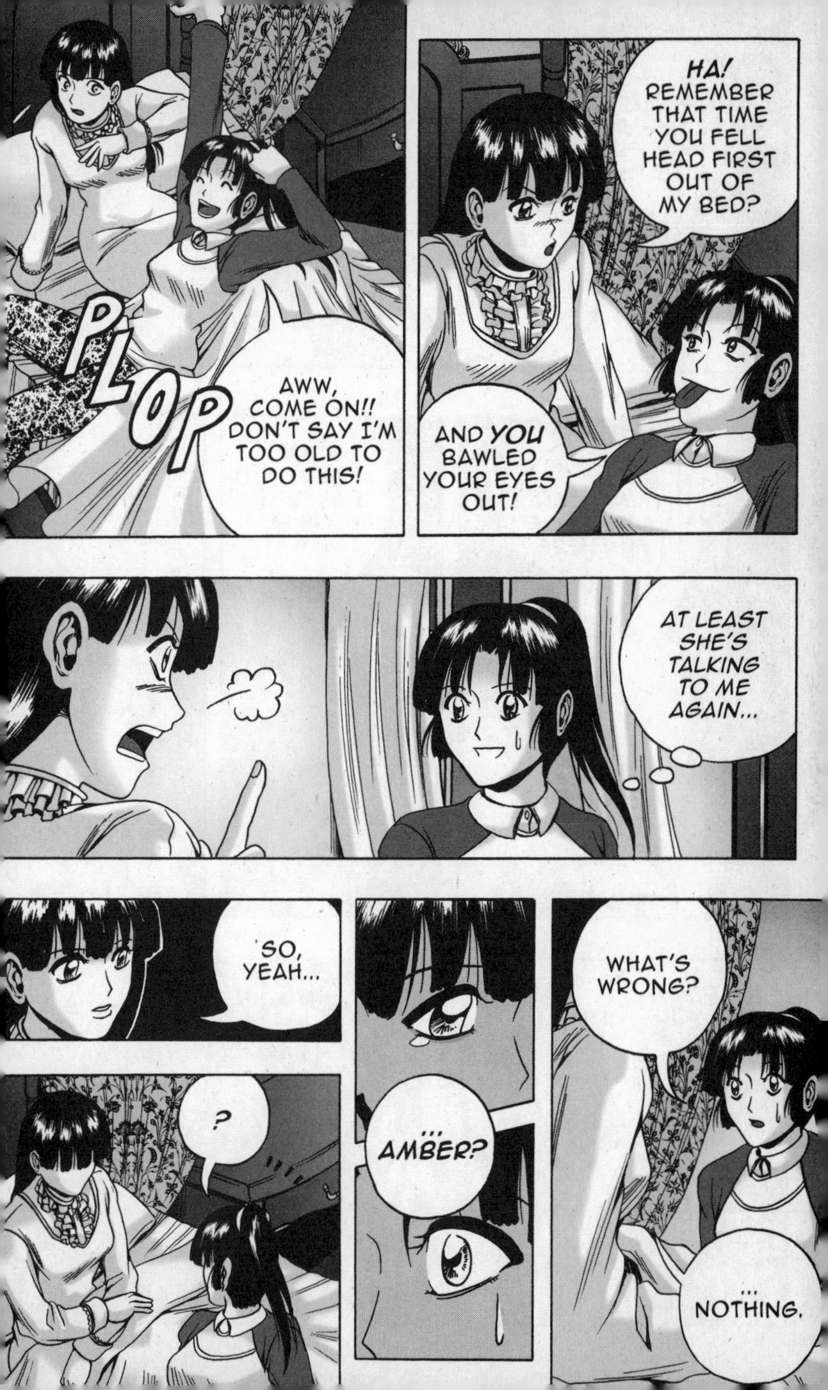
PLOP
AWW, COME ON!! DON'T SAY I'M TOO OLD TO DO THIS!
HA! REMEMBER THAT TIME YOU FELL HEAD FIRST OUT OF MY BED?
AND YOU BAWLED YOUR EYES OUT!
AT LEAST SHE'S TALKING TO ME AGAIN...
SO, YEAH...
?
...AMBER?
WHAT'S WRONG?
...NOTHING.

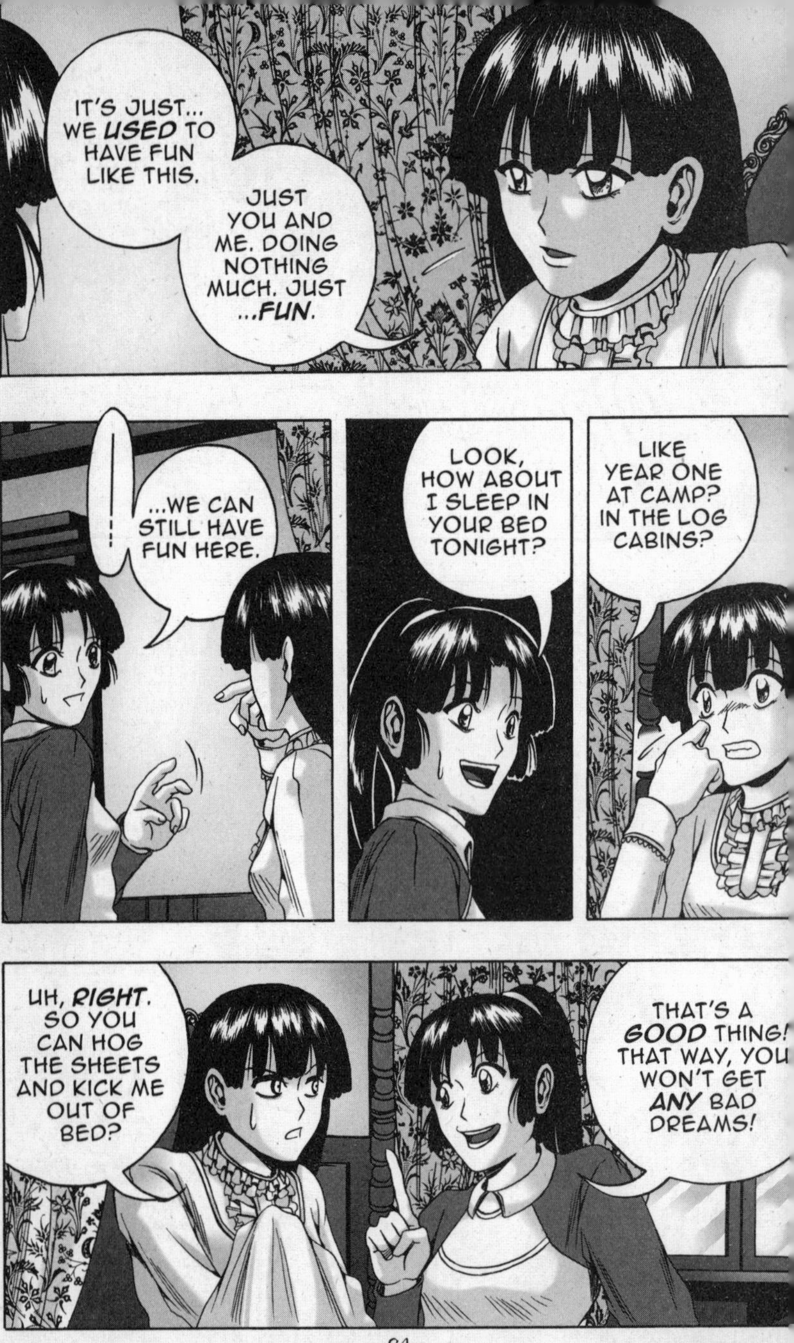
IT'S JUST... WE USED TO HAVE FUN LIKE THIS.
JUST YOU AND ME. DOING NOTHING MUCH. JUST ...FUN.
!
...WE CAN STILL HAVE FUN HERE.
LOOK, HOW ABOUT I SLEEP IN YOUR BED TONIGHT?
LIKE YEAR ONE AT CAMP? IN THE LOG CABINS?
UH, RIGHT. SO YOU CAN HOG THE SHEETS AND KICK ME OUT OF BED?
THAT'S A GOOD THING! THAT WAY, YOU WON'T GET ANY BAD DREAMS!

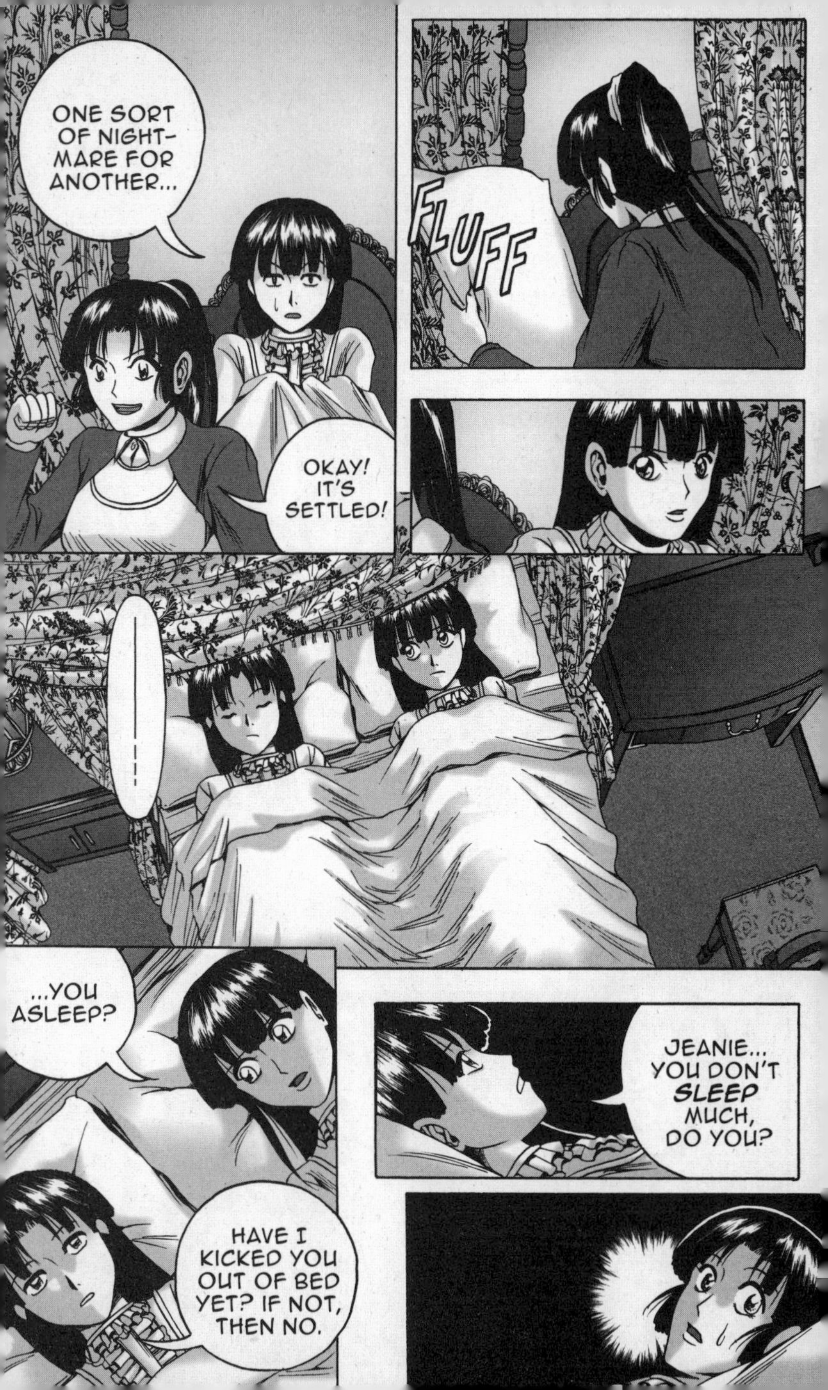

ONE SORT OF NIGHT-MARE FOR ANOTHER...
OKAY! IT'S SETTLED!
FLUFF
......
...YOU ASLEEP?
JEANIE... YOU DON'T SLEEP MUCH, DO YOU?
HAVE I KICKED YOU OUT OF BED YET? IF NOT, THEN NO.

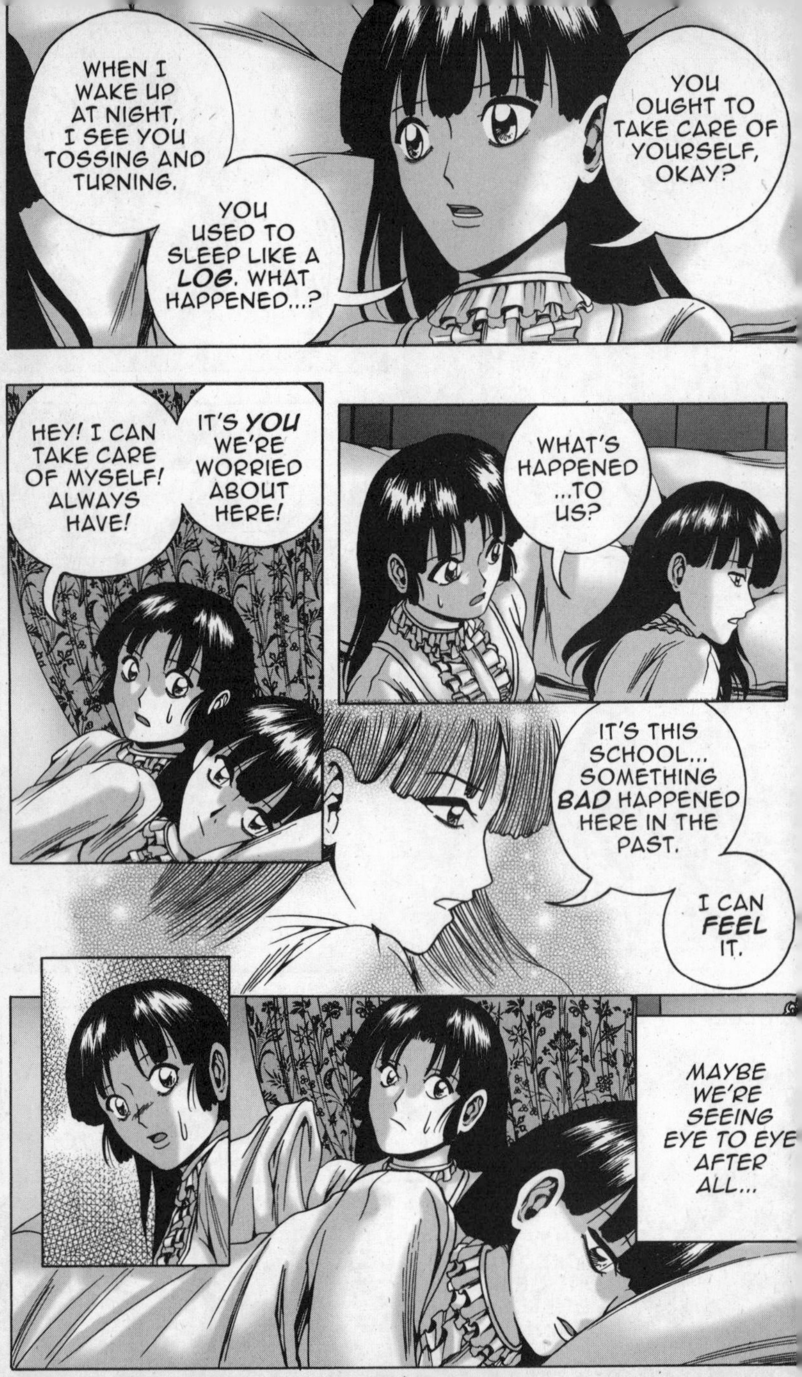
WHEN I WAKE UP AT NIGHT, I SEE YOU TOSSING AND TURNING.
YOU USED TO SLEEP LIKE A LOG. WHAT HAPPENED...?
YOU OUGHT TO TAKE CARE OF YOURSELF, OKAY?
HEY! I CAN TAKE CARE OF MYSELF! ALWAYS HAVE!
IT'S YOU WE'RE WORRIED ABOUT HERE!
WHAT'S HAPPENED ...TO US?
IT'S THIS SCHOOL... SOMETHING BAD HAPPENED HERE IN THE PAST.
I CAN FEEL IT.
MAYBE WE'RE SEEING EYE TO EYE AFTER ALL...

Chapter II

That Which Is Not Dead

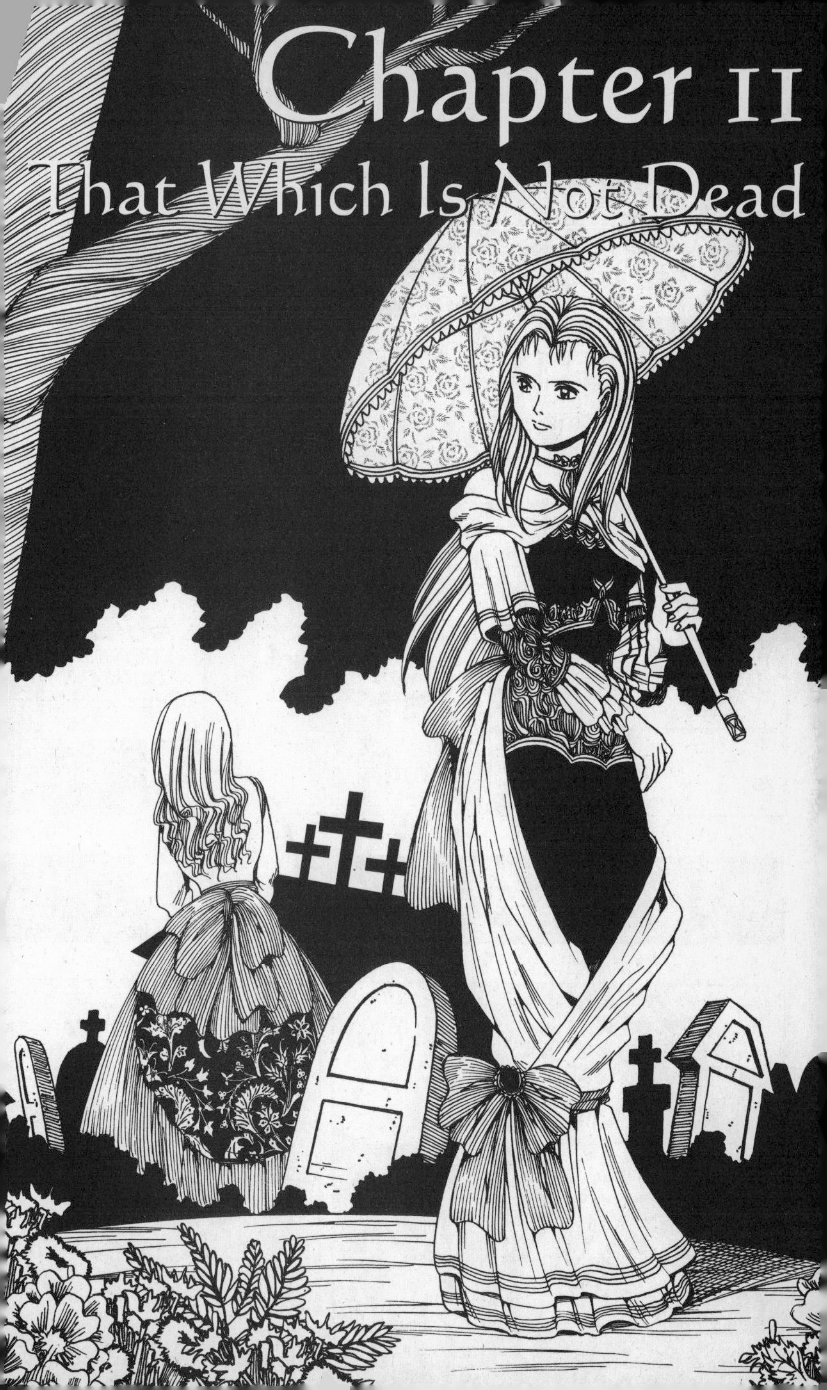

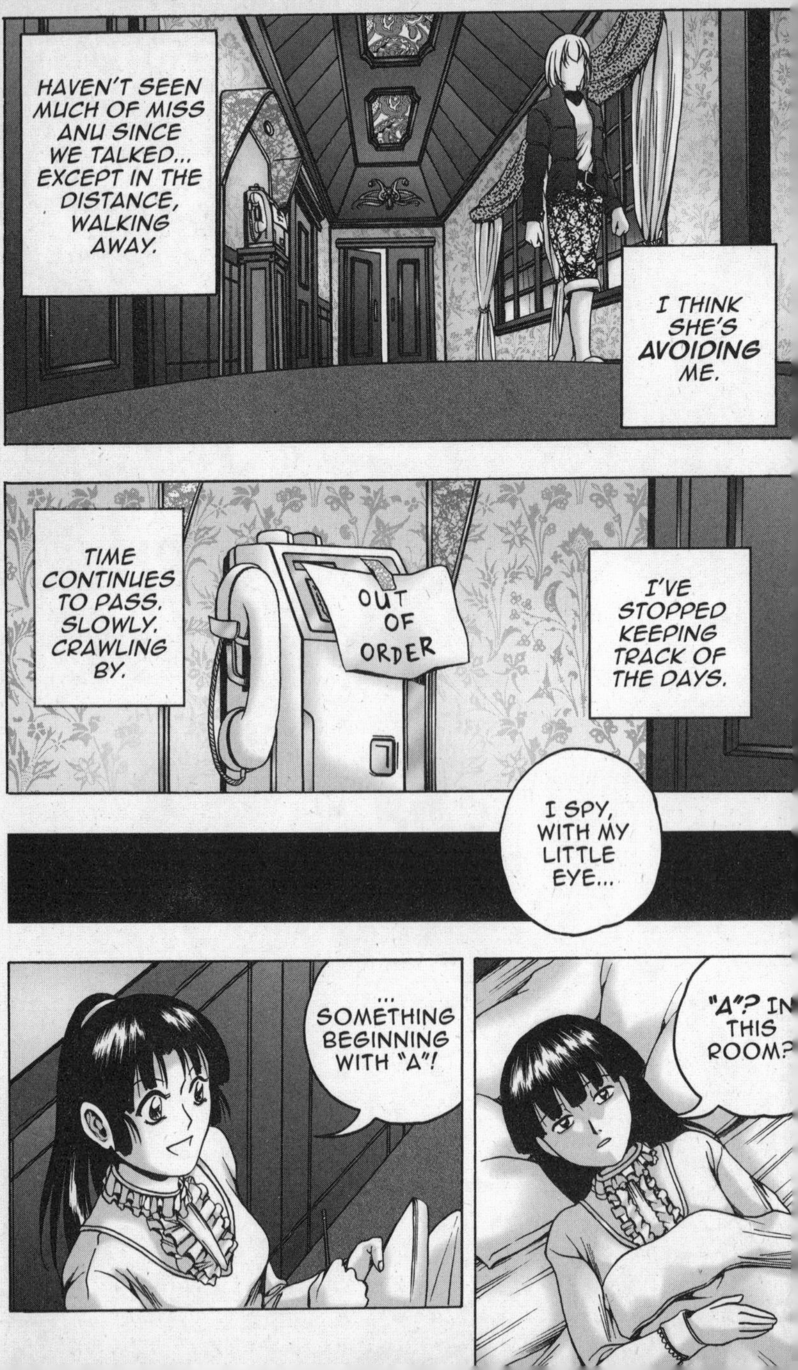
HAVEN'T SEEN MUCH OF MISS ANU SINCE WE TALKED... EXCEPT IN THE DISTANCE, WALKING AWAY.
I THINK SHE'S **AVOIDING** ME.
TIME CONTINUES TO PASS. SLOWLY. CRAWLING BY.
OUT OF ORDER
I'VE STOPPED KEEPING TRACK OF THE DAYS.
I SPY, WITH MY LITTLE EYE...
... SOMETHING BEGINNING WITH "A"!
"A"? IN THIS ROOM?

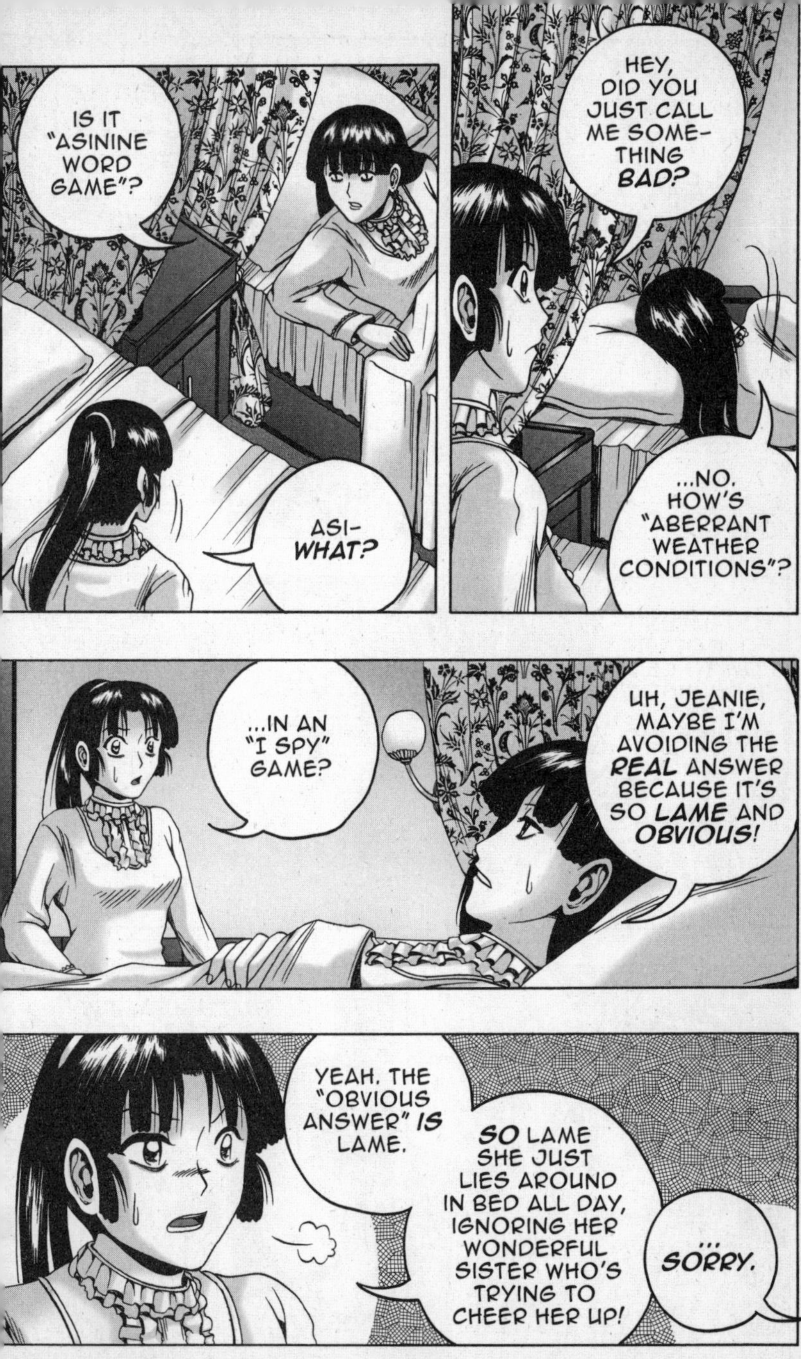
IS IT "ASININE WORD GAME"?
ASI-*WHAT?*
HEY, DID YOU JUST CALL ME SOME-THING *BAD?*
...NO. HOW'S "ABERRANT WEATHER CONDITIONS"?
...IN AN "I SPY" GAME?
UH, JEANIE, MAYBE I'M AVOIDING THE *REAL* ANSWER BECAUSE IT'S SO *LAME* AND *OBVIOUS*!
YEAH. THE "OBVIOUS ANSWER" *IS* LAME.
SO LAME SHE JUST LIES AROUND IN BED ALL DAY, IGNORING HER WONDERFUL SISTER WHO'S TRYING TO CHEER HER UP!
... *SORRY.*

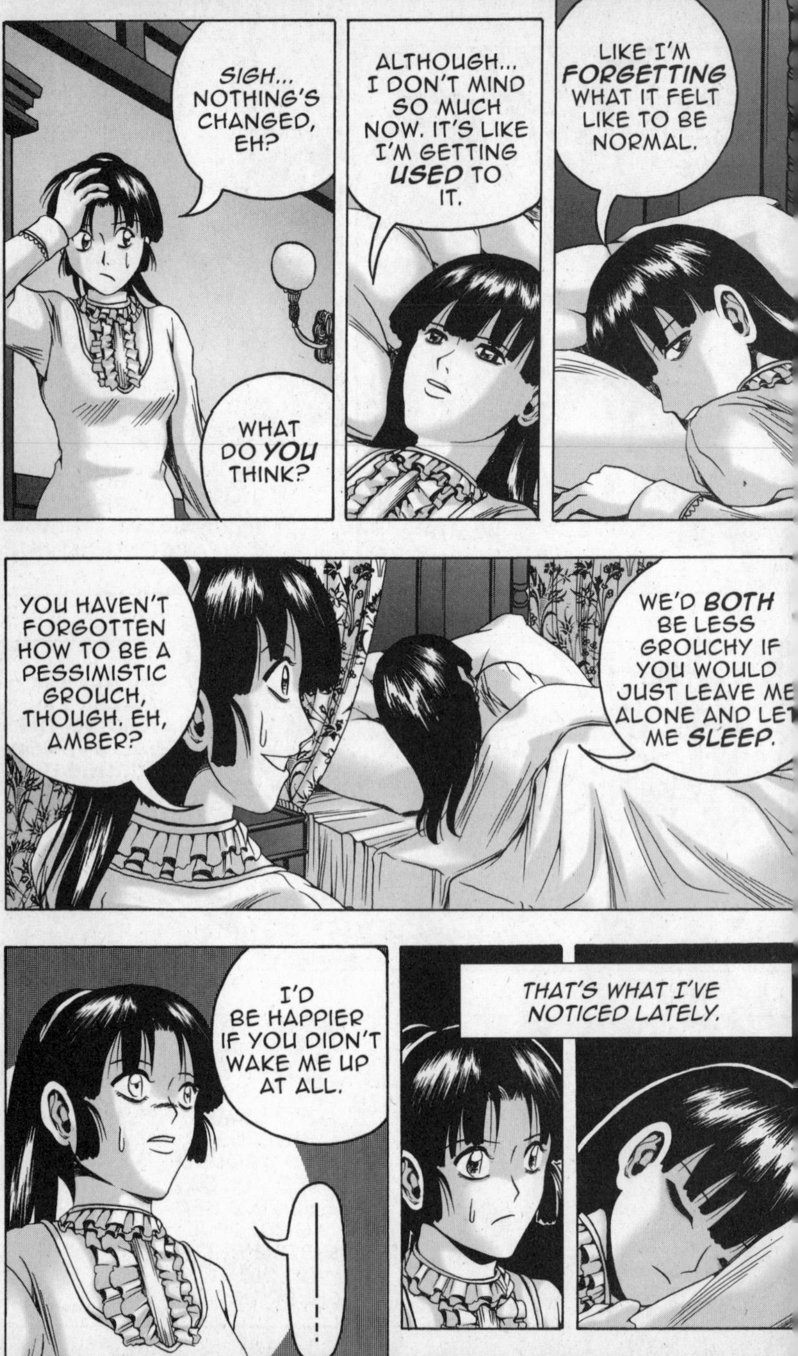
SIGH... NOTHING'S CHANGED, EH?
WHAT DO YOU THINK?
ALTHOUGH... I DON'T MIND SO MUCH NOW. IT'S LIKE I'M GETTING USED TO IT.
LIKE I'M FORGETTING WHAT IT FELT LIKE TO BE NORMAL.
YOU HAVEN'T FORGOTTEN HOW TO BE A PESSIMISTIC GROUCH, THOUGH. EH, AMBER?
WE'D BOTH BE LESS GROUCHY IF YOU WOULD JUST LEAVE ME ALONE AND LET ME SLEEP.
I'D BE HAPPIER IF YOU DIDN'T WAKE ME UP AT ALL.
......
THAT'S WHAT I'VE NOTICED LATELY.

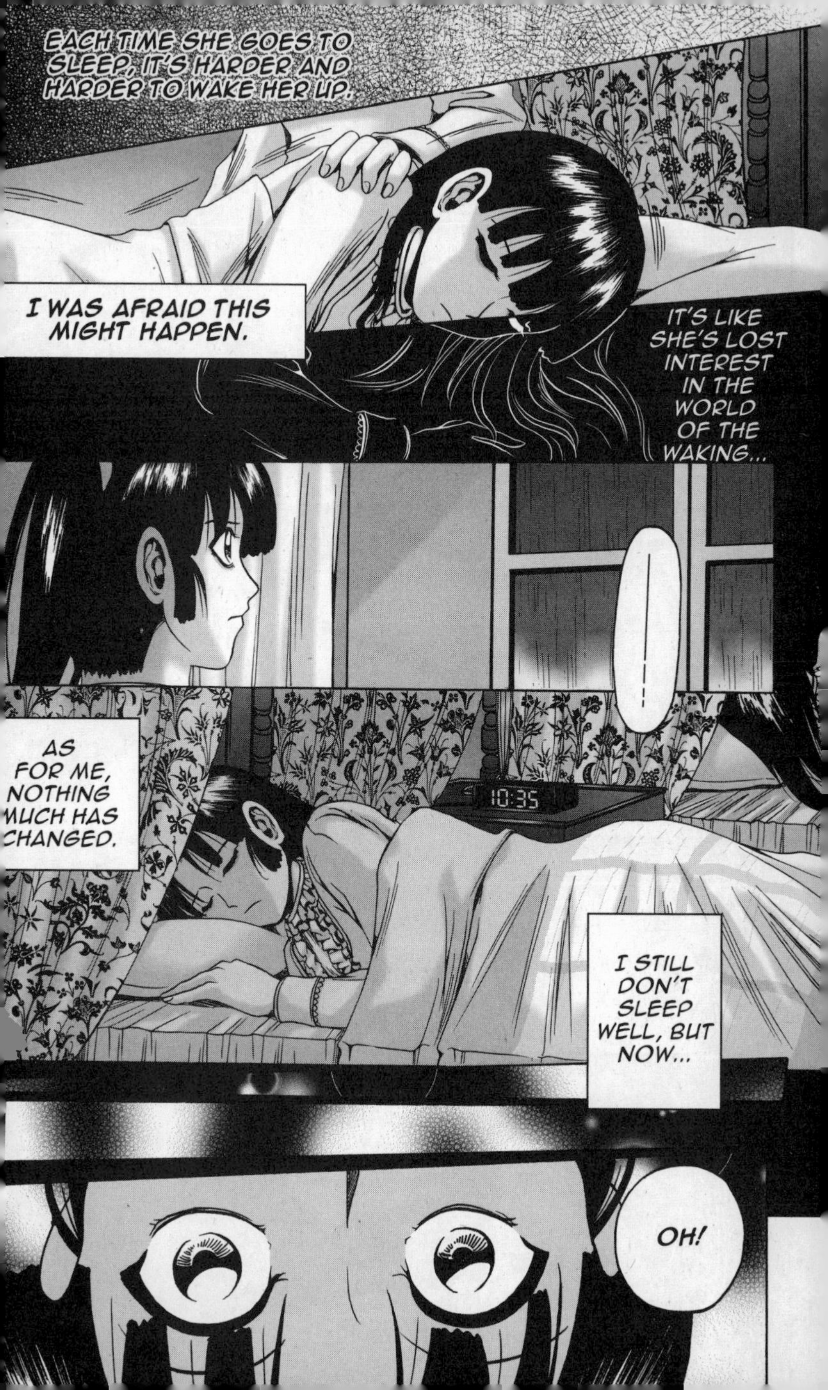
EACH TIME SHE GOES TO SLEEP, IT'S HARDER AND HARDER TO WAKE HER UP.
I WAS AFRAID THIS MIGHT HAPPEN.
IT'S LIKE SHE'S LOST INTEREST IN THE WORLD OF THE WAKING...
AS FOR ME, NOTHING MUCH HAS CHANGED.
10:35
I STILL DON'T SLEEP WELL, BUT NOW...
OH!

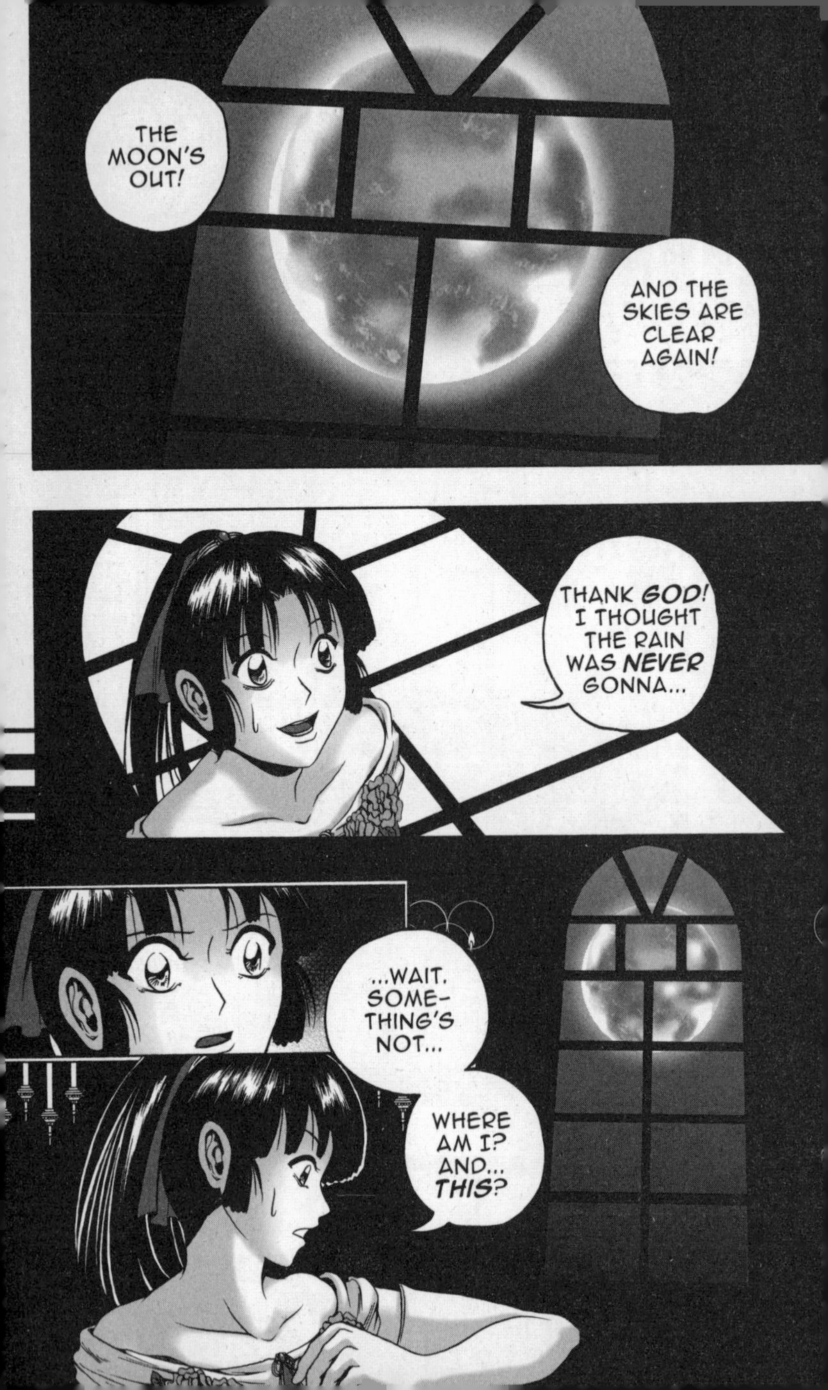
THE MOON'S OUT!
AND THE SKIES ARE CLEAR AGAIN!
THANK GOD! I THOUGHT THE RAIN WAS NEVER GONNA...
...WAIT. SOME-THING'S NOT...
WHERE AM I? AND... THIS?

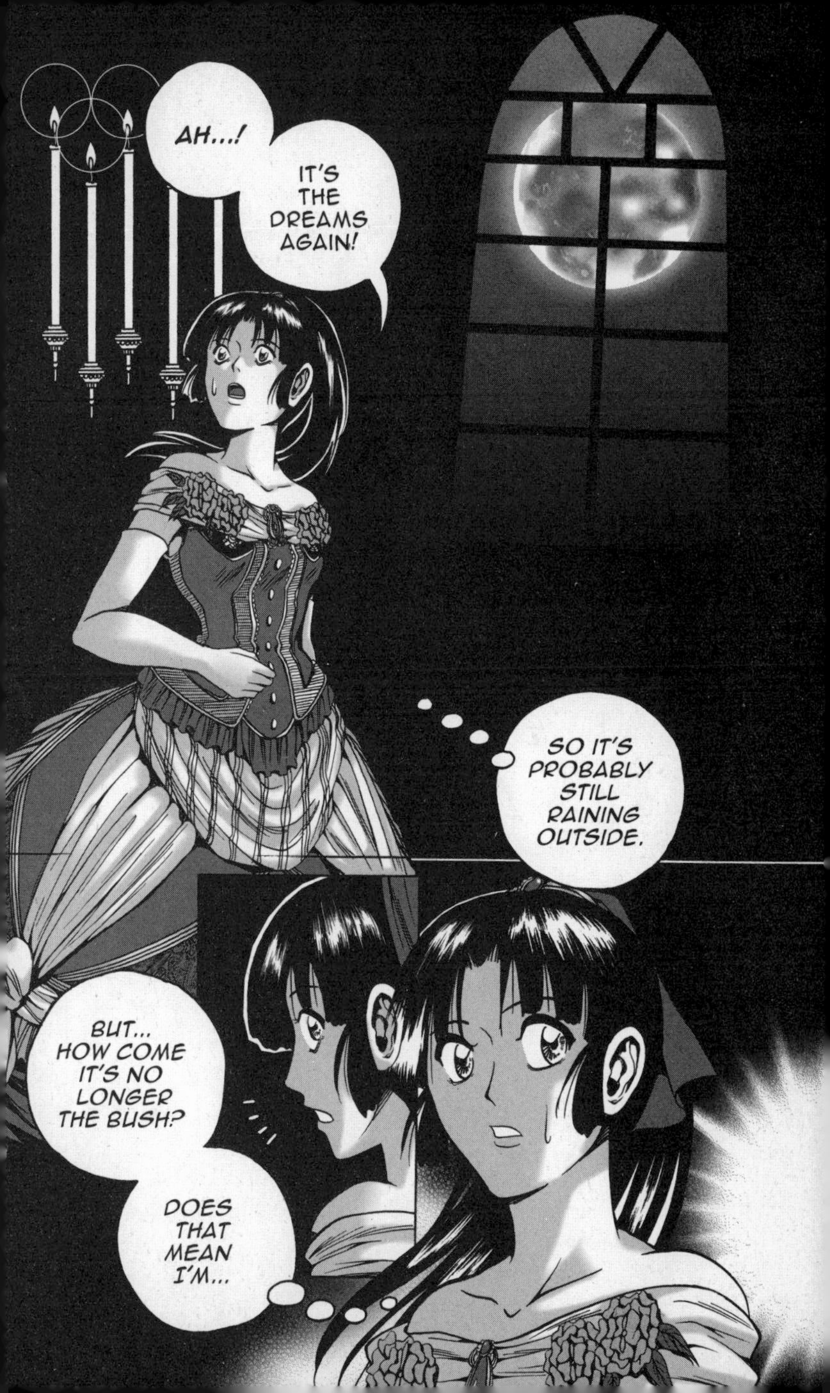
AH...!
IT'S THE DREAMS AGAIN!
SO IT'S PROBABLY STILL RAINING OUTSIDE.
BUT... HOW COME IT'S NO LONGER THE BUSH?
DOES THAT MEAN I'M...

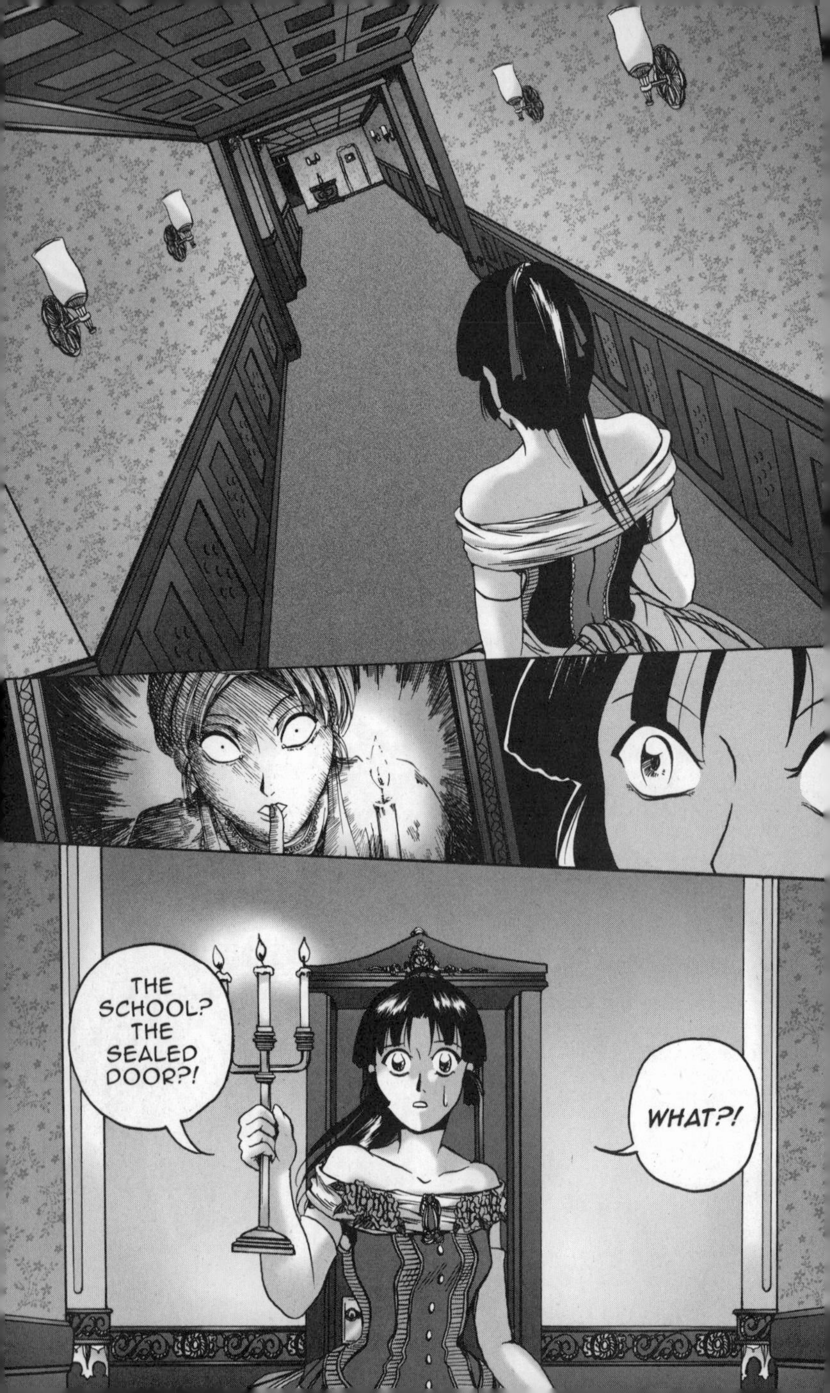
THE SCHOOL? THE SEALED DOOR?!
WHAT?!

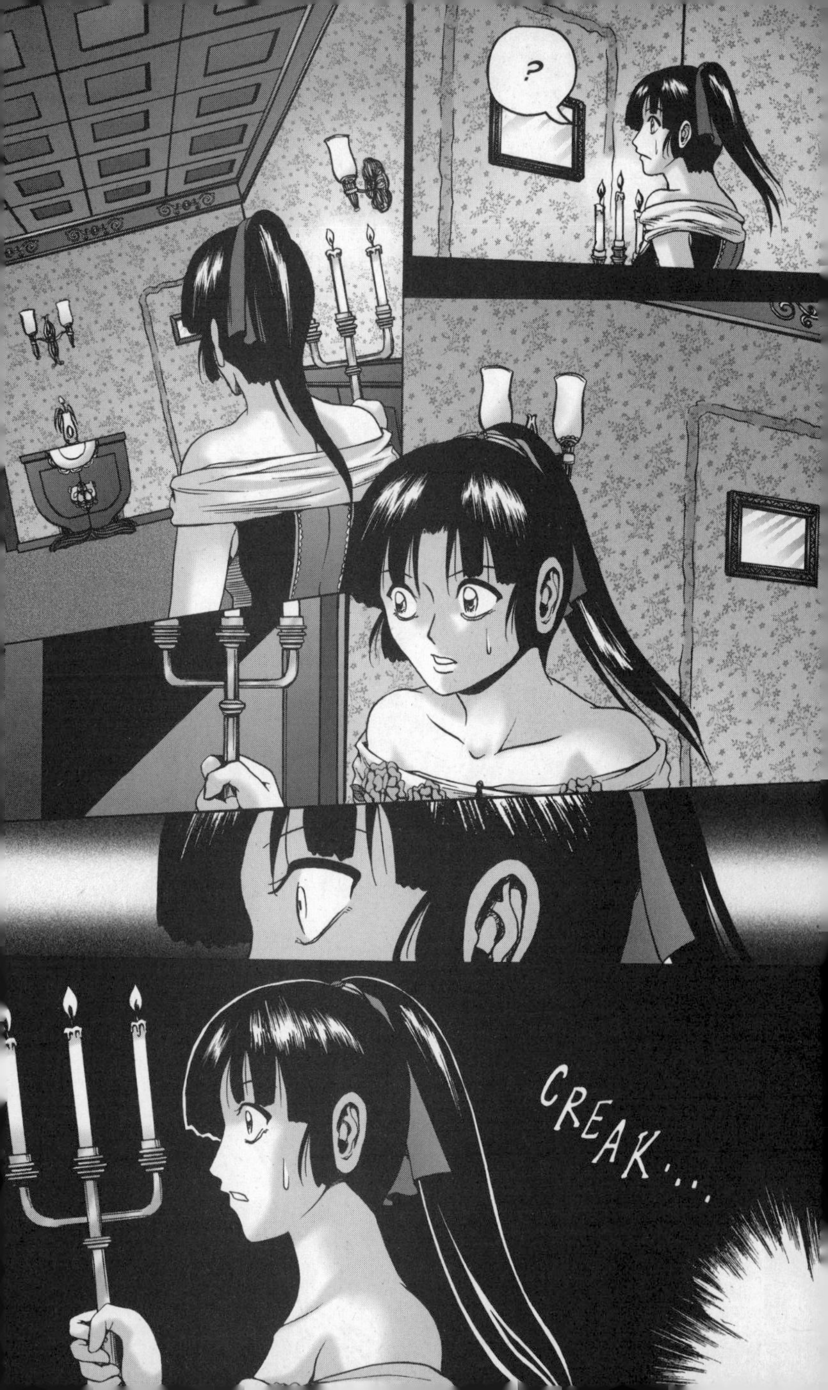
?
CREAK....

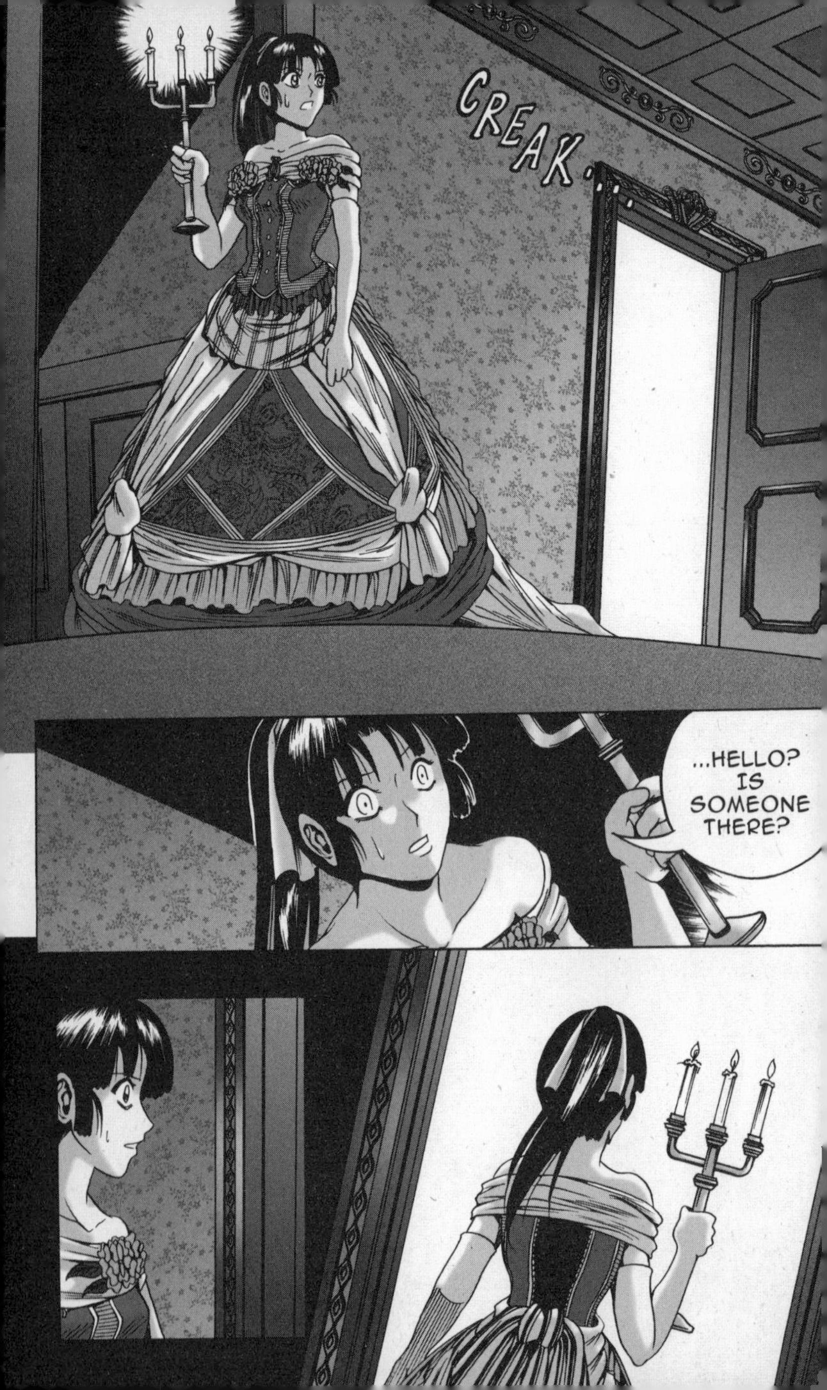
CREAK.
...HELLO? IS SOMEONE THERE?

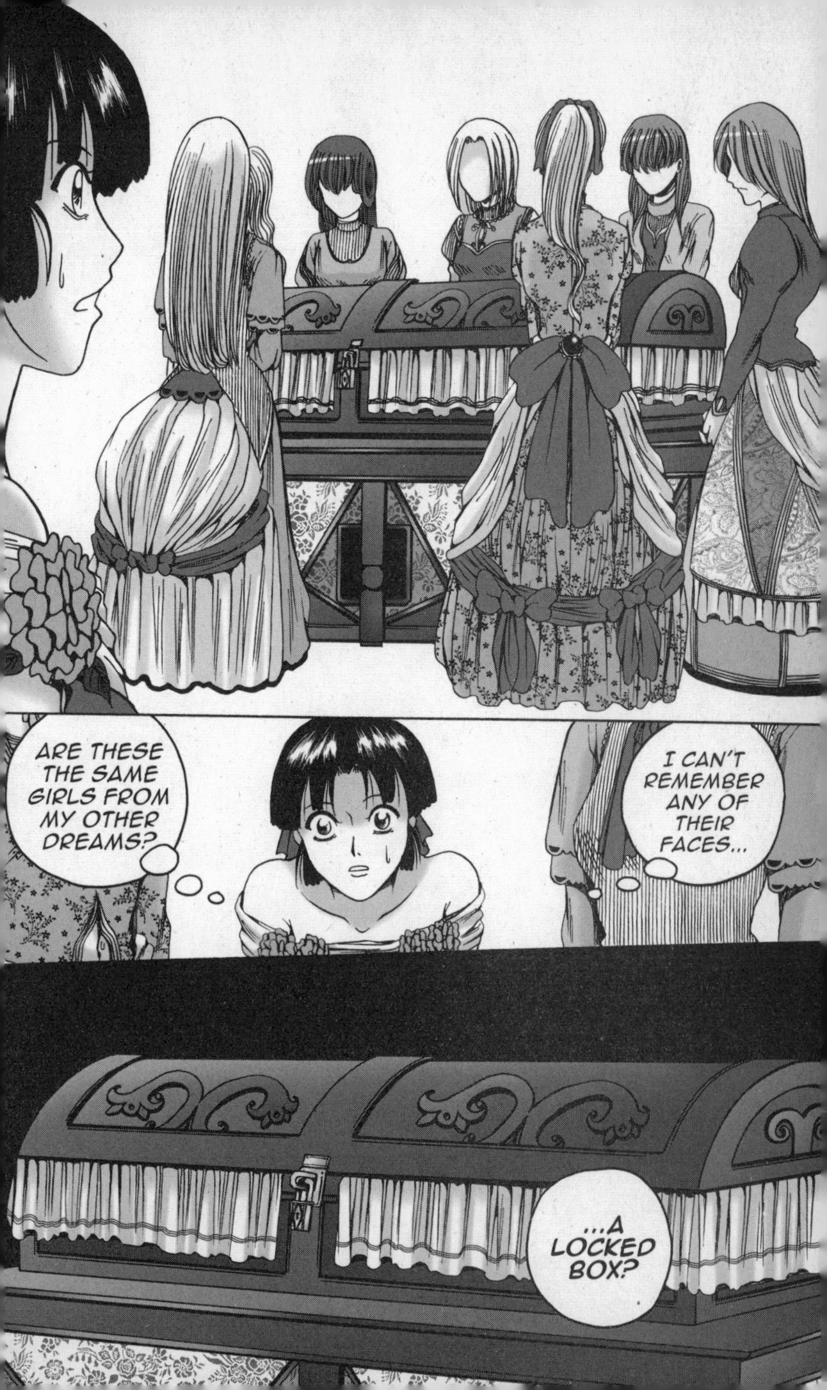
ARE THESE THE SAME GIRLS FROM MY OTHER DREAMS?
I CAN'T REMEMBER ANY OF THEIR FACES...
...A LOCKED BOX?

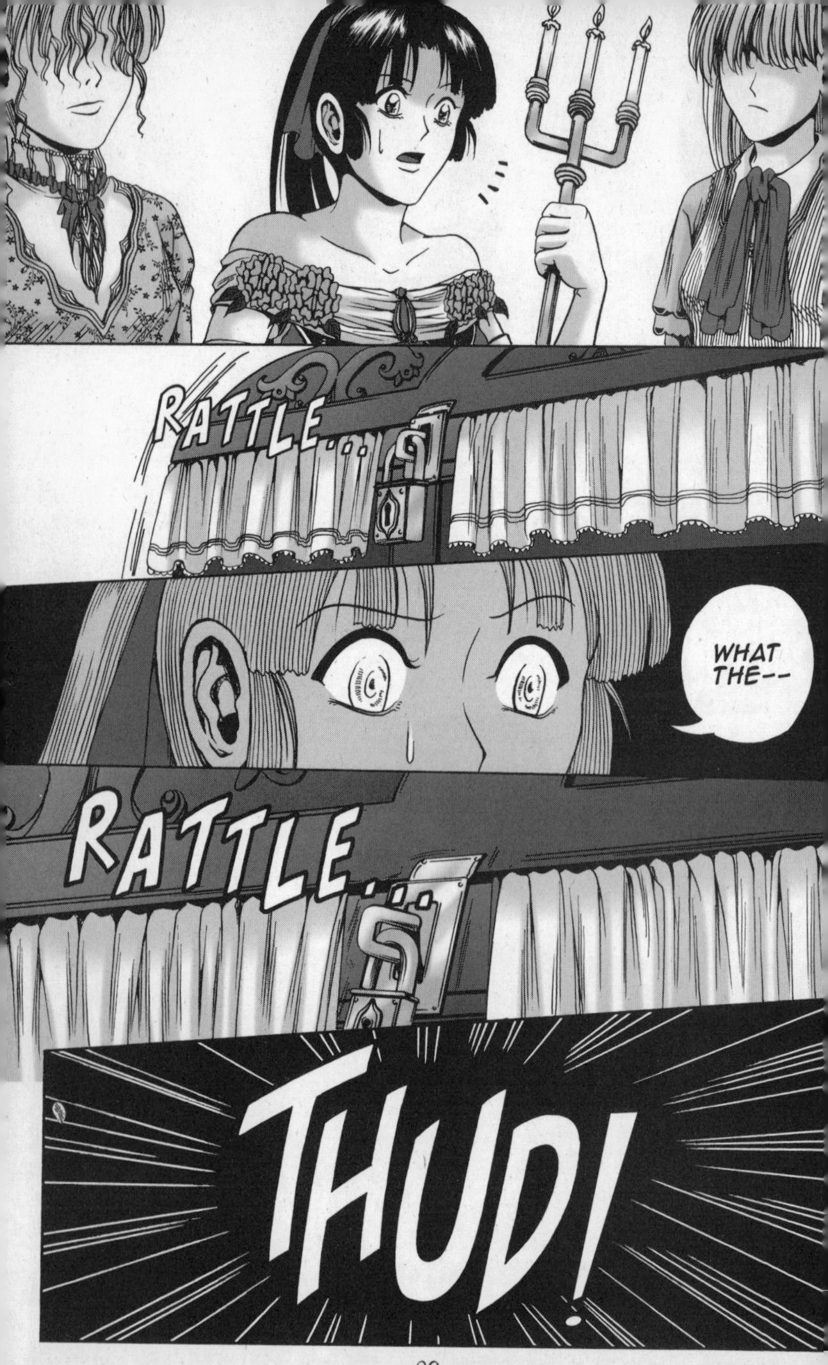
RATTLE...
WHAT THE--
RATTLE...
THUD!

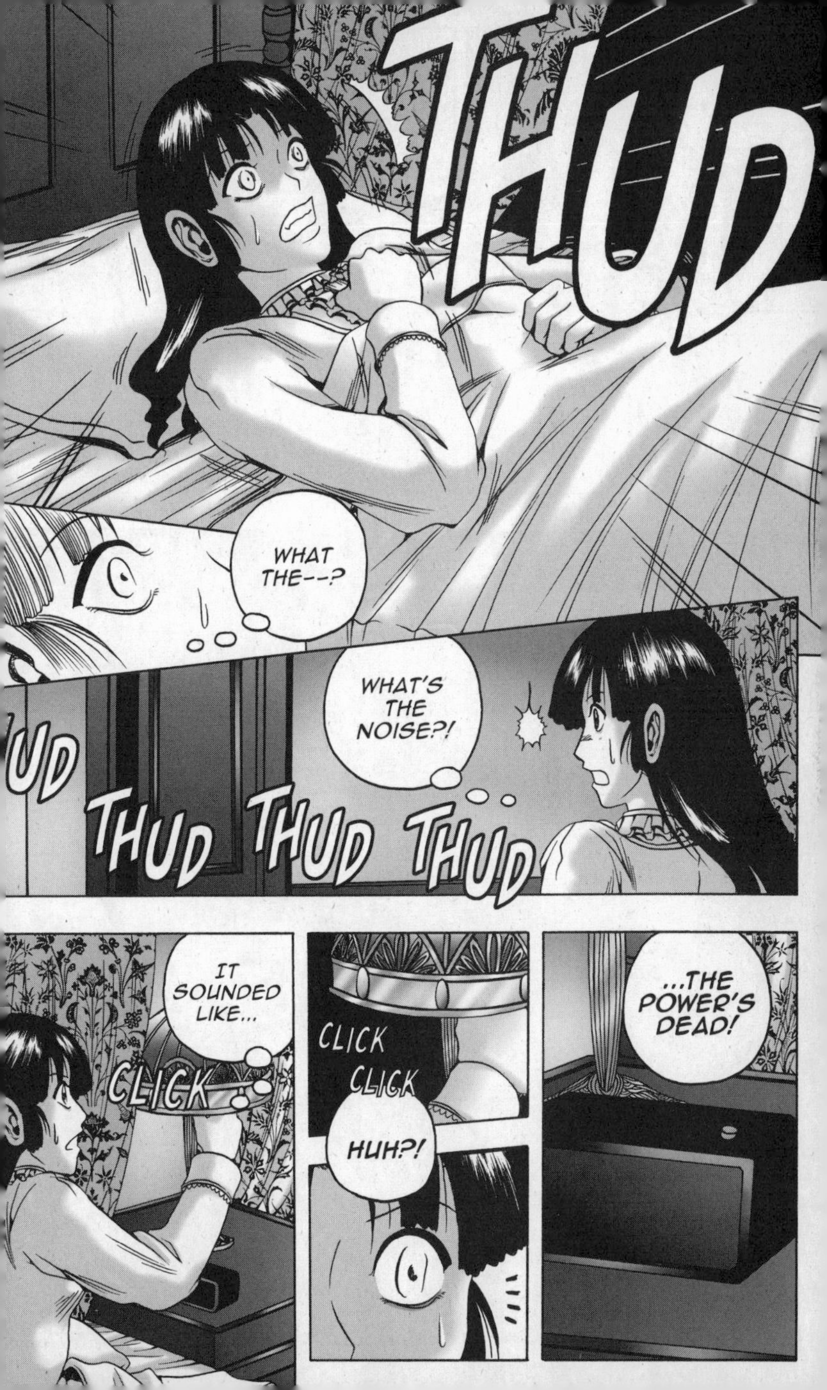
THUD
WHAT THE--?
WHAT'S THE NOISE?!
UD
THUD THUD THUD
IT SOUNDED LIKE...
CLICK
CLICK
CLICK
HUH?!
...THE POWER'S DEAD!

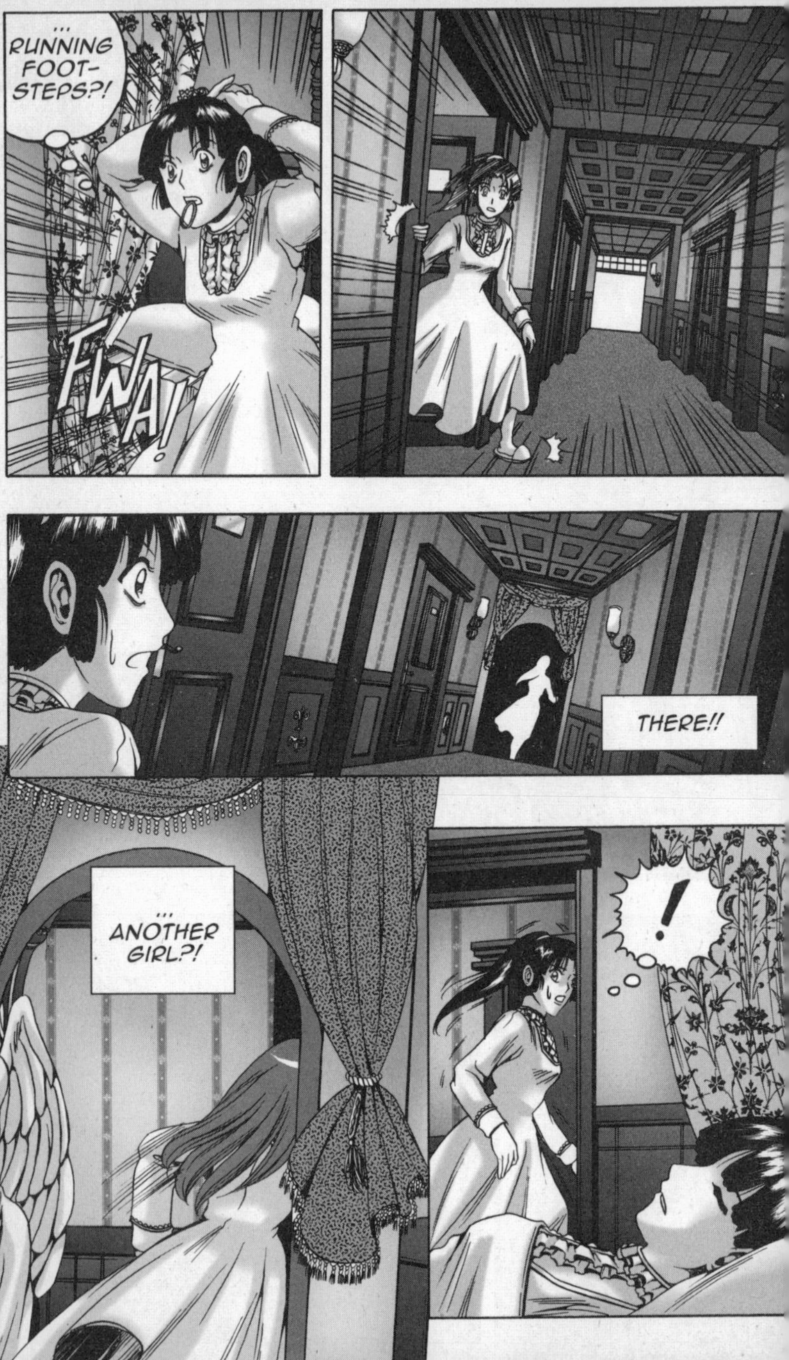
...RUNNING FOOT-STEPS?!
FWA!
THERE!!
...ANOTHER GIRL?!
!

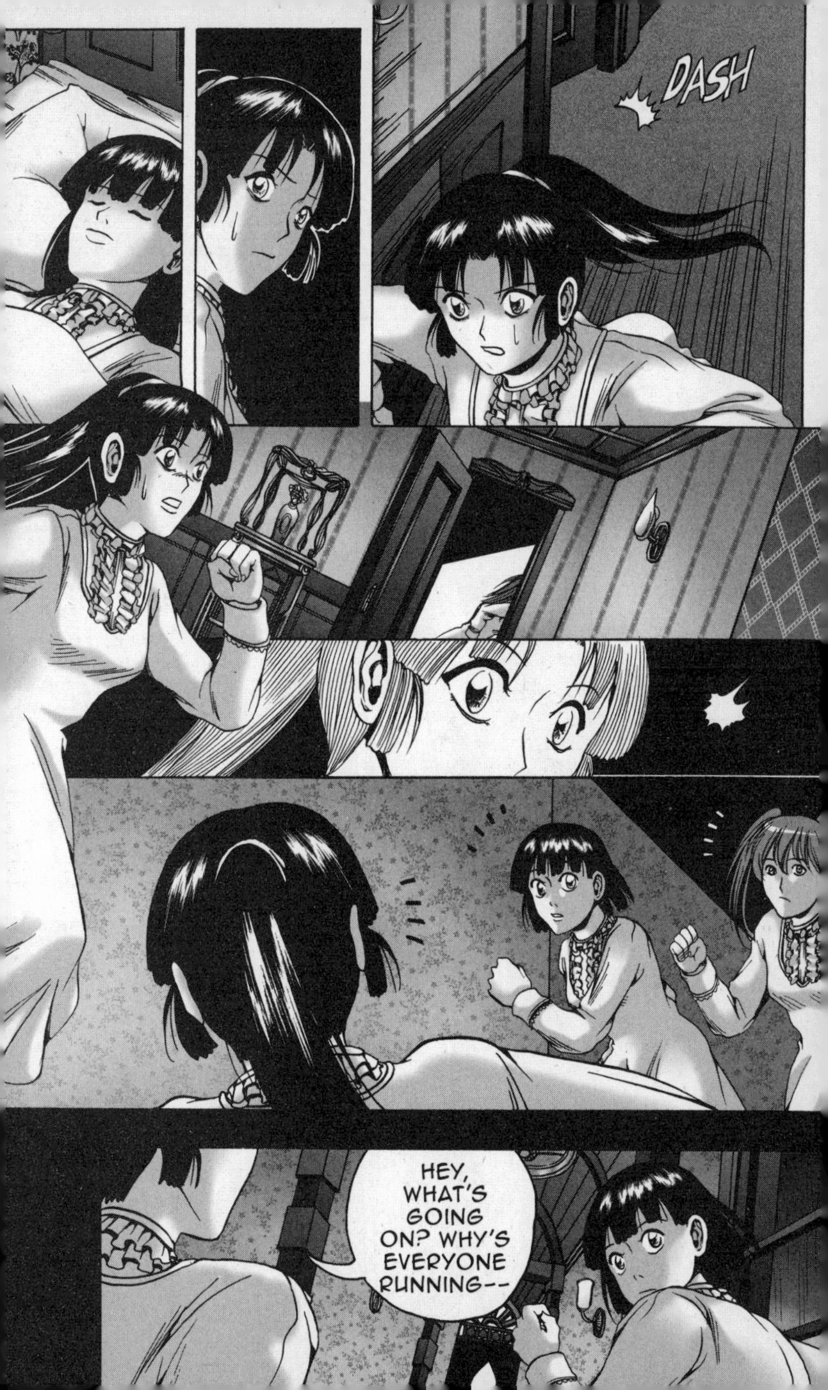
DASH
HEY, WHAT'S GOING ON? WHY'S EVERYONE RUNNING--

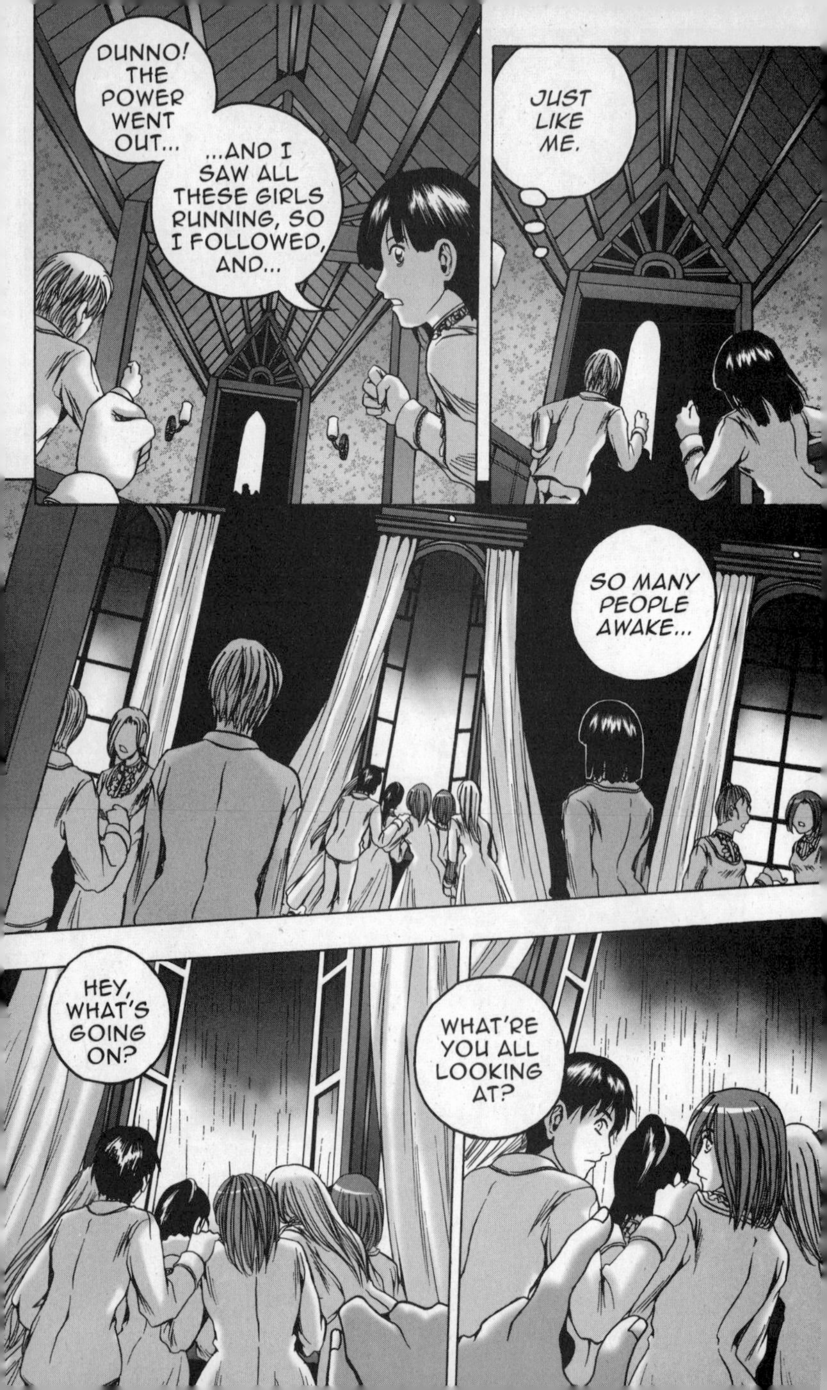
DUNNO! THE POWER WENT OUT...
...AND I SAW ALL THESE GIRLS RUNNING, SO I FOLLOWED, AND...
JUST LIKE ME.
SO MANY PEOPLE AWAKE...
HEY, WHAT'S GOING ON?
WHAT'RE YOU ALL LOOKING AT?

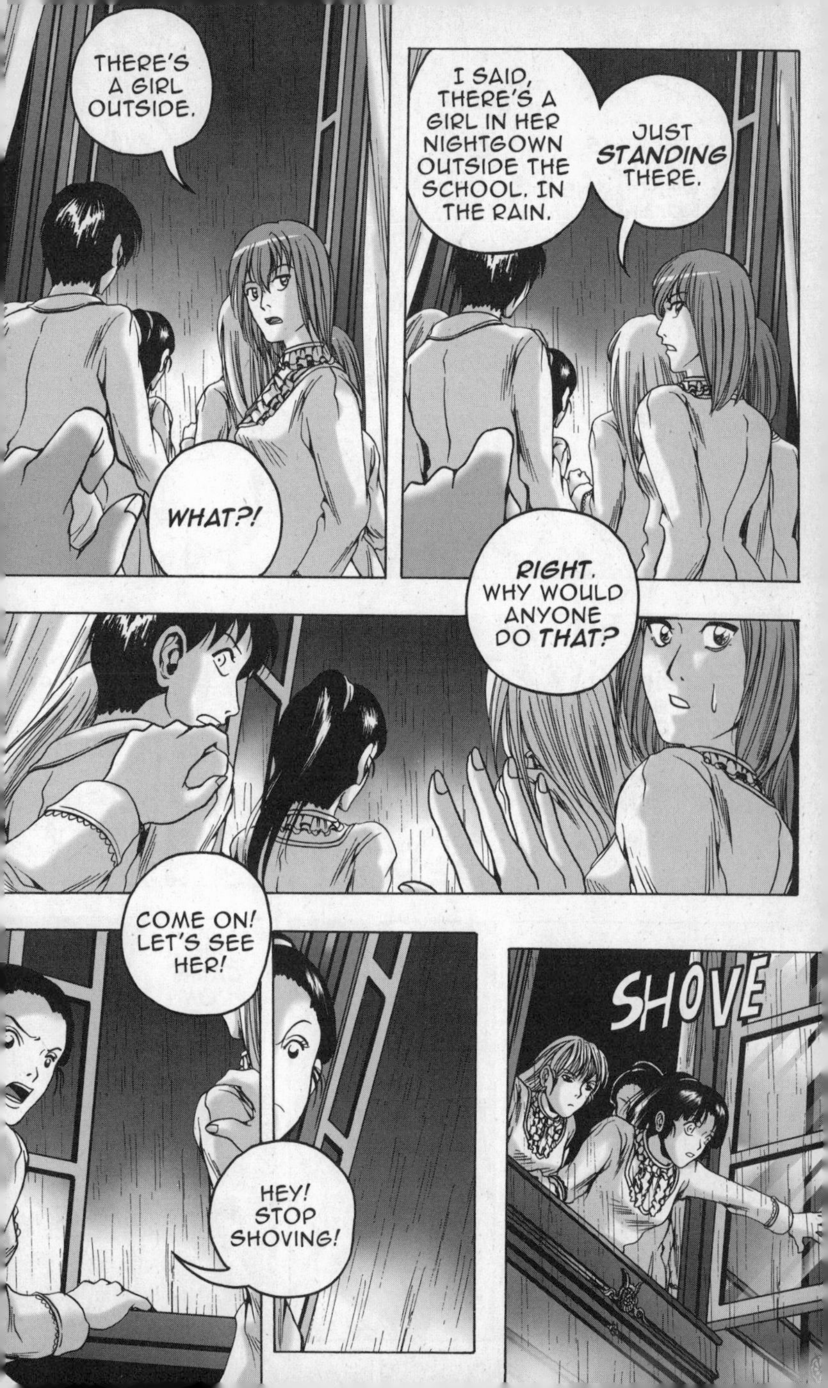
THERE'S A GIRL OUTSIDE.
WHAT?!
I SAID, THERE'S A GIRL IN HER NIGHTGOWN OUTSIDE THE SCHOOL. IN THE RAIN.
JUST STANDING THERE.
RIGHT. WHY WOULD ANYONE DO THAT?
COME ON! LET'S SEE HER!
HEY! STOP SHOVING!
SHOVE

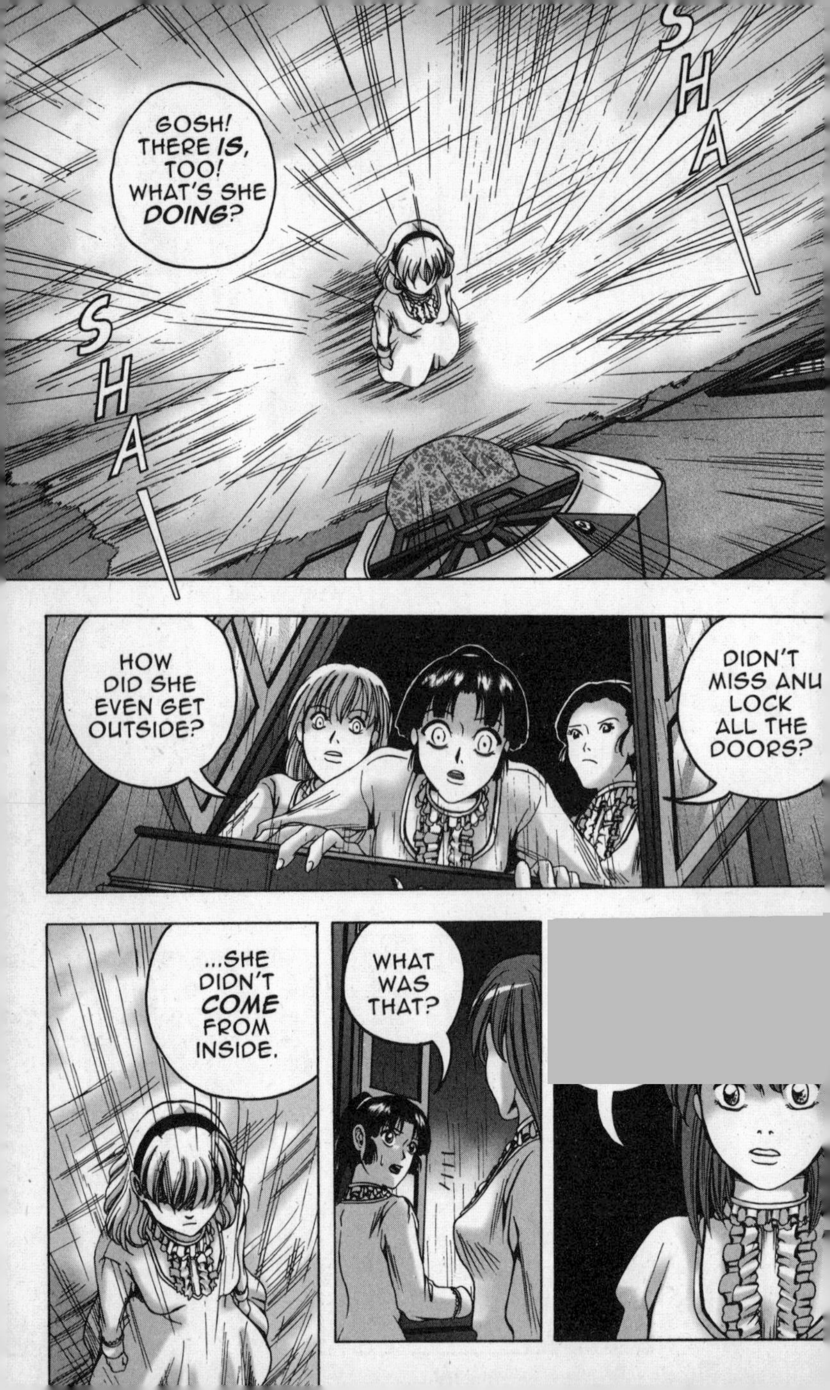
SHA
GOSH! THERE IS, TOO! WHAT'S SHE DOING?
SHA
DIDN'T MISS ANU LOCK ALL THE DOORS?
HOW DID SHE EVEN GET OUTSIDE?
WHAT WAS THAT?
...SHE DIDN'T COME FROM INSIDE.

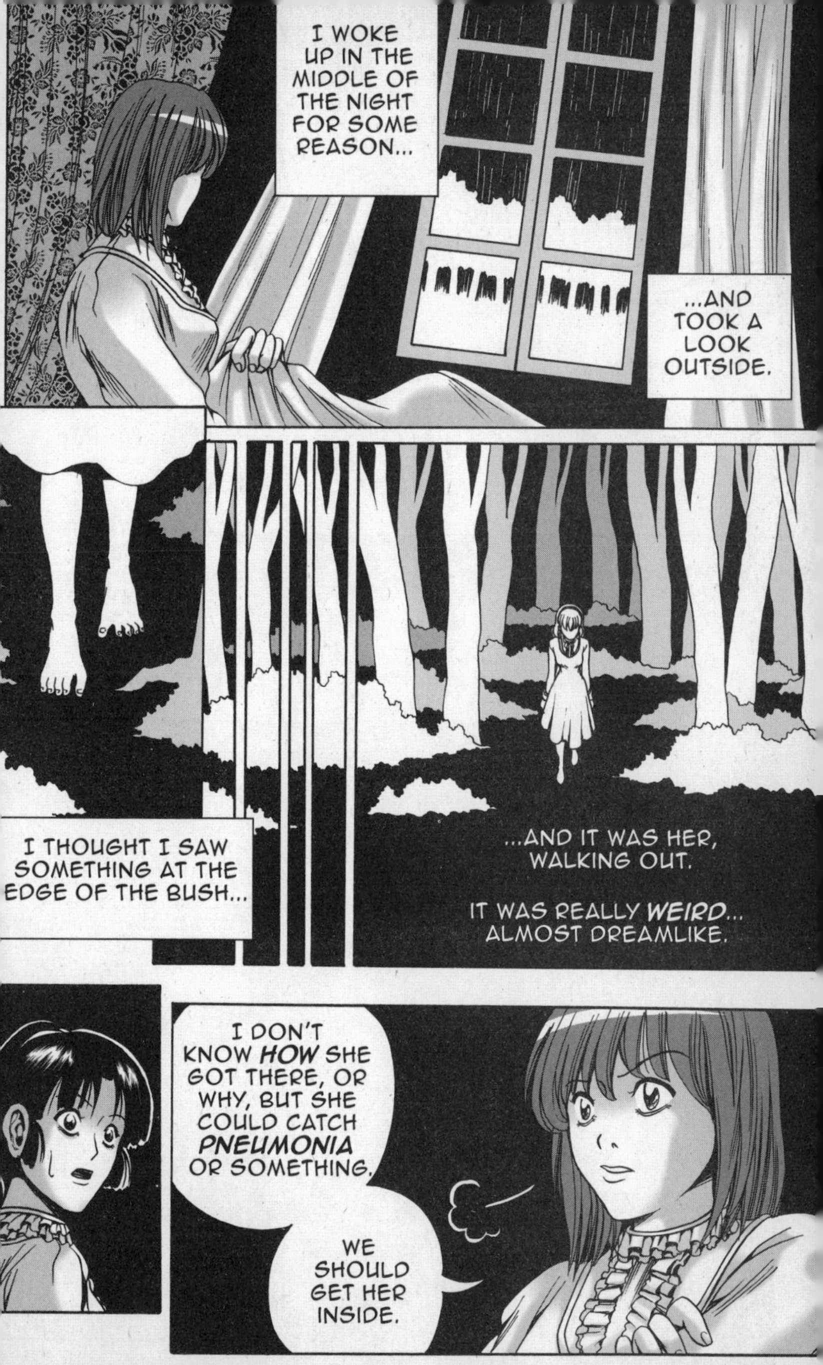
I WOKE UP IN THE MIDDLE OF THE NIGHT FOR SOME REASON...
...AND TOOK A LOOK OUTSIDE.
I THOUGHT I SAW SOMETHING AT THE EDGE OF THE BUSH...
...AND IT WAS HER, WALKING OUT.
IT WAS REALLY *WEIRD*... ALMOST DREAMLIKE.
I DON'T KNOW *HOW* SHE GOT THERE, OR WHY, BUT SHE COULD CATCH *PNEUMONIA* OR SOMETHING.
WE SHOULD GET HER INSIDE.

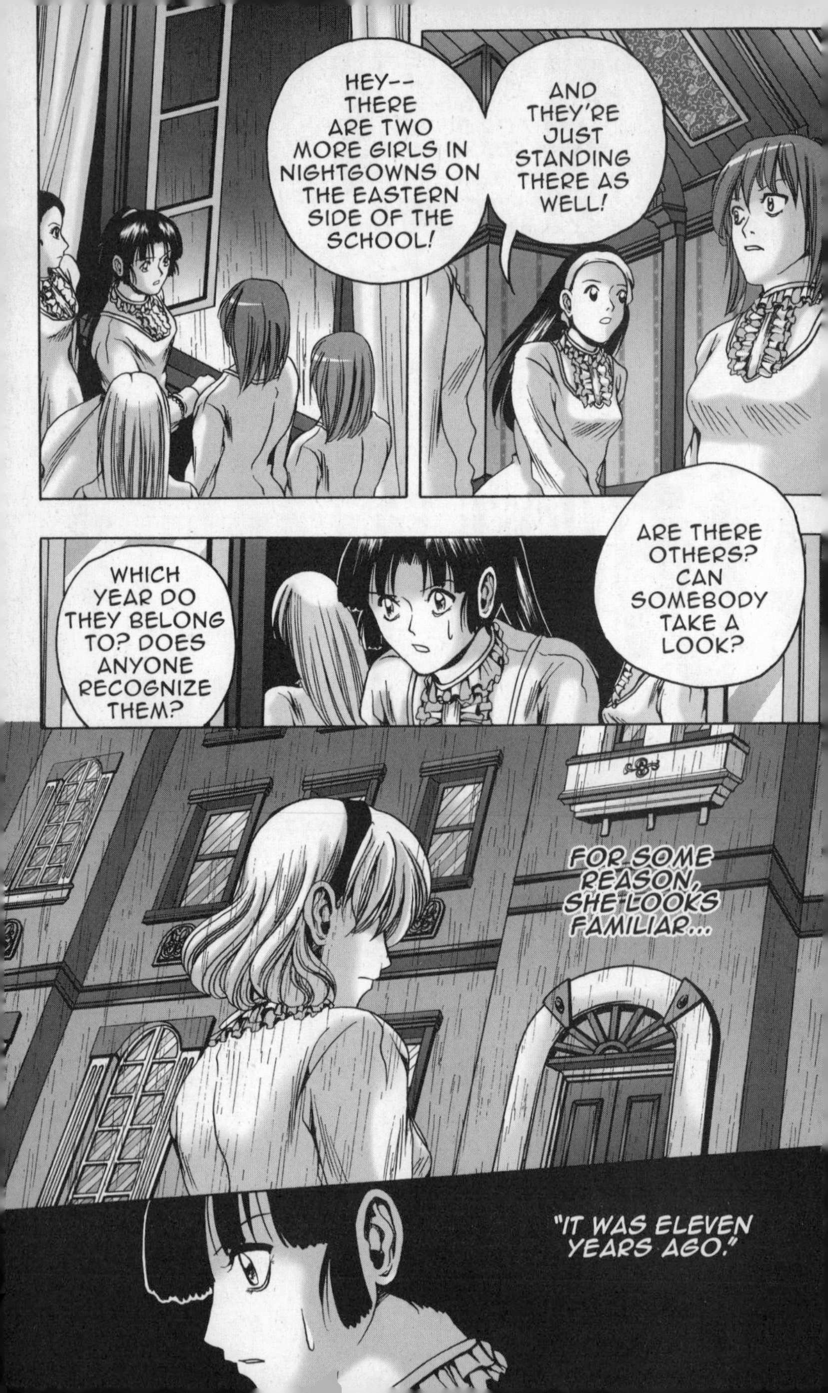
HEY-- THERE ARE TWO MORE GIRLS IN NIGHTGOWNS ON THE EASTERN SIDE OF THE SCHOOL!
AND THEY'RE JUST STANDING THERE AS WELL!
WHICH YEAR DO THEY BELONG TO? DOES ANYONE RECOGNIZE THEM?
ARE THERE OTHERS? CAN SOMEBODY TAKE A LOOK?
FOR SOME REASON, SHE LOOKS FAMILIAR...
"IT WAS ELEVEN YEARS AGO."

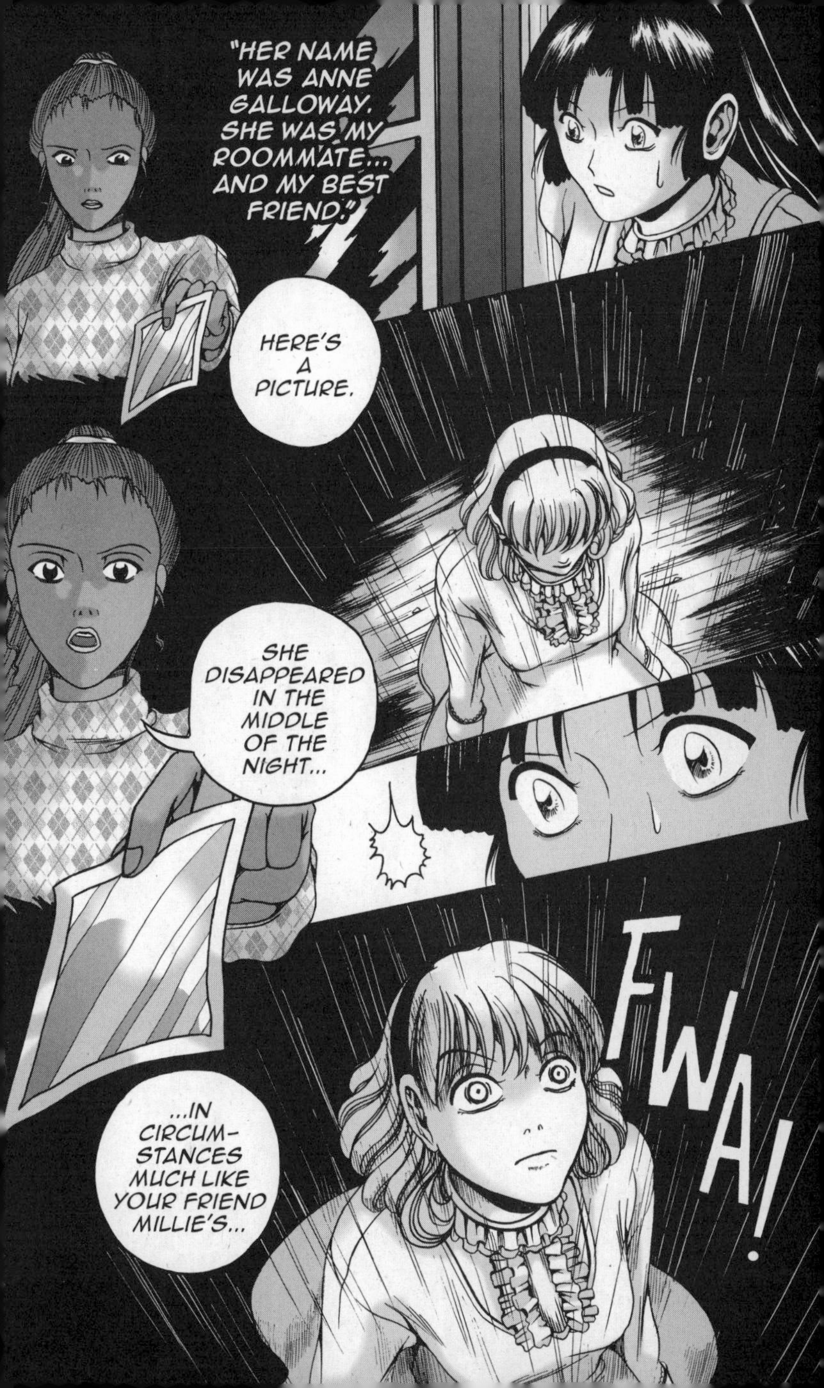
"HER NAME WAS ANNE GALLOWAY. SHE WAS MY ROOMMATE... AND MY BEST FRIEND."
HERE'S A PICTURE.
SHE DISAPPEARED IN THE MIDDLE OF THE NIGHT...
...IN CIRCUM-STANCES MUCH LIKE YOUR FRIEND MILLIE'S...
FWA!

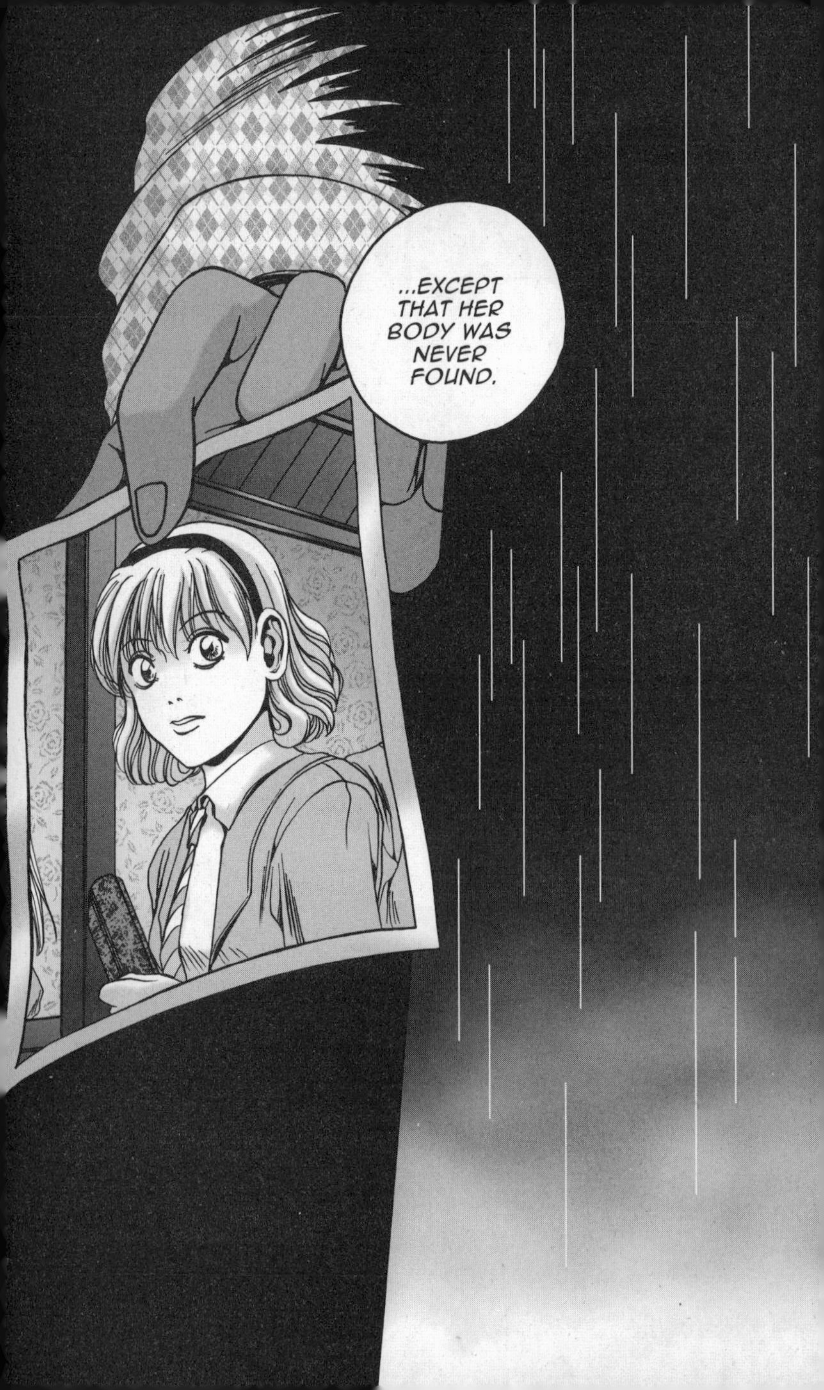
...EXCEPT THAT HER BODY WAS NEVER FOUND.

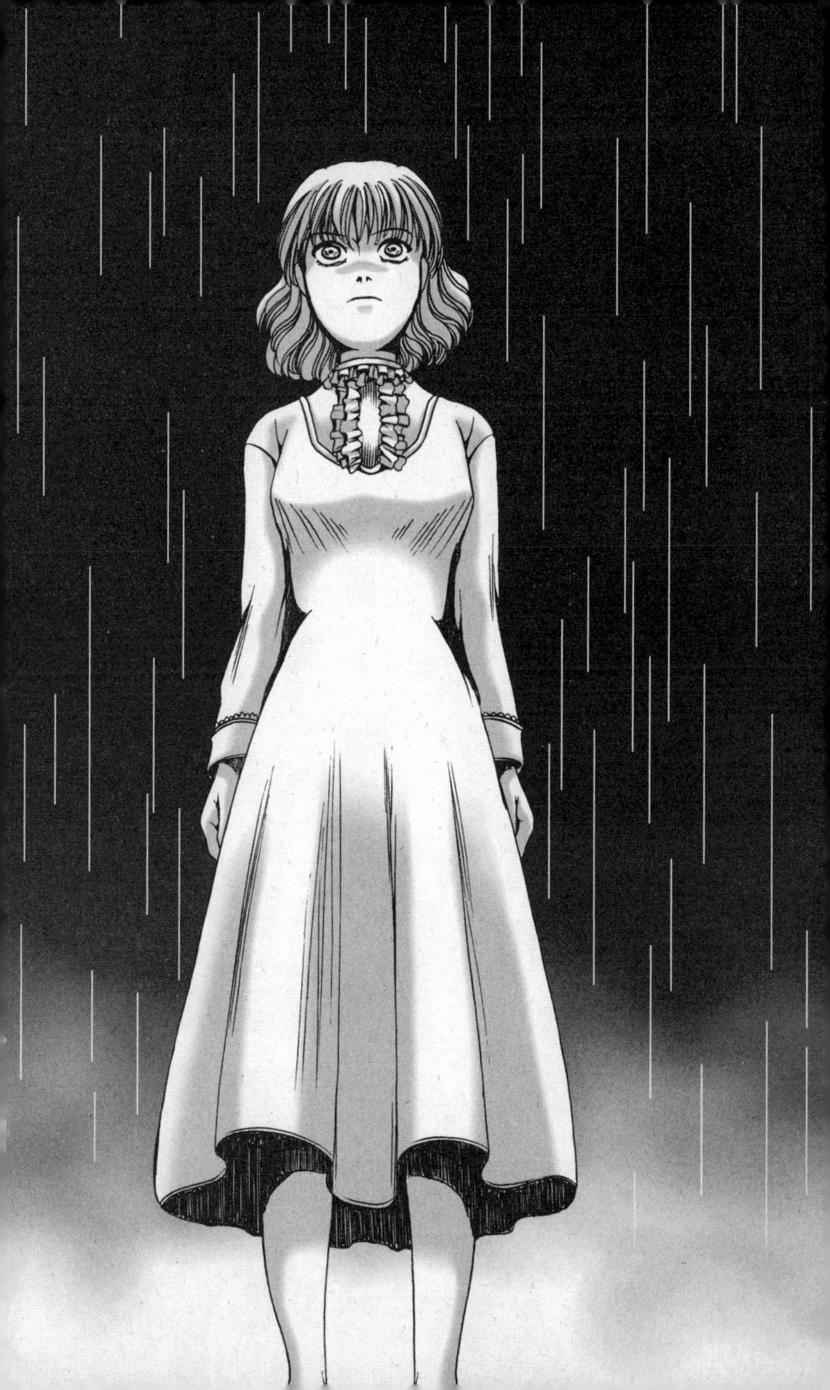

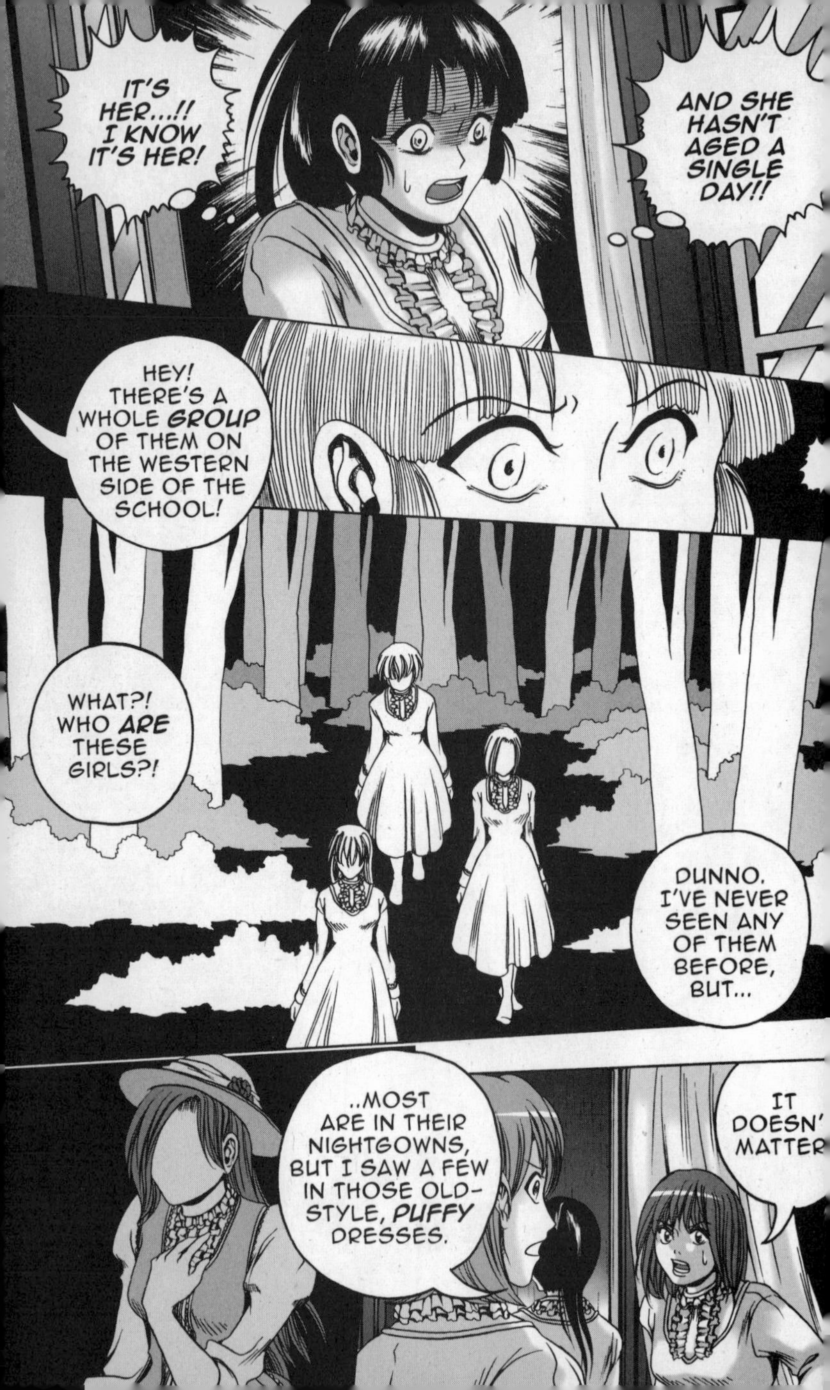
IT'S HER...!! I KNOW IT'S HER!
AND SHE HASN'T AGED A SINGLE DAY!!
HEY! THERE'S A WHOLE GROUP OF THEM ON THE WESTERN SIDE OF THE SCHOOL!
WHAT?! WHO ARE THESE GIRLS?!
DUNNO. I'VE NEVER SEEN ANY OF THEM BEFORE, BUT...
..MOST ARE IN THEIR NIGHTGOWNS, BUT I SAW A FEW IN THOSE OLD-STYLE, PUFFY DRESSES.
IT DOESN' MATTER

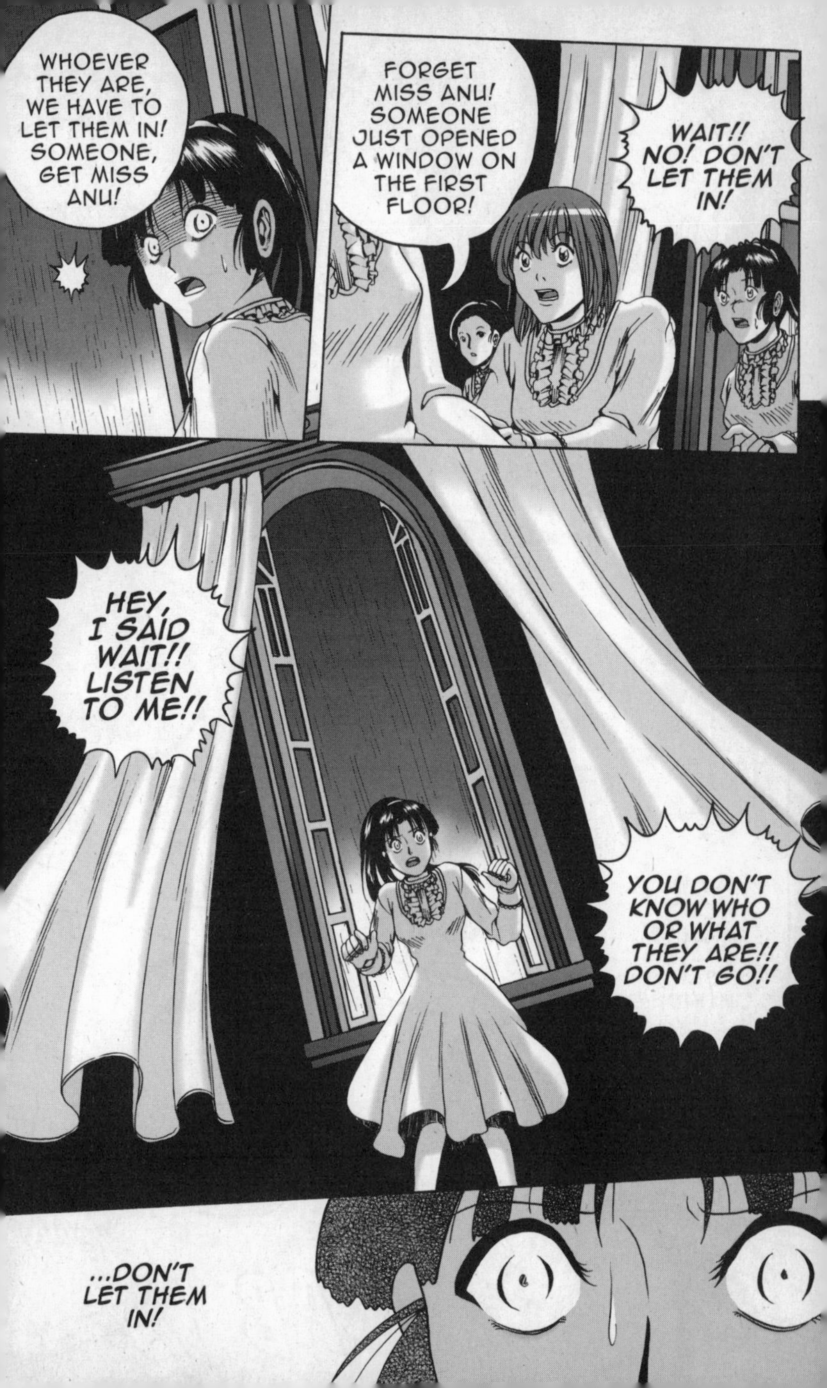
WHOEVER THEY ARE, WE HAVE TO LET THEM IN! SOMEONE, GET MISS ANU!
FORGET MISS ANU! SOMEONE JUST OPENED A WINDOW ON THE FIRST FLOOR!
WAIT!! NO! DON'T LET THEM IN!
HEY, I SAID WAIT!! LISTEN TO ME!!
YOU DON'T KNOW WHO OR WHAT THEY ARE!! DON'T GO!!
...DON'T LET THEM IN!

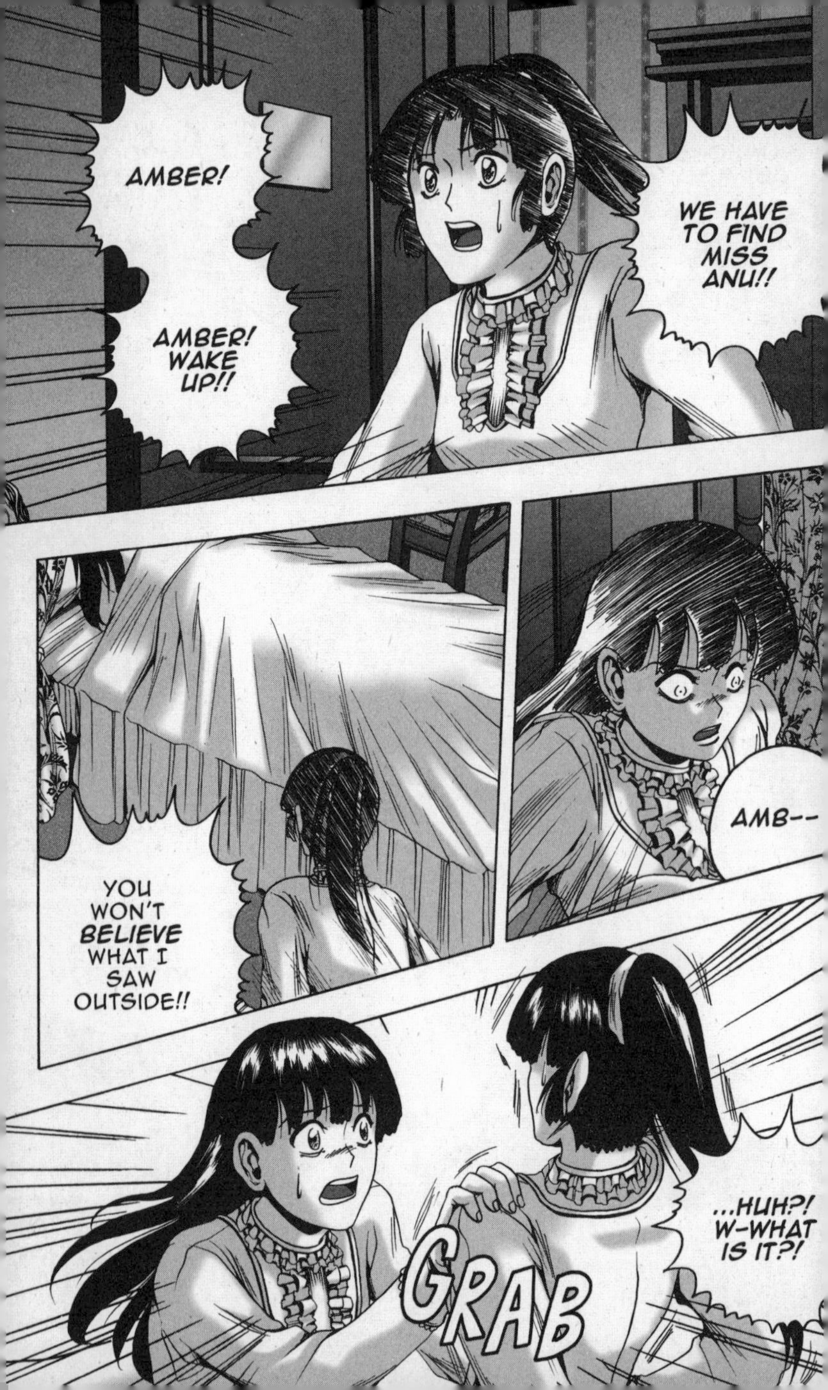
AMBER!
AMBER! WAKE UP!!
WE HAVE TO FIND MISS ANU!!
YOU WON'T BELIEVE WHAT I SAW OUTSIDE!!
AMB--
GRAB
...HUH?! W-WHAT IS IT?!

Chapter 12
Echoes of Dreams

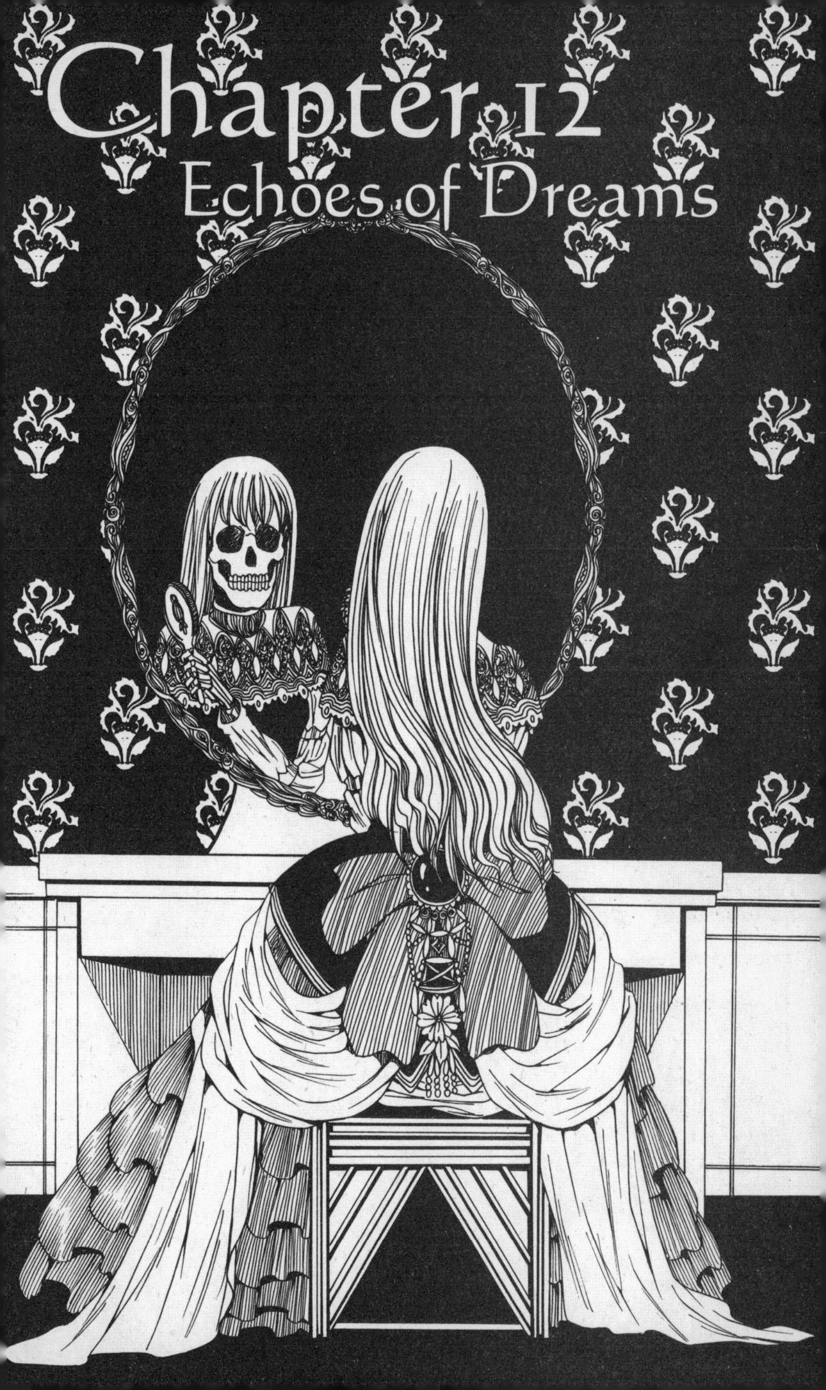

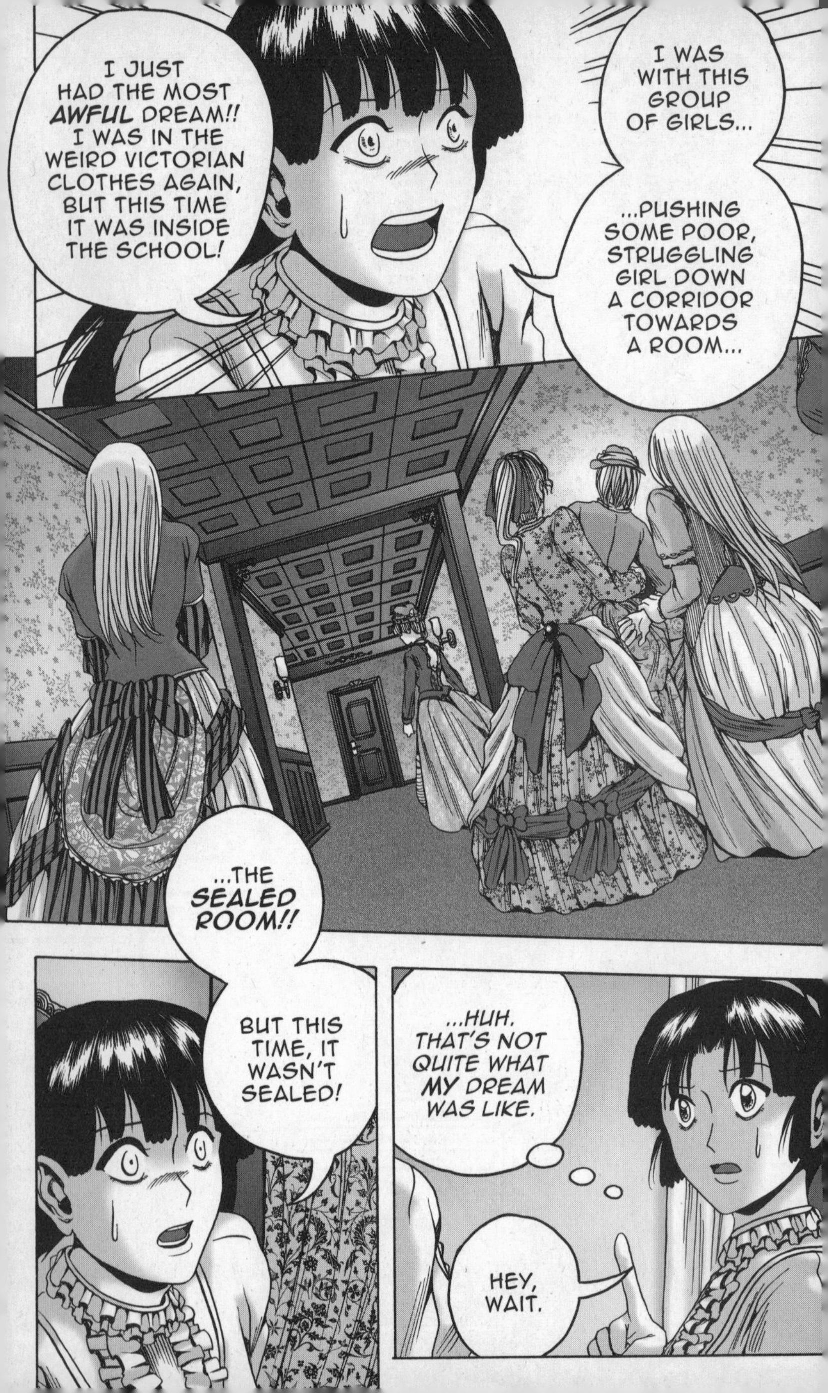
I JUST HAD THE MOST AWFUL DREAM!! I WAS IN THE WEIRD VICTORIAN CLOTHES AGAIN, BUT THIS TIME IT WAS INSIDE THE SCHOOL!
I WAS WITH THIS GROUP OF GIRLS...
...PUSHING SOME POOR, STRUGGLING GIRL DOWN A CORRIDOR TOWARDS A ROOM...
...THE SEALED ROOM!!
BUT THIS TIME, IT WASN'T SEALED!
...HUH. THAT'S NOT QUITE WHAT MY DREAM WAS LIKE.
HEY, WAIT.

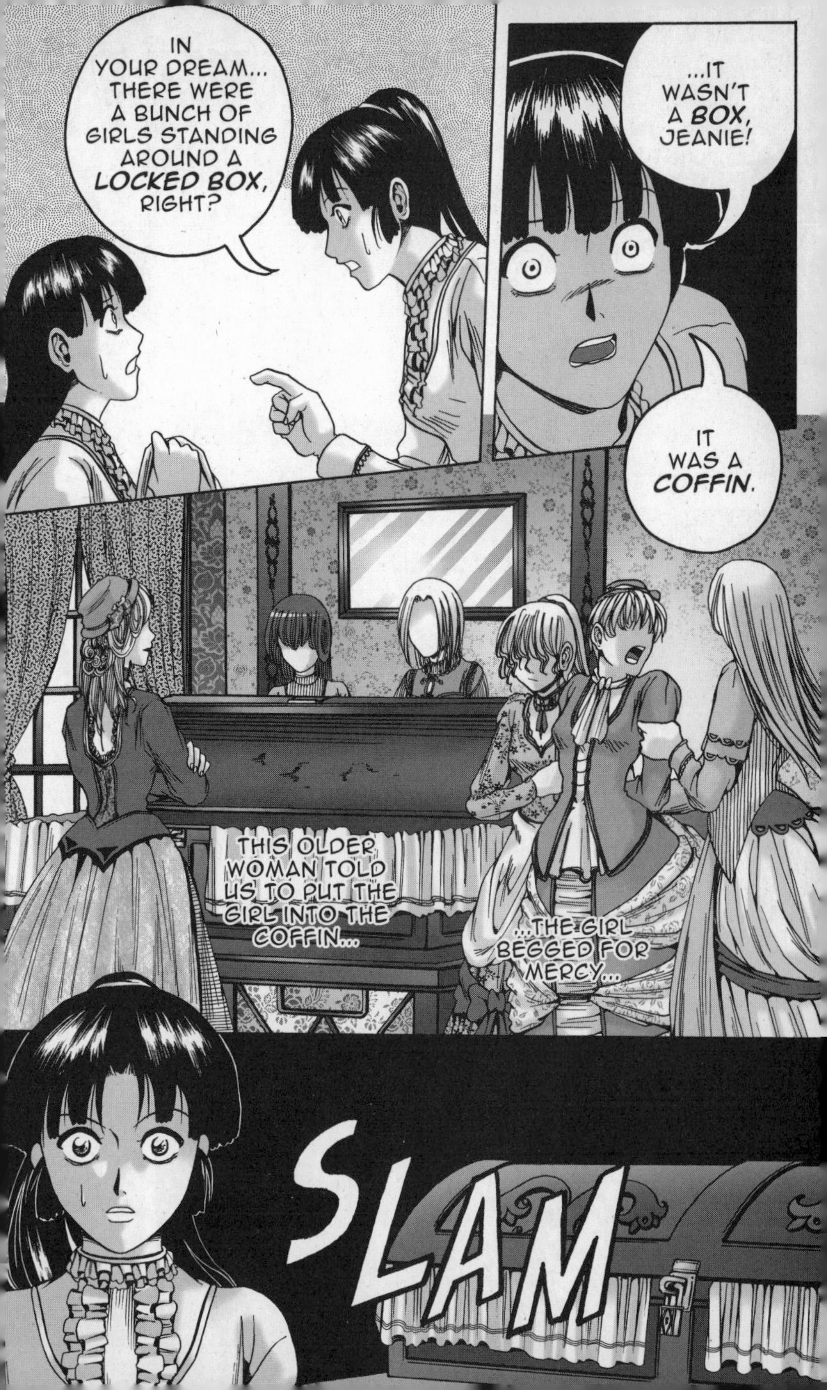
IN YOUR DREAM... THERE WERE A BUNCH OF GIRLS STANDING AROUND A LOCKED BOX, RIGHT?
...IT WASN'T A BOX, JEANIE!
IT WAS A COFFIN.
THIS OLDER WOMAN TOLD US TO PUT THE GIRL INTO THE COFFIN...
...THE GIRL BEGGED FOR MERCY...
SLAM

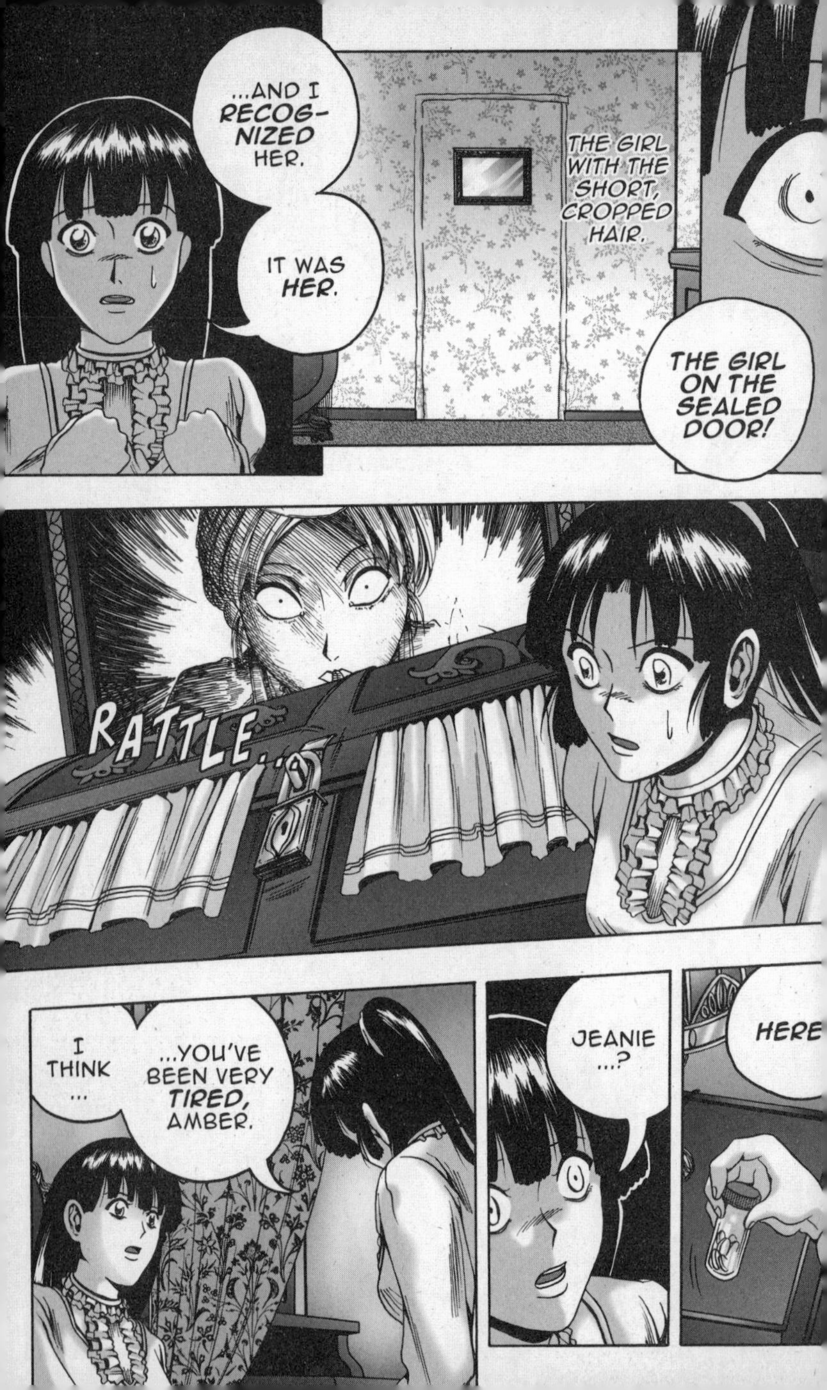

...AND I RECOG-NIZED HER.
IT WAS HER.
THE GIRL WITH THE SHORT, CROPPED HAIR.
THE GIRL ON THE SEALED DOOR!
RATTLE...
I THINK ...
...YOU'VE BEEN VERY TIRED, AMBER.
JEANIE ...?
HERE

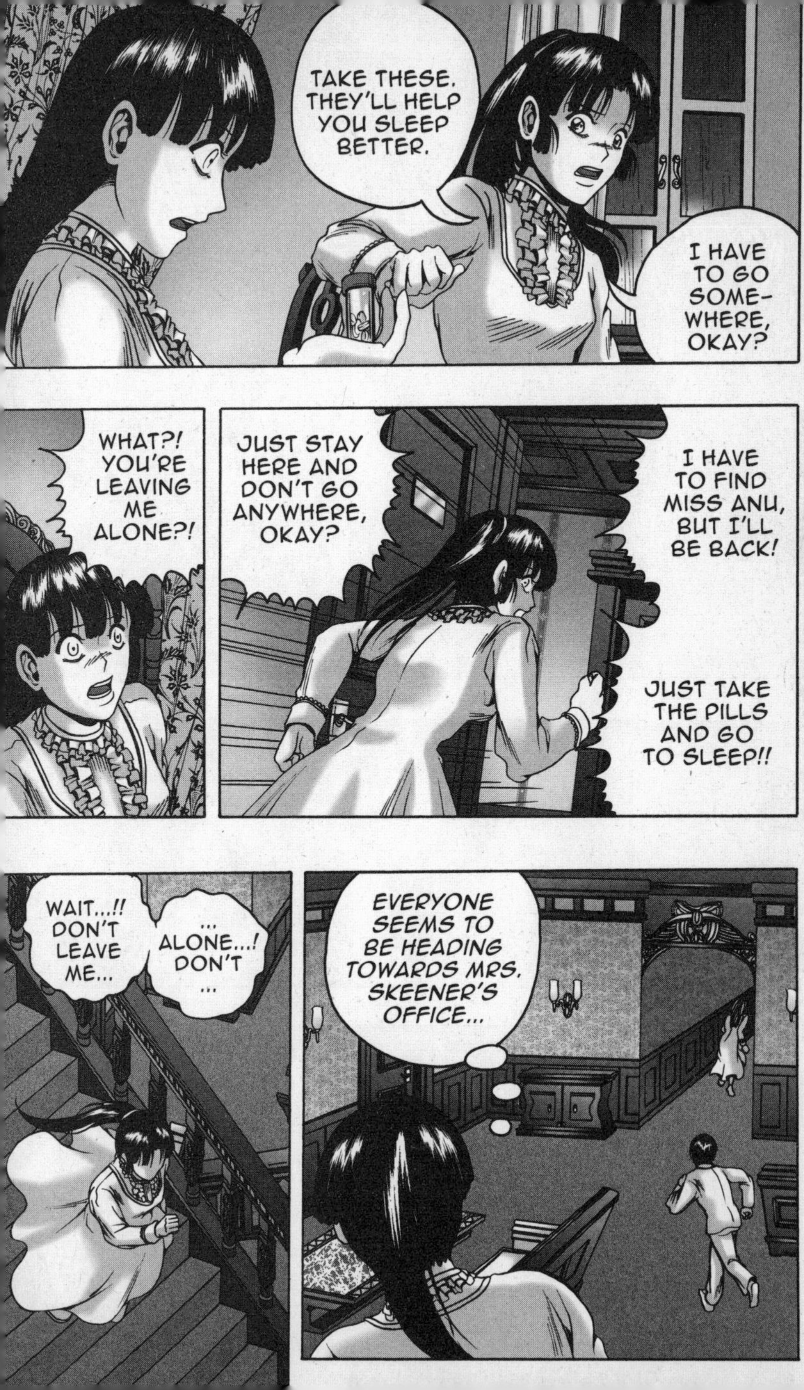
TAKE THESE. THEY'LL HELP YOU SLEEP BETTER.
I HAVE TO GO SOME-WHERE, OKAY?
WHAT?! YOU'RE LEAVING ME ALONE?!
JUST STAY HERE AND DON'T GO ANYWHERE, OKAY?
I HAVE TO FIND MISS ANU, BUT I'LL BE BACK!
JUST TAKE THE PILLS AND GO TO SLEEP!!
WAIT...!! DON'T LEAVE ME...
... ALONE...! DON'T ...
EVERYONE SEEMS TO BE HEADING TOWARDS MRS. SKEENER'S OFFICE...

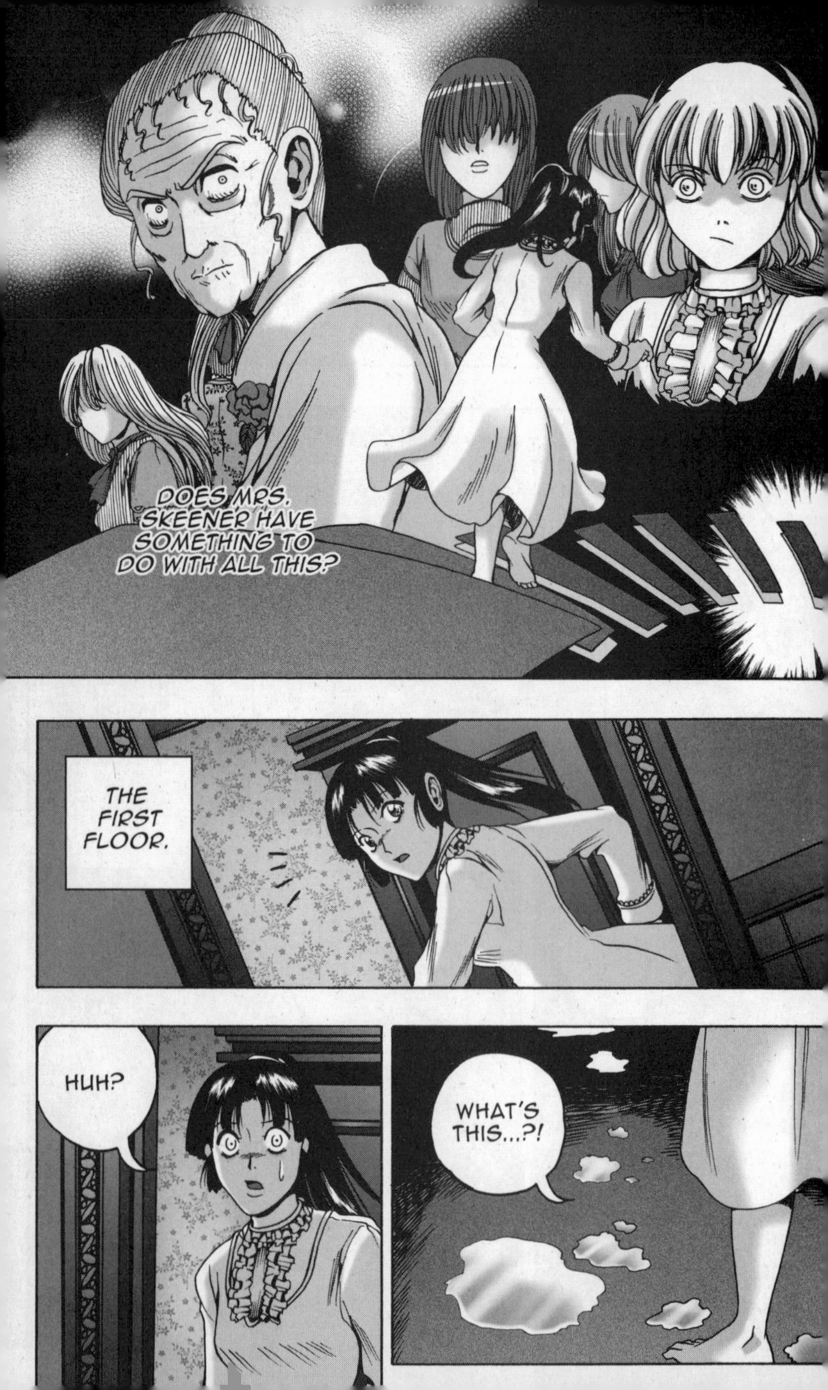
DOES MRS. SKEENER HAVE SOMETHING TO DO WITH ALL THIS?
THE FIRST FLOOR.
HUH?
WHAT'S THIS...?!

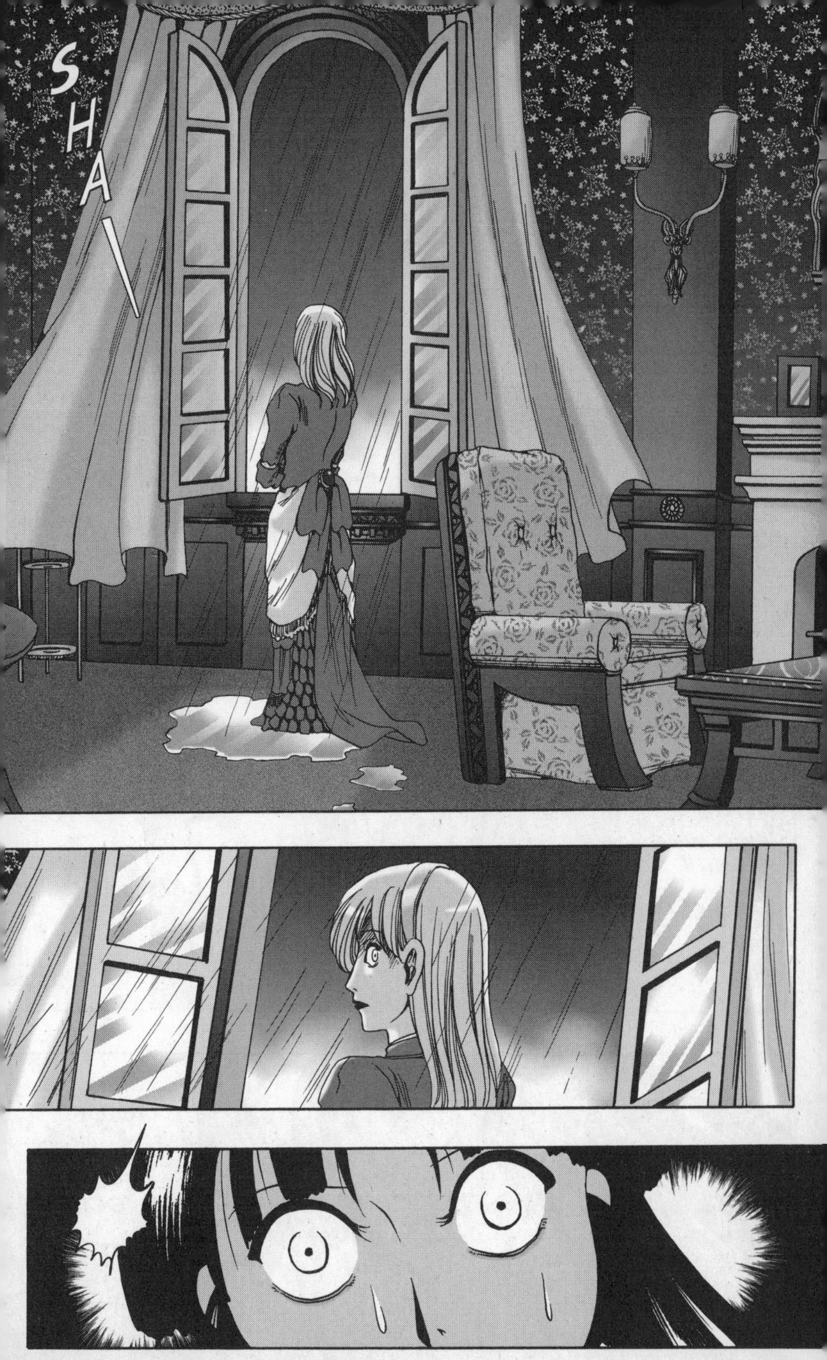
SHA

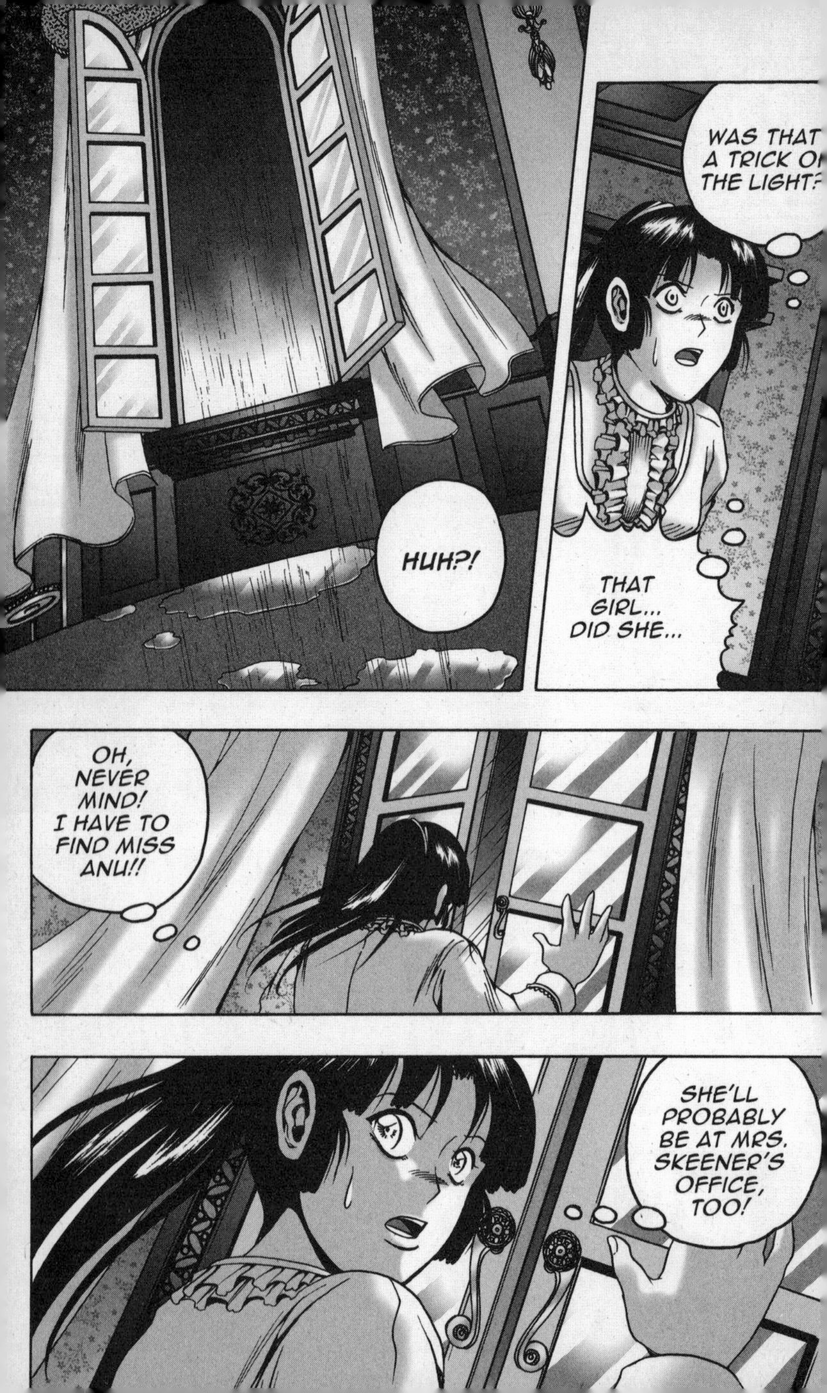
HUH?!
WAS THAT A TRICK OF THE LIGHT?
THAT GIRL... DID SHE...
OH, NEVER MIND! I HAVE TO FIND MISS ANU!!
SHE'LL PROBABLY BE AT MRS. SKEENER'S OFFICE, TOO!

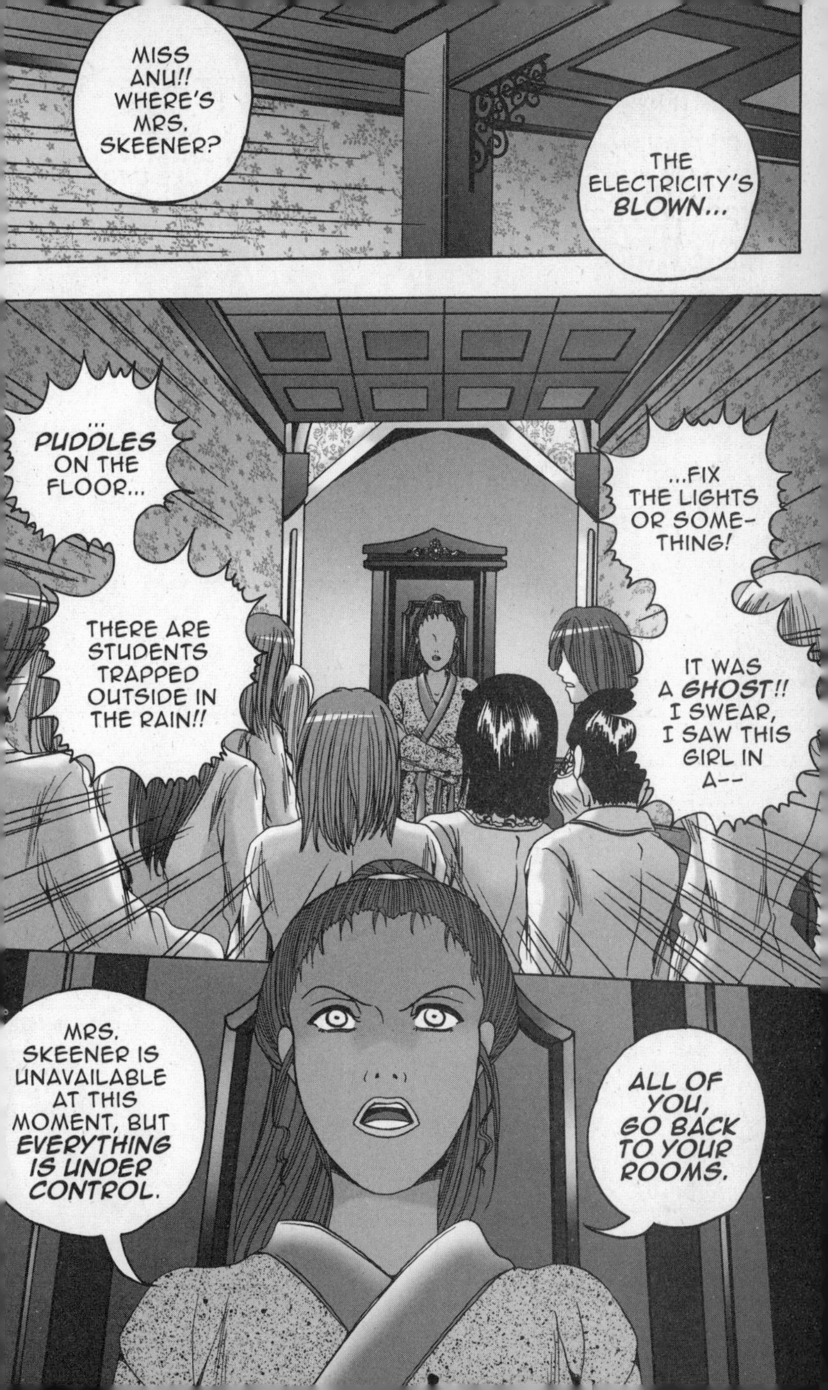
MISS ANU!! WHERE'S MRS. SKEENER?
THE ELECTRICITY'S BLOWN...
... PUDDLES ON THE FLOOR...
...FIX THE LIGHTS OR SOME-THING!
THERE ARE STUDENTS TRAPPED OUTSIDE IN THE RAIN!!
IT WAS A GHOST!! I SWEAR, I SAW THIS GIRL IN A--
MRS. SKEENER IS UNAVAILABLE AT THIS MOMENT, BUT EVERYTHING IS UNDER CONTROL.
ALL OF YOU, GO BACK TO YOUR ROOMS.

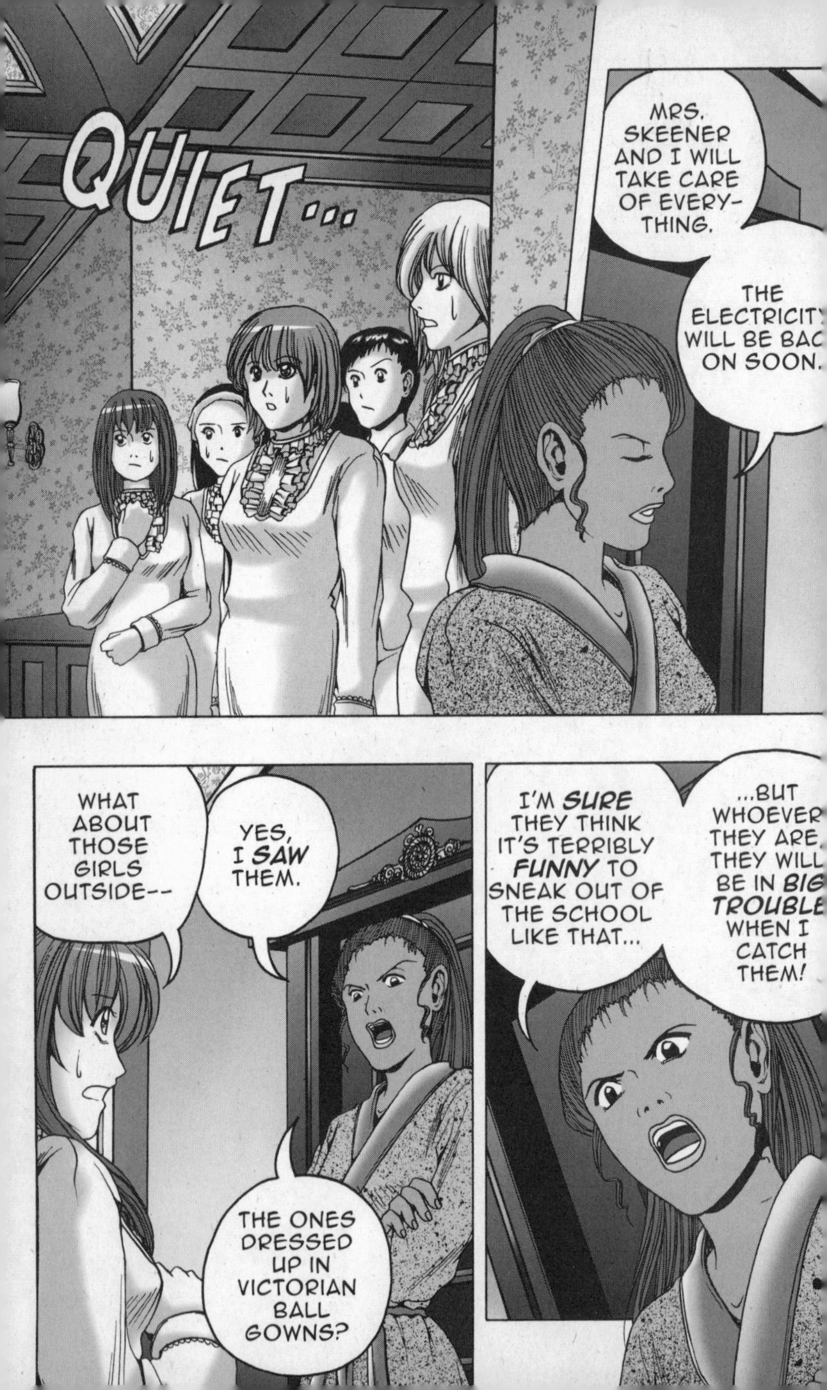

QUIET...
MRS. SKEENER AND I WILL TAKE CARE OF EVERY-THING.
THE ELECTRICITY WILL BE BAC ON SOON.
WHAT ABOUT THOSE GIRLS OUTSIDE--
YES, I SAW THEM.
THE ONES DRESSED UP IN VICTORIAN BALL GOWNS?
I'M SURE THEY THINK IT'S TERRIBLY FUNNY TO SNEAK OUT OF THE SCHOOL LIKE THAT...
...BUT WHOEVER THEY ARE, THEY WILL BE IN BIG TROUBLE WHEN I CATCH THEM!

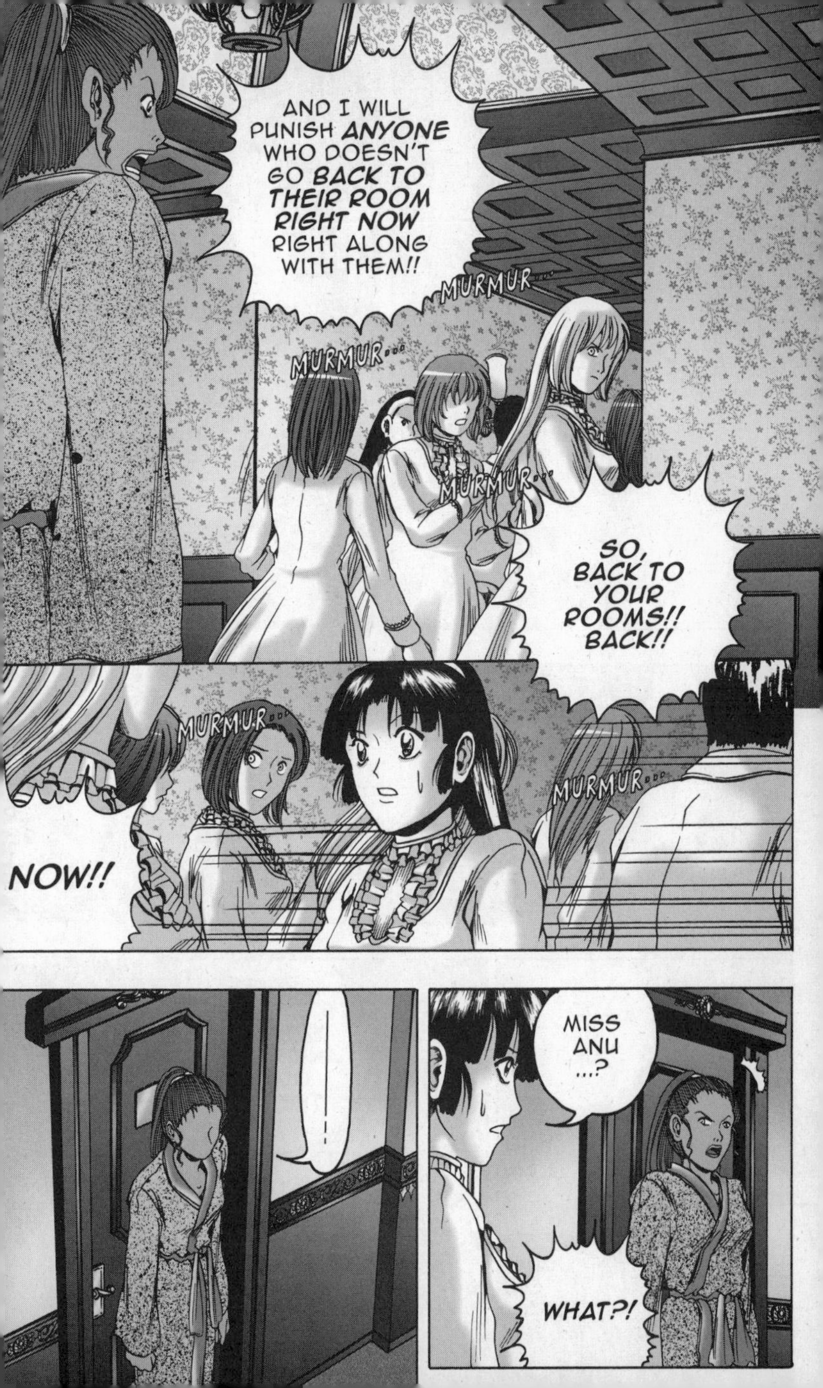
AND I WILL PUNISH ANYONE WHO DOESN'T GO BACK TO THEIR ROOM RIGHT NOW RIGHT ALONG WITH THEM!!
MURMUR...
MURMUR...
MURMUR...
SO, BACK TO YOUR ROOMS!! BACK!!
MURMUR...
MURMUR...
NOW!!
!
MISS ANU ...?
WHAT?!

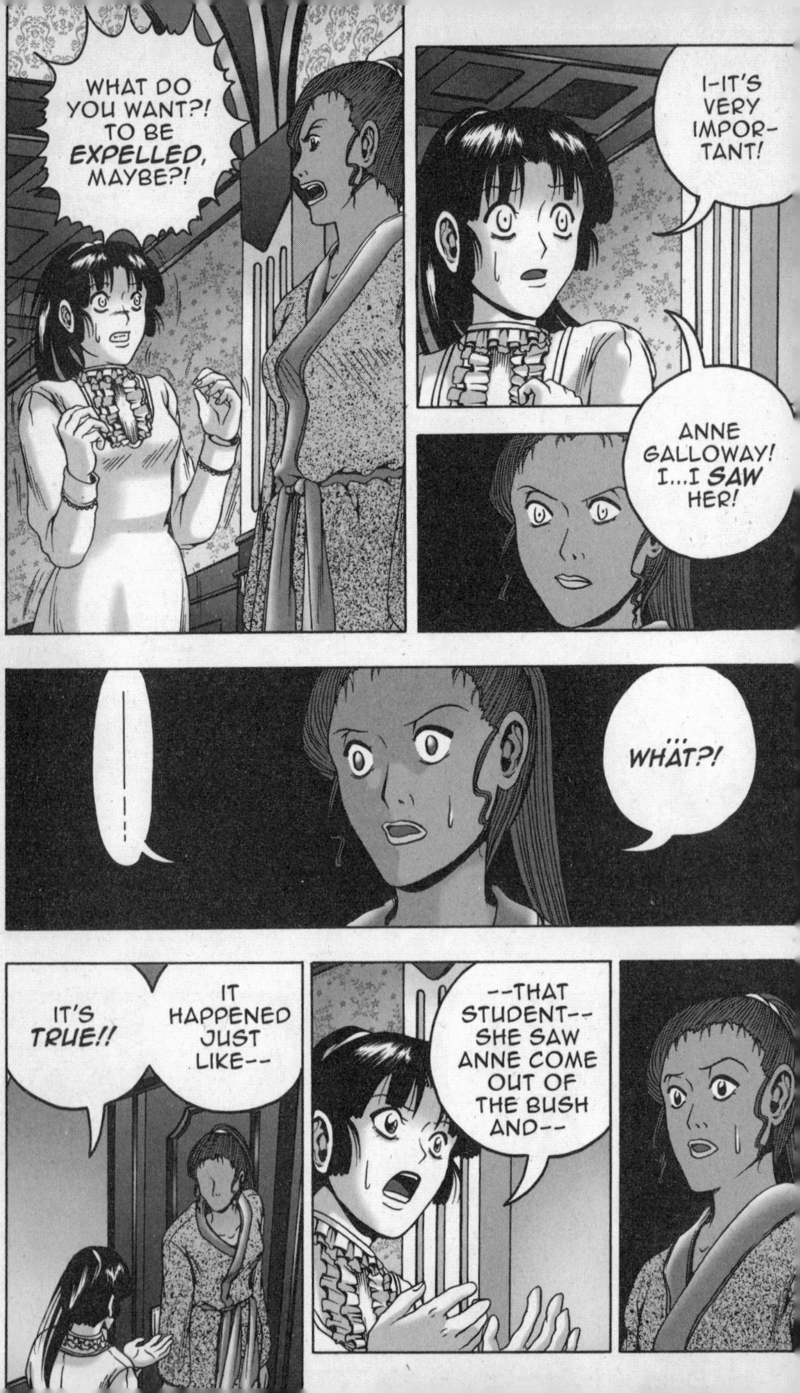
WHAT DO YOU WANT?! TO BE EXPELLED, MAYBE?!
I-IT'S VERY IMPOR-TANT!
ANNE GALLOWAY! I...I SAW HER!
--
...WHAT?!
IT'S TRUE!!
IT HAPPENED JUST LIKE--
--THAT STUDENT-- SHE SAW ANNE COME OUT OF THE BUSH AND--

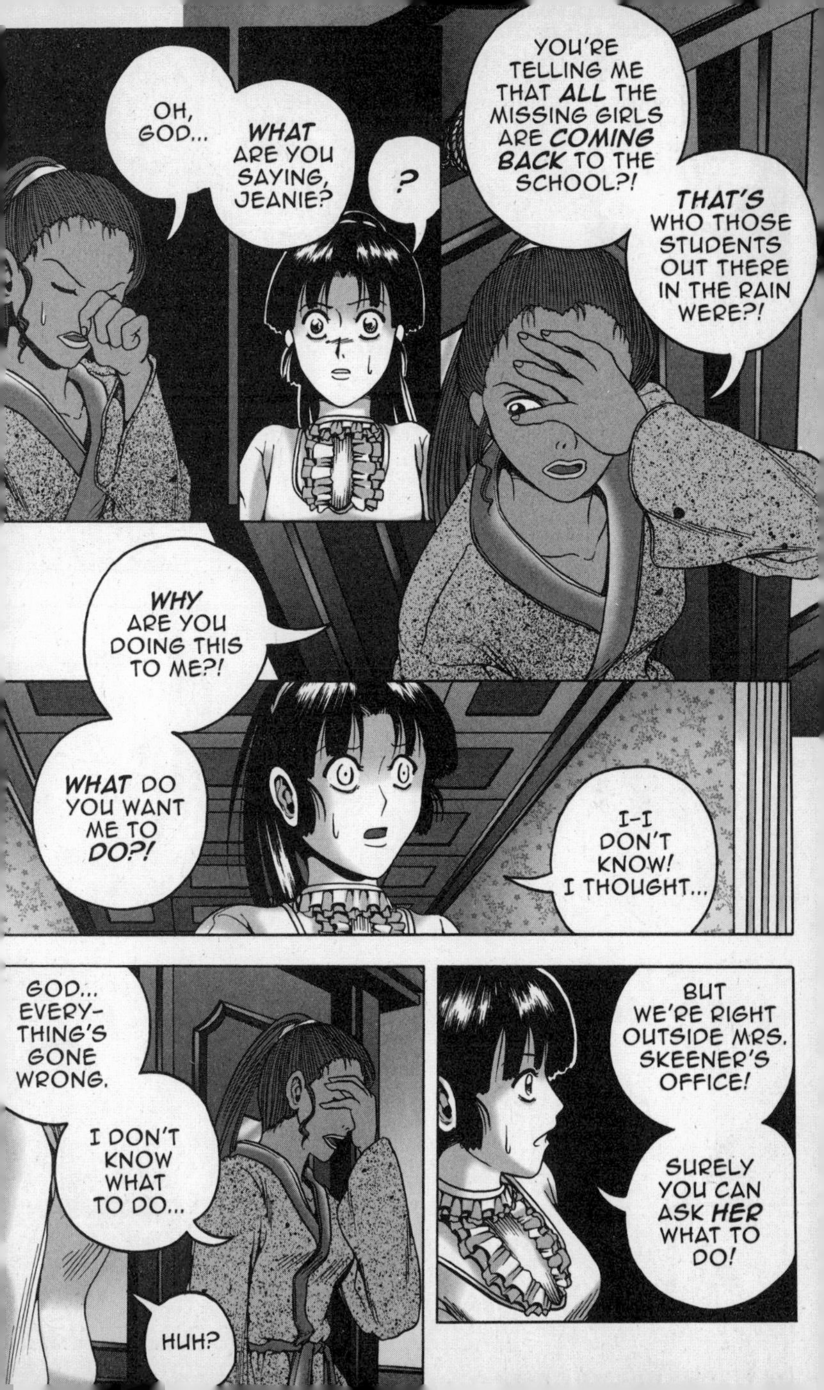
OH, GOD...
WHAT ARE YOU SAYING, JEANIE?
?
YOU'RE TELLING ME THAT ALL THE MISSING GIRLS ARE COMING BACK TO THE SCHOOL?!
THAT'S WHO THOSE STUDENTS OUT THERE IN THE RAIN WERE?!
WHY ARE YOU DOING THIS TO ME?!
WHAT DO YOU WANT ME TO DO?!
I-I DON'T KNOW! I THOUGHT...
GOD... EVERY-THING'S GONE WRONG.
I DON'T KNOW WHAT TO DO...
HUH?
BUT WE'RE RIGHT OUTSIDE MRS. SKEENER'S OFFICE!
SURELY YOU CAN ASK HER WHAT TO DO!

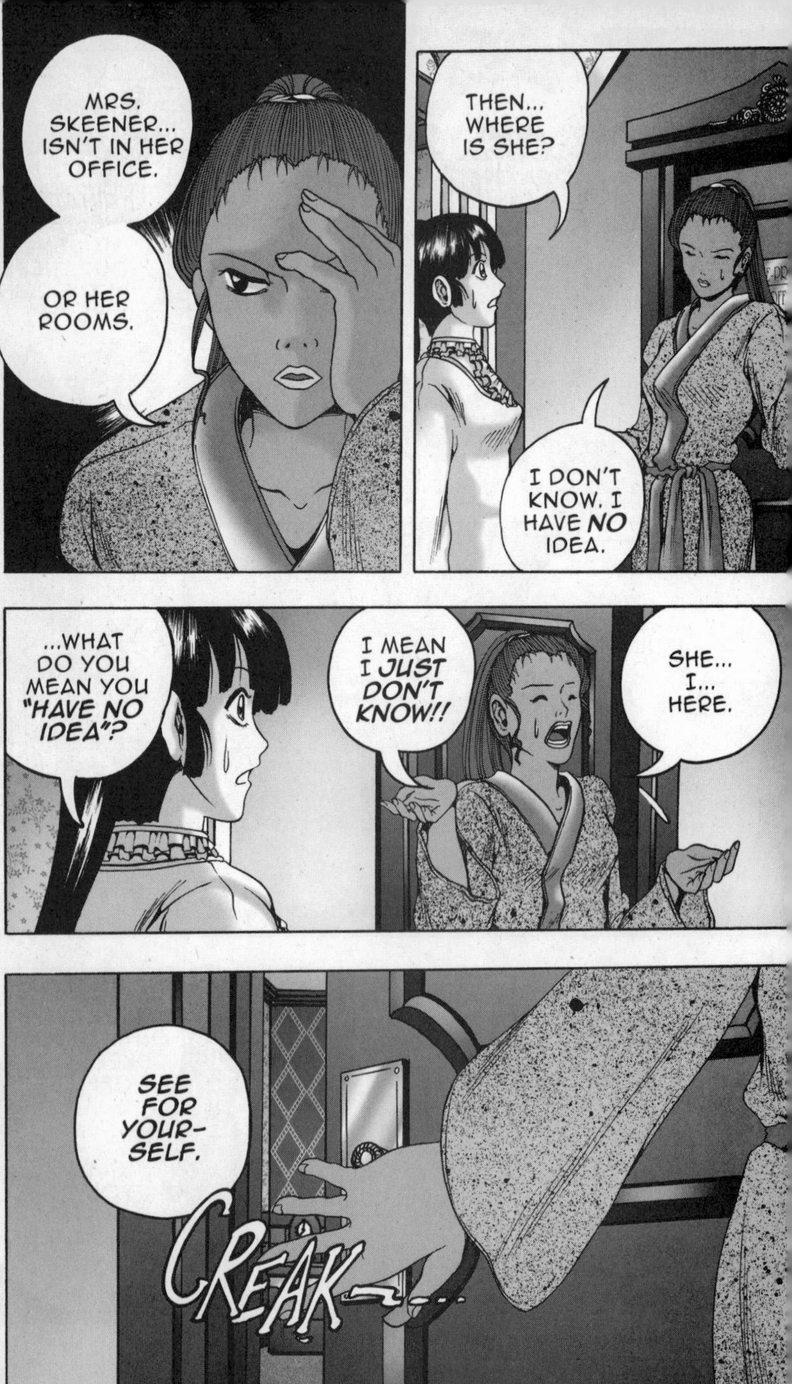
MRS. SKEENER... ISN'T IN HER OFFICE.
OR HER ROOMS.
THEN... WHERE IS SHE?
I DON'T KNOW. I HAVE NO IDEA.
...WHAT DO YOU MEAN YOU "HAVE NO IDEA"?
I MEAN I JUST DON'T KNOW!!
SHE... I... HERE.
SEE FOR YOUR-SELF.
CREAK...

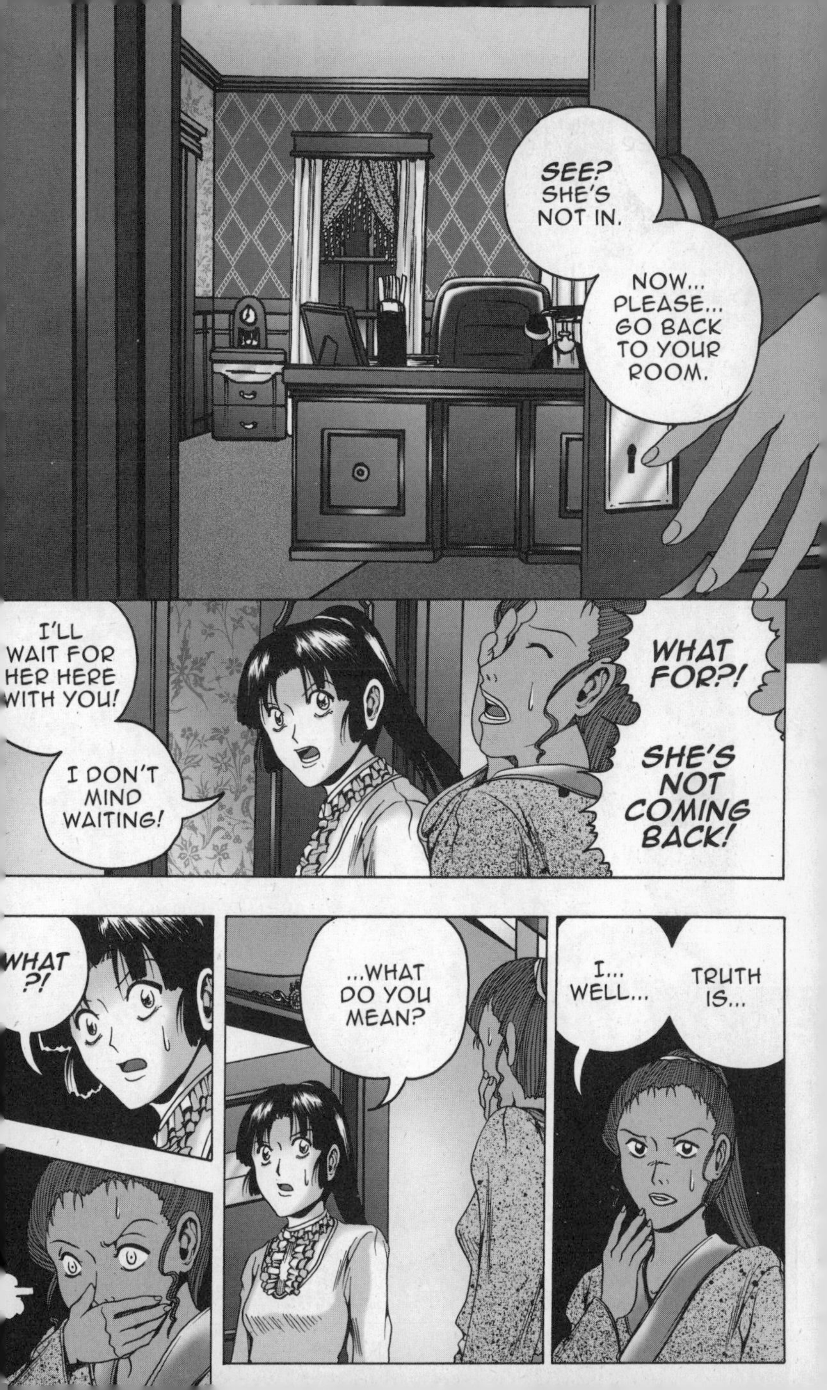
SEE? SHE'S NOT IN.
NOW... PLEASE... GO BACK TO YOUR ROOM.
I'LL WAIT FOR HER HERE WITH YOU!
I DON'T MIND WAITING!
WHAT FOR?!
SHE'S NOT COMING BACK!
WHAT?!
...WHAT DO YOU MEAN?
I... WELL...
TRUTH IS...

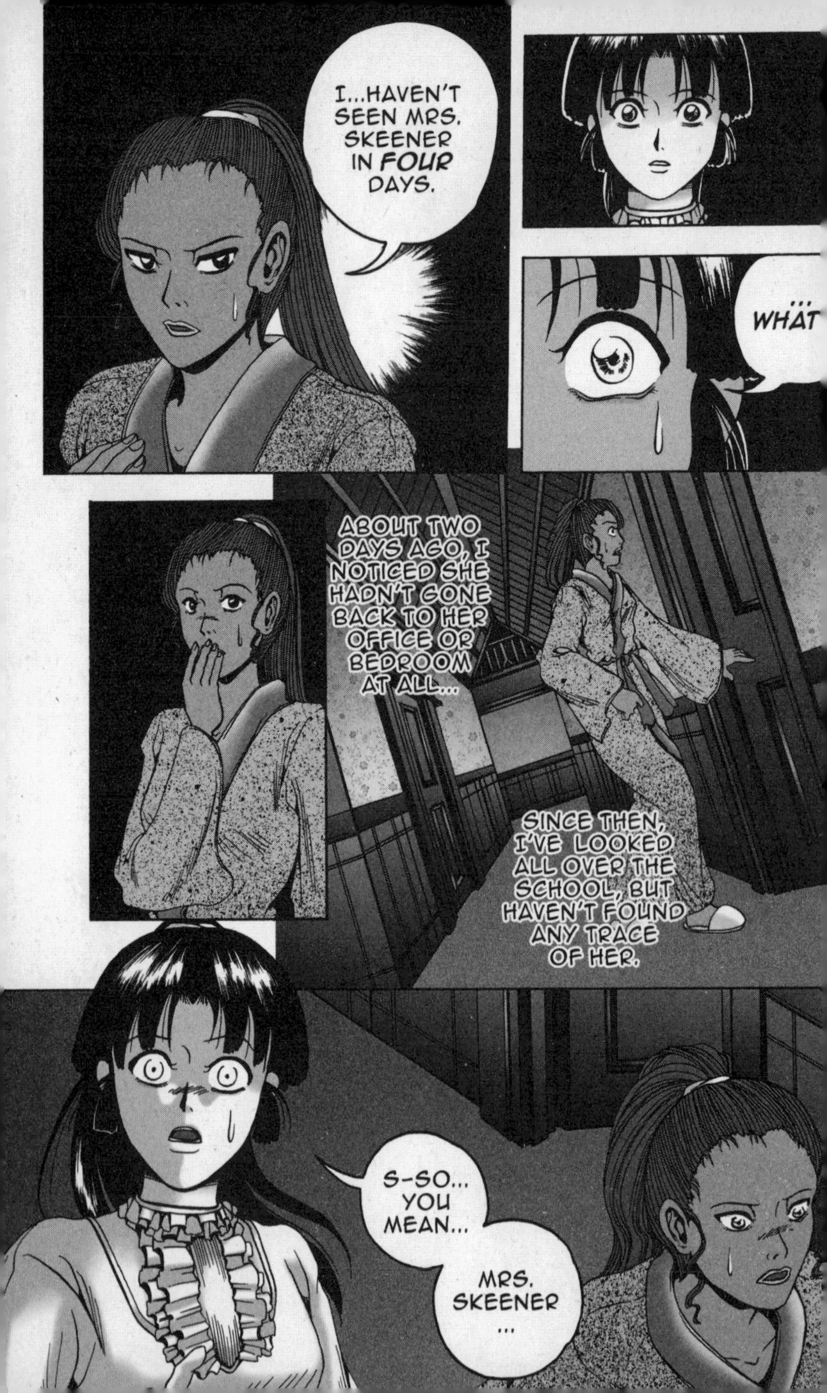
I...HAVEN'T SEEN MRS. SKEENER IN FOUR DAYS.
... WHAT
ABOUT TWO DAYS AGO, I NOTICED SHE HADN'T GONE BACK TO HER OFFICE OR BEDROOM AT ALL...
SINCE THEN, I'VE LOOKED ALL OVER THE SCHOOL, BUT HAVEN'T FOUND ANY TRACE OF HER.
S-SO... YOU MEAN...
MRS. SKEENER ...

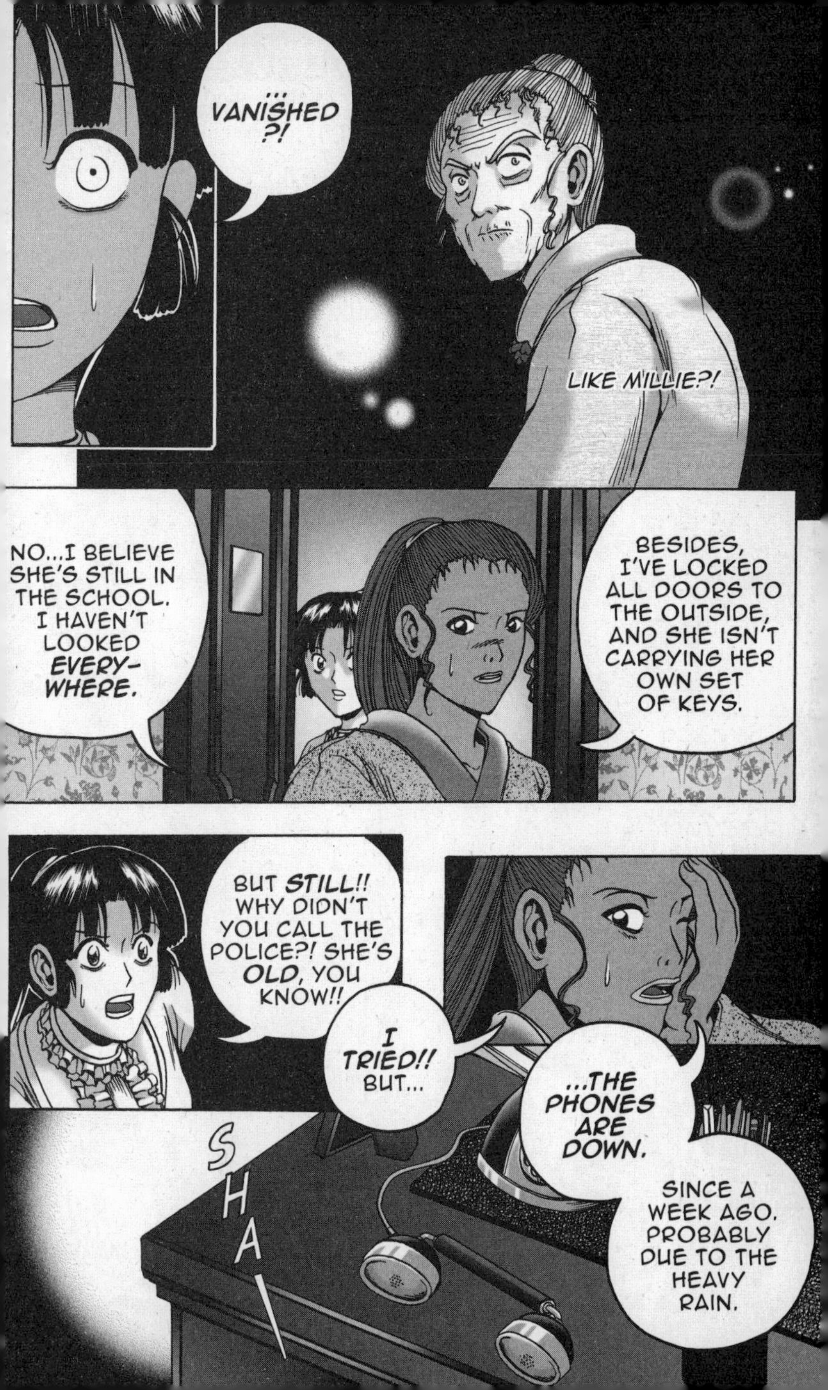
...VANISHED?!
LIKE MILLIE?!
NO...I BELIEVE SHE'S STILL IN THE SCHOOL. I HAVEN'T LOOKED *EVERY-WHERE*.
BESIDES, I'VE LOCKED ALL DOORS TO THE OUTSIDE, AND SHE ISN'T CARRYING HER OWN SET OF KEYS.
BUT *STILL*!! WHY DIDN'T YOU CALL THE POLICE?! SHE'S *OLD*, YOU KNOW!!
I TRIED!! BUT...
...THE PHONES ARE *DOWN*.
SHA
SINCE A WEEK AGO. PROBABLY DUE TO THE HEAVY RAIN.

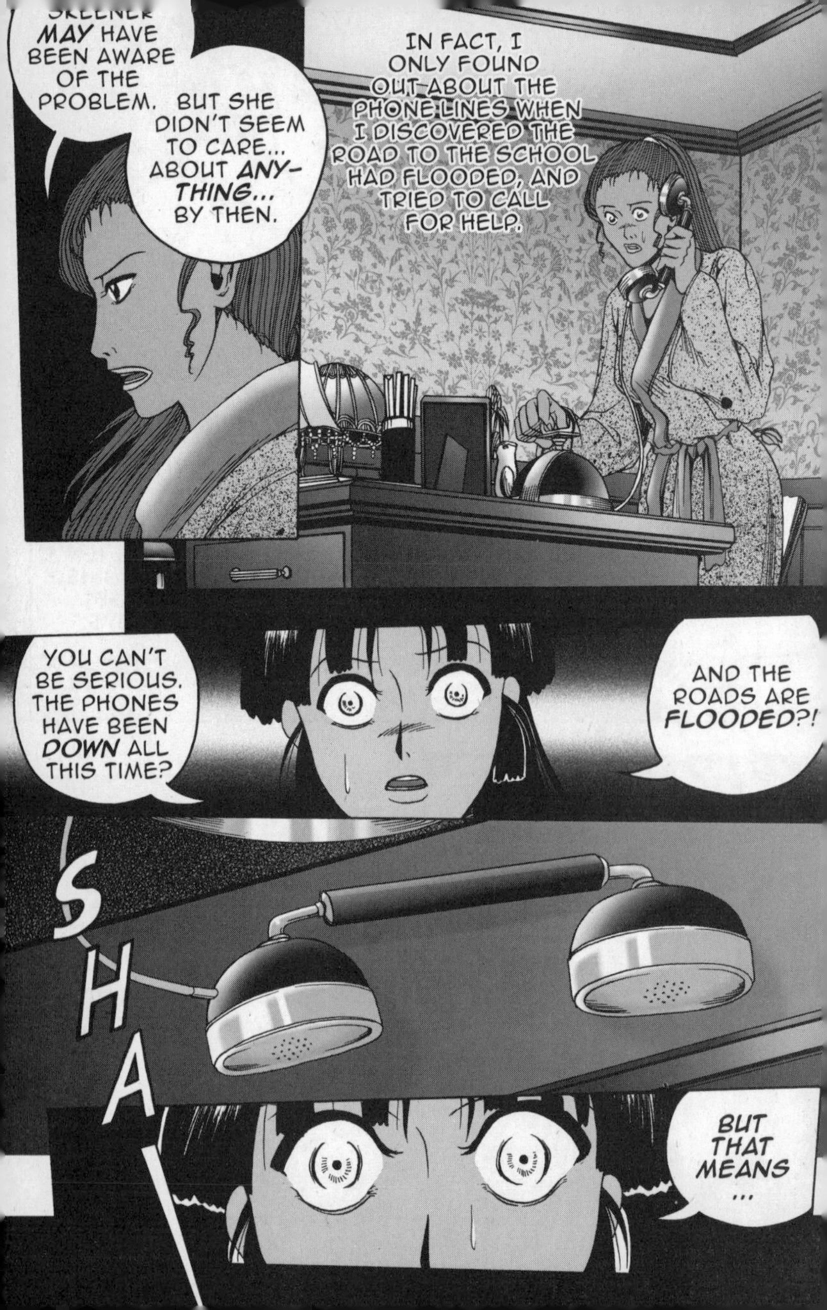
MAY HAVE BEEN AWARE OF THE PROBLEM.
BUT SHE DIDN'T SEEM TO CARE... ABOUT ANY-THING... BY THEN.
IN FACT, I ONLY FOUND OUT ABOUT THE PHONE LINES WHEN I DISCOVERED THE ROAD TO THE SCHOOL HAD FLOODED, AND TRIED TO CALL FOR HELP.
YOU CAN'T BE SERIOUS. THE PHONES HAVE BEEN DOWN ALL THIS TIME?
AND THE ROADS ARE FLOODED?!
SHA
BUT THAT MEANS ...

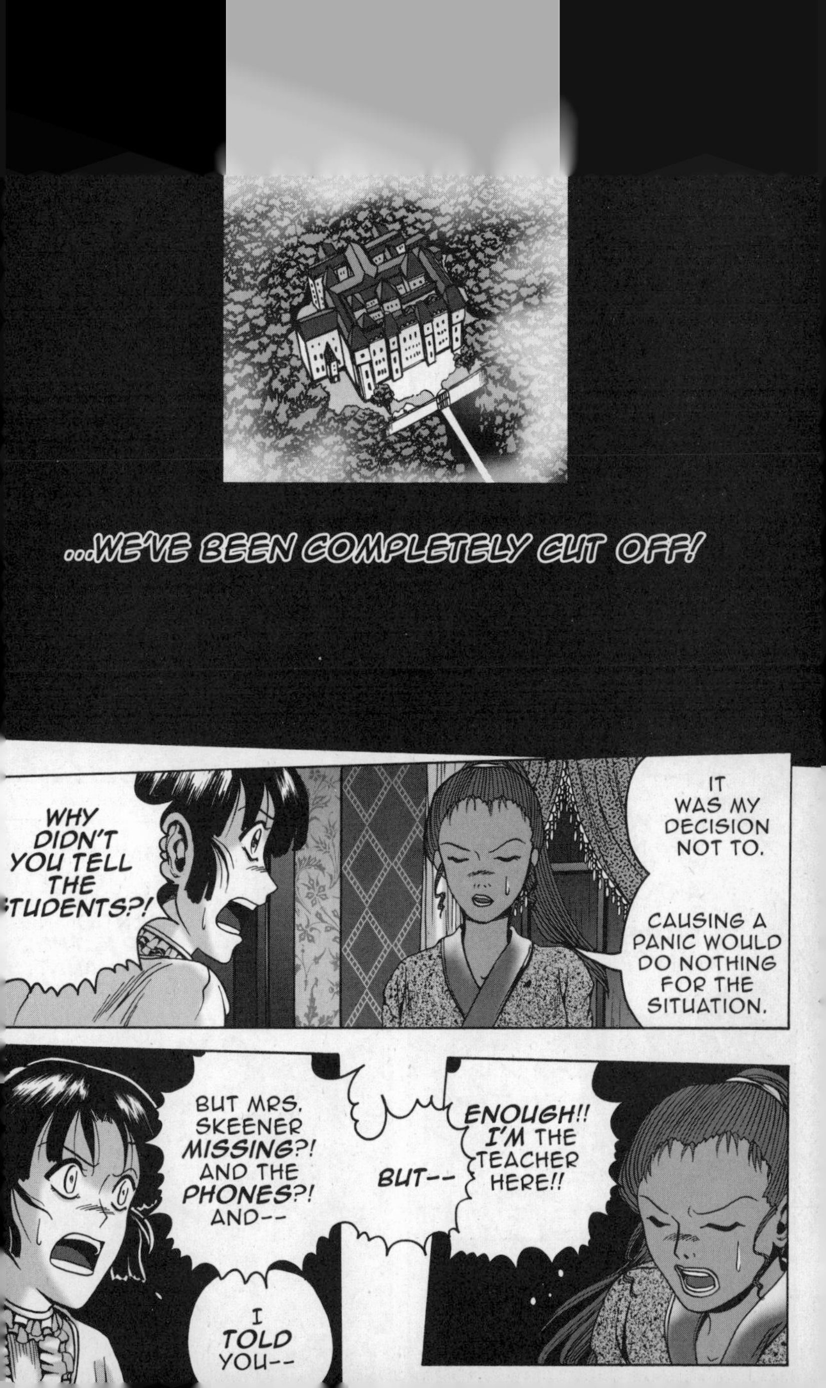
...WE'VE BEEN COMPLETELY CUT OFF!
WHY DIDN'T YOU TELL THE STUDENTS?!
IT WAS MY DECISION NOT TO.
CAUSING A PANIC WOULD DO NOTHING FOR THE SITUATION.
BUT MRS. SKEENER *MISSING*?! AND THE *PHONES*?! AND--
I *TOLD* YOU--
BUT--
ENOUGH!! I'M THE TEACHER HERE!!

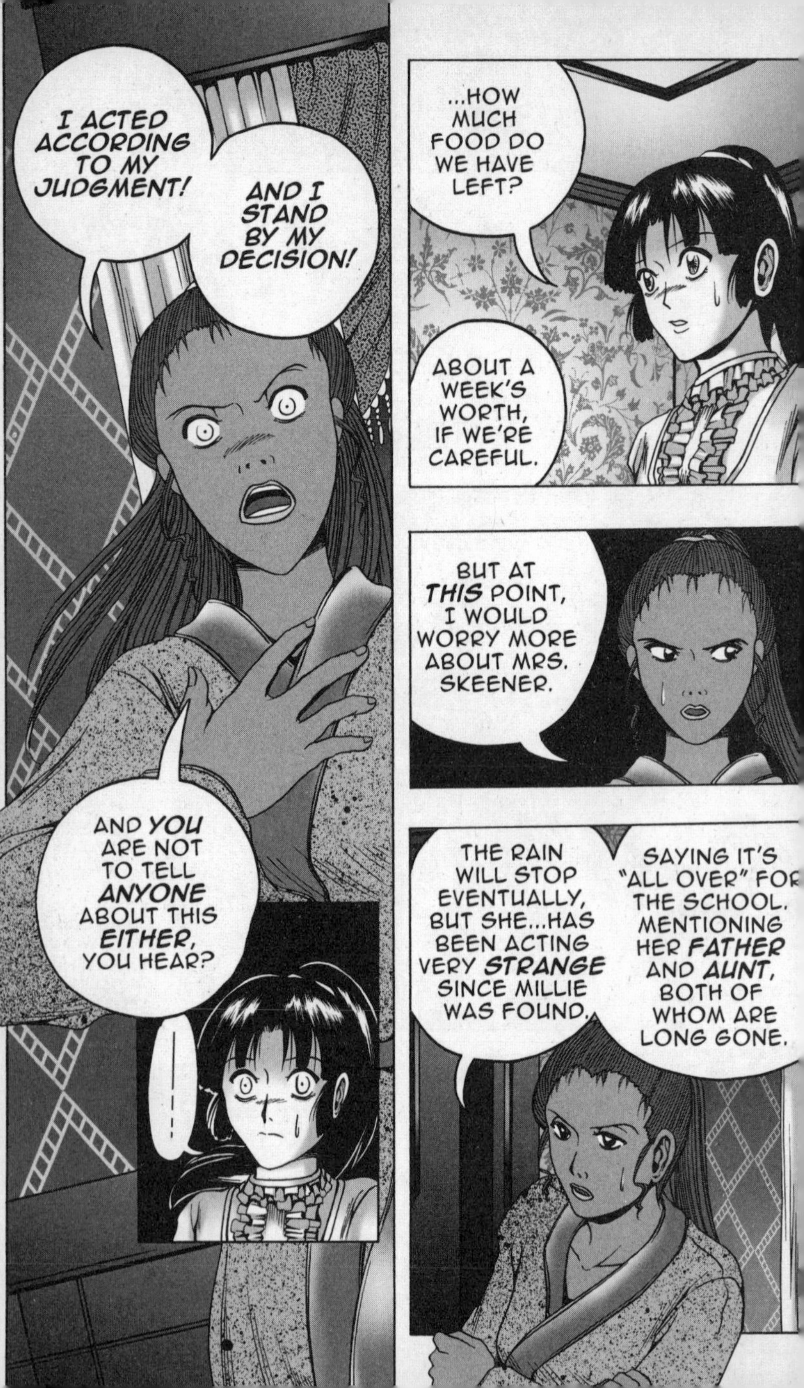
I ACTED ACCORDING TO MY JUDGMENT!
AND I STAND BY MY DECISION!
AND YOU ARE NOT TO TELL ANYONE ABOUT THIS EITHER, YOU HEAR?
...HOW MUCH FOOD DO WE HAVE LEFT?
ABOUT A WEEK'S WORTH, IF WE'RE CAREFUL.
BUT AT THIS POINT, I WOULD WORRY MORE ABOUT MRS. SKEENER.
THE RAIN WILL STOP EVENTUALLY, BUT SHE...HAS BEEN ACTING VERY STRANGE SINCE MILLIE WAS FOUND.
SAYING IT'S "ALL OVER" FOR THE SCHOOL. MENTIONING HER FATHER AND AUNT, BOTH OF WHOM ARE LONG GONE.

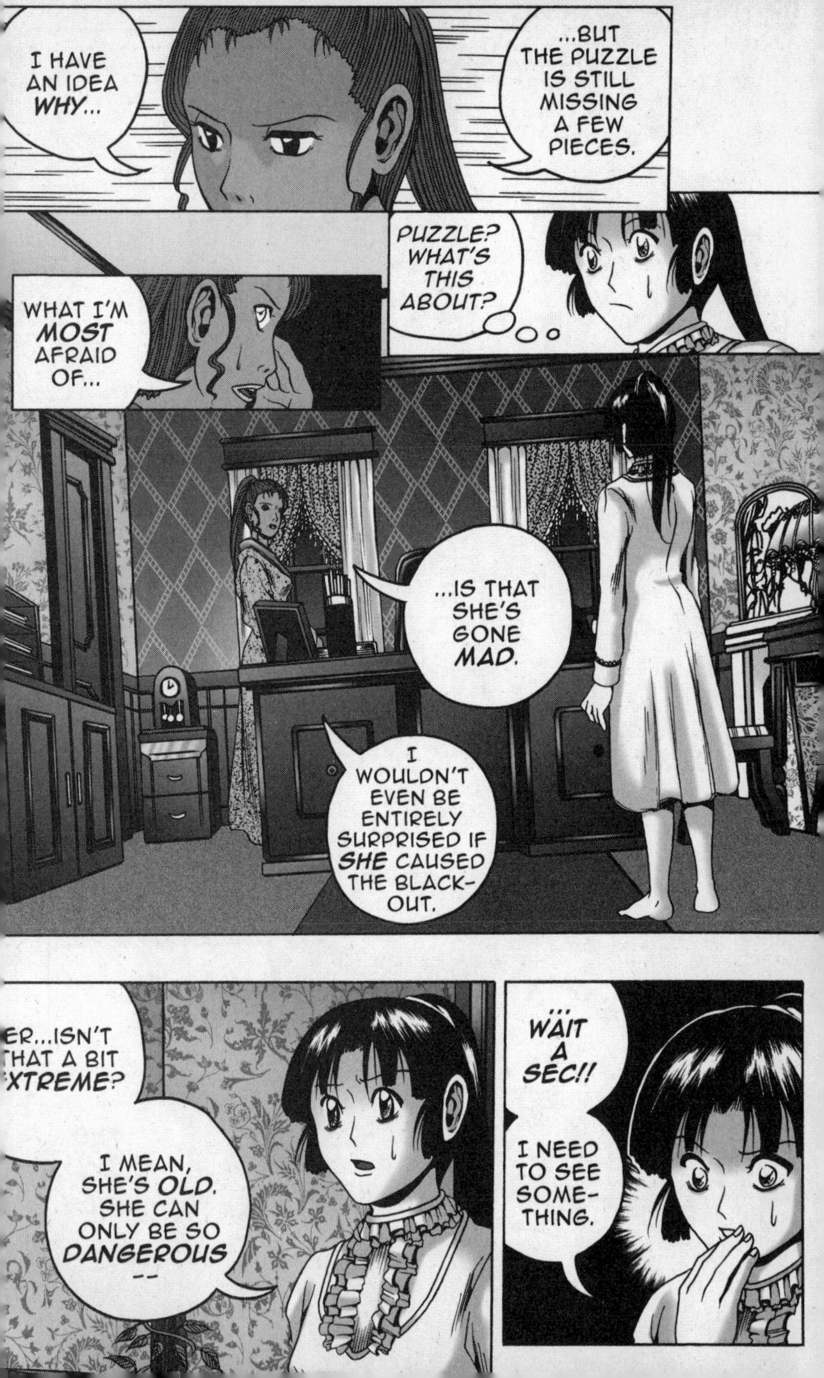
I HAVE AN IDEA *WHY*...
...BUT THE PUZZLE IS STILL MISSING A FEW PIECES.
PUZZLE? WHAT'S THIS ABOUT?
WHAT I'M *MOST* AFRAID OF...
...IS THAT SHE'S GONE *MAD*.
I WOULDN'T EVEN BE ENTIRELY SURPRISED IF *SHE* CAUSED THE BLACK-OUT.
ER...ISN'T THAT A BIT *EXTREME*?
I MEAN, SHE'S *OLD*. SHE CAN ONLY BE SO *DANGEROUS* --
... *WAIT A SEC!!*
I NEED TO SEE SOME-THING.

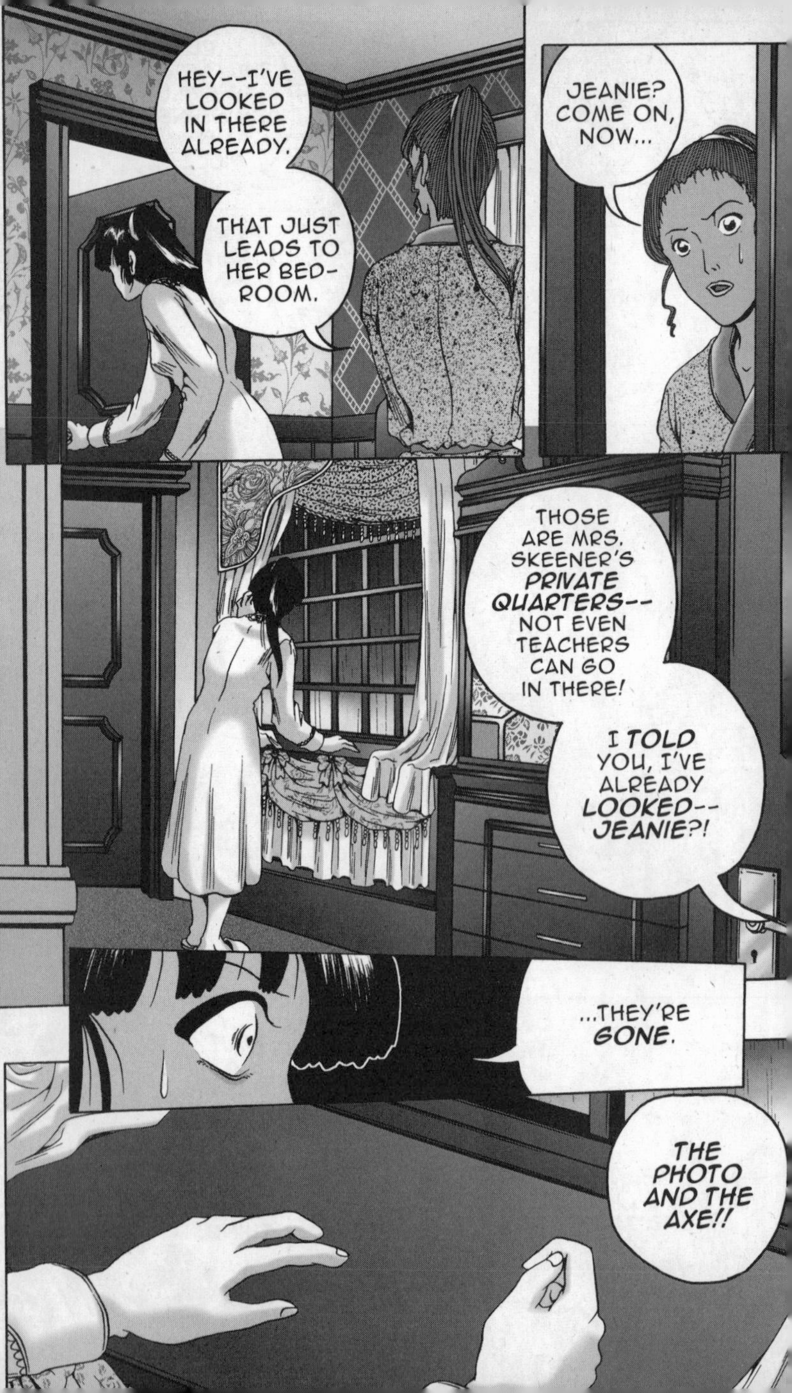
HEY--I'VE LOOKED IN THERE ALREADY.
THAT JUST LEADS TO HER BED-ROOM.
JEANIE? COME ON, NOW...
THOSE ARE MRS. SKEENER'S *PRIVATE QUARTERS*--NOT EVEN TEACHERS CAN GO IN THERE!
I *TOLD* YOU, I'VE ALREADY *LOOKED*--*JEANIE*?!
...THEY'RE *GONE*.
THE PHOTO AND THE AXE!!

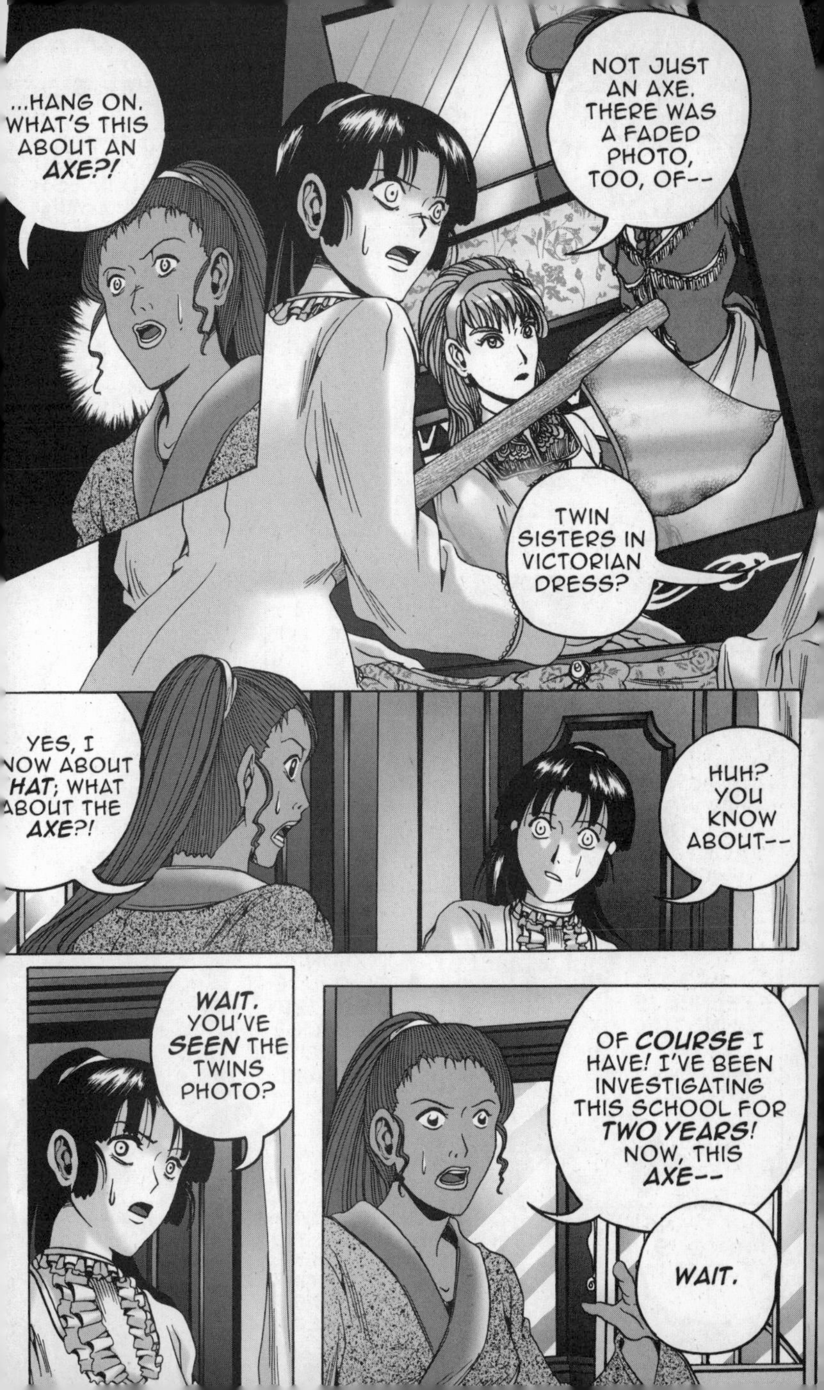

...HANG ON. WHAT'S THIS ABOUT AN *AXE?!*
NOT JUST AN AXE. THERE WAS A FADED PHOTO, TOO, OF--
TWIN SISTERS IN VICTORIAN DRESS?
YES, I NOW ABOUT *HAT*; WHAT BOUT THE *AXE*?!
HUH? YOU KNOW ABOUT--
WAIT. YOU'VE *SEEN* THE TWINS PHOTO?
OF *COURSE* I HAVE! I'VE BEEN INVESTIGATING THIS SCHOOL FOR *TWO YEARS!* NOW, THIS *AXE--*
WAIT.

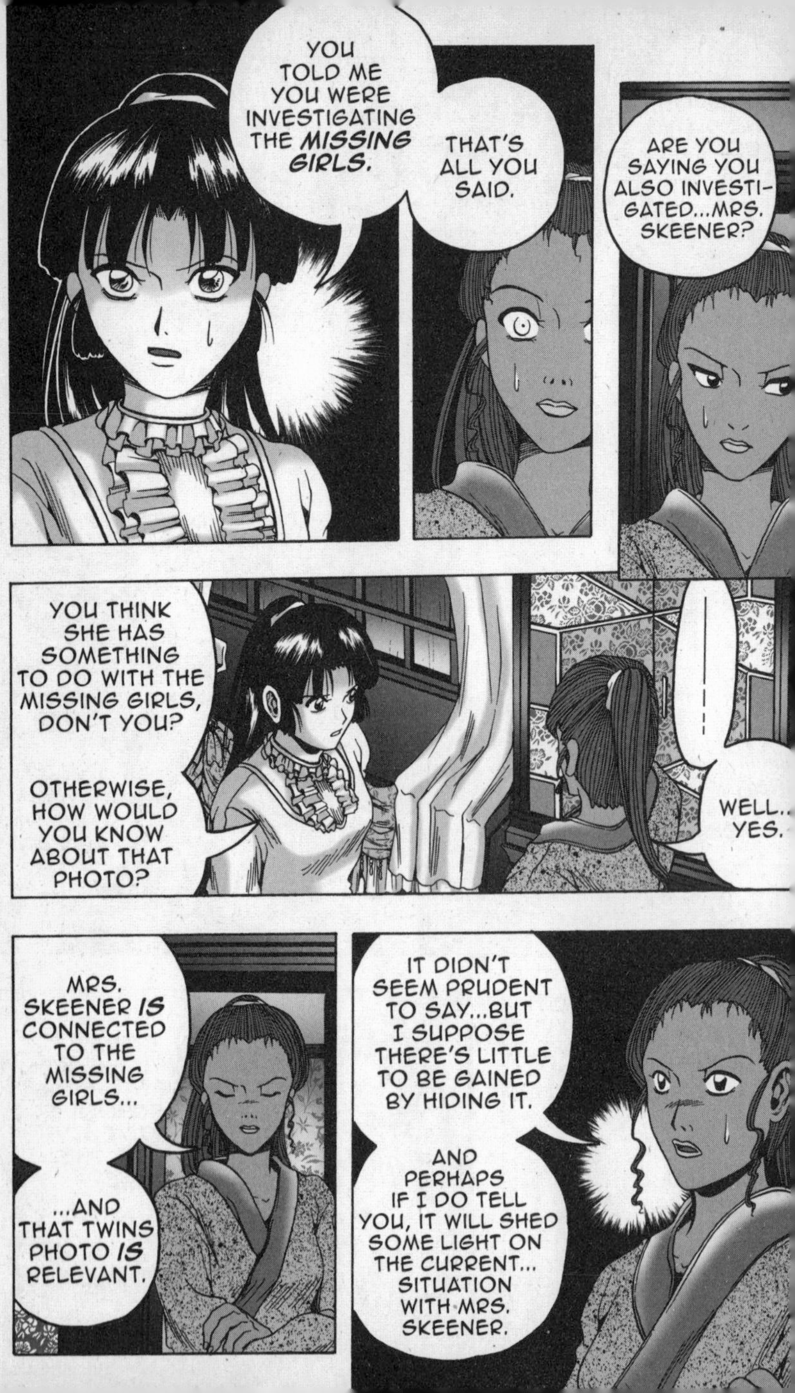
YOU TOLD ME YOU WERE INVESTIGATING THE *MISSING GIRLS.*
THAT'S ALL YOU SAID.
ARE YOU SAYING YOU ALSO INVESTI-GATED...MRS. SKEENER?
YOU THINK SHE HAS SOMETHING TO DO WITH THE MISSING GIRLS, DON'T YOU?
OTHERWISE, HOW WOULD YOU KNOW ABOUT THAT PHOTO?
......
WELL... YES.
MRS. SKEENER *IS* CONNECTED TO THE MISSING GIRLS...
...AND THAT TWINS PHOTO *IS* RELEVANT.
IT DIDN'T SEEM PRUDENT TO SAY...BUT I SUPPOSE THERE'S LITTLE TO BE GAINED BY HIDING IT.
AND PERHAPS IF I DO TELL YOU, IT WILL SHED SOME LIGHT ON THE CURRENT... SITUATION WITH MRS. SKEENER.

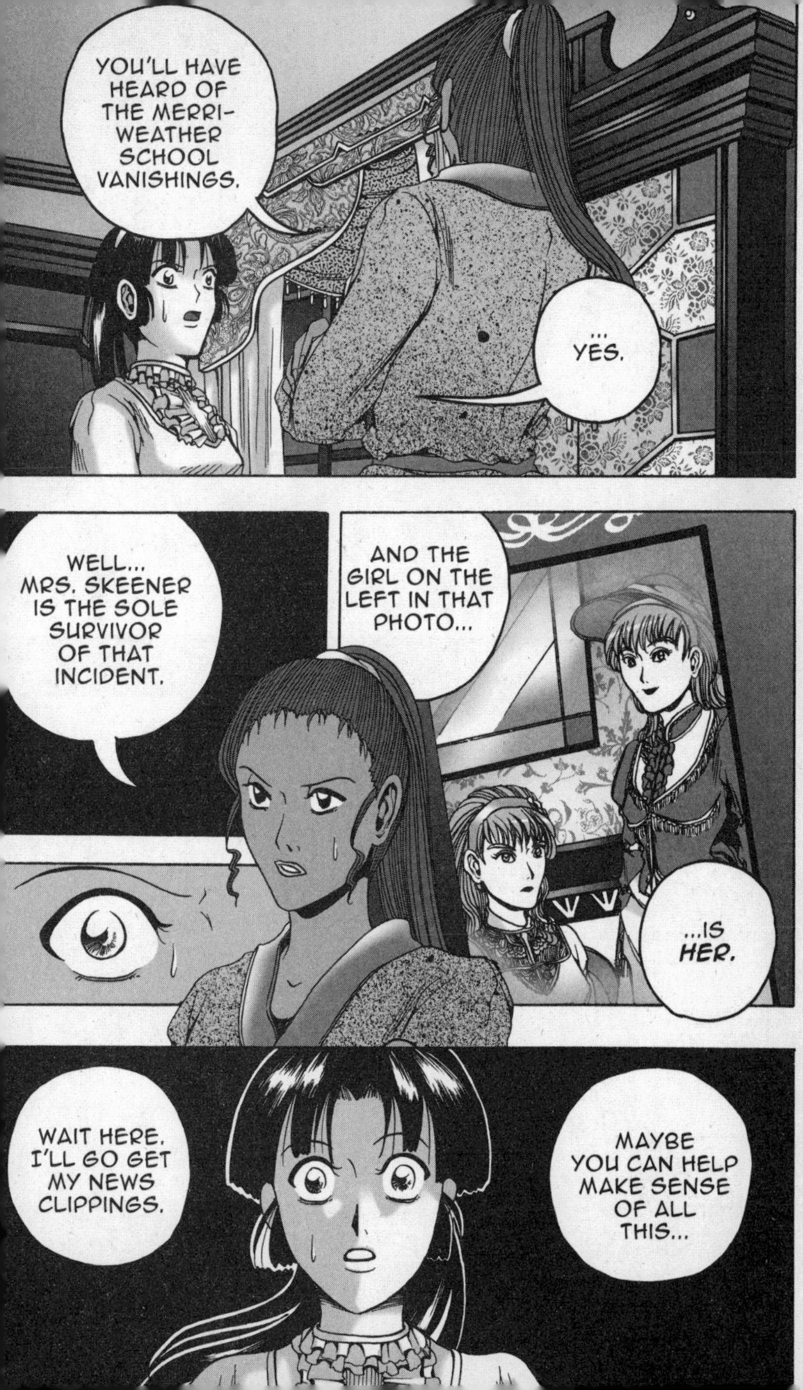
YOU'LL HAVE HEARD OF THE MERRI-WEATHER SCHOOL VANISHINGS.
... YES.
WELL... MRS. SKEENER IS THE SOLE SURVIVOR OF THAT INCIDENT.
AND THE GIRL ON THE LEFT IN THAT PHOTO...
...IS **HER.**
WAIT HERE. I'LL GO GET MY NEWS CLIPPINGS.
MAYBE YOU CAN HELP MAKE SENSE OF ALL THIS...

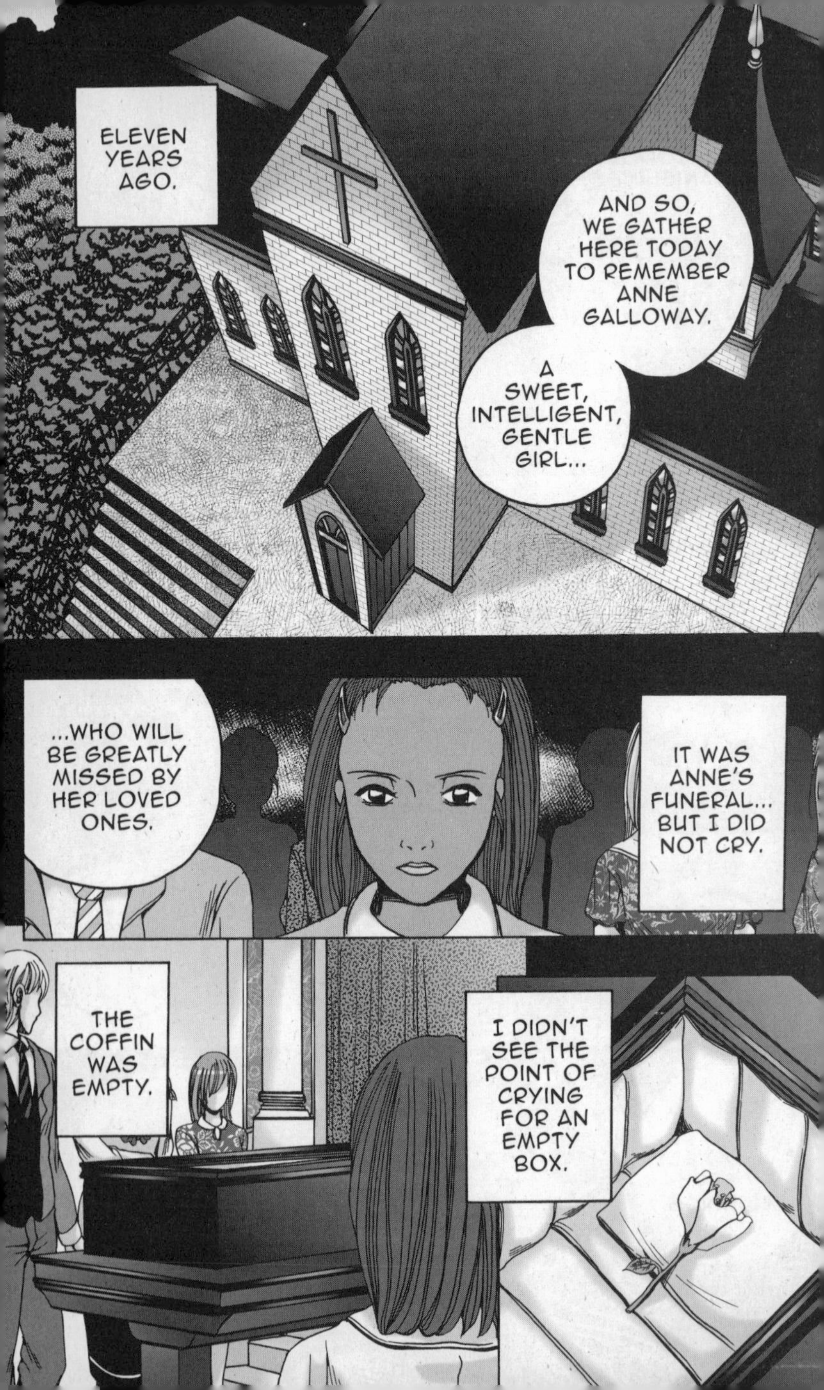
ELEVEN YEARS AGO.
AND SO, WE GATHER HERE TODAY TO REMEMBER ANNE GALLOWAY.
A SWEET, INTELLIGENT, GENTLE GIRL...
...WHO WILL BE GREATLY MISSED BY HER LOVED ONES.
IT WAS ANNE'S FUNERAL... BUT I DID NOT CRY.
THE COFFIN WAS EMPTY.
I DIDN'T SEE THE POINT OF CRYING FOR AN EMPTY BOX.

Chapter 13
What Miss Anu Knows

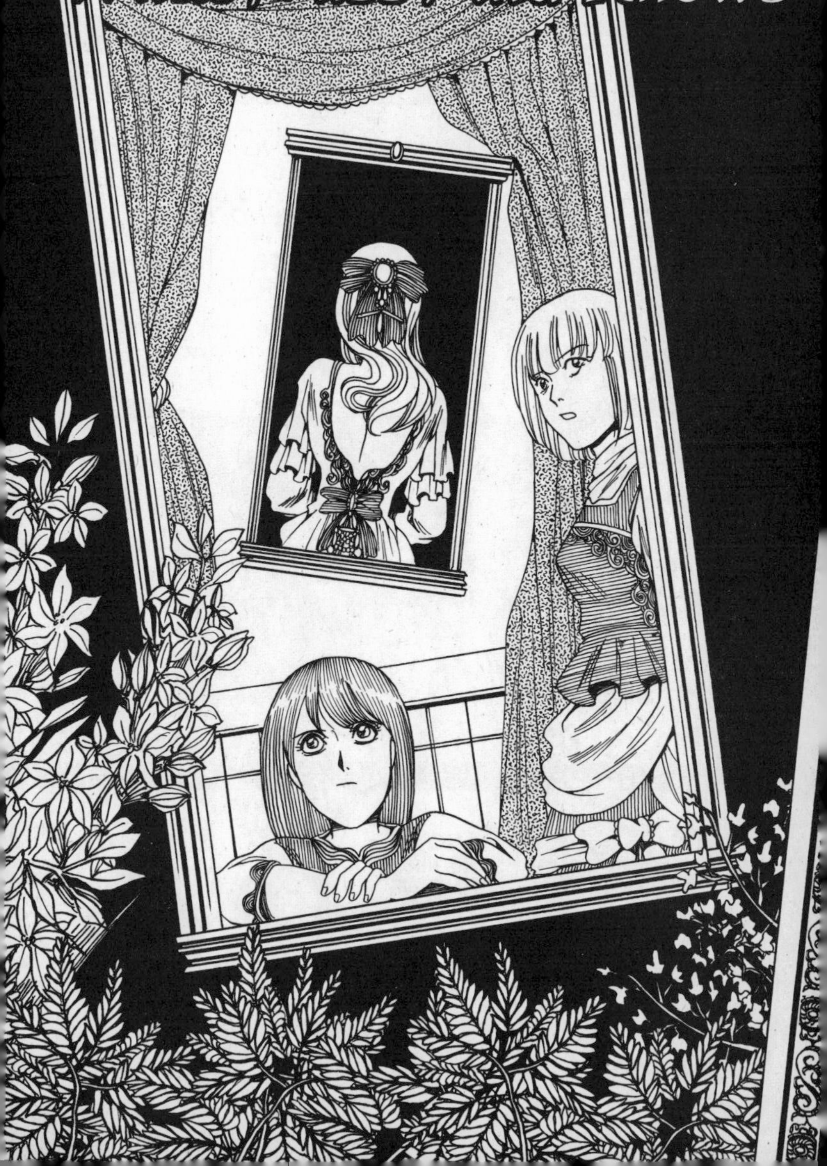

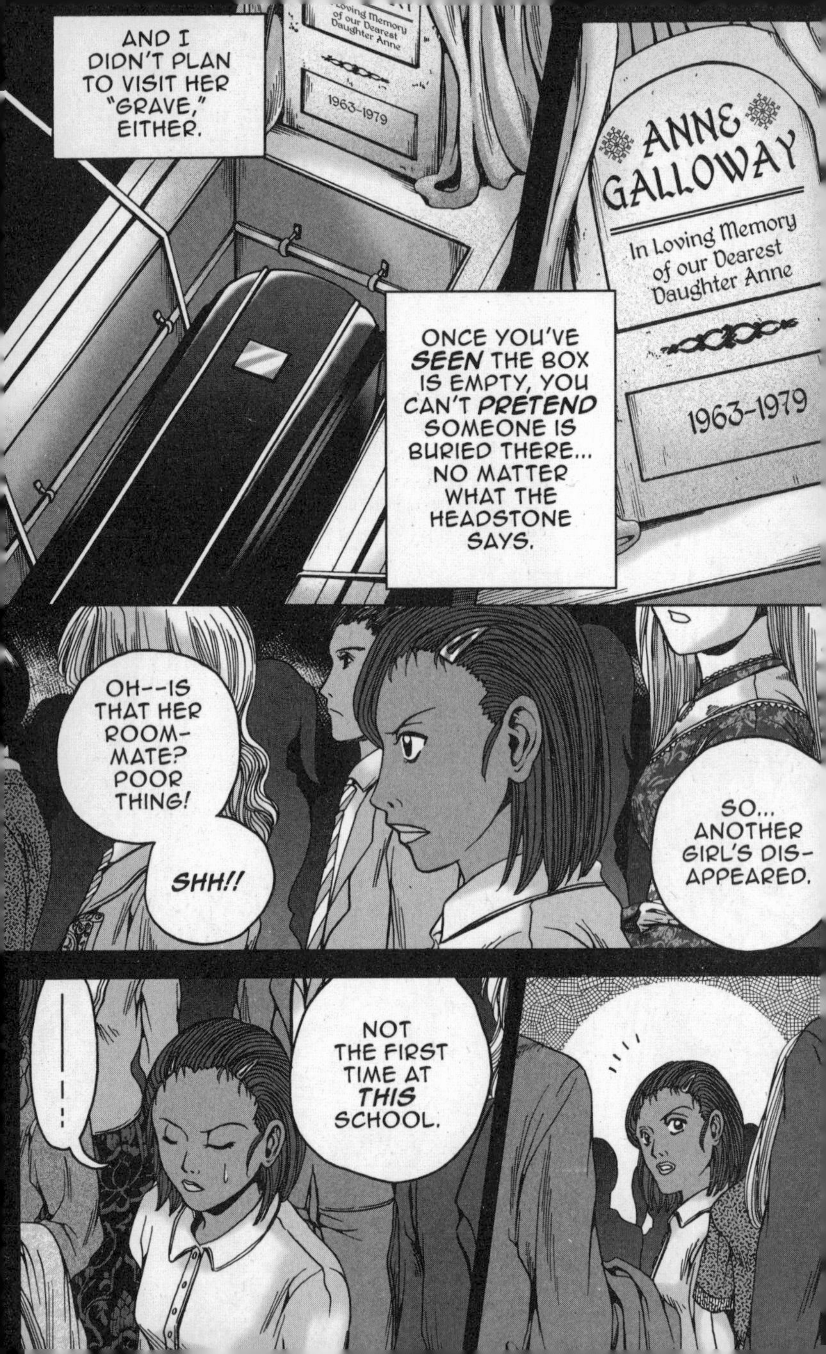
AND I DIDN'T PLAN TO VISIT HER "GRAVE," EITHER.
In Loving Memory of our Dearest Daughter Anne
1963-1979
ANNE GALLOWAY
In Loving Memory of our Dearest Daughter Anne
1963-1979
ONCE YOU'VE *SEEN* THE BOX IS EMPTY, YOU CAN'T *PRETEND* SOMEONE IS BURIED THERE... NO MATTER WHAT THE HEADSTONE SAYS.
OH--IS THAT HER ROOM-MATE? POOR THING!
SHH!!
SO... ANOTHER GIRL'S DIS-APPEARED.

NOT THE FIRST TIME AT *THIS* SCHOOL.

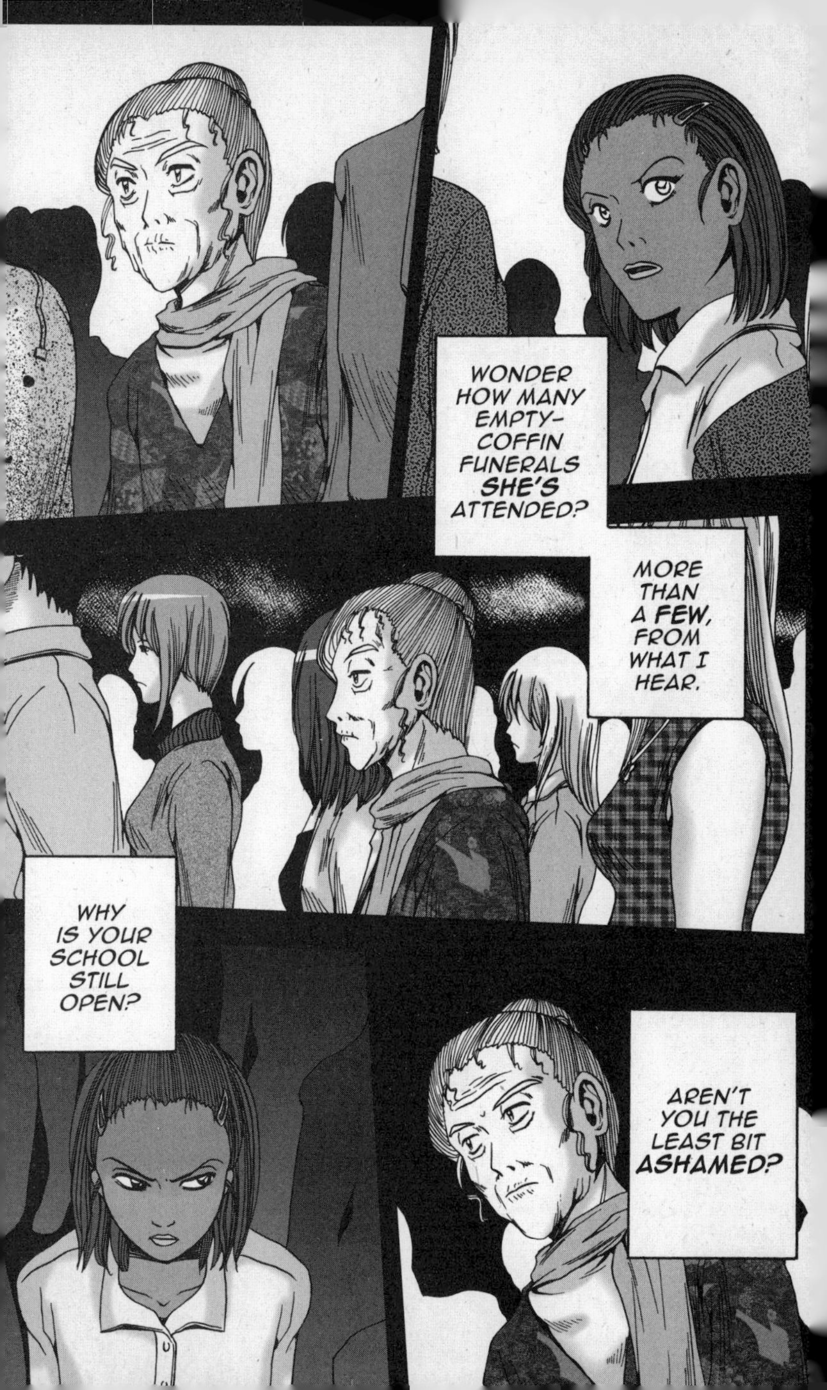
WONDER HOW MANY EMPTY-COFFIN FUNERALS **SHE'S** ATTENDED?
MORE THAN A **FEW**, FROM WHAT I HEAR.
WHY IS YOUR SCHOOL STILL OPEN?
AREN'T YOU THE LEAST BIT **ASHAMED?**

DON'T ALL THOSE STUDENTS MEAN **ANYTHING** TO YOU?

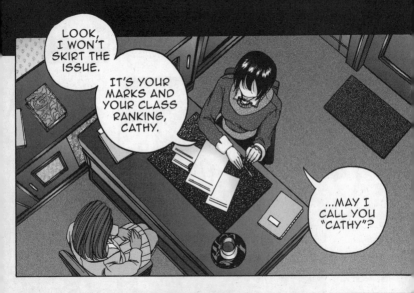

LOOK, I WON'T SKIRT THE ISSUE.

IT'S YOUR MARKS AND YOUR CLASS RANKING, CATHY.

...MAY I CALL YOU "CATHY"?

YOU USED TO BE AT THE TOP OF YOUR CLASS.

YOU SAID YOU WANTED TO BE A NUCLEAR PHYSICIST ALONG WITH ANNE.

YOU WORKED SO HARD FOR YOUR GOALS.

WHAT HAPPENED?

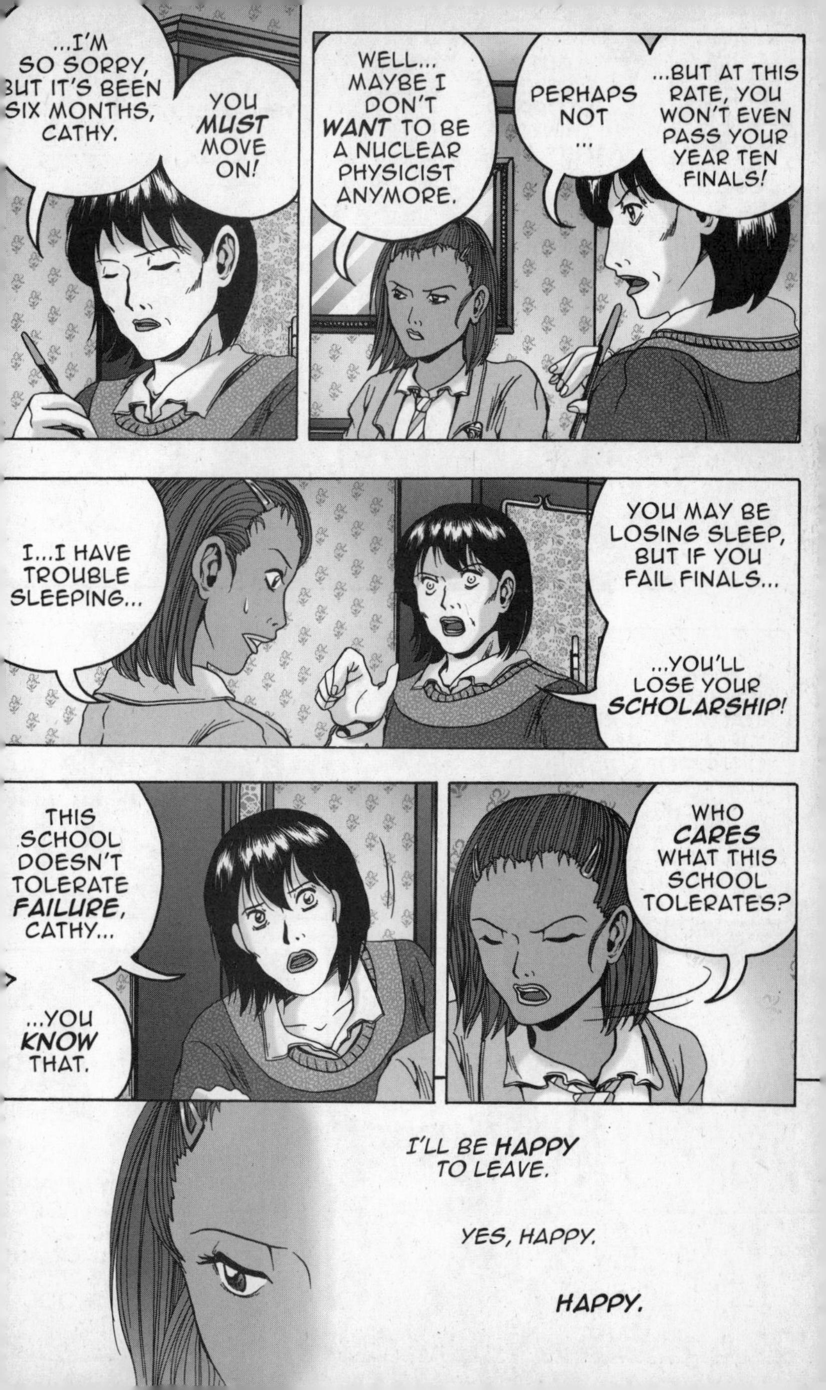
...I'M SO SORRY, BUT IT'S BEEN SIX MONTHS, CATHY.
YOU *MUST* MOVE ON!
WELL... MAYBE I DON'T *WANT* TO BE A NUCLEAR PHYSICIST ANYMORE.
PERHAPS NOT ...
...BUT AT THIS RATE, YOU WON'T EVEN PASS YOUR YEAR TEN FINALS!
I...I HAVE TROUBLE SLEEPING...
YOU MAY BE LOSING SLEEP, BUT IF YOU FAIL FINALS...
...YOU'LL LOSE YOUR *SCHOLARSHIP*!
THIS SCHOOL DOESN'T TOLERATE *FAILURE*, CATHY...
...YOU *KNOW* THAT.
WHO *CARES* WHAT THIS SCHOOL TOLERATES?
I'LL BE *HAPPY* TO LEAVE.
YES, HAPPY.
HAPPY.

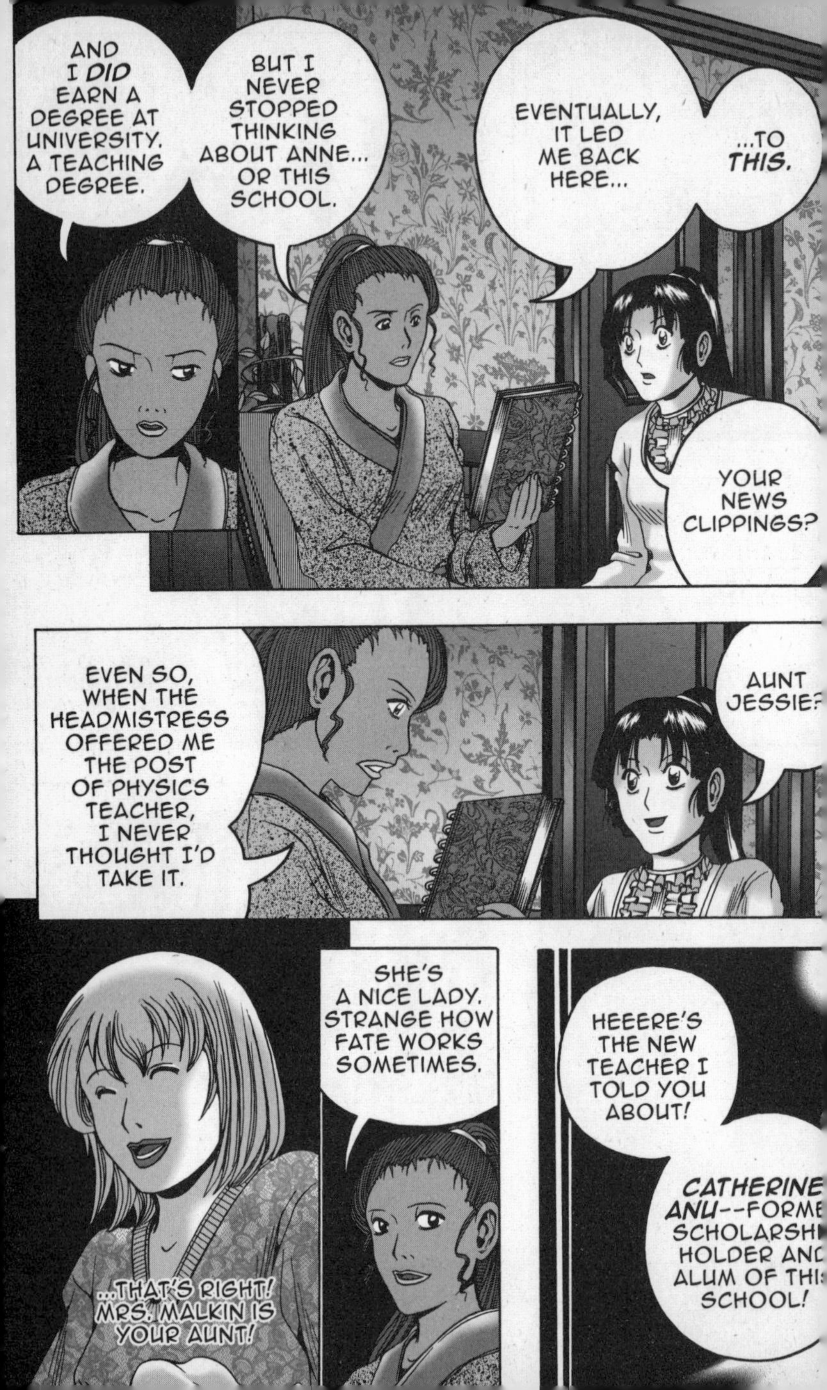
AND I *DID* EARN A DEGREE AT UNIVERSITY. A TEACHING DEGREE.
BUT I NEVER STOPPED THINKING ABOUT ANNE... OR THIS SCHOOL.
EVENTUALLY, IT LED ME BACK HERE...
...TO *THIS.*
YOUR NEWS CLIPPINGS?
EVEN SO, WHEN THE HEADMISTRESS OFFERED ME THE POST OF PHYSICS TEACHER, I NEVER THOUGHT I'D TAKE IT.
AUNT JESSIE?
...THAT'S RIGHT! MRS. MALKIN IS YOUR AUNT!
SHE'S A NICE LADY. STRANGE HOW FATE WORKS SOMETIMES.
HEEERE'S THE NEW TEACHER I TOLD YOU ABOUT!
CATHERINE ANU--FORME SCHOLARSHI HOLDER AND ALUM OF THI SCHOOL!

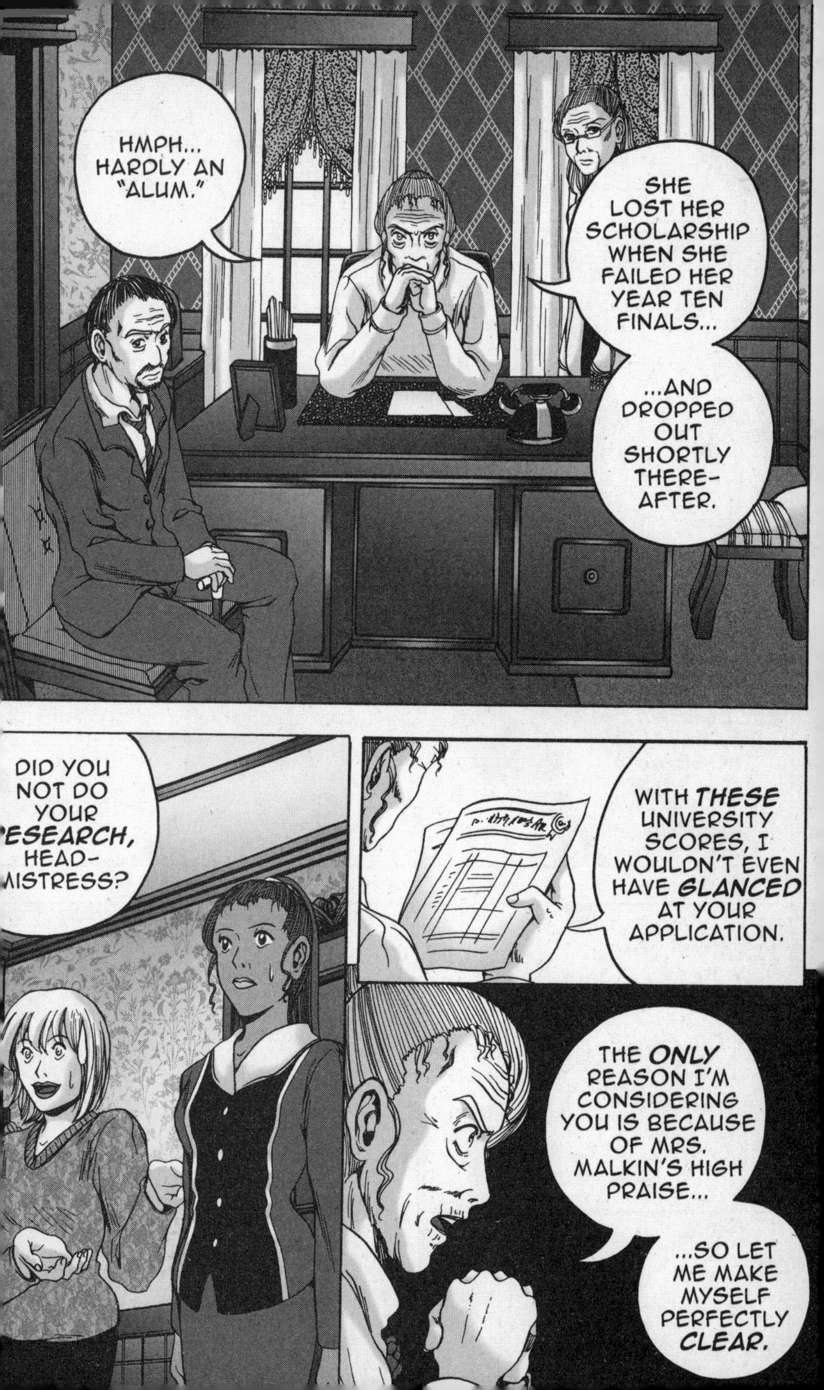

HMPH... HARDLY AN "ALUM."
SHE LOST HER SCHOLARSHIP WHEN SHE FAILED HER YEAR TEN FINALS...
...AND DROPPED OUT SHORTLY THERE-AFTER.
DID YOU NOT DO YOUR ESEARCH, HEAD-MISTRESS?
WITH *THESE* UNIVERSITY SCORES, I WOULDN'T EVEN HAVE *GLANCED* AT YOUR APPLICATION.
THE *ONLY* REASON I'M CONSIDERING YOU IS BECAUSE OF MRS. MALKIN'S HIGH PRAISE...
...SO LET ME MAKE MYSELF PERFECTLY *CLEAR.*

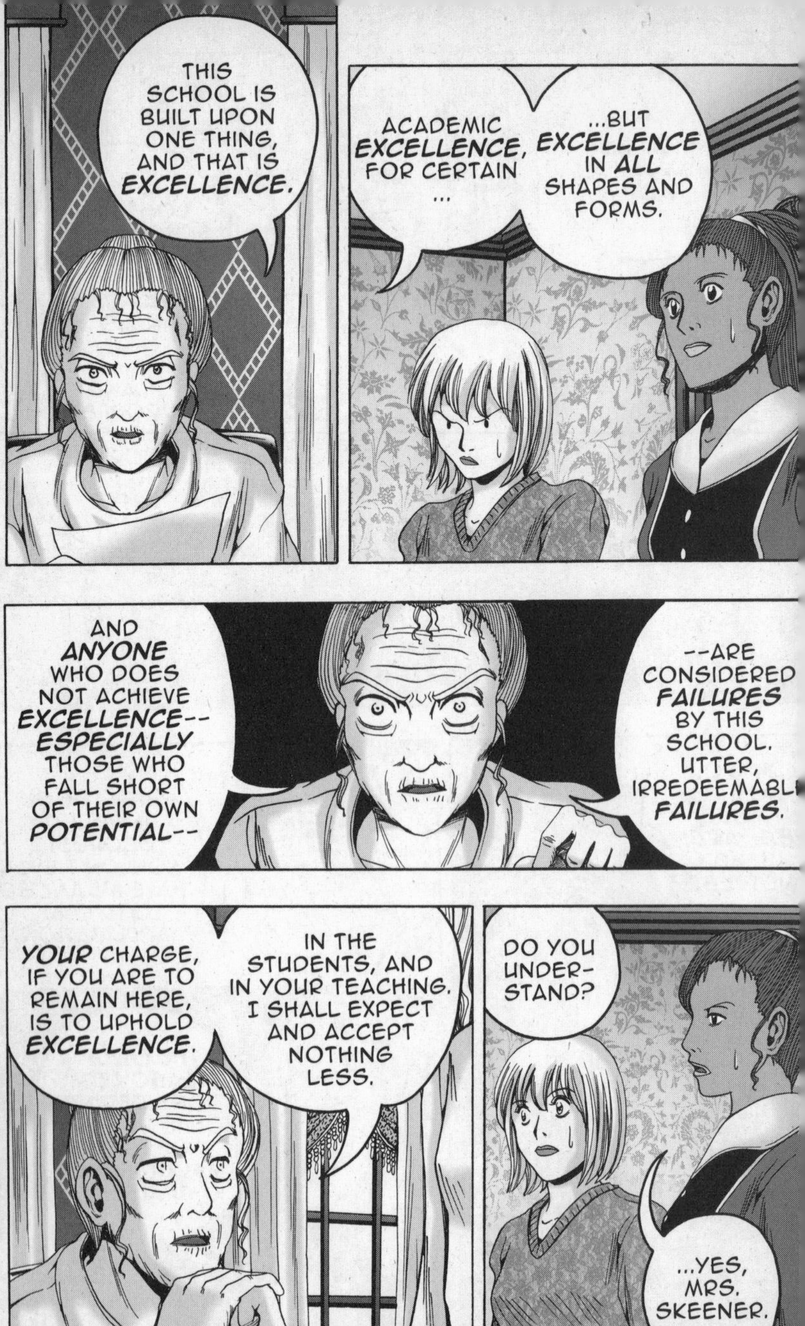
THIS SCHOOL IS BUILT UPON ONE THING, AND THAT IS EXCELLENCE.
ACADEMIC EXCELLENCE, FOR CERTAIN ...
...BUT EXCELLENCE IN ALL SHAPES AND FORMS.
AND ANYONE WHO DOES NOT ACHIEVE EXCELLENCE-- ESPECIALLY THOSE WHO FALL SHORT OF THEIR OWN POTENTIAL--
--ARE CONSIDERED FAILURES BY THIS SCHOOL. UTTER, IRREDEEMABL FAILURES.
YOUR CHARGE, IF YOU ARE TO REMAIN HERE, IS TO UPHOLD EXCELLENCE.
IN THE STUDENTS, AND IN YOUR TEACHING. I SHALL EXPECT AND ACCEPT NOTHING LESS.
DO YOU UNDER- STAND?
...YES, MRS. SKEENER.

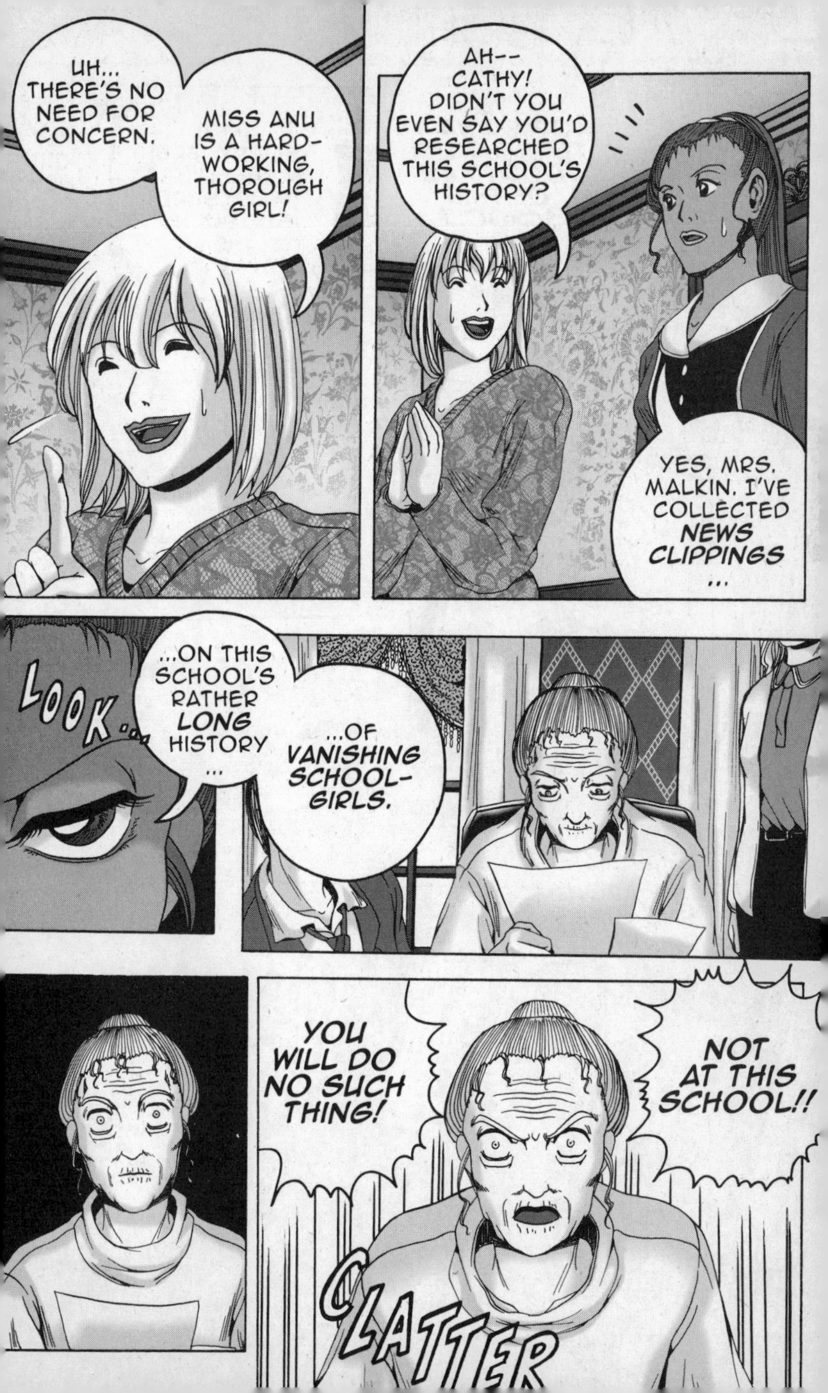
UH... THERE'S NO NEED FOR CONCERN.
MISS ANU IS A HARD-WORKING, THOROUGH GIRL!
AH-- CATHY! DIDN'T YOU EVEN SAY YOU'D RESEARCHED THIS SCHOOL'S HISTORY?
YES, MRS. MALKIN. I'VE COLLECTED NEWS CLIPPINGS ...
LOOK...
...ON THIS SCHOOL'S RATHER LONG HISTORY ...
...OF VANISHING SCHOOL-GIRLS.
YOU WILL DO NO SUCH THING!
NOT AT THIS SCHOOL!!
CLATTER

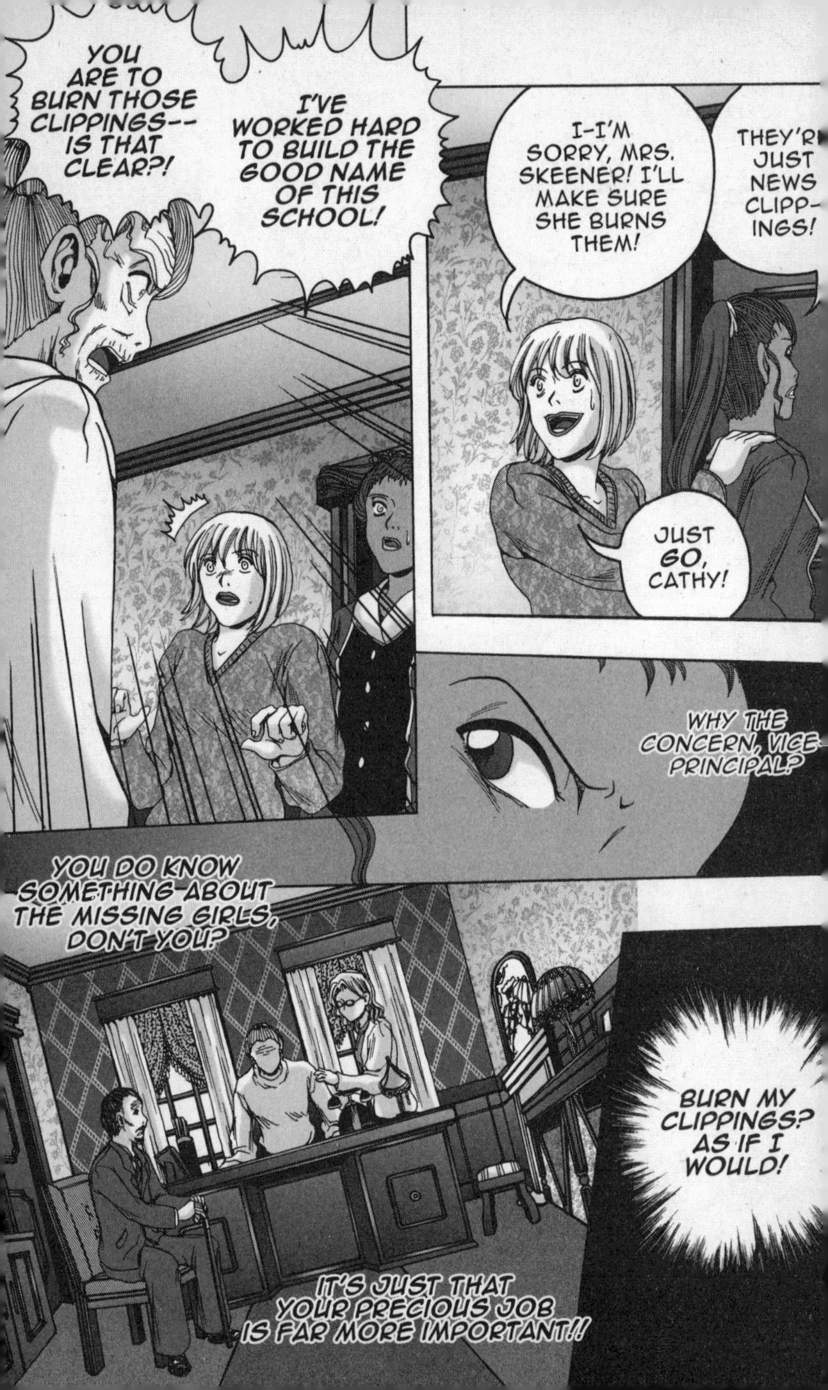
YOU ARE TO BURN THOSE CLIPPINGS-- IS THAT CLEAR?!
I'VE WORKED HARD TO BUILD THE GOOD NAME OF THIS SCHOOL!
I-I'M SORRY, MRS. SKEENER! I'LL MAKE SURE SHE BURNS THEM!
THEY'R JUST NEWS CLIPP-INGS!
JUST GO, CATHY!
WHY THE CONCERN, VICE PRINCIPAL?
YOU DO KNOW SOMETHING ABOUT THE MISSING GIRLS, DON'T YOU?
BURN MY CLIPPINGS? AS IF I WOULD!
IT'S JUST THAT YOUR PRECIOUS JOB IS FAR MORE IMPORTANT!!

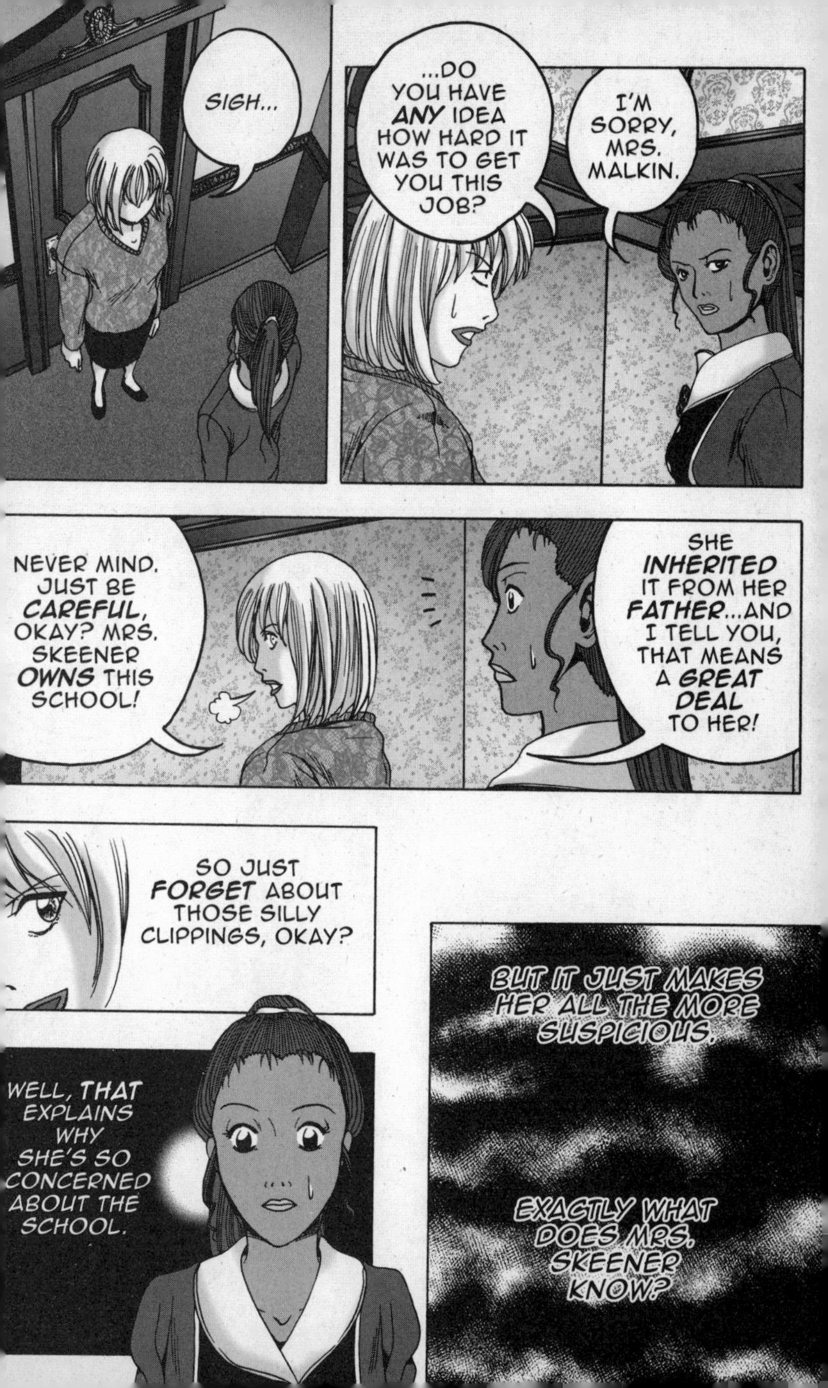
SIGH...
...DO YOU HAVE ANY IDEA HOW HARD IT WAS TO GET YOU THIS JOB?
I'M SORRY, MRS. MALKIN.
NEVER MIND. JUST BE CAREFUL, OKAY? MRS. SKEENER OWNS THIS SCHOOL!
SHE INHERITED IT FROM HER FATHER...AND I TELL YOU, THAT MEANS A GREAT DEAL TO HER!
SO JUST FORGET ABOUT THOSE SILLY CLIPPINGS, OKAY?
WELL, THAT EXPLAINS WHY SHE'S SO CONCERNED ABOUT THE SCHOOL.
BUT IT JUST MAKES HER ALL THE MORE SUSPICIOUS.
EXACTLY WHAT DOES MRS. SKEENER KNOW?

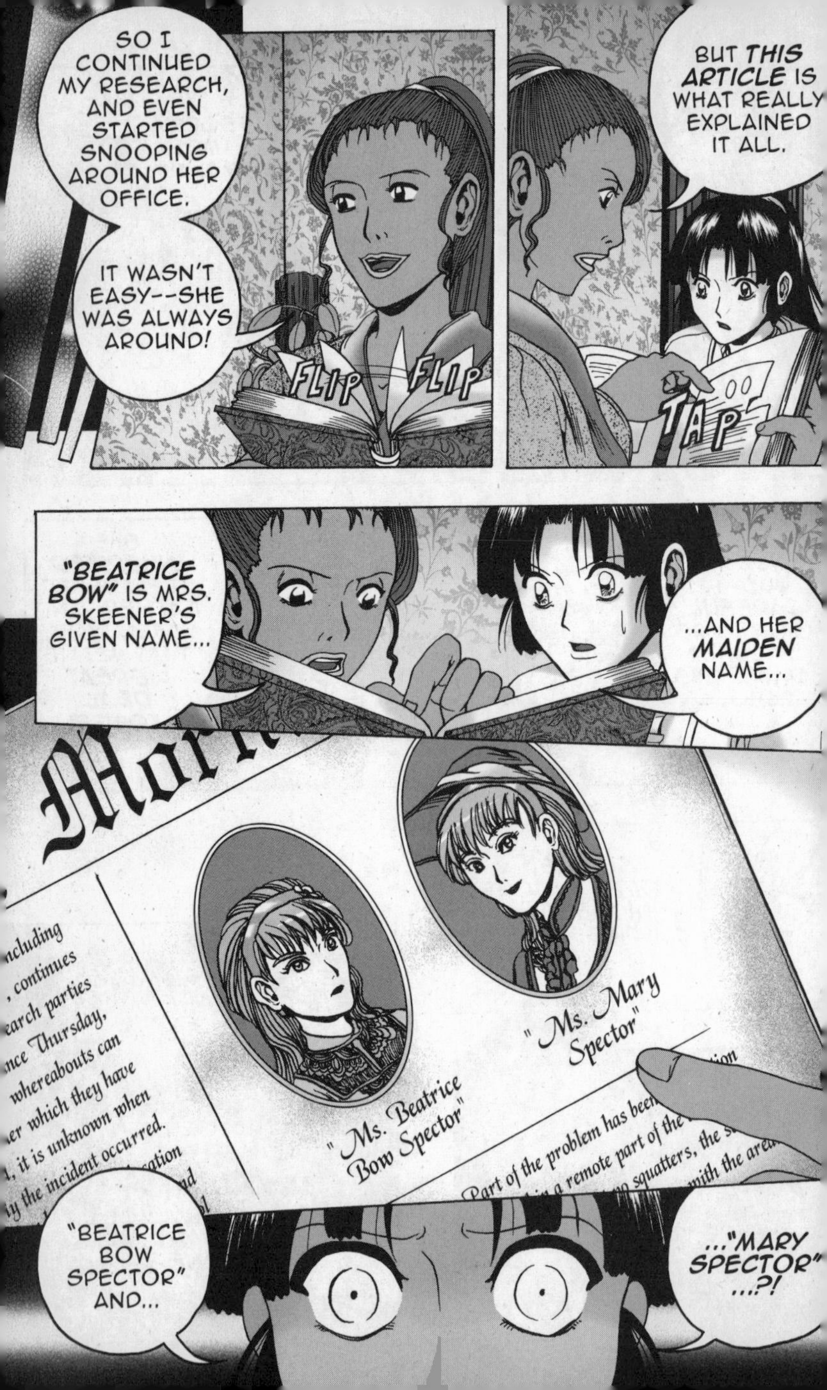
SO I CONTINUED MY RESEARCH, AND EVEN STARTED SNOOPING AROUND HER OFFICE.
IT WASN'T EASY--SHE WAS ALWAYS AROUND!
FLIP FLIP
BUT *THIS ARTICLE* IS WHAT REALLY EXPLAINED IT ALL.
TAP
"*BEATRICE BOW*" IS MRS. SKEENER'S GIVEN NAME...
...AND HER *MAIDEN* NAME...
, continues
whereabouts can
which they have
it is unknown when
the incident occurred.
"Ms. Beatrice Bow Spector"
"Ms. Mary Spector"
Part of the problem has been
a remote part of the
squatters,
with the area
"BEATRICE BOW SPECTOR" AND...
..."MARY SPECTOR" ...?!

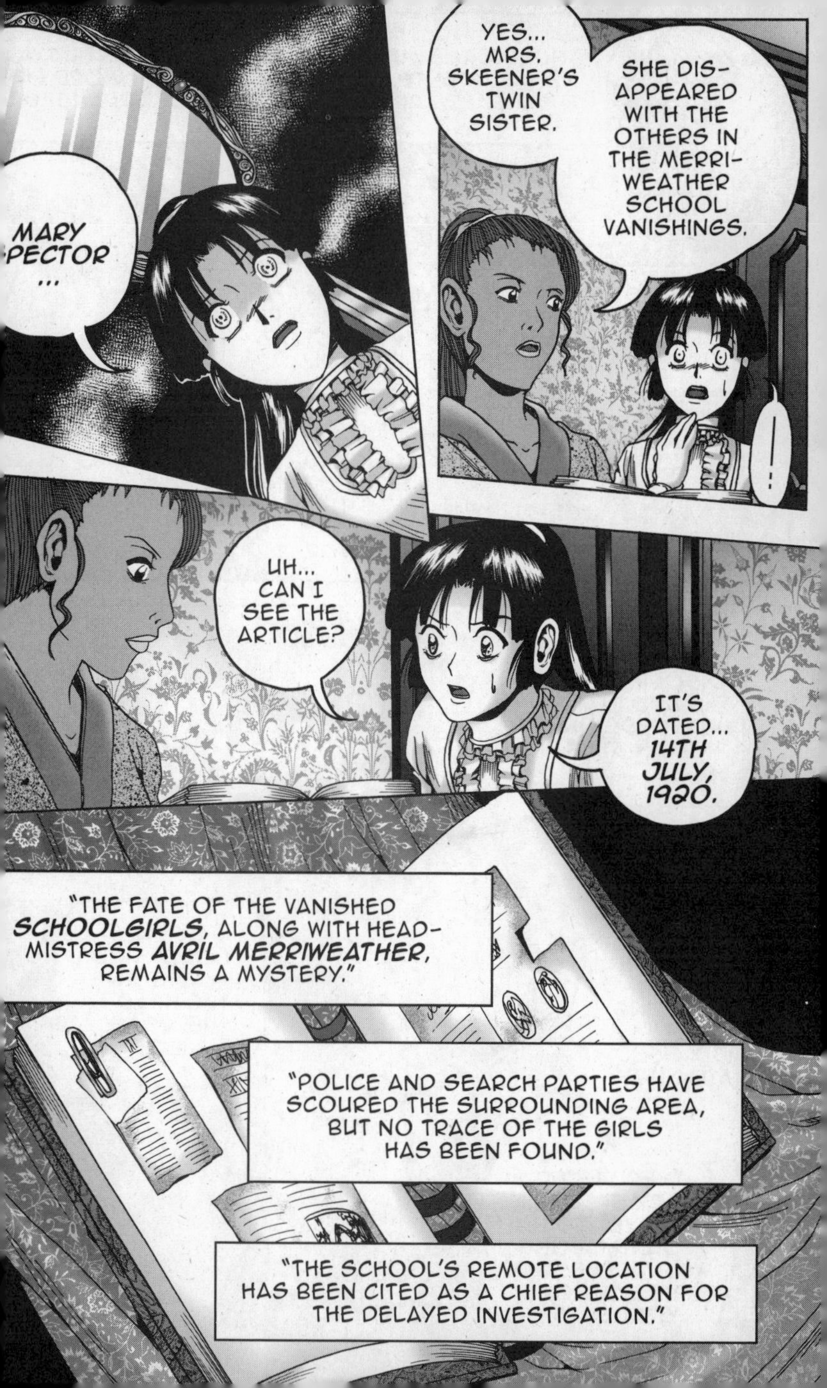
MARY
PECTOR
...
YES... MRS. SKEENER'S TWIN SISTER.
SHE DIS-APPEARED WITH THE OTHERS IN THE MERRI-WEATHER SCHOOL VANISHINGS.
!
UH... CAN I SEE THE ARTICLE?
IT'S DATED... 14TH JULY, 1920.
"THE FATE OF THE VANISHED SCHOOLGIRLS, ALONG WITH HEAD-MISTRESS AVRIL MERRIWEATHER, REMAINS A MYSTERY."
"POLICE AND SEARCH PARTIES HAVE SCOURED THE SURROUNDING AREA, BUT NO TRACE OF THE GIRLS HAS BEEN FOUND."
"THE SCHOOL'S REMOTE LOCATION HAS BEEN CITED AS A CHIEF REASON FOR THE DELAYED INVESTIGATION."

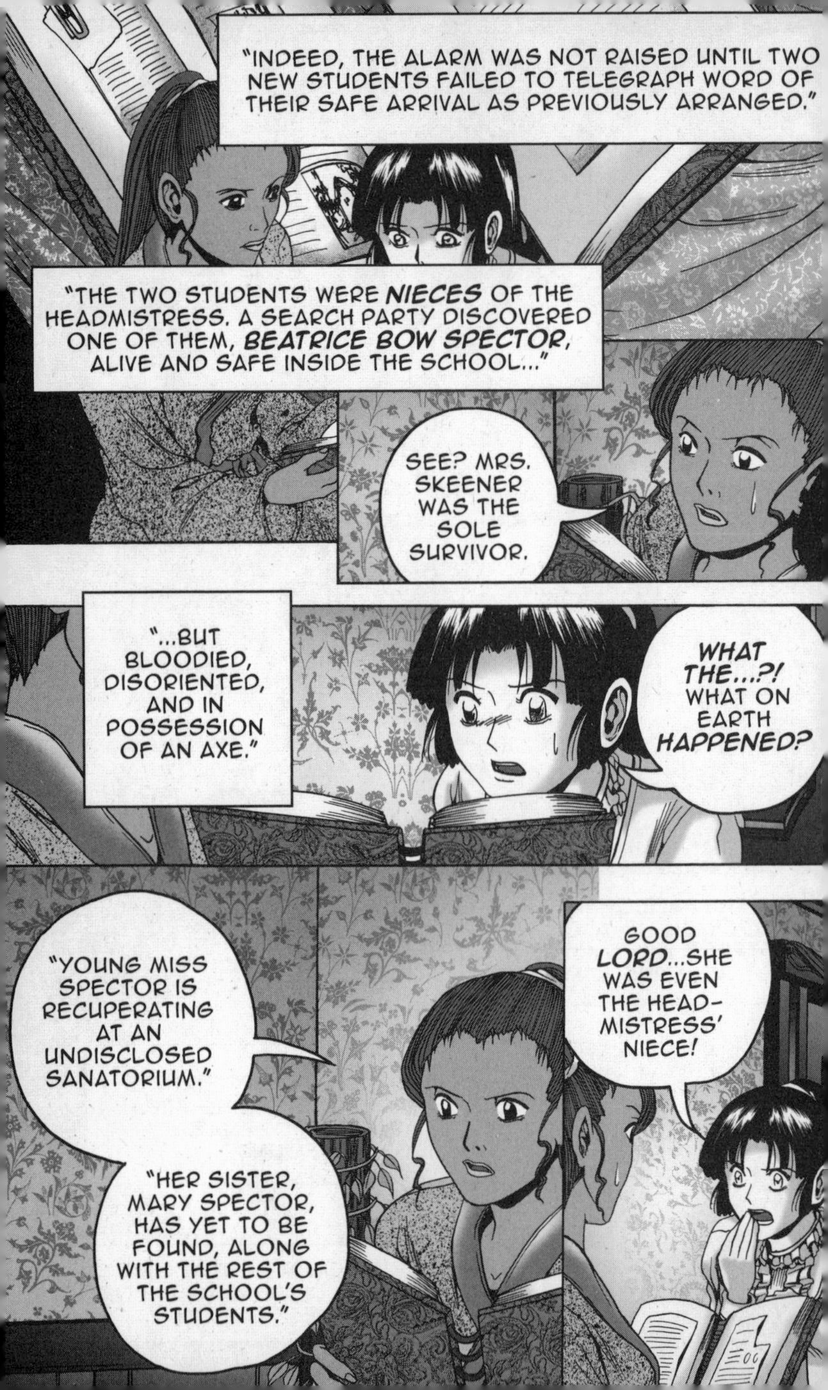
"INDEED, THE ALARM WAS NOT RAISED UNTIL TWO NEW STUDENTS FAILED TO TELEGRAPH WORD OF THEIR SAFE ARRIVAL AS PREVIOUSLY ARRANGED."
"THE TWO STUDENTS WERE ***NIECES*** OF THE HEADMISTRESS. A SEARCH PARTY DISCOVERED ONE OF THEM, ***BEATRICE BOW SPECTOR***, ALIVE AND SAFE INSIDE THE SCHOOL..."
SEE? MRS. SKEENER WAS THE SOLE SURVIVOR.
"...BUT BLOODIED, DISORIENTED, AND IN POSSESSION OF AN AXE."
WHAT THE...?! WHAT ON EARTH ***HAPPENED?***
"YOUNG MISS SPECTOR IS RECUPERATING AT AN UNDISCLOSED SANATORIUM."
"HER SISTER, MARY SPECTOR, HAS YET TO BE FOUND, ALONG WITH THE REST OF THE SCHOOL'S STUDENTS."
GOOD ***LORD***...SHE WAS EVEN THE HEAD-MISTRESS' NIECE!

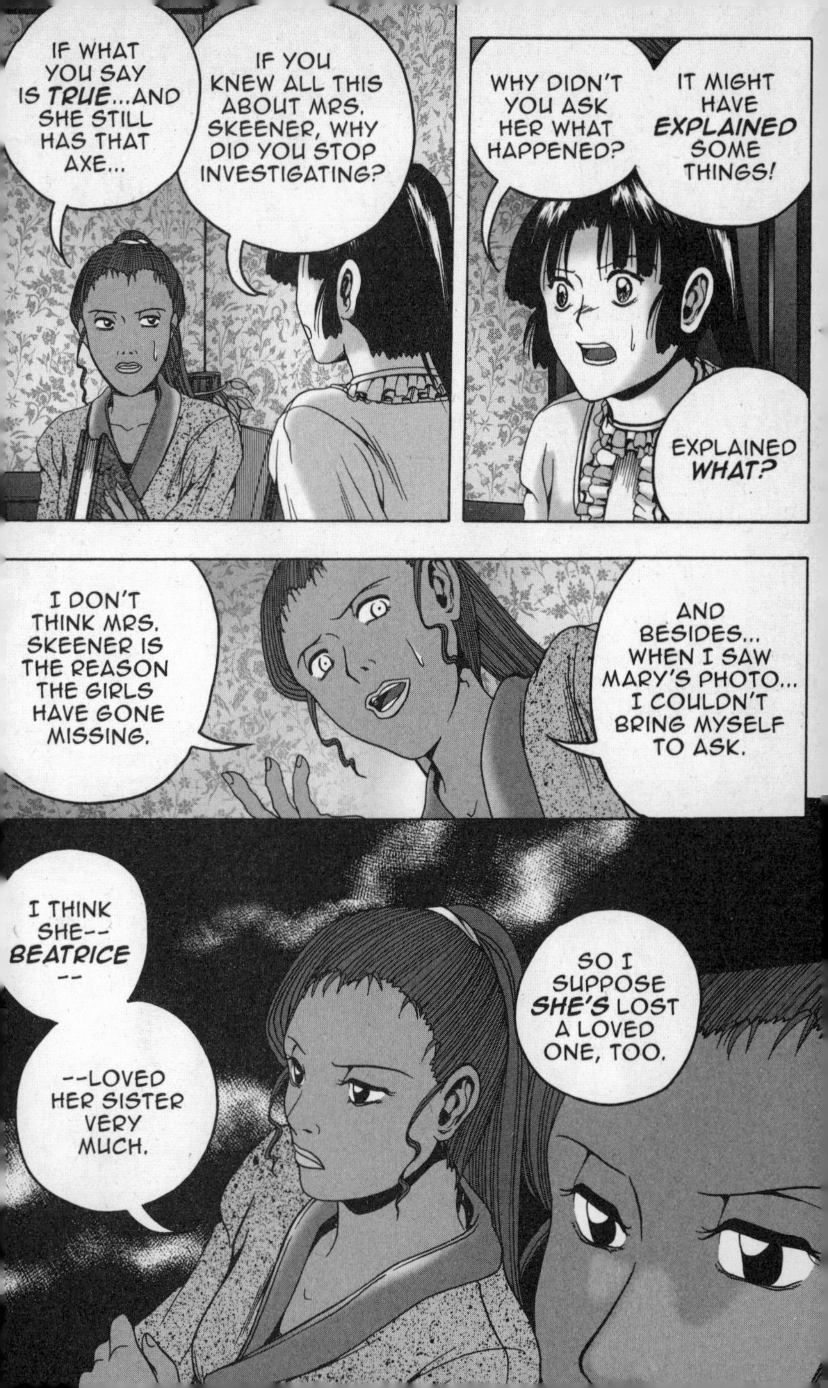
IF WHAT YOU SAY IS ***TRUE***...AND SHE STILL HAS THAT AXE...
IF YOU KNEW ALL THIS ABOUT MRS. SKEENER, WHY DID YOU STOP INVESTIGATING?
WHY DIDN'T YOU ASK HER WHAT HAPPENED?
IT MIGHT HAVE ***EXPLAINED*** SOME THINGS!
EXPLAINED ***WHAT?***
I DON'T THINK MRS. SKEENER IS THE REASON THE GIRLS HAVE GONE MISSING.
AND BESIDES... WHEN I SAW MARY'S PHOTO... I COULDN'T BRING MYSELF TO ASK.
I THINK SHE-- ***BEATRICE*** --
--LOVED HER SISTER VERY MUCH.
SO I SUPPOSE ***SHE'S*** LOST A LOVED ONE, TOO.

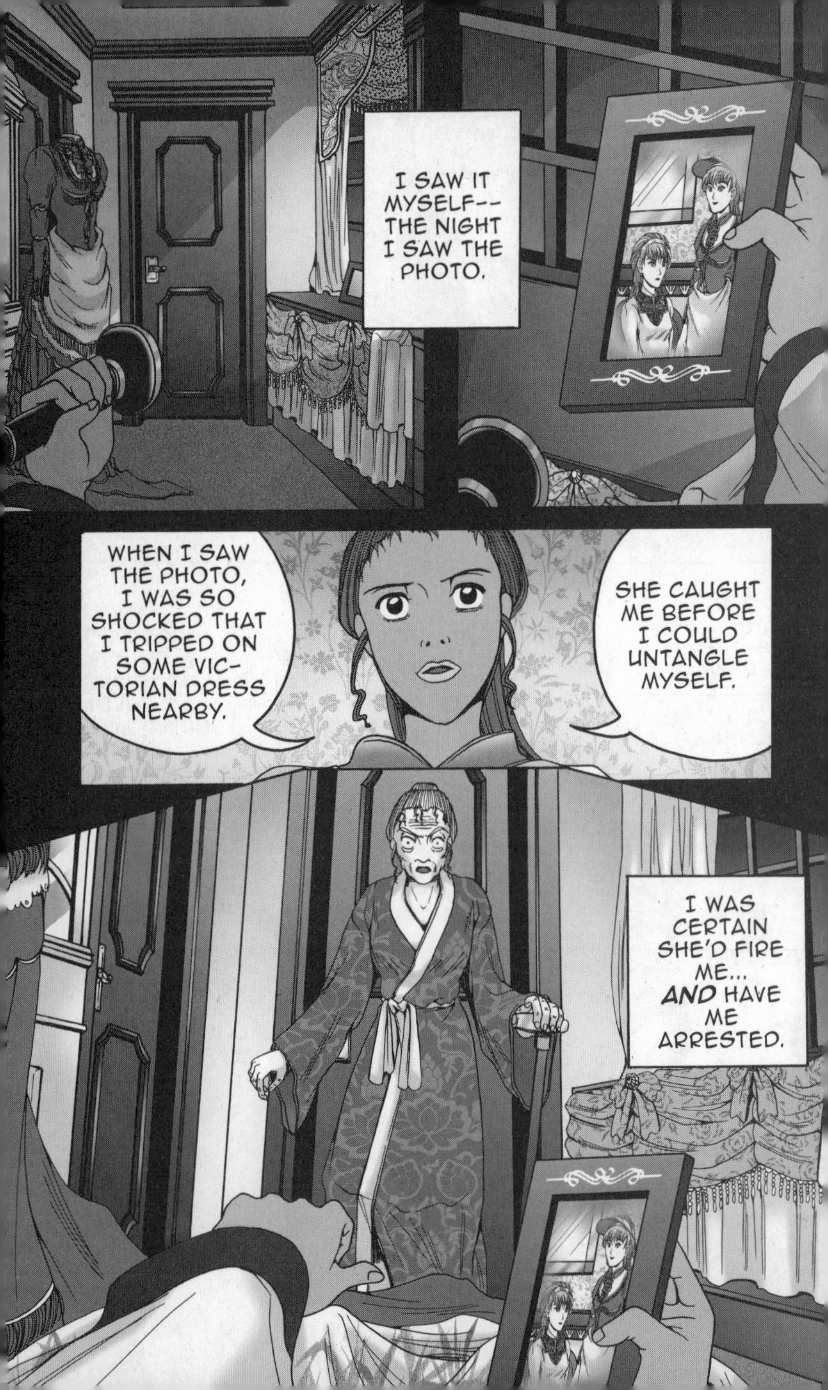
I SAW IT MYSELF-- THE NIGHT I SAW THE PHOTO.
WHEN I SAW THE PHOTO, I WAS SO SHOCKED THAT I TRIPPED ON SOME VIC-TORIAN DRESS NEARBY.
SHE CAUGHT ME BEFORE I COULD UNTANGLE MYSELF.
I WAS CERTAIN SHE'D FIRE ME... **AND** HAVE ME ARRESTED.

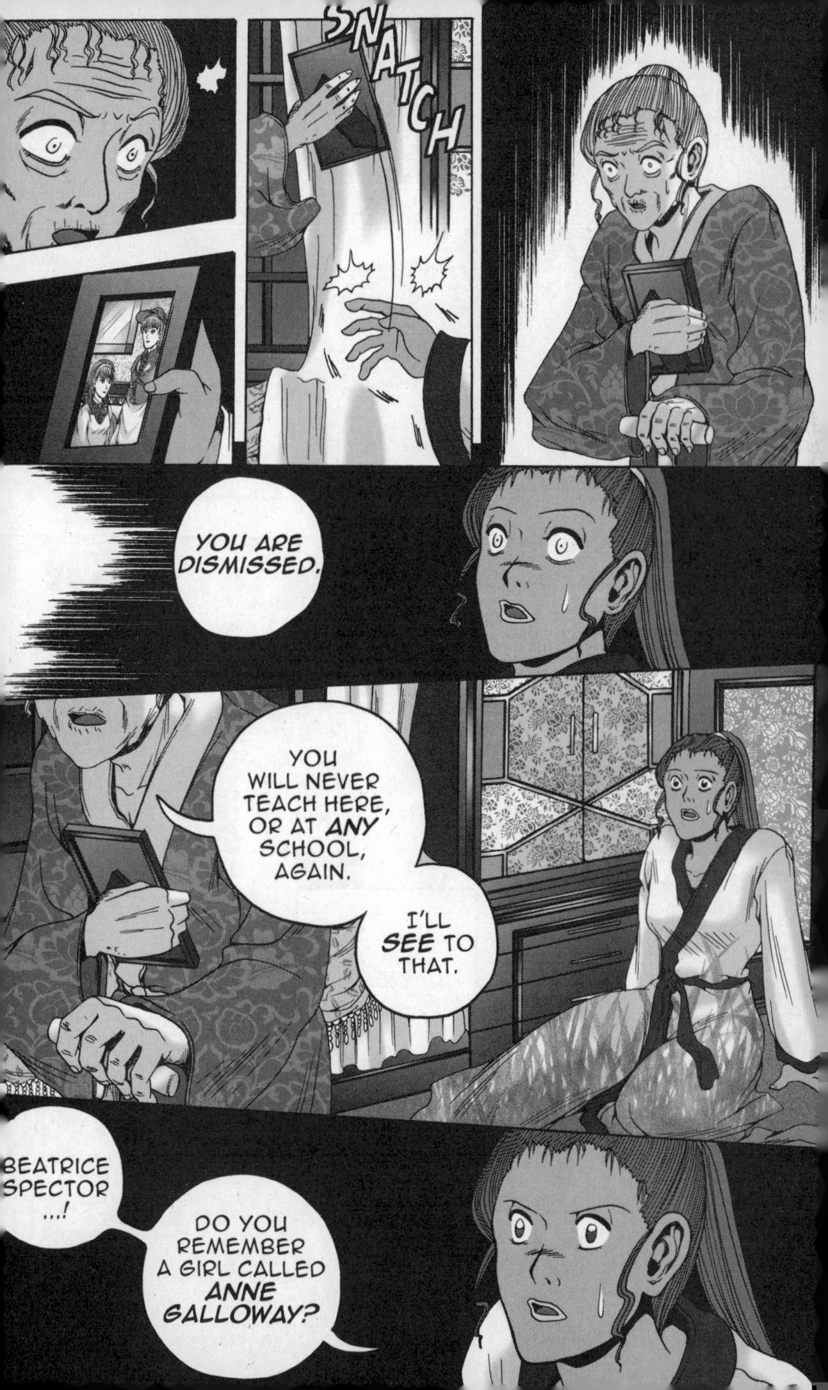
SNATCH
YOU ARE DISMISSED.
YOU WILL NEVER TEACH HERE, OR AT ANY SCHOOL, AGAIN.
I'LL SEE TO THAT.
BEATRICE SPECTOR ...!
DO YOU REMEMBER A GIRL CALLED ANNE GALLOWAY?

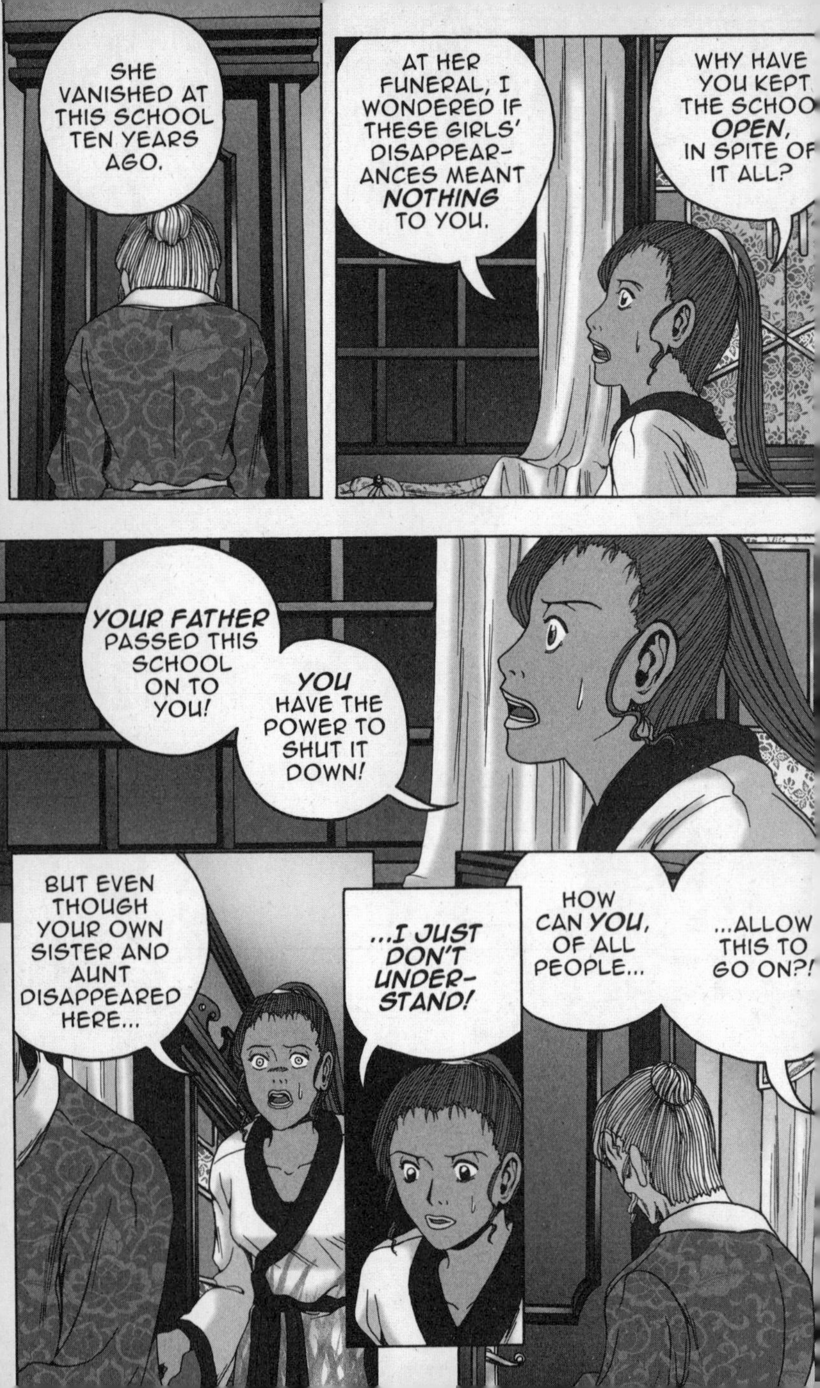
SHE VANISHED AT THIS SCHOOL TEN YEARS AGO.
AT HER FUNERAL, I WONDERED IF THESE GIRLS' DISAPPEARANCES MEANT *NOTHING* TO YOU.
WHY HAVE YOU KEPT THE SCHOO *OPEN*, IN SPITE OF IT ALL?
YOUR FATHER PASSED THIS SCHOOL ON TO YOU!
YOU HAVE THE POWER TO SHUT IT DOWN!
BUT EVEN THOUGH YOUR OWN SISTER AND AUNT DISAPPEARED HERE...
...I JUST DON'T UNDERSTAND!
HOW CAN *YOU*, OF ALL PEOPLE...
...ALLOW THIS TO GO ON?!

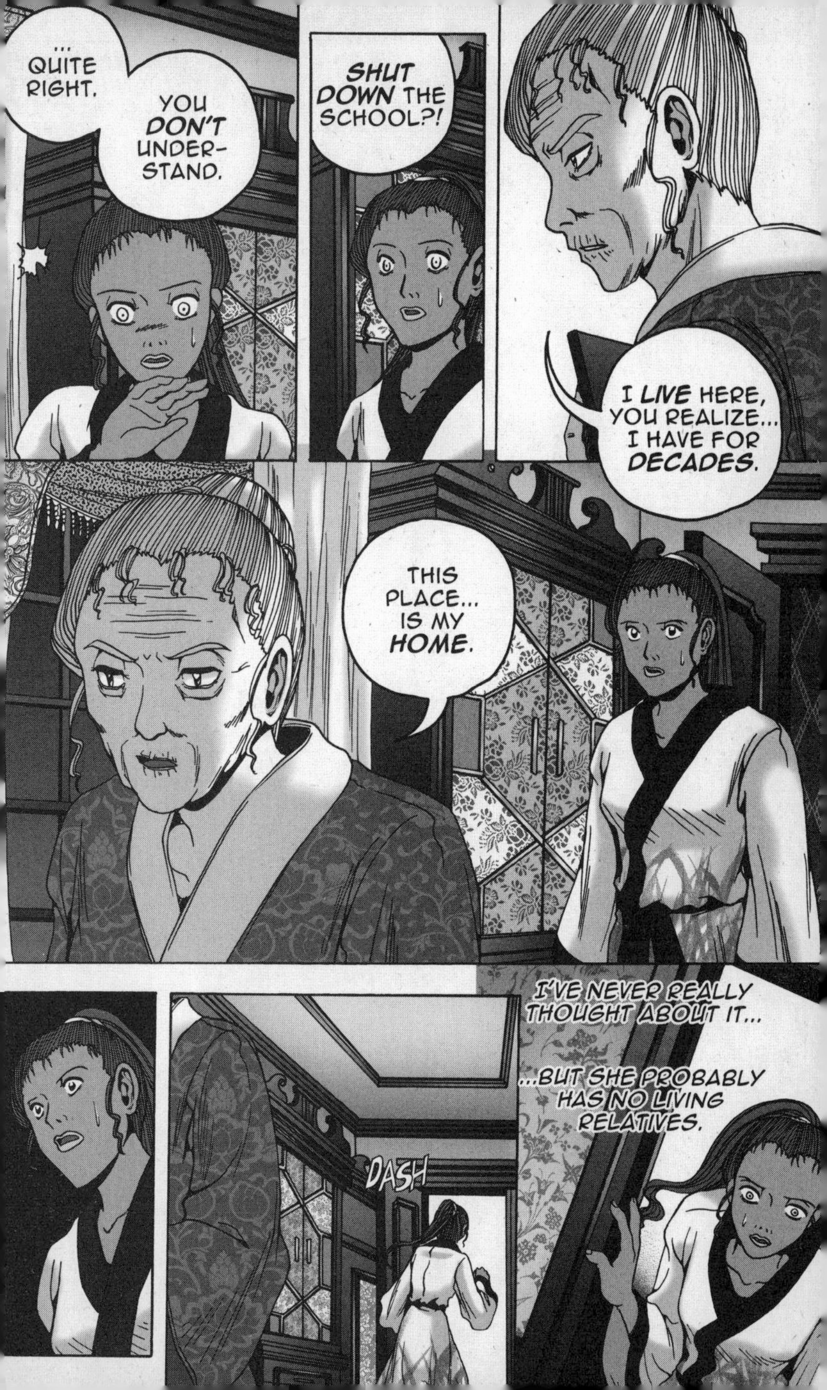

... QUITE RIGHT.
YOU DON'T UNDER-STAND.
SHUT DOWN THE SCHOOL?!
I LIVE HERE, YOU REALIZE... I HAVE FOR DECADES.
THIS PLACE... IS MY HOME.
DASH
I'VE NEVER REALLY THOUGHT ABOUT IT...
...BUT SHE PROBABLY HAS NO LIVING RELATIVES.

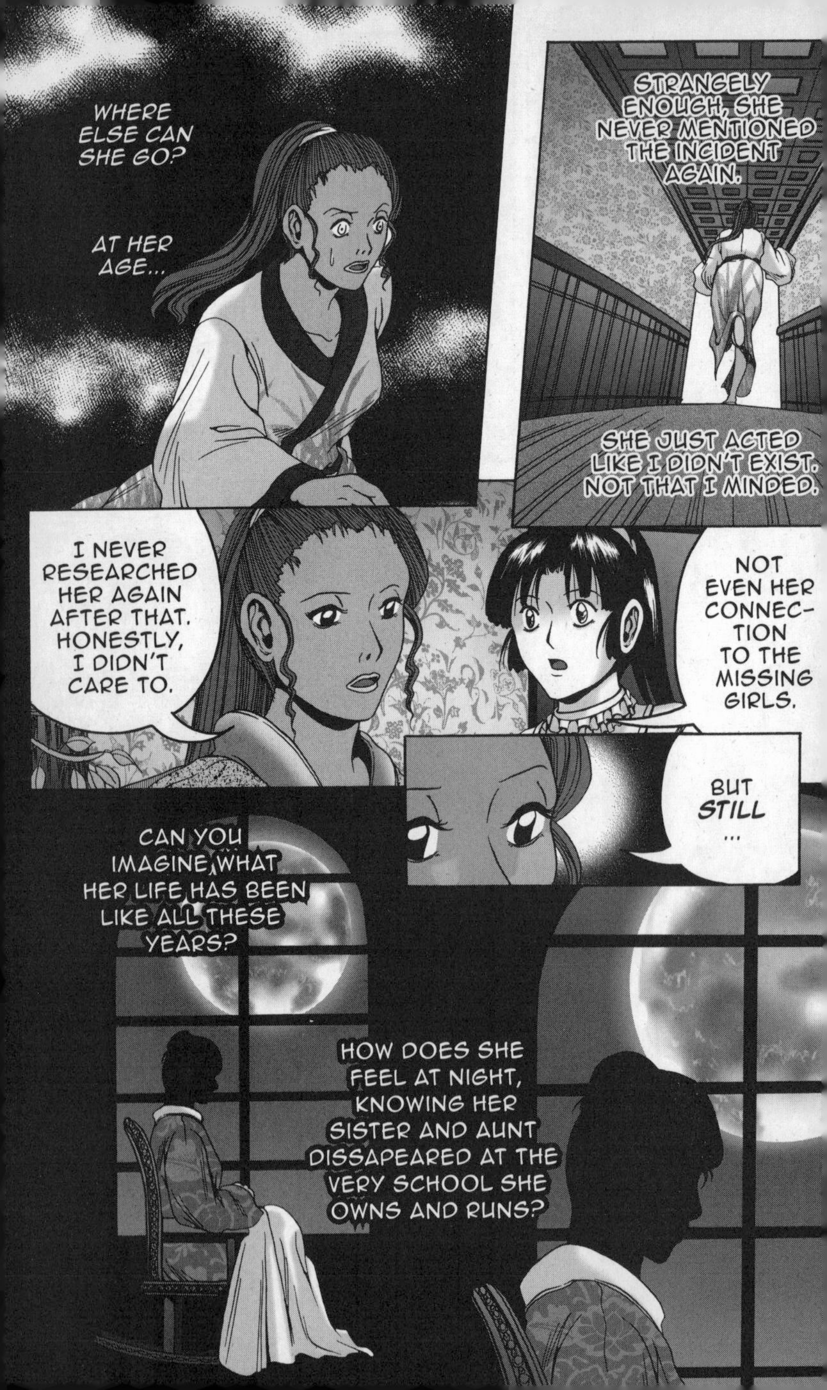

WHERE ELSE CAN SHE GO?
AT HER AGE...
STRANGELY ENOUGH, SHE NEVER MENTIONED THE INCIDENT AGAIN.
SHE JUST ACTED LIKE I DIDN'T EXIST. NOT THAT I MINDED.
I NEVER RESEARCHED HER AGAIN AFTER THAT. HONESTLY, I DIDN'T CARE TO.
NOT EVEN HER CONNECTION TO THE MISSING GIRLS.
BUT STILL ...
CAN YOU IMAGINE WHAT HER LIFE HAS BEEN LIKE ALL THESE YEARS?
HOW DOES SHE FEEL AT NIGHT, KNOWING HER SISTER AND AUNT DISSAPEARED AT THE VERY SCHOOL SHE OWNS AND RUNS?

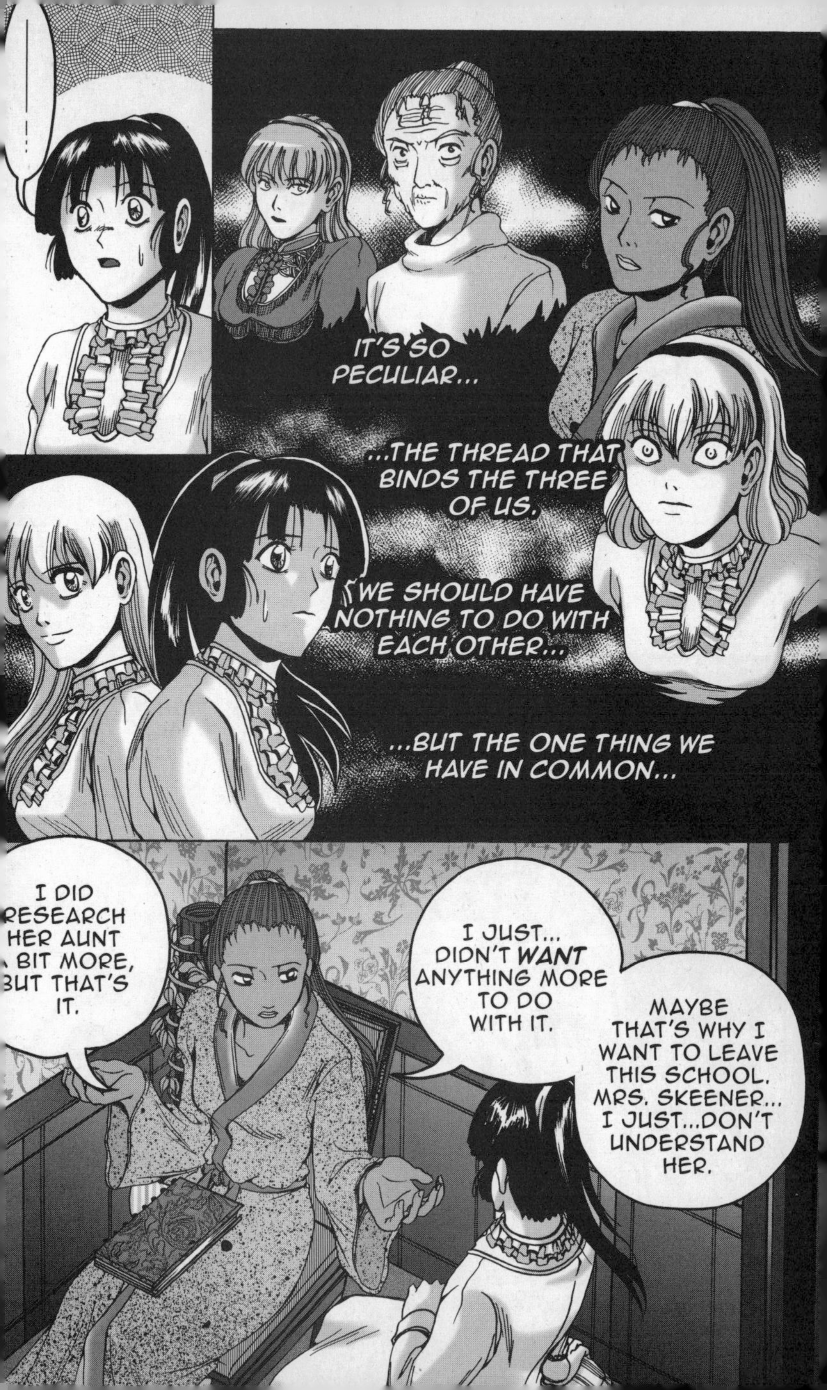

!
IT'S SO PECULIAR...
...THE THREAD THAT BINDS THE THREE OF US.
WE SHOULD HAVE NOTHING TO DO WITH EACH OTHER...
...BUT THE ONE THING WE HAVE IN COMMON...
I DID RESEARCH HER AUNT A BIT MORE, BUT THAT'S IT.
I JUST... DIDN'T WANT ANYTHING MORE TO DO WITH IT.
MAYBE THAT'S WHY I WANT TO LEAVE THIS SCHOOL. MRS. SKEENER... I JUST...DON'T UNDERSTAND HER.

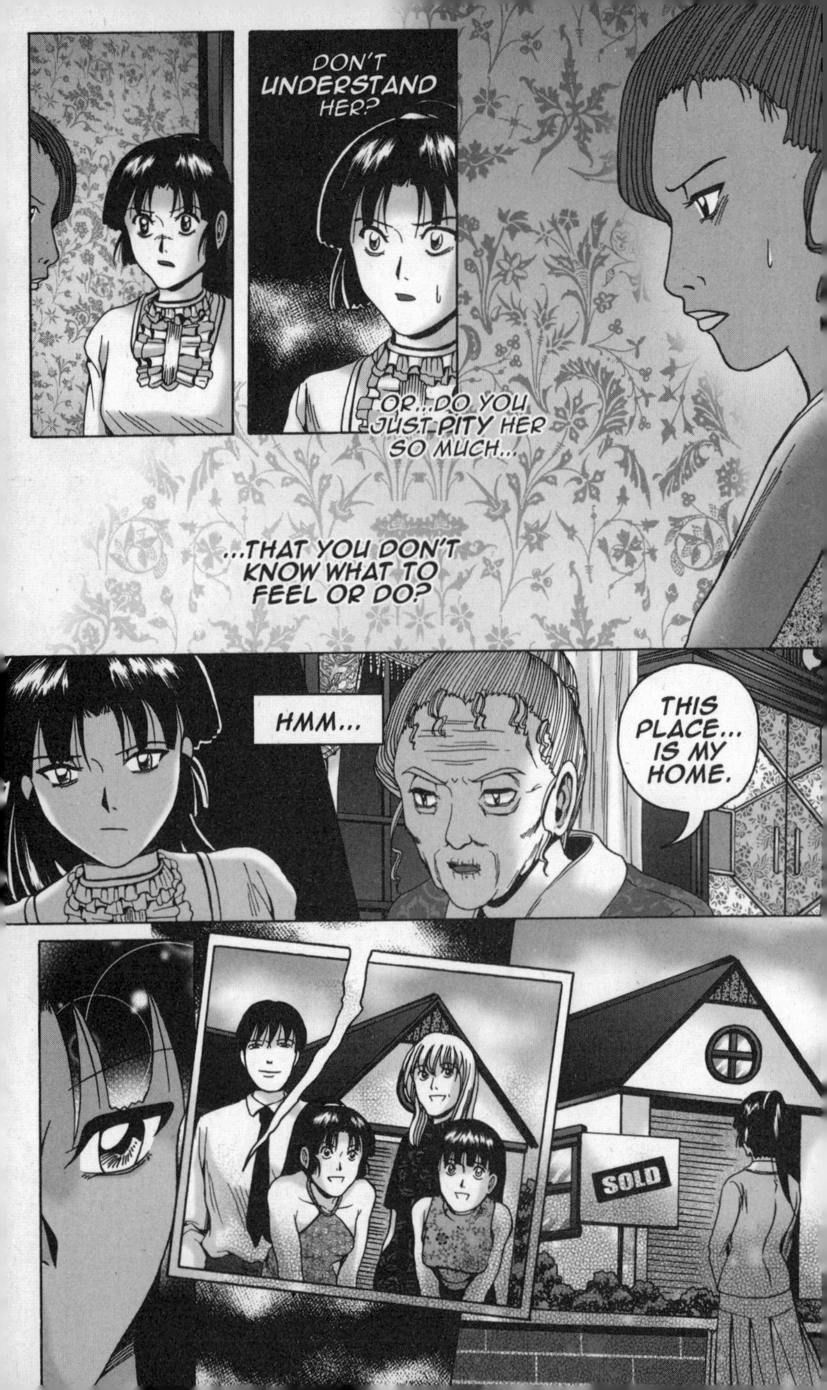
DON'T UNDERSTAND HER?
OR...DO YOU JUST PITY HER SO MUCH...
...THAT YOU DON'T KNOW WHAT TO FEEL OR DO?
HMM...
THIS PLACE... IS MY HOME.
SOLD

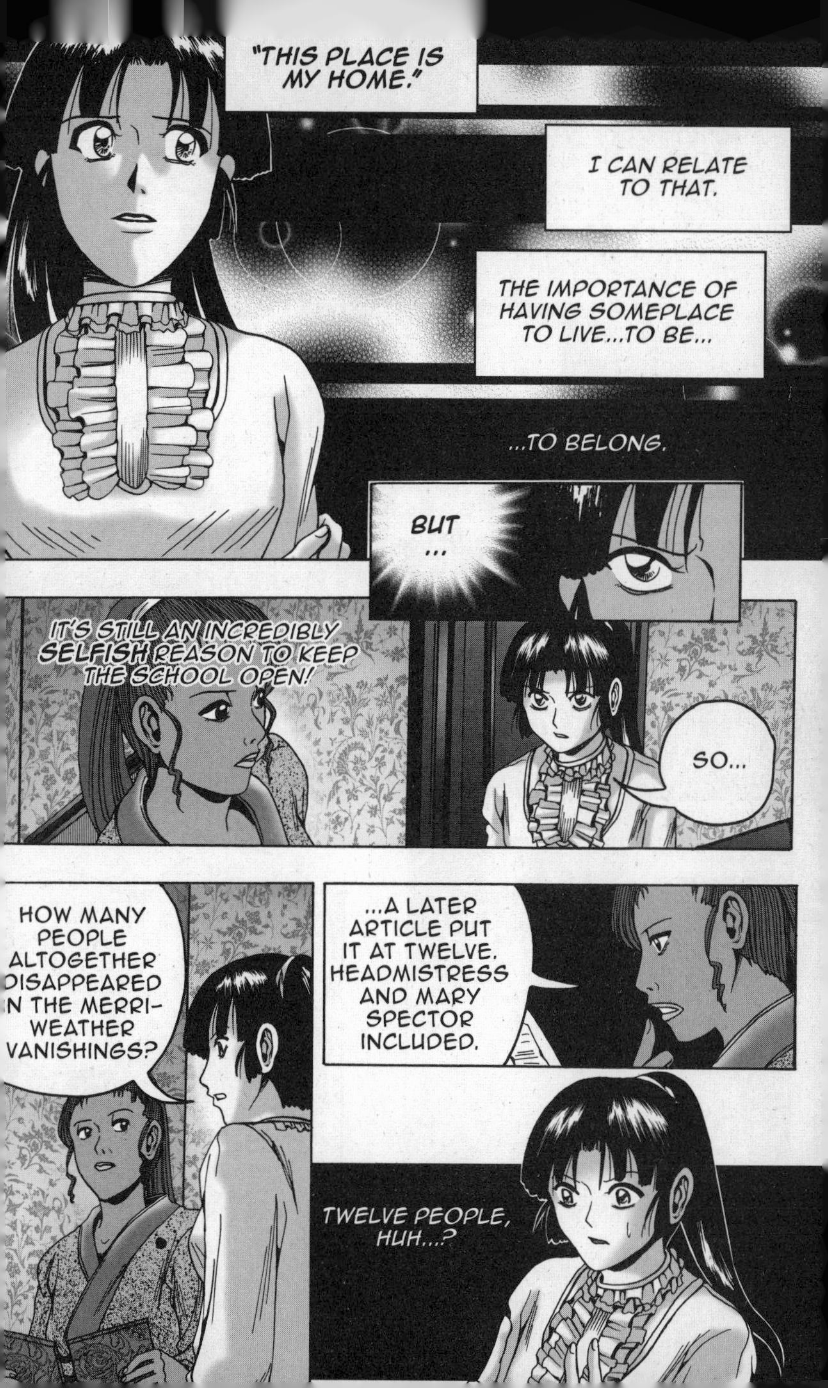
"THIS PLACE IS MY HOME."
I CAN RELATE TO THAT.
THE IMPORTANCE OF HAVING SOMEPLACE TO LIVE...TO BE...
...TO BELONG.
BUT ...
IT'S STILL AN INCREDIBLY SELFISH REASON TO KEEP THE SCHOOL OPEN!
SO...
HOW MANY PEOPLE ALTOGETHER DISAPPEARED IN THE MERRI-WEATHER VANISHINGS?
...A LATER ARTICLE PUT IT AT TWELVE. HEADMISTRESS AND MARY SPECTOR INCLUDED.
TWELVE PEOPLE, HUH...?

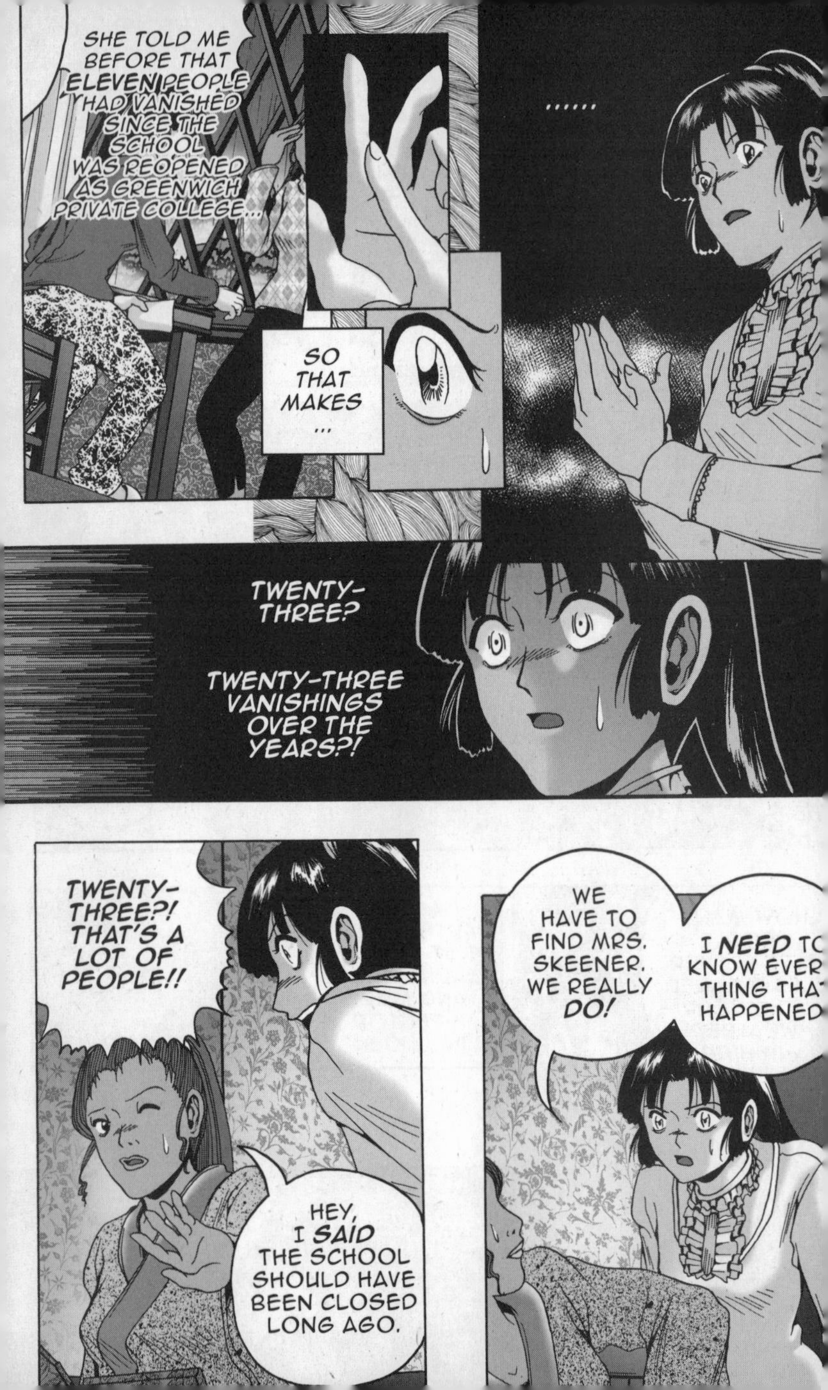
SHE TOLD ME BEFORE THAT ELEVEN PEOPLE HAD VANISHED SINCE THE SCHOOL WAS REOPENED AS GREENWICH PRIVATE COLLEGE...
SO THAT MAKES ...
......
TWENTY-THREE?
TWENTY-THREE VANISHINGS OVER THE YEARS?!
TWENTY-THREE?! THAT'S A LOT OF PEOPLE!!
HEY, I SAID THE SCHOOL SHOULD HAVE BEEN CLOSED LONG AGO.
WE HAVE TO FIND MRS. SKEENER. WE REALLY DO!
I NEED TO KNOW EVERYTHING THAT HAPPENED

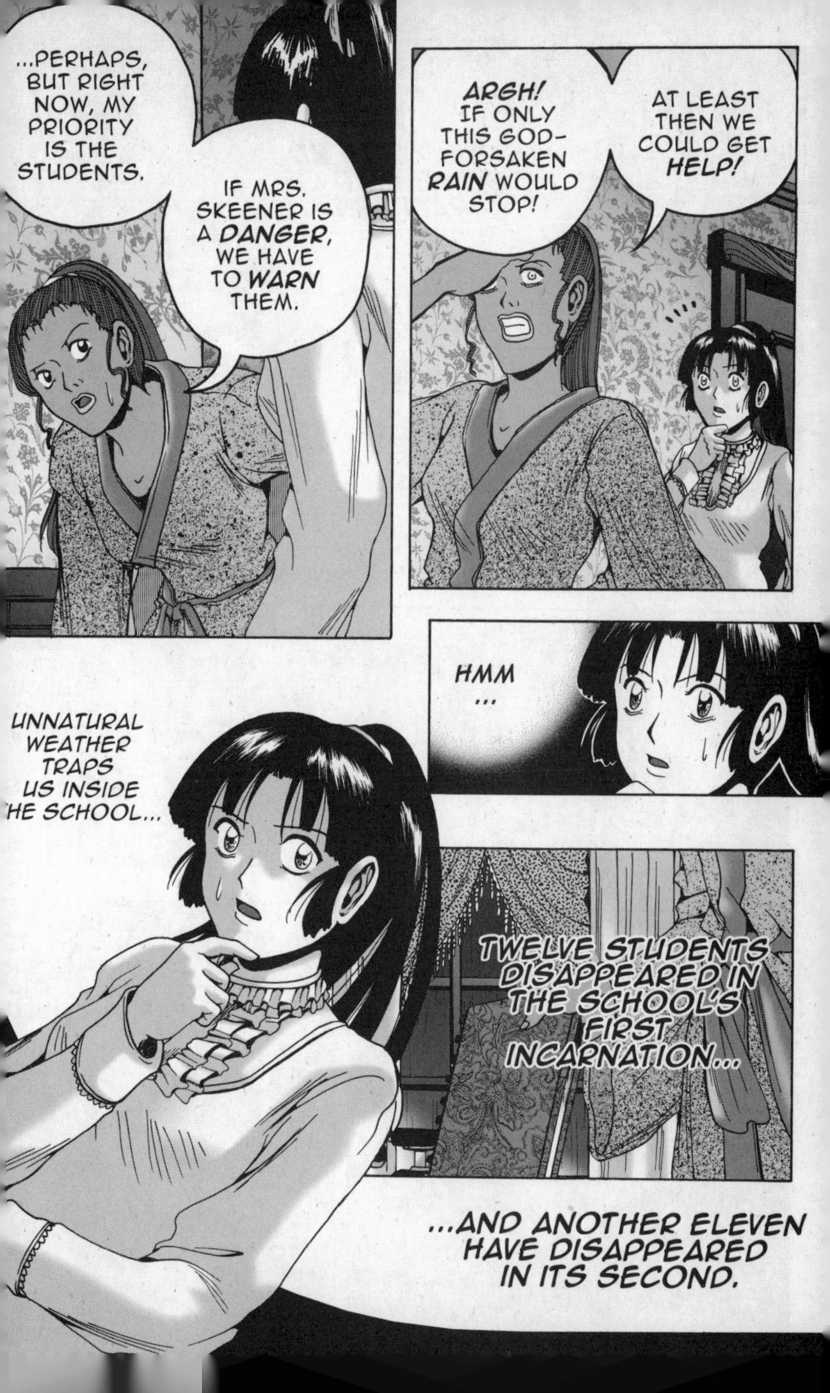
...PERHAPS, BUT RIGHT NOW, MY PRIORITY IS THE STUDENTS.
IF MRS. SKEENER IS A DANGER, WE HAVE TO WARN THEM.
ARGH! IF ONLY THIS GOD-FORSAKEN RAIN WOULD STOP!
AT LEAST THEN WE COULD GET HELP!
...
HMM ...
UNNATURAL WEATHER TRAPS US INSIDE THE SCHOOL...
TWELVE STUDENTS DISAPPEARED IN THE SCHOOL'S FIRST INCARNATION...
...AND ANOTHER ELEVEN HAVE DISAPPEARED IN ITS SECOND.

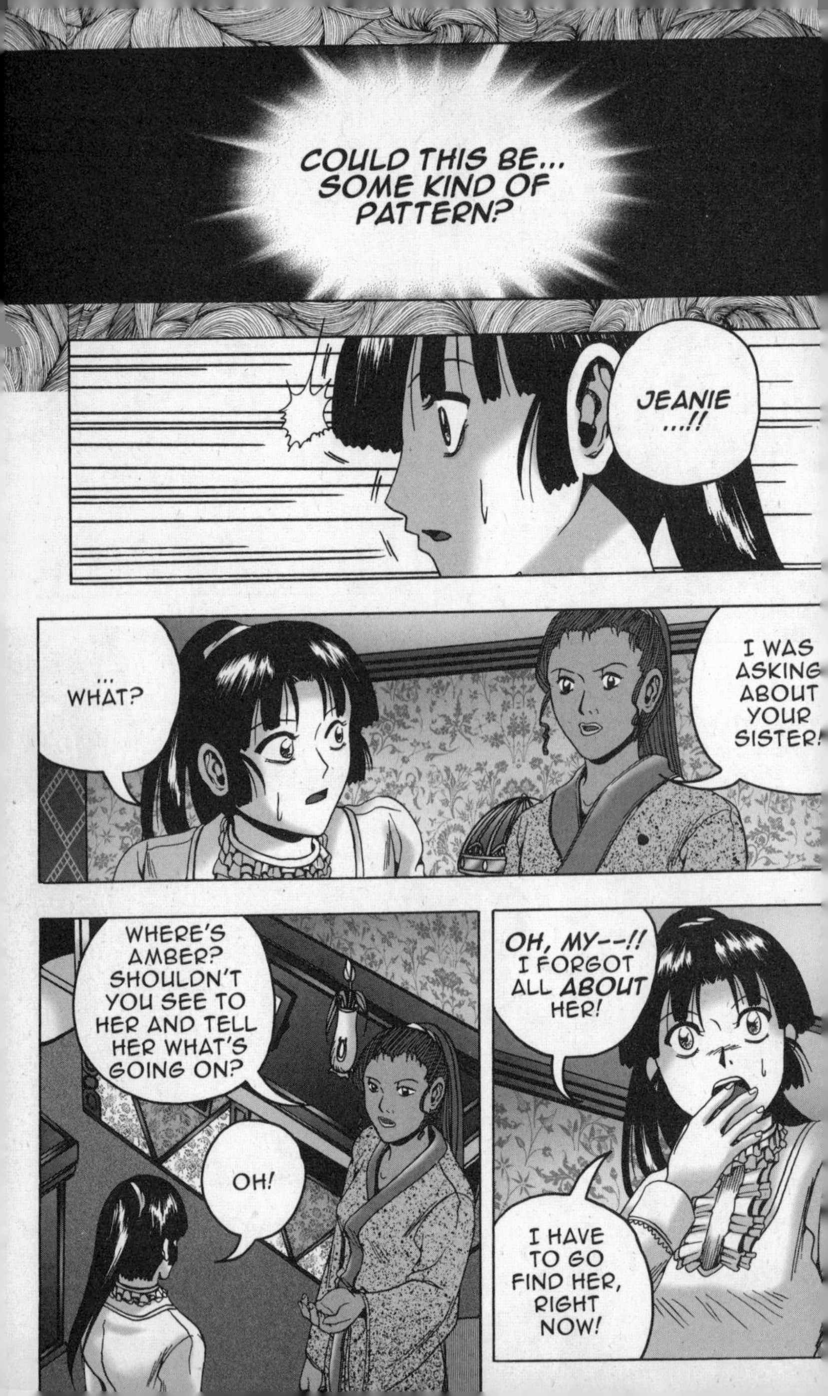
COULD THIS BE... SOME KIND OF PATTERN?
JEANIE ...!!
... WHAT?
I WAS ASKING ABOUT YOUR SISTER!
WHERE'S AMBER? SHOULDN'T YOU SEE TO HER AND TELL HER WHAT'S GOING ON?
OH!
OH, MY--!! I FORGOT ALL ABOUT HER!
I HAVE TO GO FIND HER, RIGHT NOW!

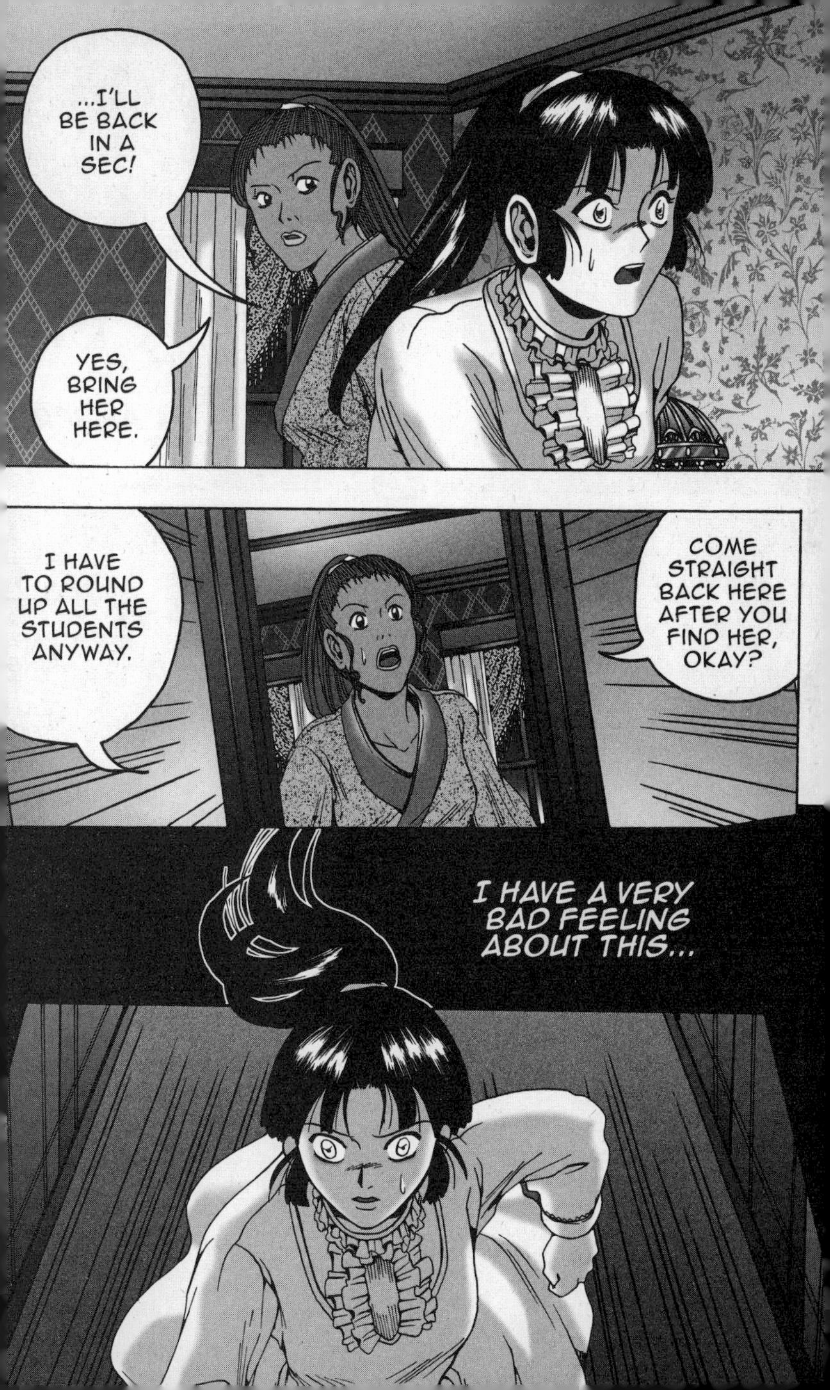
...I'LL BE BACK IN A SEC!
YES, BRING HER HERE.
I HAVE TO ROUND UP ALL THE STUDENTS ANYWAY.
COME STRAIGHT BACK HERE AFTER YOU FIND HER, OKAY?
I HAVE A VERY BAD FEELING ABOUT THIS...

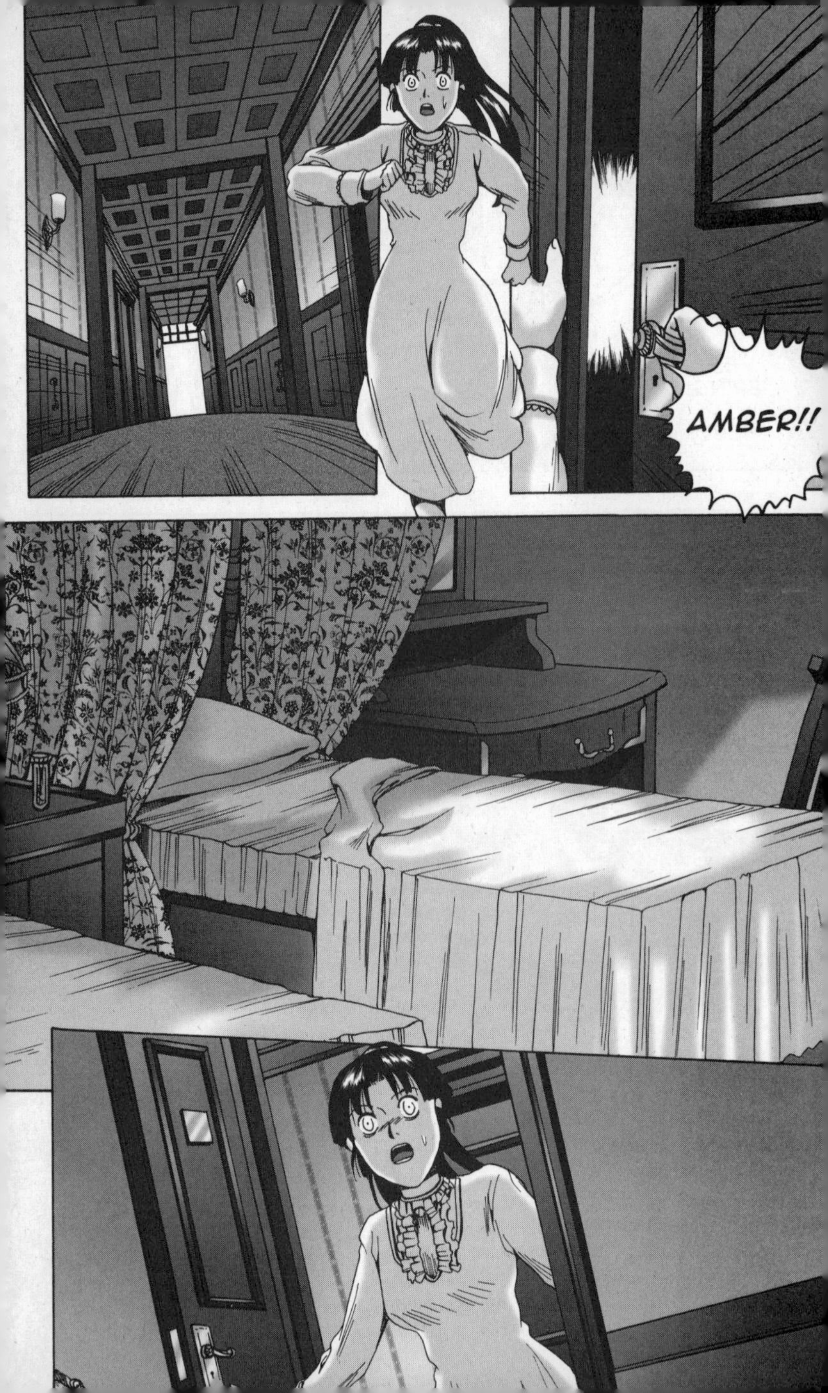
AMBER!!

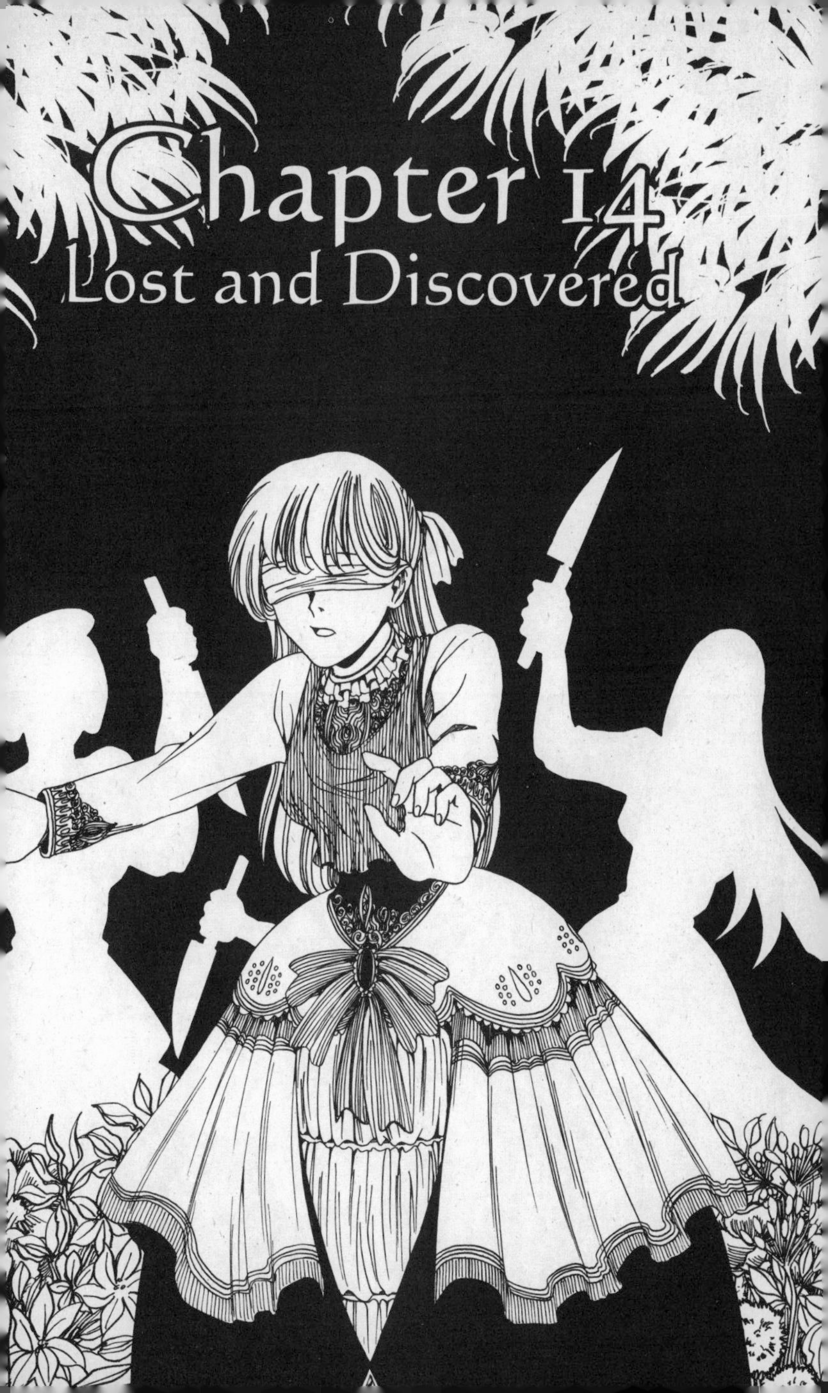
Chapter 14
Lost and Discovered

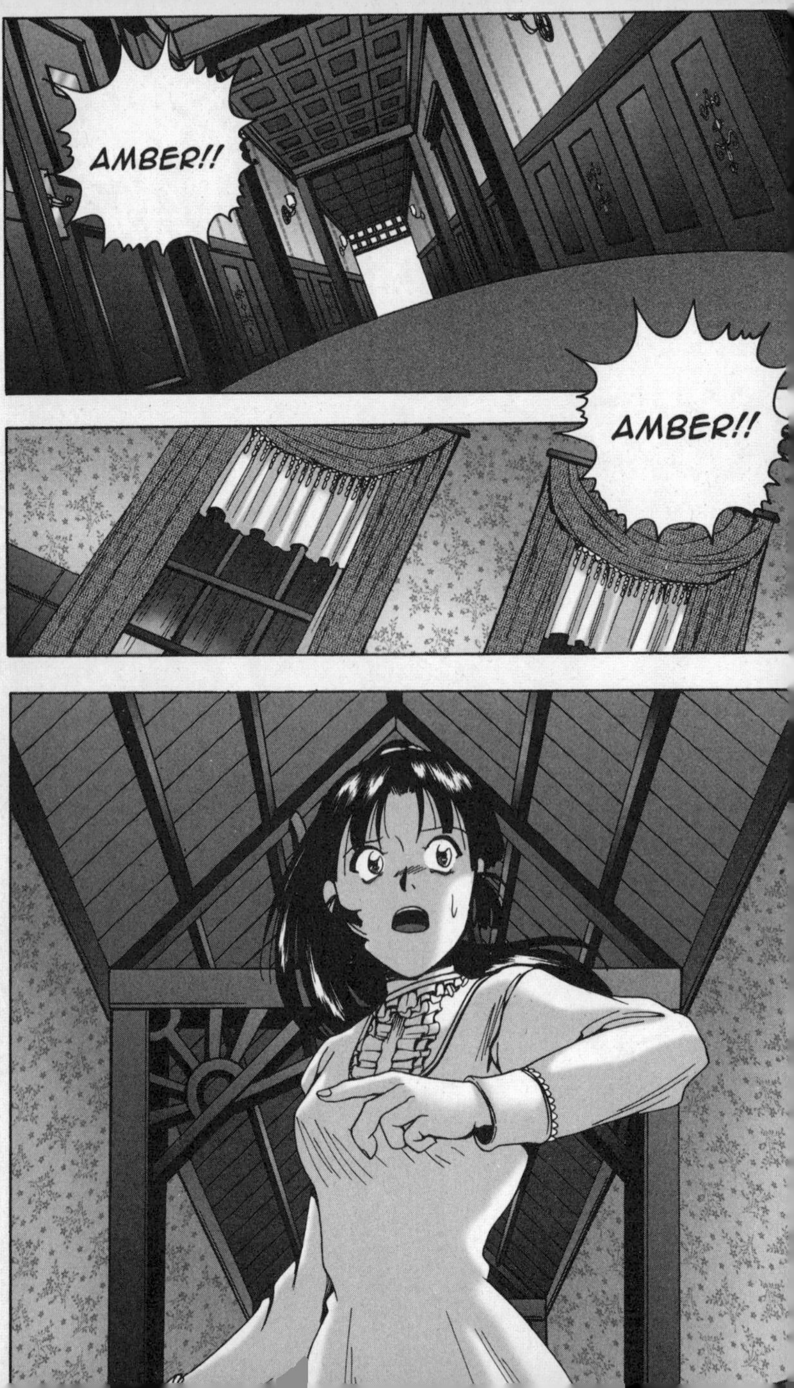
AMBER!!
AMBER!!

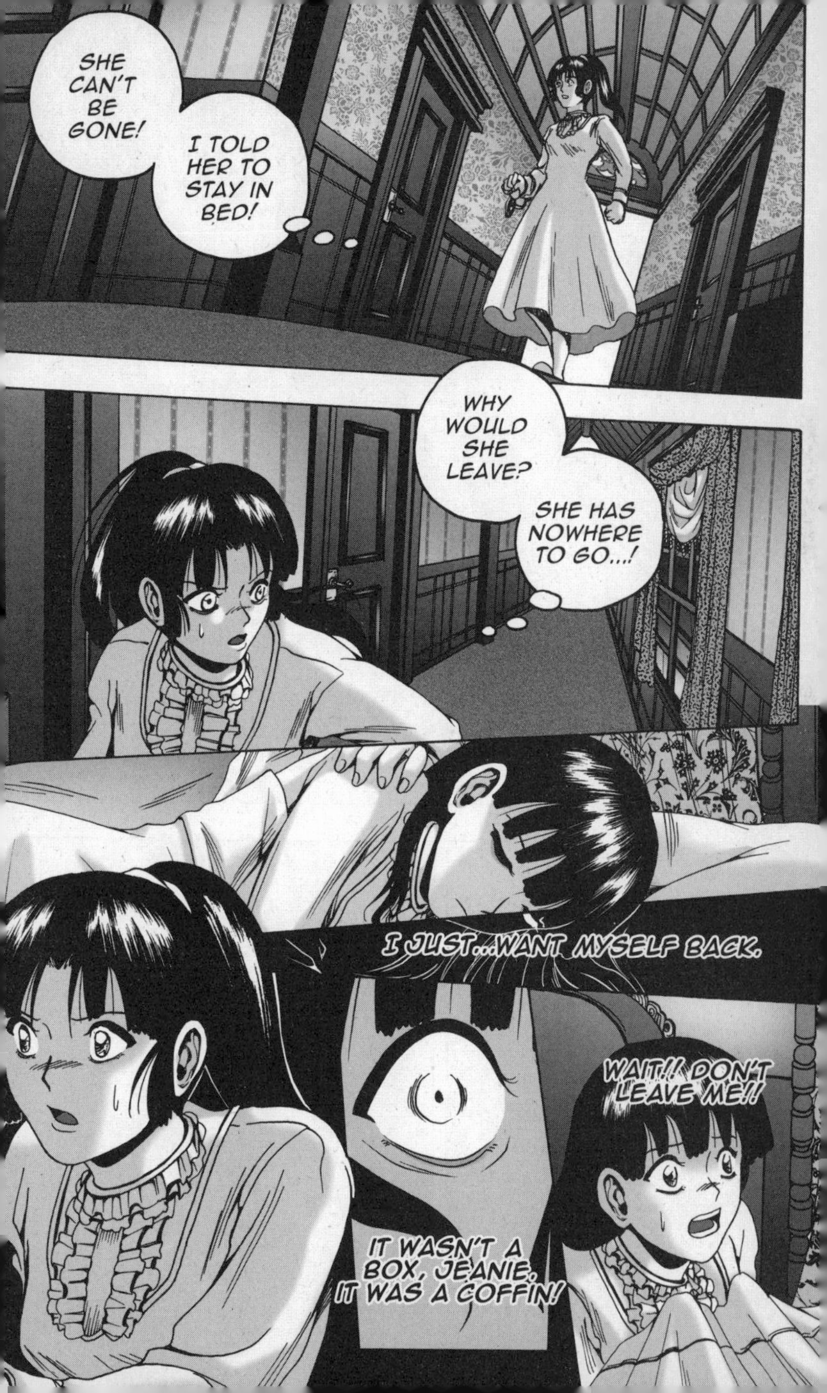
SHE CAN'T BE GONE!
I TOLD HER TO STAY IN BED!
WHY WOULD SHE LEAVE?
SHE HAS NOWHERE TO GO...!
I JUST...WANT MYSELF BACK.
WAIT!! DON'T LEAVE ME!!
IT WASN'T A BOX, JEANIE, IT WAS A COFFIN!

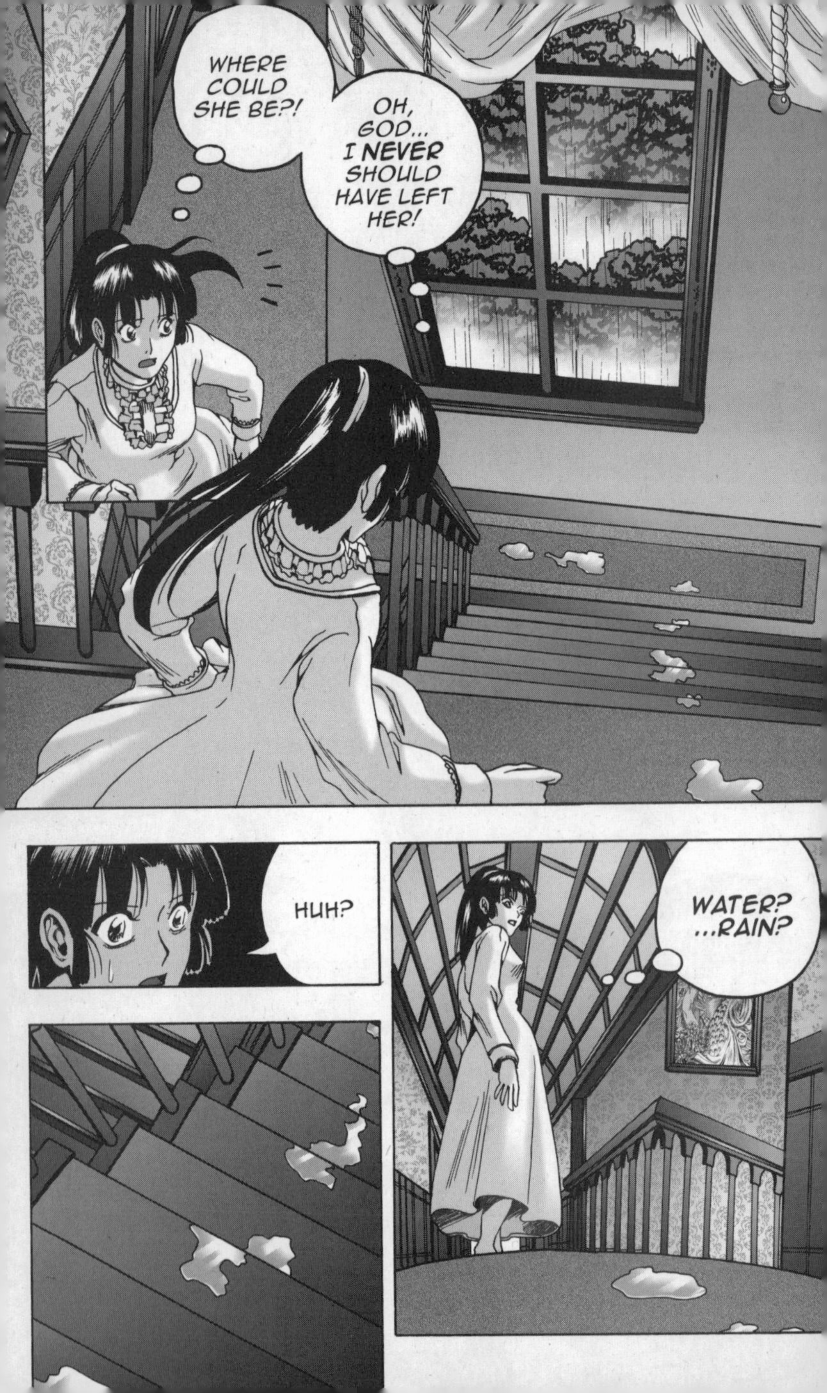
WHERE COULD SHE BE?!
OH, GOD... I NEVER SHOULD HAVE LEFT HER!
HUH?
WATER? ...RAIN?

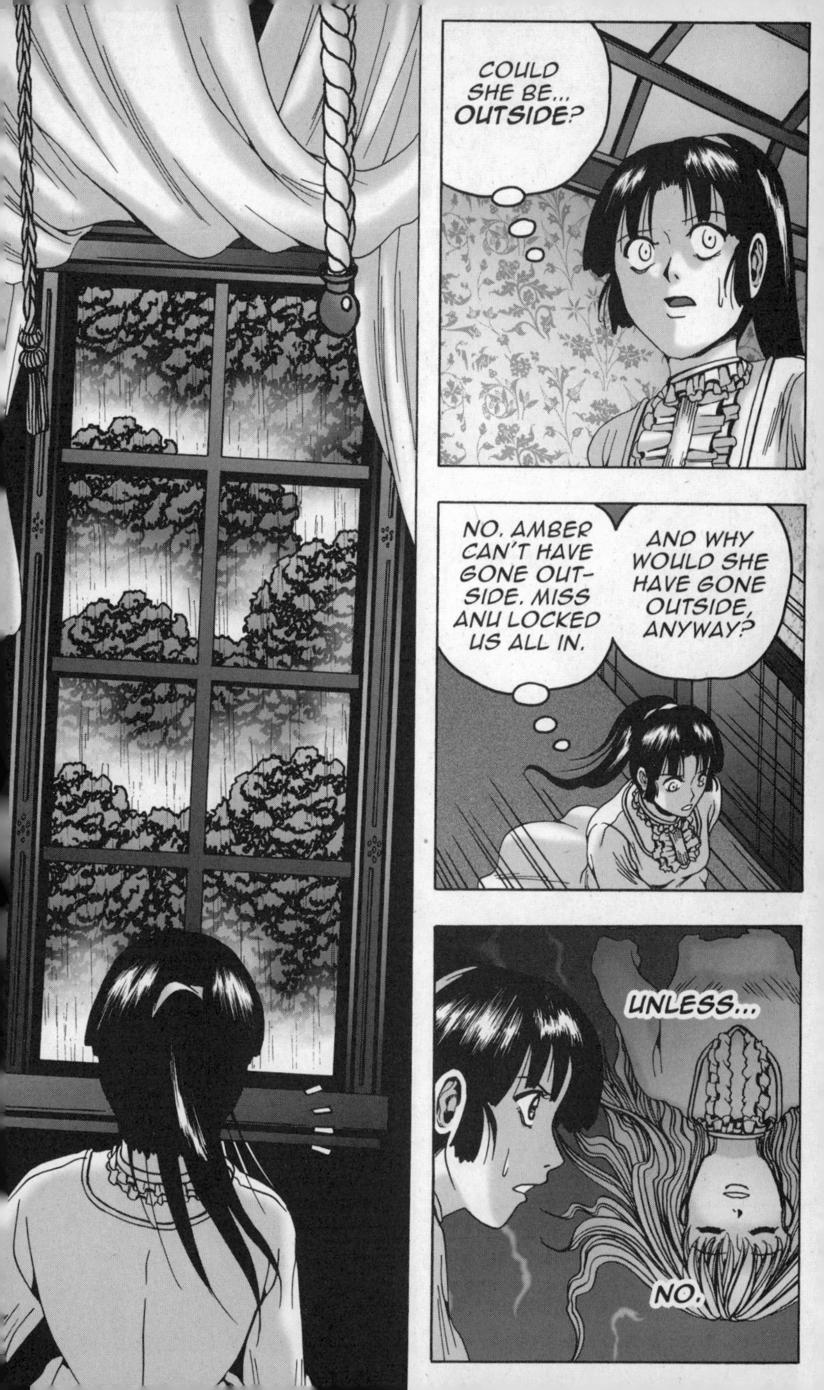
COULD SHE BE... OUTSIDE?
NO. AMBER CAN'T HAVE GONE OUT-SIDE. MISS ANU LOCKED US ALL IN.
AND WHY WOULD SHE HAVE GONE OUTSIDE, ANYWAY?
UNLESS...
NO.

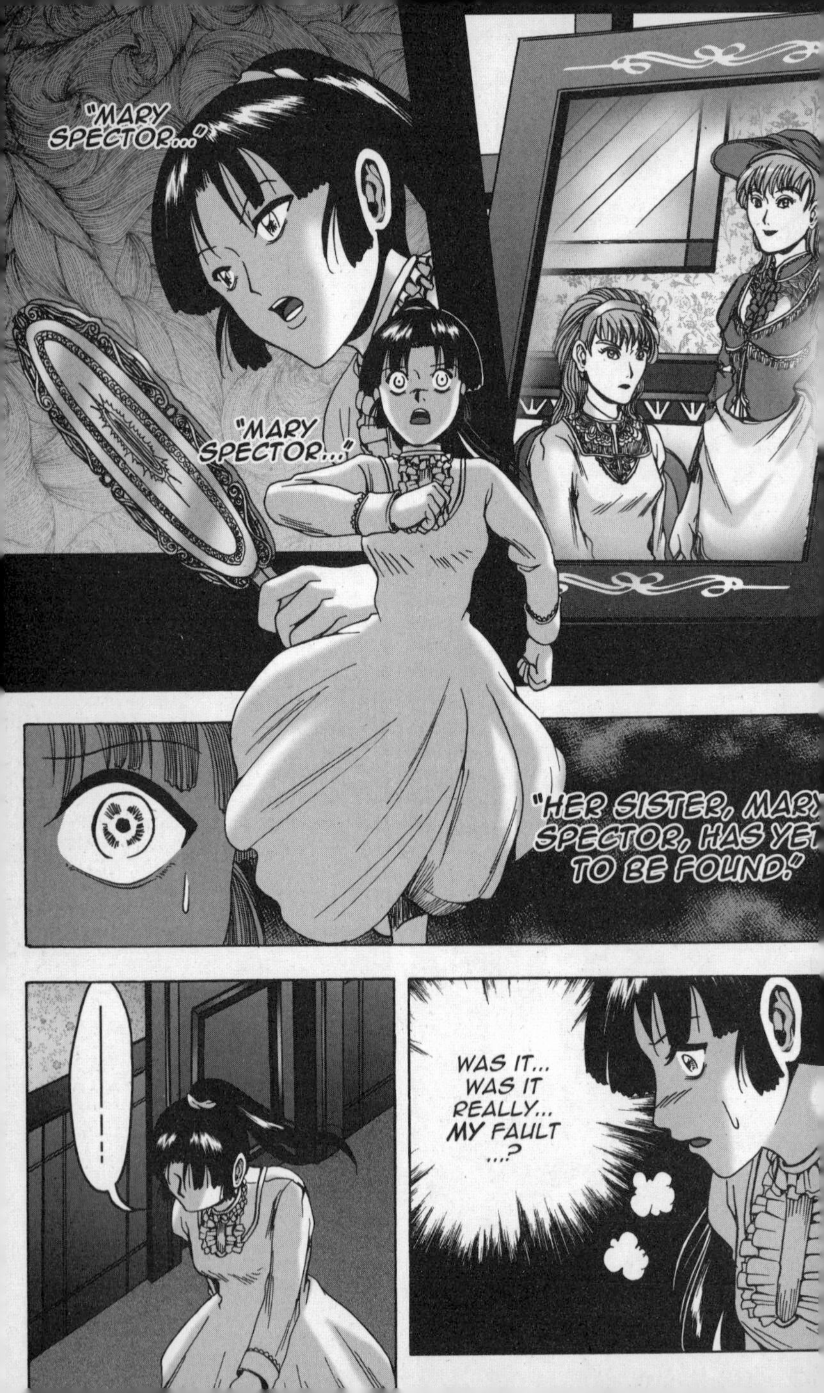
"MARY SPECTOR..."
"MARY SPECTOR..."
"HER SISTER, MARY SPECTOR, HAS YET TO BE FOUND."
!
WAS IT... WAS IT REALLY... MY FAULT ...?

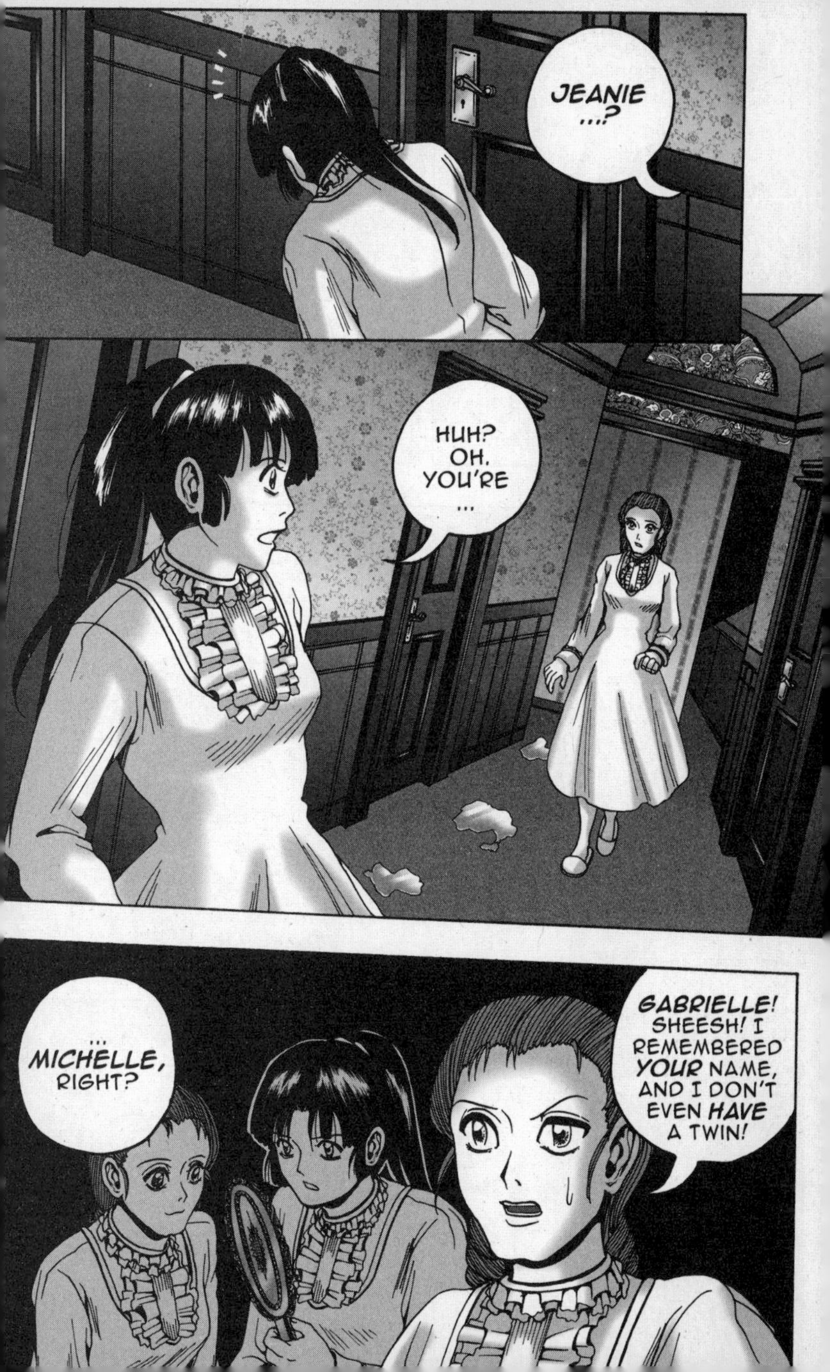

JEANIE ...?
HUH? OH. YOU'RE ...
... MICHELLE, RIGHT?
GABRIELLE! SHEESH! I REMEMBERED YOUR NAME, AND I DON'T EVEN HAVE A TWIN!

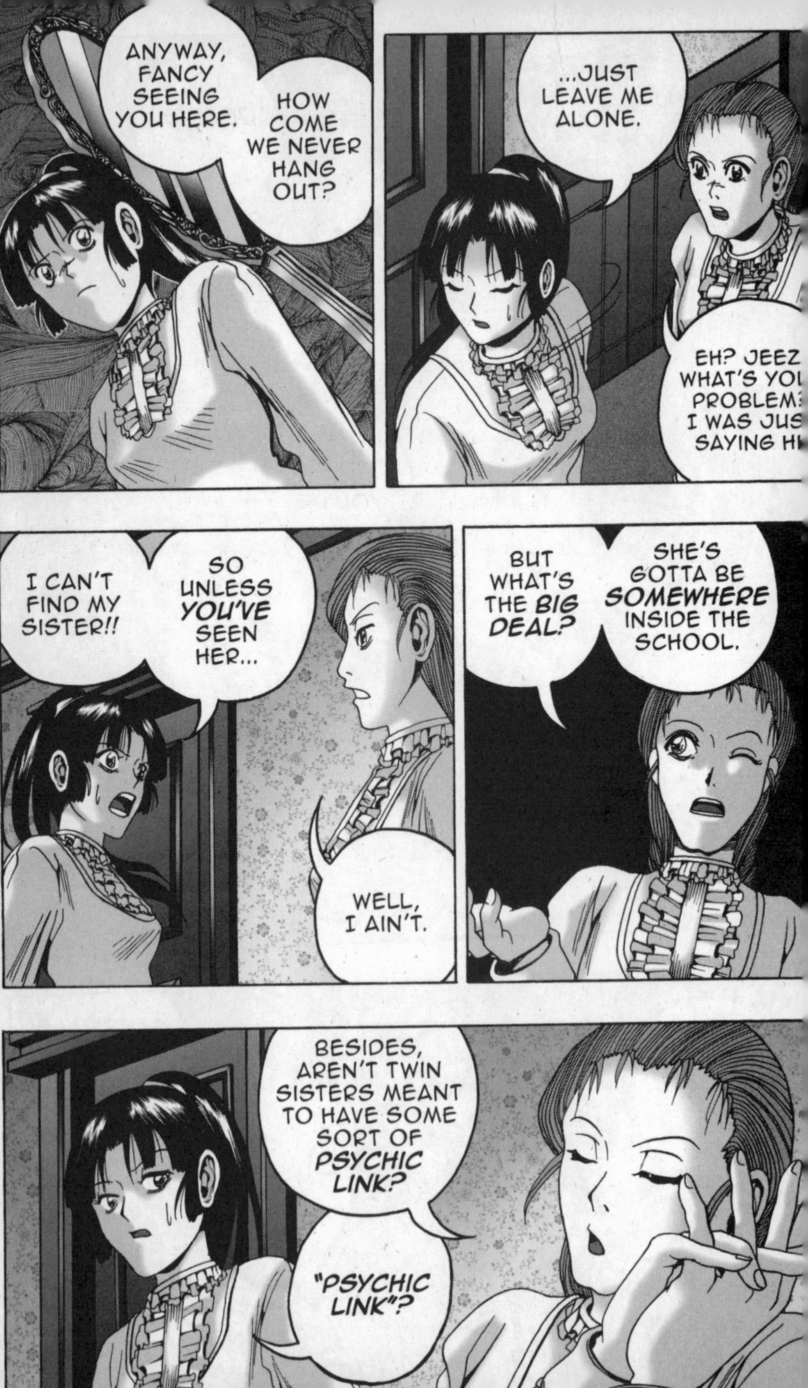

ANYWAY, FANCY SEEING YOU HERE.
HOW COME WE NEVER HANG OUT?
...JUST LEAVE ME ALONE.
EH? JEEZ WHAT'S YO PROBLEM? I WAS JUS SAYING H
I CAN'T FIND MY SISTER!!
SO UNLESS *YOU'VE* SEEN HER...
WELL, I AIN'T.
BUT WHAT'S THE *BIG DEAL?*
SHE'S GOTTA BE *SOMEWHERE* INSIDE THE SCHOOL.
BESIDES, AREN'T TWIN SISTERS MEANT TO HAVE SOME SORT OF *PSYCHIC LINK?*
"PSYCHIC LINK"?

WELL, IF *YOU* DON'T KNOW WHERE SHE IS...

...HOW WOULD ANYONE *ELSE* KNOW?

YOU KNOW ...

AMBER AND I HAVE ALWAYS DONE EVERYTHING TOGETHER, SINCE WE WERE KIDS.

PEOPLE ALWAYS SAY WE'RE "INSEPARABLE," BUT... WE'VE NEVER BEEN REALLY CLOSE.

I MEAN, WE DID HANG AROUND WITH THE SAME PEOPLE AT SCHOOL...

...BUT EVEN THAT WAS MORE A CASE OF ME MAKING FRIENDS, AND AMBER TAGGING ALONG.

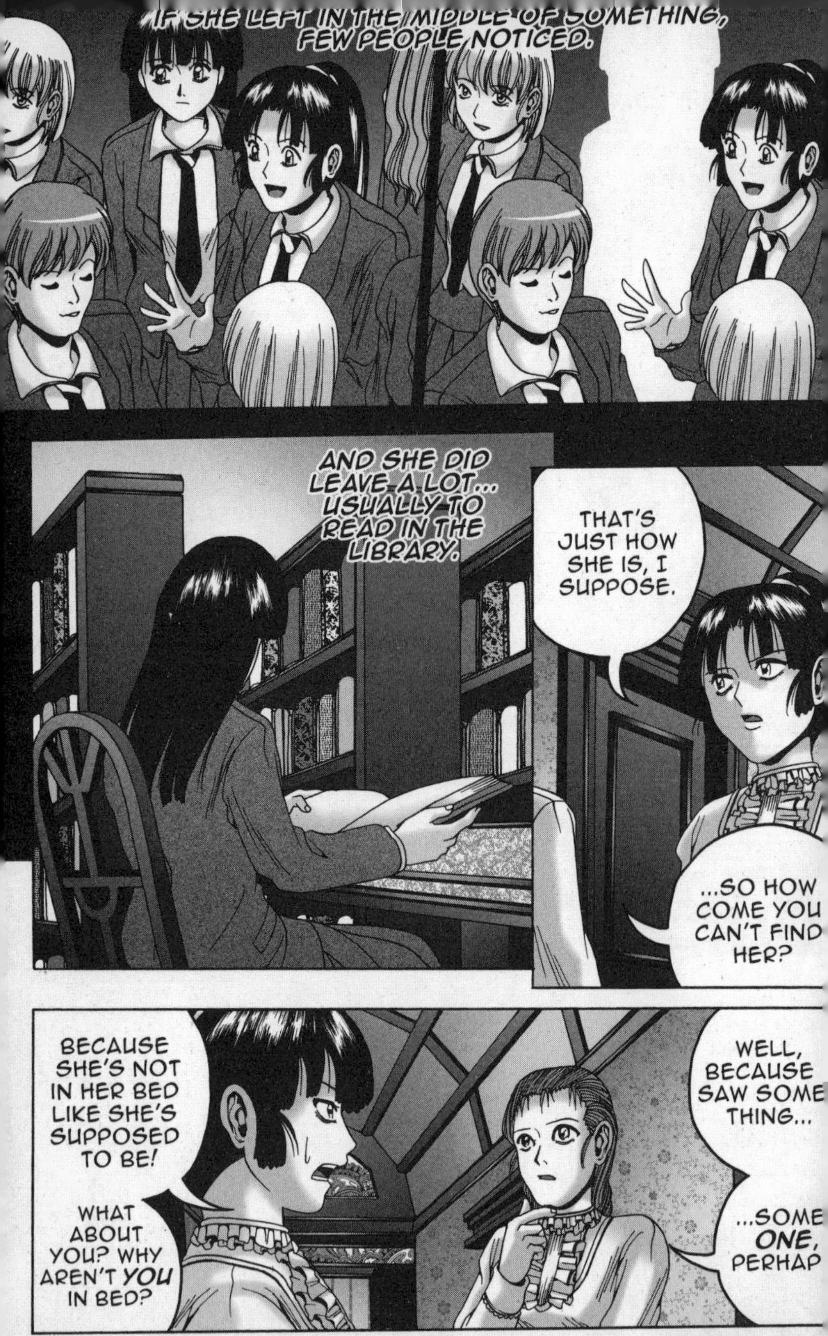

IF SHE LEFT IN THE MIDDLE OF SOMETHING, FEW PEOPLE NOTICED.
AND SHE DID LEAVE A LOT... USUALLY TO READ IN THE LIBRARY.
THAT'S JUST HOW SHE IS, I SUPPOSE.
...SO HOW COME YOU CAN'T FIND HER?
BECAUSE SHE'S NOT IN HER BED LIKE SHE'S SUPPOSED TO BE!
WHAT ABOUT YOU? WHY AREN'T YOU IN BED?
WELL, BECAUSE SAW SOME THING...
...SOME ONE, PERHAP

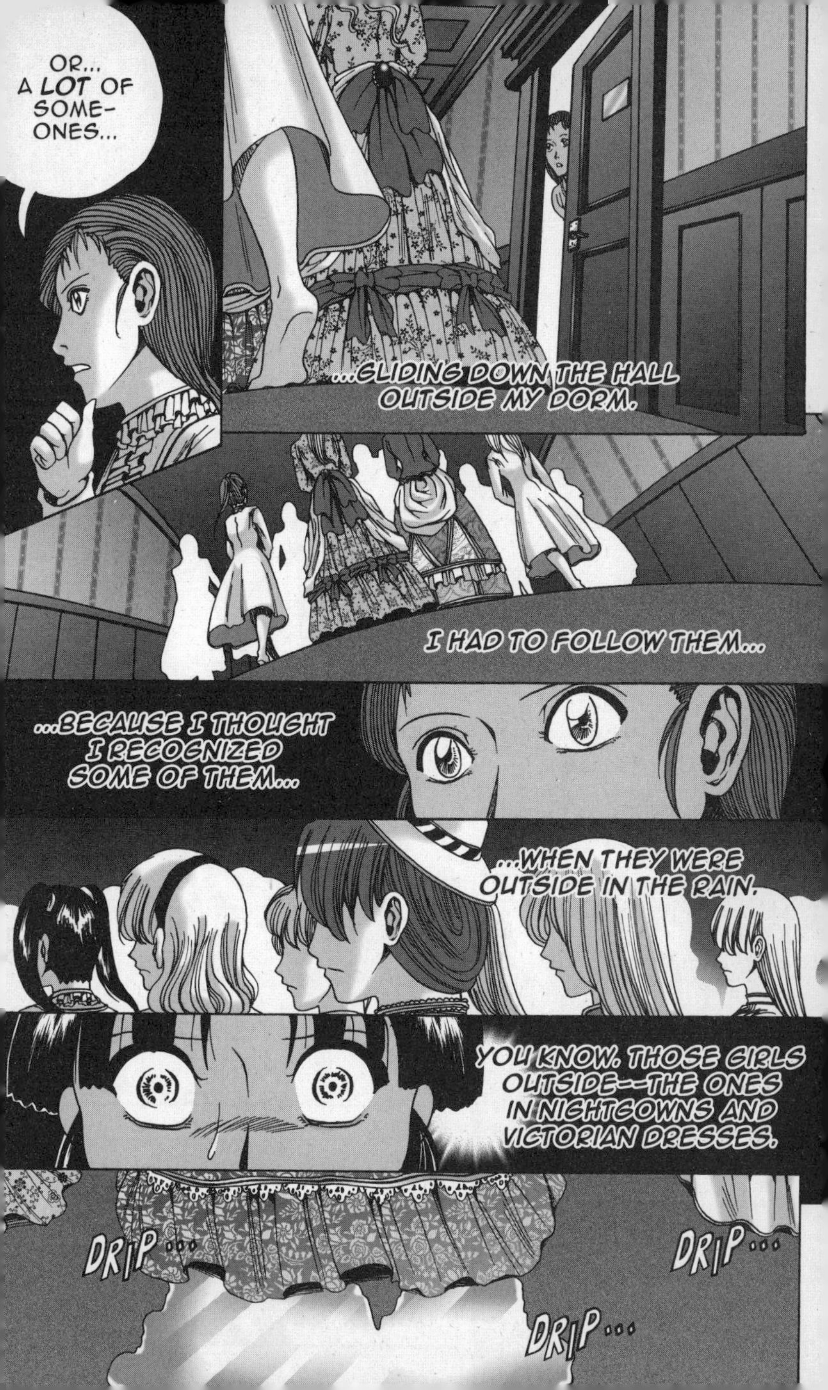
OR... A LOT OF SOME-ONES...
...GLIDING DOWN THE HALL OUTSIDE MY DORM.
I HAD TO FOLLOW THEM...
...BECAUSE I THOUGHT I RECOGNIZED SOME OF THEM...
...WHEN THEY WERE OUTSIDE IN THE RAIN.
YOU KNOW. THOSE GIRLS OUTSIDE--THE ONES IN NIGHTGOWNS AND VICTORIAN DRESSES.
DRIP...
DRIP...
DRIP...

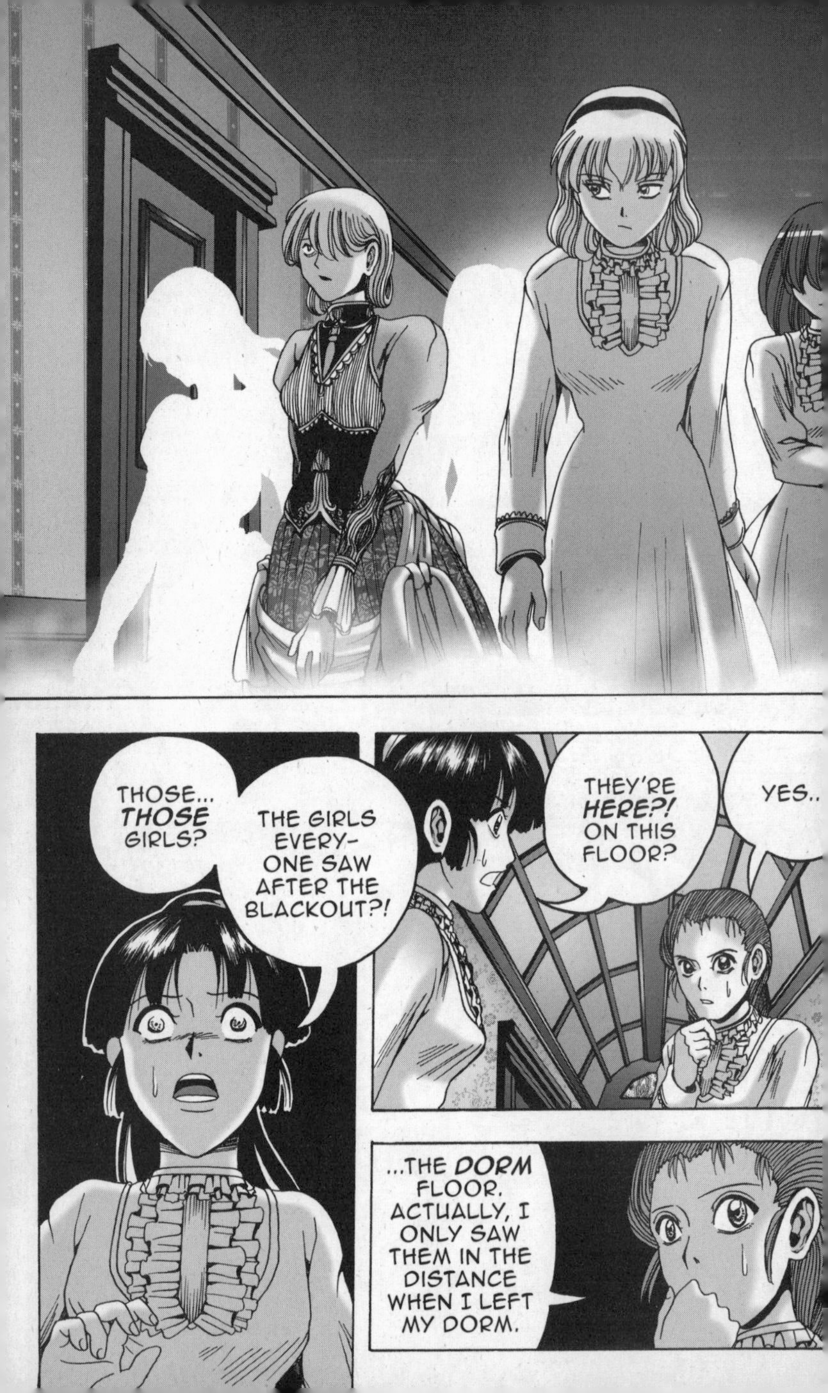
THOSE... *THOSE* GIRLS?
THE GIRLS EVERY-ONE SAW AFTER THE BLACKOUT?!
THEY'RE *HERE?!* ON THIS FLOOR?
YES...
...THE *DORM* FLOOR. ACTUALLY, I ONLY SAW THEM IN THE DISTANCE WHEN I LEFT MY DORM.

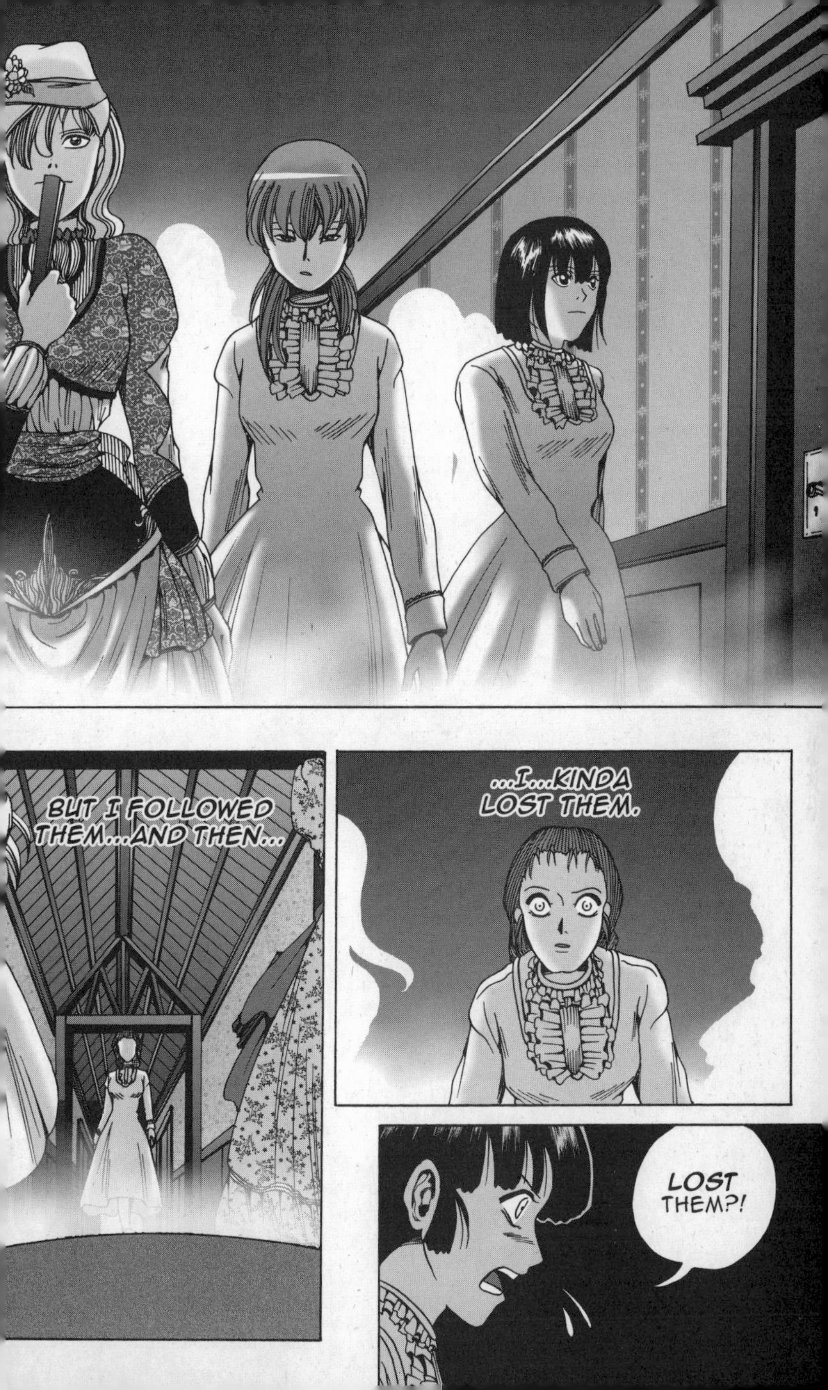
BUT I FOLLOWED THEM...AND THEN...
...I...KINDA LOST THEM.
LOST THEM?!

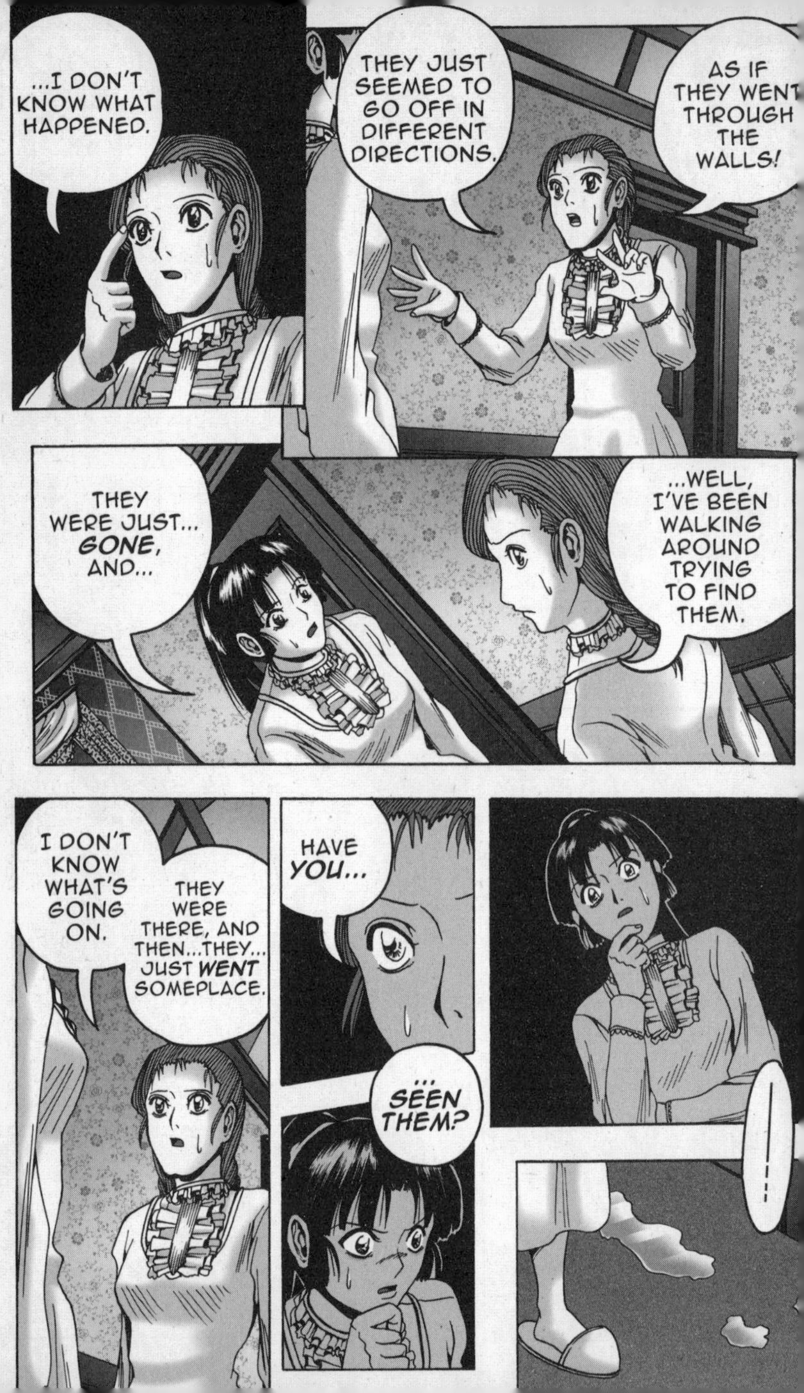
...I DON'T KNOW WHAT HAPPENED.
THEY JUST SEEMED TO GO OFF IN DIFFERENT DIRECTIONS.
AS IF THEY WENT THROUGH THE WALLS!
THEY WERE JUST... *GONE*, AND...
...WELL, I'VE BEEN WALKING AROUND TRYING TO FIND THEM.
I DON'T KNOW WHAT'S GOING ON.
THEY WERE THERE, AND THEN...THEY... JUST *WENT* SOMEPLACE.
HAVE *YOU*...
...*SEEN THEM?*
.........!!

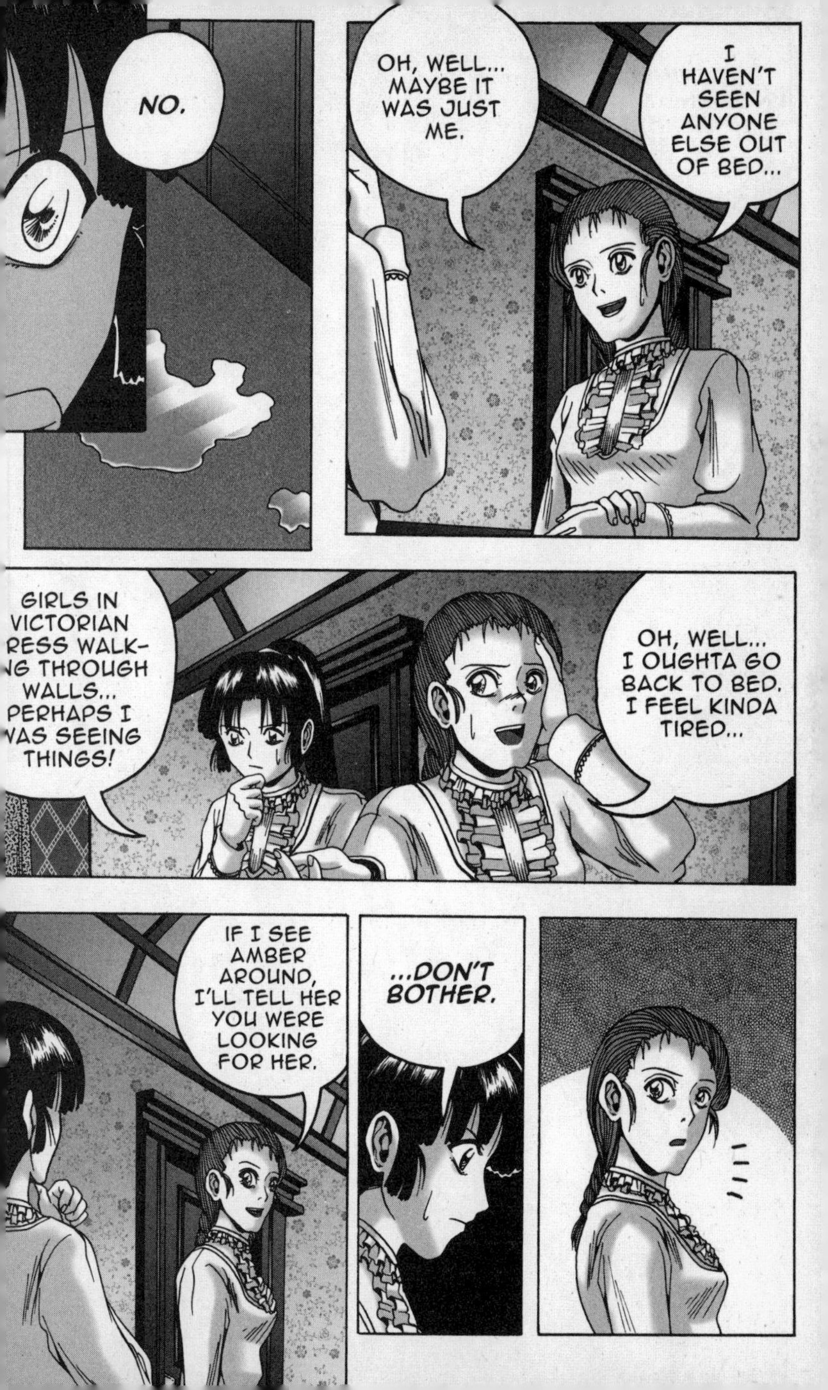
NO.
OH, WELL... MAYBE IT WAS JUST ME.
I HAVEN'T SEEN ANYONE ELSE OUT OF BED...
GIRLS IN VICTORIAN RESS WALK- NG THROUGH WALLS... PERHAPS I VAS SEEING THINGS!
OH, WELL... I OUGHTA GO BACK TO BED. I FEEL KINDA TIRED...
IF I SEE AMBER AROUND, I'LL TELL HER YOU WERE LOOKING FOR HER.
...DON'T BOTHER.

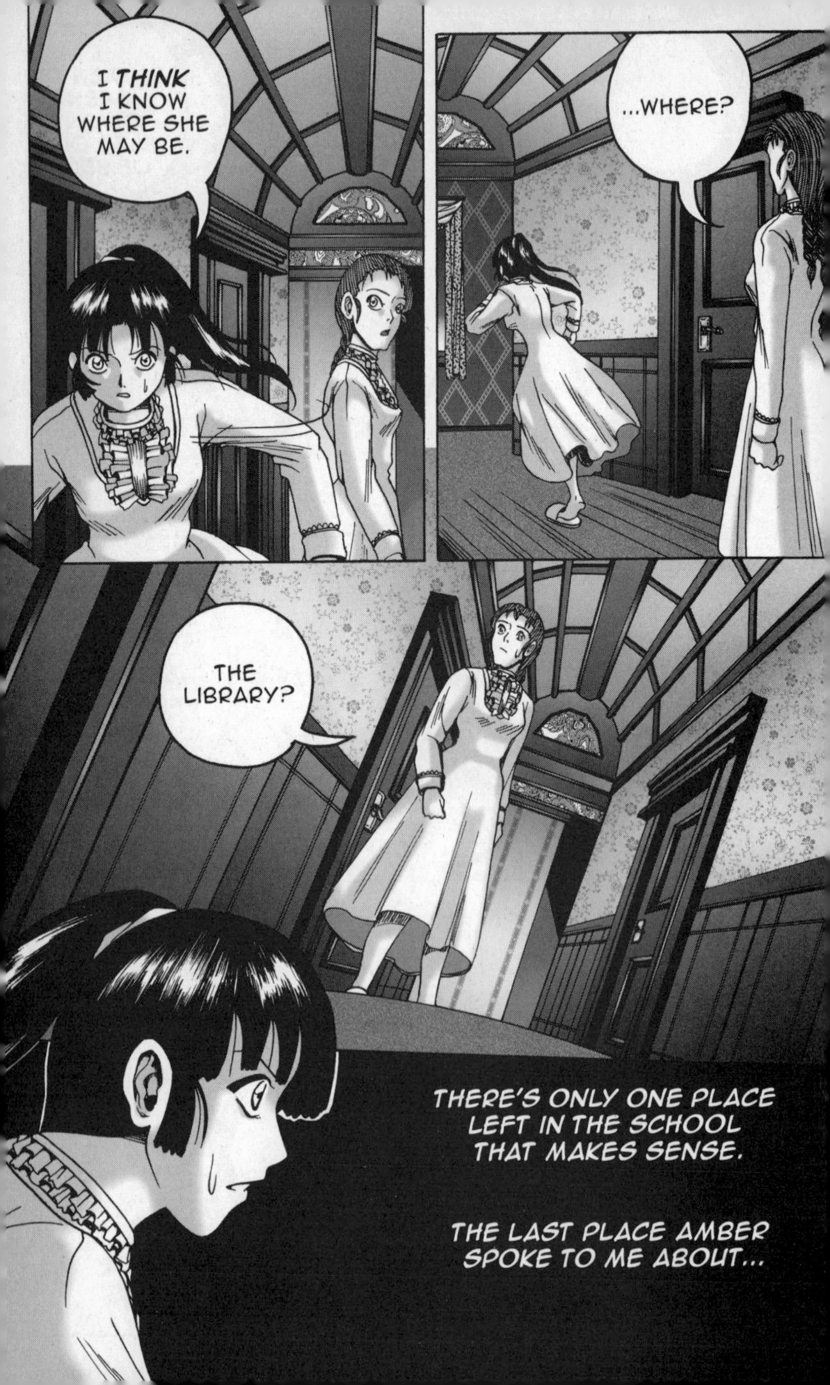
I *THINK* I KNOW WHERE SHE MAY BE.
...WHERE?
THE LIBRARY?
THERE'S ONLY ONE PLACE LEFT IN THE SCHOOL THAT MAKES SENSE.
THE LAST PLACE AMBER SPOKE TO ME ABOUT...

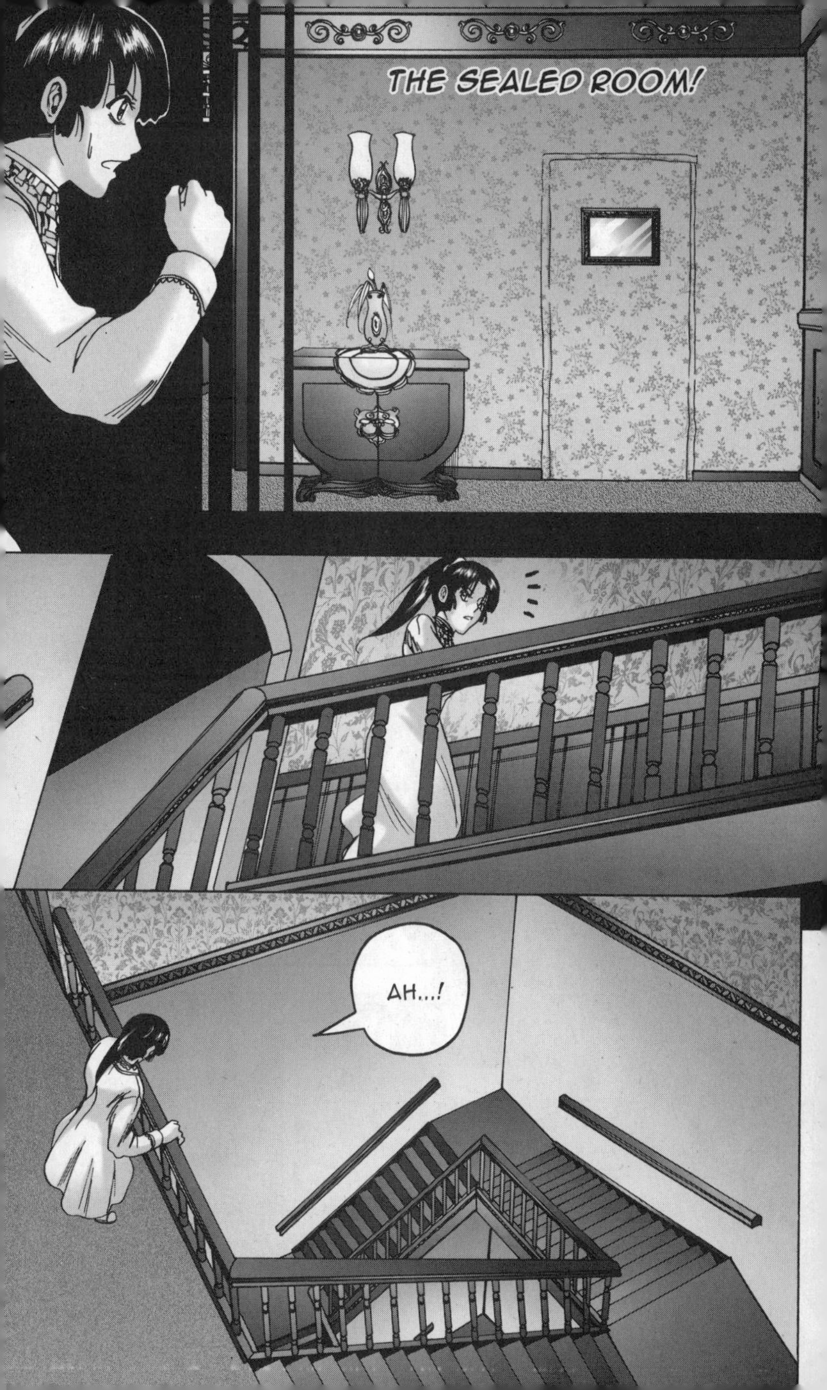
THE SEALED ROOM!
AH...!

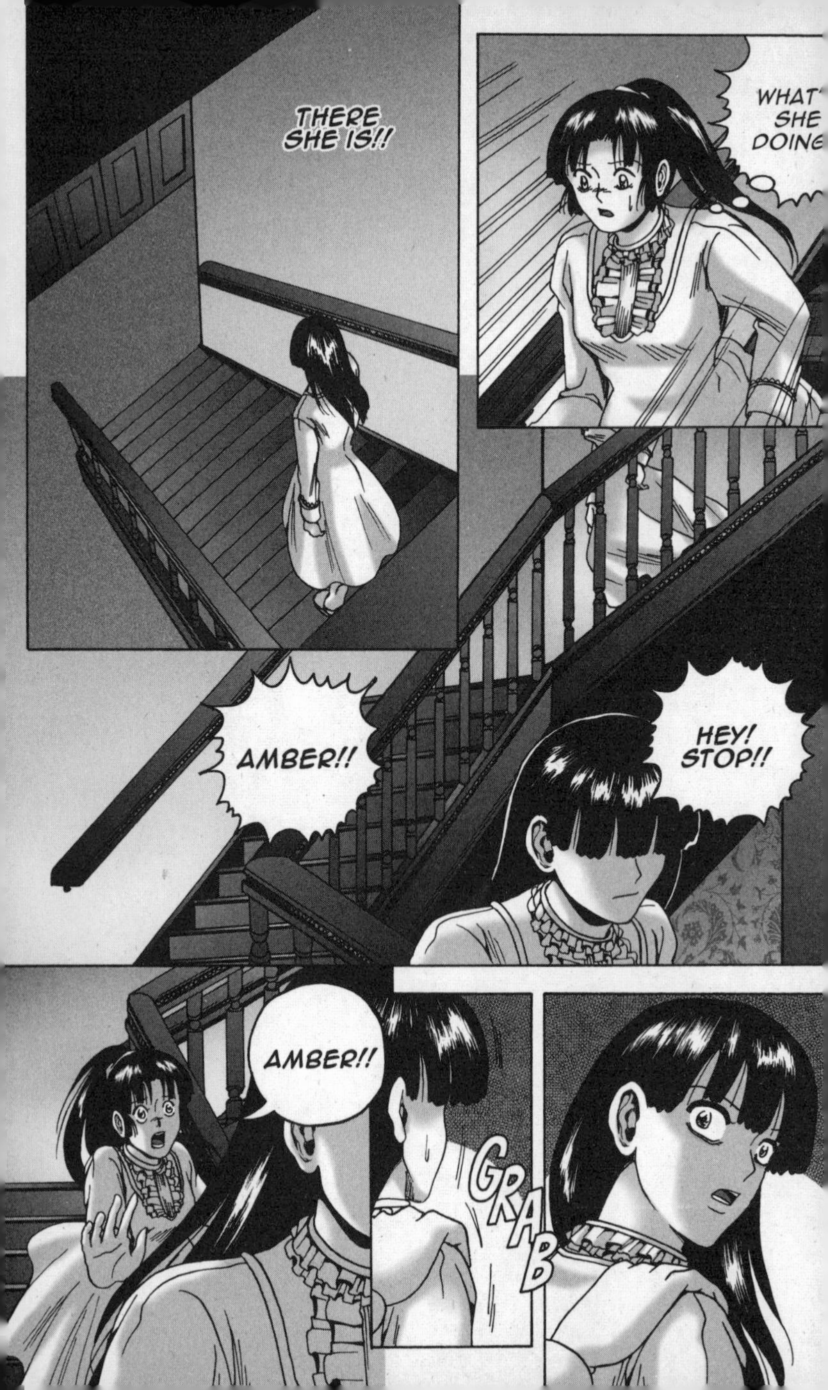
THERE SHE IS!!
WHAT' SHE DOING
AMBER!!
HEY! STOP!!
AMBER!!
GRAB

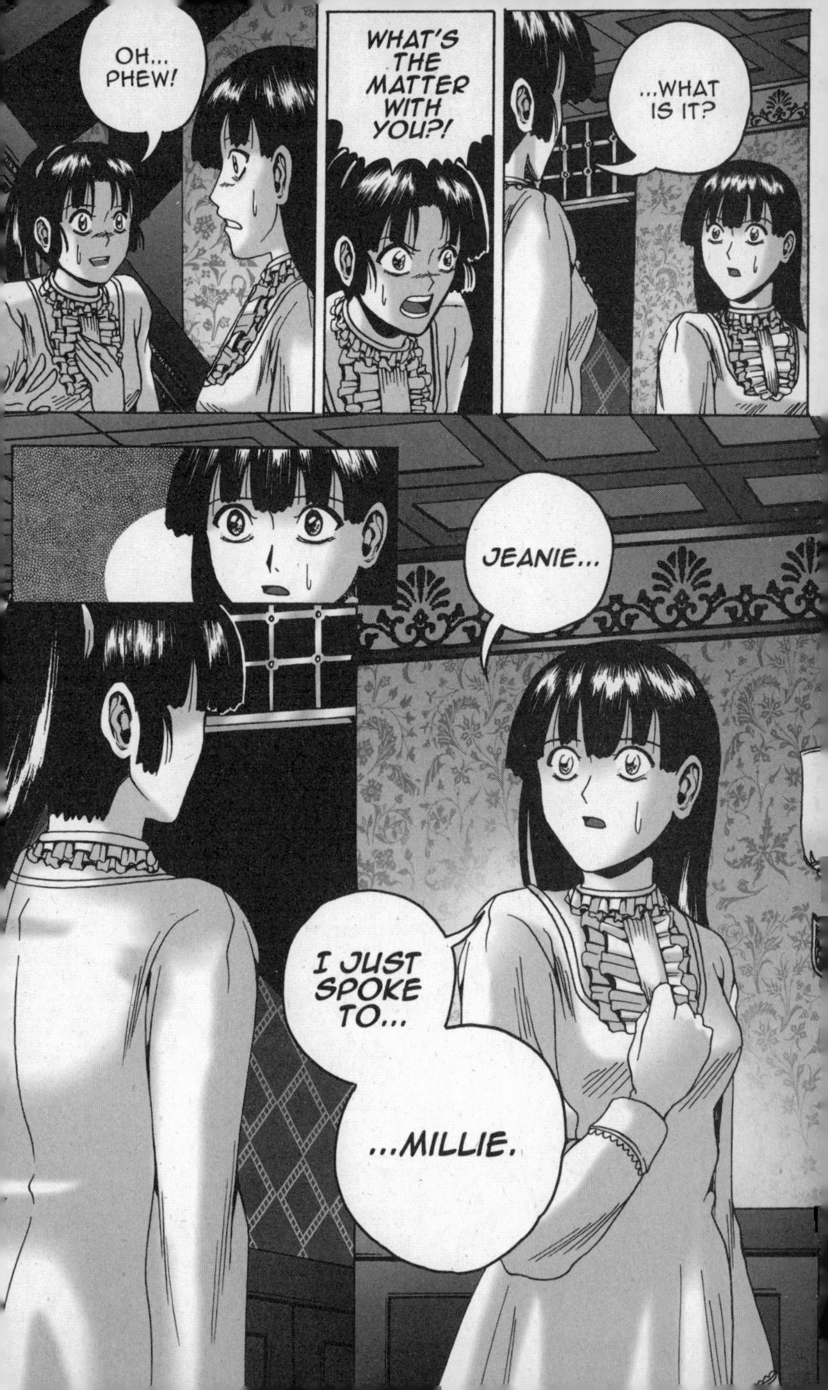
OH... PHEW!
WHAT'S THE MATTER WITH YOU?!
...WHAT IS IT?
JEANIE...
I JUST SPOKE TO...
...MILLIE.

To be continued In...

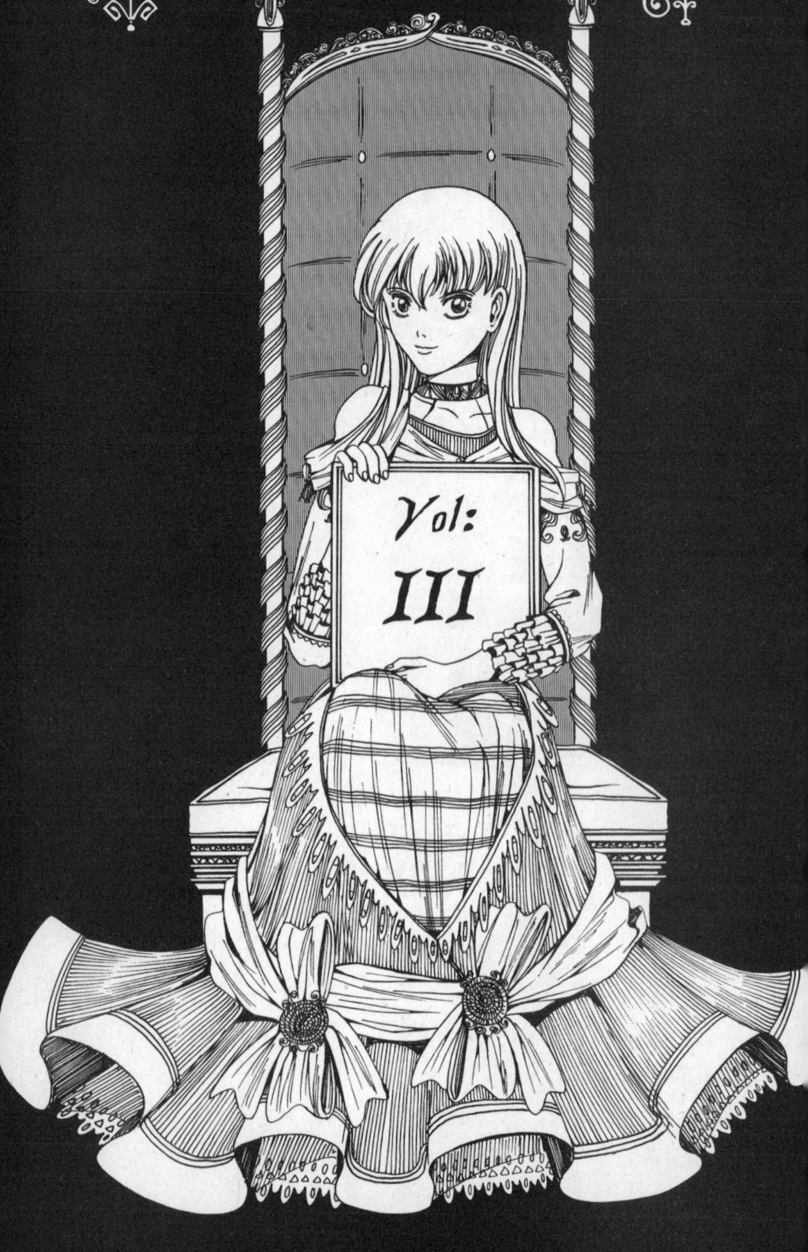
Vol:
III

The Dreaming: Volume III...

What did Millie say to Amber, and what is the real mystery behind the school, especially with the return of the missing girls? Why have they come back, and is there more to this supernatural mystery than just the school itself? The answers to these questions lie in the third and final volume of The Dreaming, as the girls and Miss Anu finally break down the door to the sealed room...

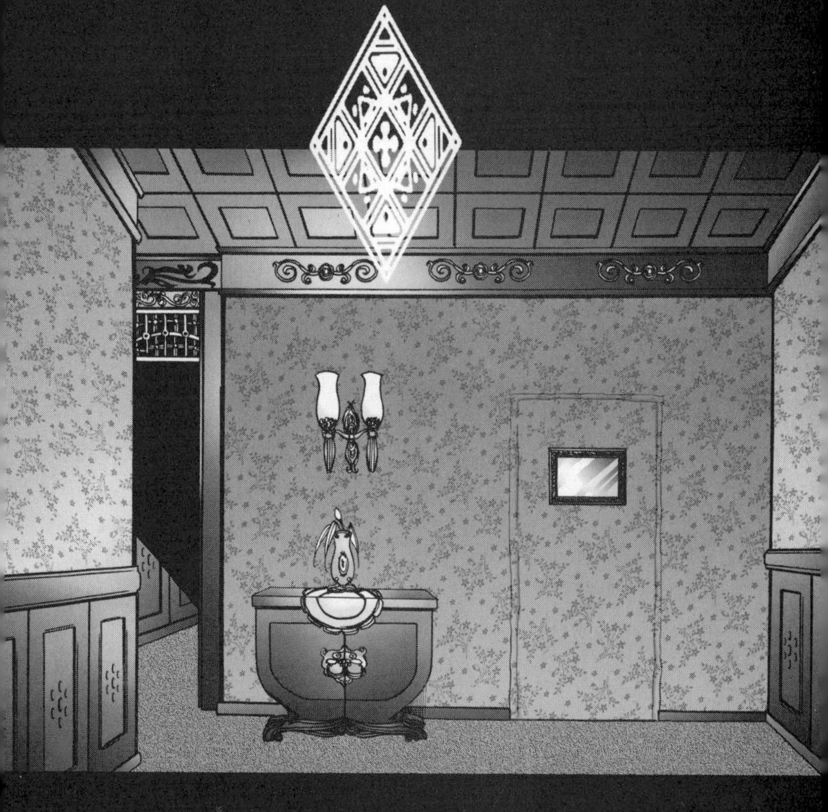

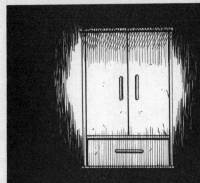

The Haunted Linen Cupboard... (Part 2)

* cue "Twilight Zone" music *

Somewhere deep inside the school, there exists a haunted linen cupboard.

Creepy polka music plays when you walk past it...

HEY! DO YOU HEAR ACCORDIAN MUSIC?!

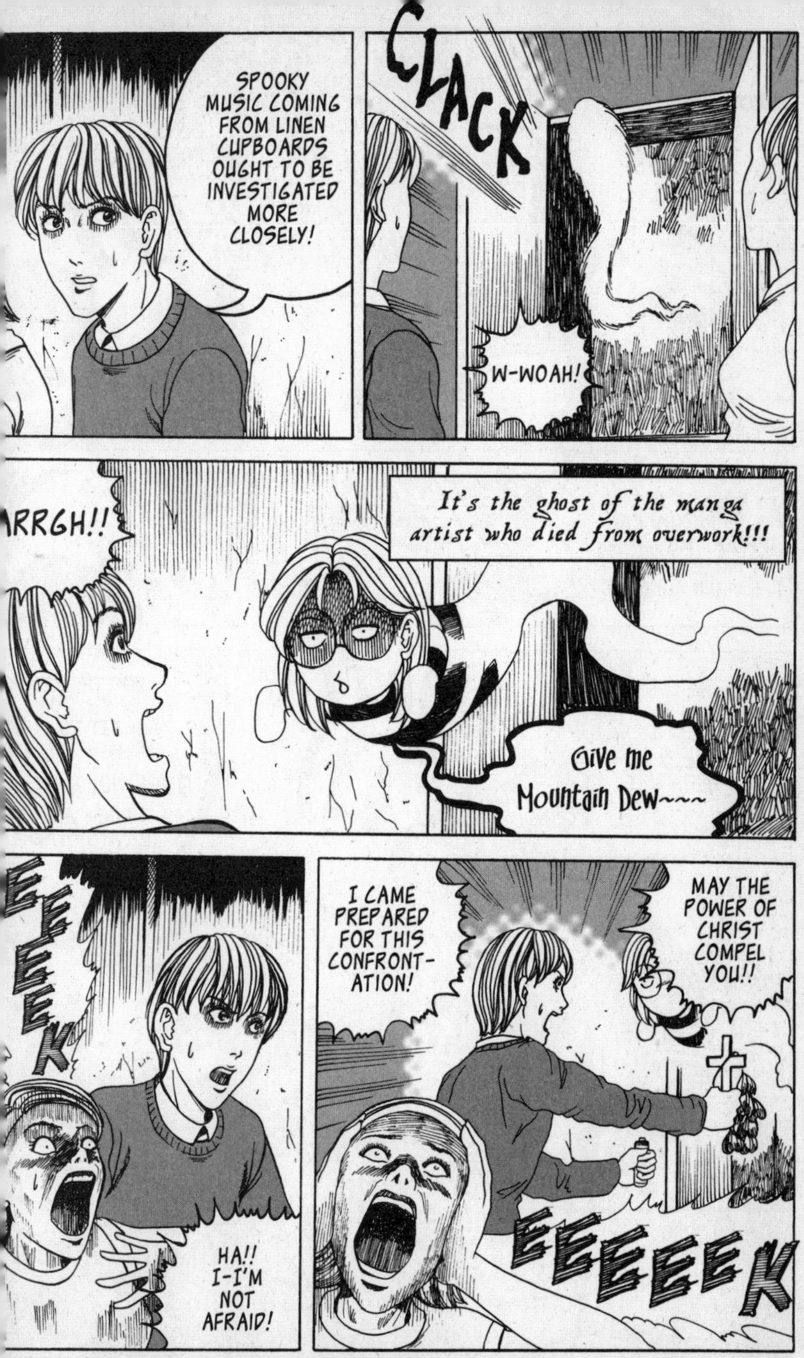
SPOOKY MUSIC COMING FROM LINEN CUPBOARDS OUGHT TO BE INVESTIGATED MORE CLOSELY!
CLACK
W-WOAH!
RRGH!!
It's the ghost of the manga artist who died from overwork!!!
Give me Mountain Dew~~~
EEEEEK
HA!! I-I'M NOT AFRAID!
I CAME PREPARED FOR THIS CONFRONT-ATION!
MAY THE POWER OF CHRIST COMPEL YOU!!
EEEEEEK

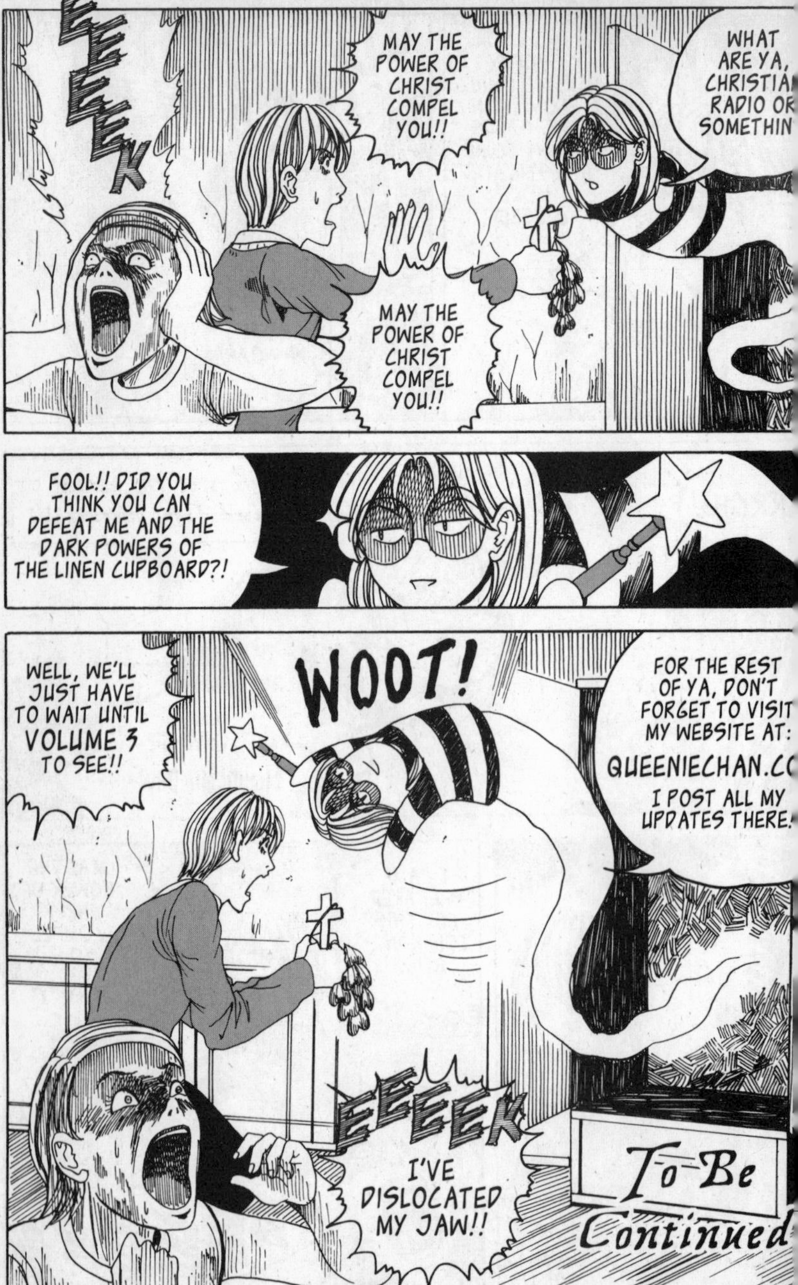
EEEEK
MAY THE POWER OF CHRIST COMPEL YOU!!
MAY THE POWER OF CHRIST COMPEL YOU!!
WHAT ARE YA, CHRISTIA RADIO OR SOMETHIN
FOOL!! DID YOU THINK YOU CAN DEFEAT ME AND THE DARK POWERS OF THE LINEN CUPBOARD?!
WELL, WE'LL JUST HAVE TO WAIT UNTIL VOLUME 3 TO SEE!!
WOOT!
FOR THE REST OF YA, DON'T FORGET TO VISIT MY WEBSITE AT: QUEENIECHAN.C I POST ALL MY UPDATES THERE.
EEEEK
I'VE DISLOCATED MY JAW!!
To Be Continued...

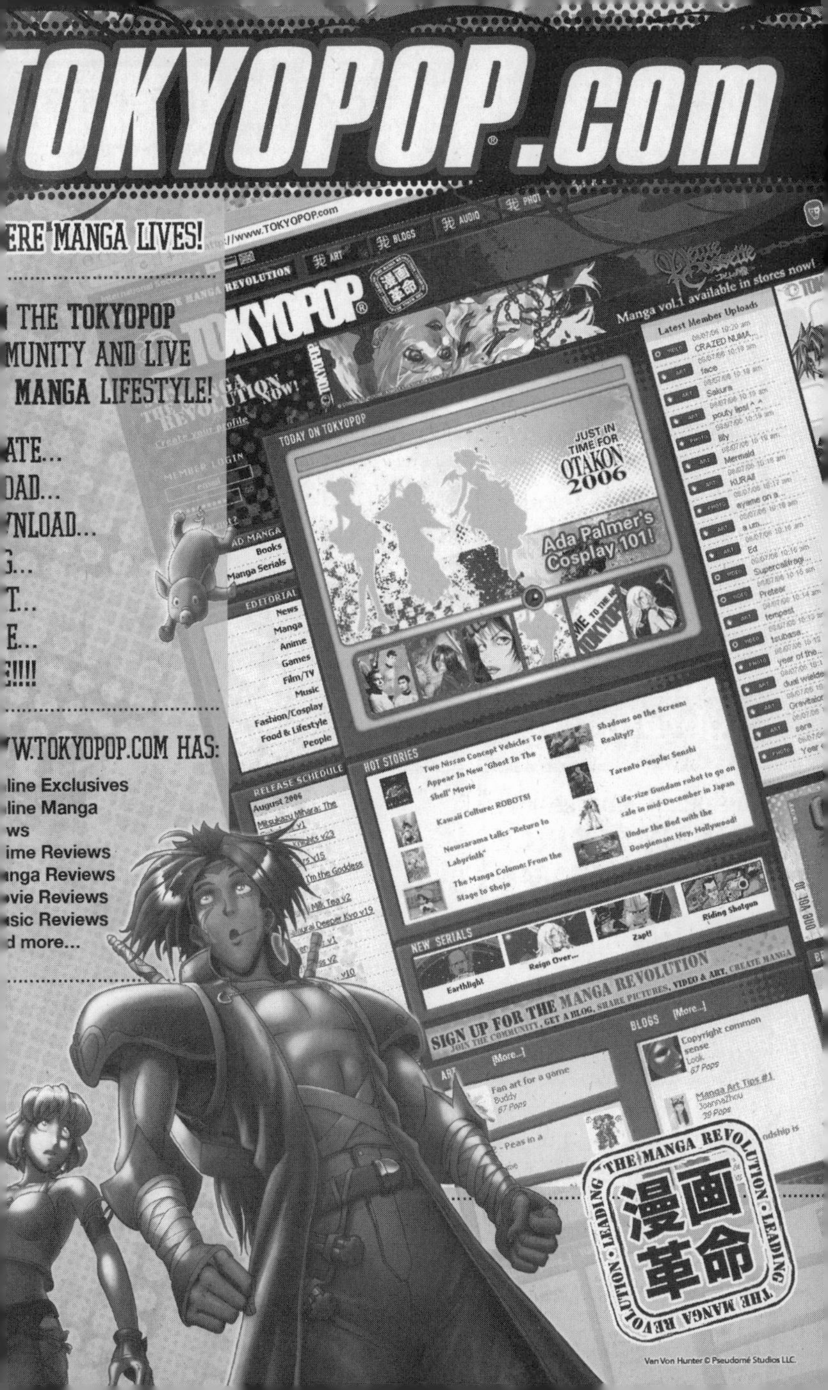

TOKYOPOP.com
ERE MANGA LIVES!
THE TOKYOPOP
MUNITY AND LIVE
MANGA LIFESTYLE!
ATE...
DAD...
VNLOAD...
G...
T...
E...
E!!!!
W.TOKYOPOP.COM HAS:
line Exclusives
line Manga
ws
ime Reviews
nga Reviews
vie Reviews
sic Reviews
d more...
http://www.TOKYOPOP.com
MANGA REVOLUTION
ART
BLOGS
AUDIO
TOKYOPOP
漫画革命
Manga vol.1 available in stores now!
Latest Member Uploads
TODAY ON TOKYOPOP
JUST IN TIME FOR OTAKON 2006
Ada Palmer's Cosplay 101!
Books
Manga Serials
EDITORIAL
News
Manga
Anime
Games
Film/TV
Music
Fashion/Cosplay
Food & Lifestyle
People
RELEASE SCHEDULE
August 2006
HOT STORIES
Two Nissan Concept Vehicles To Appear In New "Ghost In The Shell" Movie
Kawaii Culture: ROBOTS!
Newsarama talks "Return to Labyrinth"
The Manga Column: From the Stage to Shojo
Shadows on the Screen: Reality!?
Tarento People: Senshi
Life-size Gundam robot to go on sale in mid-December in Japan
Under the Bed with the Boogieman: Hey, Hollywood!
Riding Shotgun
Zap!
NEW SERIALS
Earthlight
Reign Over...
SIGN UP FOR THE MANGA REVOLUTION
JOIN THE COMMUNITY, GET A BLOG, SHARE PICTURES, VIDEO & ART, CREATE MANGA
BLOGS
[More...]
Copyright common sense
Manga Art Tips #1
ART
Fan art for a game
THE MANGA REVOLUTION • LEADING • 漫画革命
Van Von Hunter © Pseudomé Studios LLC.